INTERNATIONAL TRADE

INTERNATIONAL
TRADE

BY

F. W. TAUSSIG, Ph.D., Litt.D., Ll.D.

HENRY LEE PROFESSOR OF ECONOMICS
IN HARVARD UNIVERSITY

REPRINTS OF ECONOMIC CLASSICS

AUGUSTUS M. KELLEY · PUBLISHERS
NEW YORK · 1966

FIRST PUBLISHED 1927

REPRINTED 1966 BY PERMISSION OF
THE MACMILLAN COMPANY

LIBRARY OF CONGRESS CATALOGUE CARD NUMBER

66 - 19696

PRINTED IN THE UNITED STATES OF AMERICA
by SENTRY PRESS, NEW YORK, N. Y. 10019

PREFACE

THIS volume is divided into three parts. Part I takes up the theory of international trade. It restates views commonly held, with some amplifications and corrections. Part II is directed to ascertaining how far the actual commerce between nations proceeds in accord with that theory — how far the abstract conclusions are verified in the observed phenomena. Part III examines the characteristics of international trade between countries not having the same monetary standard; the previous Parts having been concerned with trade between countries having the same (gold) standard.

Part I follows in the main the lines of analysis and exposition which Ricardo initiated. The theorems are presented in a numerical form similar to that which he was the first to use. And not merely is Ricardo's method of exposition followed; the deduced conclusions are of the same kind as his. No part of that remarkable man's work was more original than his brief but pregnant analysis of international trade, and none has dominated the course of subsequent discussion so largely. His loyal disciple, the younger Mill, began the task of supplementing and enlarging the Ricardian theory; subsequent writers have elaborated and refined still further; yet always — so far as they have done anything constructive, — on the same fundamental lines.[1] I cannot pretend to have made any contribution of large significance in this part of the field; tho I hope that something in the way of enrichment may be found. The task of preparing a systematic statement has led not merely to the repetition and elaboration of propositions well understood, but also to some conclusions which previous writers seem to have ignored.

[1] See the remarkable comments on the literature of the subject, both mathematical and non-mathematical, by Edgeworth, in his essays on International Values, printed in Volume 2 of his Collected Papers. Compare with this the rounded and searching treatment of the same literature, old and new, by Professor J. W. Angell, in his book on The Theory of International Prices, a book which unfortunately did not reach me until the text of the present volume had been completed.

It is the simpler and more fundamental aspects of the theory which have been chiefly dealt with. Some refinements that bulk large in the literature of the subject have been disregarded. I have directed attention to the leading principles, and with a view to their practical significance rather than their theoretical nicety. More especially, those have been developed for which there seemed to be a possibility of applying the processes of test and verification undertaken in the second Part. Some intricate and much discussed elaborations of theory, especially on the play of demand and on the effects of import and export taxes, have been almost entirely ignored.

To the conversant reader an explanation is due, and perhaps an apology, for the simplicity of Part I and for the way in which the illustrative figures are used. The procedure followed can hardly be dignified by calling it mathematical, since only the simplest operations in arithmetic are carried on. My inability to use the methods of higher mathematics prevents me from following beyond the initial stages the elaborated treatment which has been applied to the subject by a long succession of 19th century writers. The excuse which I would offer for handling the problems in ways that must seem elementary to the mathematical economists is two-fold. First, with the tools at my command I have tried to grapple with parts of the subject at large which do not seem to have received attention from those better equipped; and thereby perhaps something has been added to the theoretic framework. And second, I have some hope that the very simplicity of the computations and illustrations of this book will contribute to their practical significance. In order to come as close as possible to actuality, the theoretic conclusions have here been worked out in terms of prices and money incomes. By thus pushing them to the stage of concreteness and verisimilitude, they have been made more amenable to test, verification, correction.

In Part II, which takes up these processes of verification, I have departed farther from the beaten track. The pure theory of international trade constitutes only the initial stage toward the ascertainment of the things we wish in the end to know. Such indeed is the case with the whole of the pure theory of economics, which can be called "the" theory rather than "a" theory, solely on the ground that no other has been put forward which is generalized, consistent, intellectually satisfactory. After all, what we wish to attain is not a neat logical structure, but an understanding of the actualities. We must inquire whether the facts conform to the elaborated theorems; must make sure that nothing has been forgotten in the premises, nothing has been erroneous in the reasoning. It is incumbent on the economist to follow a procedure similar to that used in the natural sciences. The physicist or biologist who believes that he has hit on a generalization which conforms to the regularities of the external world uses it merely as a working hypothesis. He proceeds to test it by observation and experiment. The economist should do the same for his hypotheses. In economics this task is more difficult than in most natural sciences, because the economist is debarred from the method which has proved in them by far the most serviceable, that of experiment. He cannot experiment; he can resort to observation only. Observation, however, he must utilize to the utmost — thru history, description, statistics. In so doing he may or may not find confirmation of his hypotheses. Quite probably he will find partial confirmation only; he will have occasion, to a greater or less extent, for revision, amendment, restatement.

The task of verification and correction has constituted the most laborious and difficult portion of this book. Yet I am well aware that much more remains to be done, and can only hope that others will carry the same sort of inquiry to better fruition. The difficulties which I have encountered have been due in no small part to the inadequacy of the available data, and especially to the lack of statistical material put together in such way as to throw light on the validity of the theoretic conclusions. Something will be gained if I have succeeded in calling the attention of statisticians to the problems that arise and to the sort of information that is needed. In every direction — not only from the statisticians, but from the historians, annalists, men of affairs — economic science needs more and more of well sifted material, for the confirmation (or confutation, as the case may be) of its hypothetical generalizations.

In Part III, which deals with international trade under dislocated exchanges, I have unfortunately been compelled to confine myself in the main to theoretic reasoning. Even more than for Part II, the statistical material, abundant tho it is, does not dovetail with the theoretic frame work. Little of it is in such form that the hypotheses can be either substantiated or overthrown. I am aware, however, that not all that is available has been here examined; further patient research might have made possible substantive results of greater scope. A wish to present for the consideration of the expert certain new trains of thought must serve as a further excuse for my failure to carry out to the full the same method of treatment in this Part as in the preceding.

A more important restriction of the scope of the book is the elimination of all discussion, or nearly all, of the controversy about protection and free trade. On this matter I have said so much elsewhere that it seemed otiose to go into it again.[1] The intellectual problems raised by it are much simpler than many others in the subject at large; while the historic and descriptive aspects are quite too extensive for full treatment in the present book. Some ways in which the general theory of international trade bears on the controversy regarding protection are considered in one place or another, especially in Chapters 13 and 16.

Finally a word may be said on another limitation of the scope of the book. It is strictly an inquiry on a particular phase of the system of private property and capitalistic enterprise. It assumes that system to exist, for good or ill, and examines merely in what way it works. There is no attempt to evaluate this phase of it, or any other; to consider how far it is satisfactory or in what ways it might be mended. I have abundant sympathy with those who question whether the situation as thus laid bare by cold-blooded analysis is satisfactory. What we see is the working of international trade thru the medium of money payments, and of money movements this way and that; thru shifting prices and incomes, slow and painful adjustments, friction and uncertainty and waste motion; obscure forces with which men struggle blindly and unavailingly. But these unwelcome features appear in every part of the existing economic and social organization. The whole capitalistic system is on trial; and not least, its monetary machinery. It is not at all inconceivable that international trade should be conducted thru a process quite different from that now in use and examined in these pages. There might be direct and conscious barter between nations, in place of that veiled barter which so mystifies the ordinary man. Speculations of this kind are beyond the scope of the present volume, which accepts the world as it is and simply examines in what way trade is now carried on between the several countries.

---

[1] I refer the reader to my Tariff History of the United States (8th ed., 1923); Some Aspects of the Tariff Question (2nd ed., 1916); and the volume of collected papers entitled The Tariff, Free Trade and Reciprocity.

I have to express my indebtedness to two of my colleagues, Mr. Edwin Frickey and Mr. II. D. White, for most helpful aid and advice in revising the manuscript and correcting the proof sheets. The Bureau of International Research of Harvard University and Radcliffe College, under a grant from the Laura Spelman Memorial Foundation, has made appropriations for research on special problems and for clerical service which have greatly facilitated my work. I hope that the results as here presented will be found to justify the enlightened policy of thus aiding scientific research.

F. W. TAUSSIG

CONTENTS

PART I

THEORY

CHAPTER I   PAGES

THREE CASES   3–6

Preliminary assumptions. Three kinds of differences in cost:
absolute, equal, and comparative differences, 3.

CHAPTER 2

CASE I — ABSOLUTE DIFFERENCES IN COST   7–18

Barter of two commodities under the simplest conditions, 7.
The barter terms of trade, 8. Trade conducted with use of
money, 11. Domestic supply price, 11. Various possibilities
in exchange of two commodities produced with absolute differences in costs, 12. The gain from exchange greater to the
country of higher money wages, 14. Absolute differences in cost
found mainly in trade between tropical and temperate countries, 17.

CHAPTER 3

CASE II — EQUAL DIFFERENCES IN COST   19–22

Commodities produced with equal differences in labor cost
will not be exchanged, 19. What the situation is when money
is used and domestic supply prices are computed, 20. Money
wages adjust themselves to differences in effectiveness of labor,
21.

CHAPTER 4

CASE III — COMPARATIVE COSTS   23–33

Two forms of comparative advantage in production: superior
advantage, inferior disadvantage, 23. How comparative advantages operate under barter; how when trade is conducted
with money, 24. Effect of changes in demand on the barter

xi

terms of trade, 27. Changes in the barter terms of trade reflected in changes of commodity incomes, 28. In what sense it can be said that the barter terms become more or less favorable, 29. Effect of elasticity of demand for foreign commodities on the barter terms of trade, 31. Elasticity of demand for domestic goods a modifying factor, 32.

CHAPTER 5

WAGES AND PRICES IN DIFFERENT COUNTRIES. DOMESTIC PRICES AND INTERNATIONAL PRICES 34–42

Distinction between international goods and domestic goods, 34. High money wages do not necessarily cause high prices, 35. What determines the range of money wages, of real wages, 36. High money wages not necessarily correlative with prosperity. A common fallacy: that there is a tendency to international equalization of money wages, 38. Relations of money wages and domestic prices, 40. Movements of domestic prices, as distinct from international prices, best revealed by movements of money incomes, 41.

CHAPTER 6

WAGES NOT UNIFORM. NON-COMPETING GROUPS 43–60

Prices of commodities within a country are not in accord with the quantities of labor necessary for their production, 43. How a lower wages cost can convert a comparative disadvantage in terms of labor cost into a comparative advantage. Persistence of differences in wages cost is possible because of the existence of non-competing groups of laborers, 44. International trade not affected by this factor unless there be differences between countries as regards the hierarchy of non-competing groups, 47. The relative positions of non-competing groups and the forces determining the numbers in each group, 52. Relation of reciprocal international demand and reciprocal domestic demand, 54. Illustrations of the influence of non-competing groups on international trade furnished by the chemical industries of Germany in latter part of 19th century, 57; by the industries using much unskilled labor in the United States during the same period, 58.

CHAPTER 7

CAPITAL AND INTEREST 61–75

Cost of raw materials may be resolved into wages and interest, and hence is not an independent factor, 61. Interest charges, when they bear in the same way on commodities in each country, do not alter the conditions of trade if merely the rate of interest is different, 62; nor if they act on some only of the commodities produced, 63; nor if they act on some more than on others, 64. But differences in the rate of interest do influence international trade in so far as different quantities of capital are used in the production of different commodities, 65. The quantitative importance of this influence, 67. Another aspect of the influence of capital and interest: capital is used more effectively in some countries than in others, 68. Some comparisons and illustrations of the existence of a comparative advantage secured because of the more effective use of capital, 71. Lower transportation costs by railway illustrate the possibilities of more effective use of capital, 73.

CHAPTER 8

VARYING COSTS; DIMINISHING RETURNS; INCREASING RETURNS   76-87

Trade in commodities produced with varying costs, 76. Connection between varying costs, international trade, and rent, 77. Varying costs are found in manufacturing industries as well as in agriculture. The human element is the main cause of variations of cost in industry, but not in agriculture, 80. Superior powers of production resting on physical causes are not transferable; those ascribable to the personal element are capable of being transferred, 81. One of the effects of this difference on international trade illustrated by the operation of protective duties, 82. Meaning of "increasing returns," 83. Internal and external economies, 84. Advantages resting on human causes are cumulative, but do not persist indefinitely. How this affects international trade, 85. Some problems as to mining industries, 86.

CHAPTER 9

VARYING ADVANTAGES   88-96

Various possibilities of barter when more than two commodities are being exchanged. Illustrations under varying relations of comparative effectiveness of production, 88. Variation in barter terms of trade arising from changes of demand, 90. Influence of total demand for all imports on the barter terms of trade. How new conditions of trade arising from changes in demand are brought about thru the mechanism of money prices and money incomes, 92.

CONTENTS

CHAPTER 10

PAGES

TWO COUNTRIES COMPETING IN A THIRD 97–107

Various combinations of barter possible when two countries or more compete in a third, 97. An increase in demand in one of the countries for any one of the commodities affects the barter terms of trade of all countries, 98. Two ways in which a country obtains its commodities cheaper thru foreign trade, 101. Examples of more complicated variants of barter among three countries, 102. The same variants considered in terms of money prices and money incomes, 104.

CHAPTER 11

NON-MERCHANDISE TRANSACTIONS. TRIBUTES, INDEMNITIES, TOURIST EXPENSES 108–122

Increasing importance of international payments arising out of non-merchandise transactions, 108. Illustration of the change in barter terms of trade brought about by foreign payments for which no *quid pro quo* is obtained, 109. The terms "favorable" and "unfavorable" balance of trade, 111. Payment of a tribute or indemnity is costly in two ways: a country parts with a quantity of goods, and it obtains its imports on less favorable terms, 112. Distinction between the gross barter terms of trade and the net barter terms of trade, 113. Illustration of the effect on both gross and net barter terms of a change in elasticity of demand for one of the imported commodities. "Invisible" items in the balance of payments not alike in their effects on the barter terms of trade, 114. Effect of indemnities and of tourist expenditures contrasted, 117. Gifts and charitable remittances, 121.

CHAPTER 12

NON-MERCHANDISE TRANSACTIONS, FURTHER CONSIDERED. LOANS AND INTEREST PAYMENTS; FREIGHT CHARGES . . . 123–140

Foreign loans by individuals cause a flow of specie from the lending country, 123. Qualification of this statement if foreign loans are linked directly with commodity exports, 124. The borrowing country secures a double gain from the capital movement: an additional supply of imported goods, and the procurement of all imports on barter terms more favorable than before, 127. Interest payments, as they accumulate, tend to reduce the gain. When annual interest payments finally exceed annual borrowings, the double gain shifts from borrowers to lenders, 128. The changes operate thru flow of specie and modification of money

prices and money incomes, 129. Irregularity of capital exports,
129. A country in the early states of borrowing has an excess of
imports; in the later stages an excess of exports, 130. A precise
balancing of the losses and gains arising out of the shifts from
more to less favorable barter terms of trade is impossible, 131.
Freight payments in the international balance sheet, 132.
Freight payments affect the barter terms of trade in a manner
similar to payment of tourists' expenditures. Payment for
freight services no more signify a loss to a country than payments
for merchandise imports, 134. Circumstances under which the
burden of shipping charges may be transferred to the exporting
country, 135. The practise of valuing imports C. I. F. and
exports F. O. B. leads to some statistical difficulties, 136. Illustrations from the trade between Australia and Great Britain;
between United States and Great Britain, 137.

CHAPTER 13

DUTIES ON IMPORTS AND THE BARTER TERMS OF TRADE . . 141–148

Effects of a revenue tax on imports, 141; the barter terms of
trade become more favorable to the country imposing the tax. A
protective tax on imports exerts a similar influence, 144. The
loss in other directions must be balanced against this gain from
more favorable barter terms, 145. In any case the gain is certain
only when other countries do not resort to similar duties, 147.
The position of the United States with regard to these possibilities, 148.

PART II

PROBLEMS OF VERIFICATION

CHAPTER 14

INTRODUCTORY 151–160

The abstract method of analysis useful only as a preliminary
approach, 151. Some aspects of international trade patently in
accord with theory, 152. Is there a tendency to world-wide
equalization of prices and wages? 153. Persistence of wide differences in prices and wages illustrated by Great Britain and India;
by Great Britain and the Continent of Europe, 154. High or low
money wages are not a factor in promoting or retarding international trade, 155. Differences in wages and prices between
Western Europe and the Orient, and their relation to the deductions of theory, 156.

CONTENTS

CHAPTER 15

PAGES

DIFFERENCES IN LABOR COSTS 161–177

Labor cost and cost as understood by accountants, 161. Some international comparisons of the effectiveness of labor in coal mining; in brick making, 162. Comparison of beer production in the United States and Germany, 166. Iron production per worker in the United States and in Great Britain, 167; superiority of American production, and reasons for it, 168. British and American tin plate production; sugar refining, 170; butter; ice, 171. Effectiveness of hand and machine production of glass in Belgium, Sweden, and the United States, 171. American and Japanese cotton spinning and weaving, 174.

CHAPTER 16

COMPARATIVE ADVANTAGES AND PROTECTIVE TARIFFS IN THE UNITED STATES 178–196

Effects of protective legislation in the United States can be understood only on the basis of the principle of comparative advantage, 178. Factors which secure for the United States such an advantage in agricultural commodities, 179. How the interplay of physical and human factors combines to bring about or to take away a comparative advantage in the beet sugar industry, 183; in flax and flax seed cultivation, 186; in the iron and steel industry, 188. The United States has a comparative advantage in those industries in which the processes of manufacture can be standardized, 189. The textile industries, 192. The American aptitude in the use of machinery, 193.

CHAPTER 17

INTERNATIONAL PAYMENTS IN RELATION TO MONETARY SYSTEMS 197–214

Acceptance of some form of the quantity theory of money essential to the theory of international trade, 197. The influence of specie movements on the range of prices of paramount significance, 198. Is the total of the medium of exchange sensitive to gold movements? 199. Discount policy of banks primarily affected by flow of specie. The volume of deposits in relation to specie reserves, 201. Sensitiveness of monetary system to specie movement in Great Britain, 203; in Canada, 205; in the United States from 1879 to 1914, 206. An inflow of specie may follow, not precede, a rise in prices, 207. Degrees of sensitiveness in Continental monetary systems, 210. United States post-war monetary conditions under the Federal Reserve System, 213.

CHAPTER 18

THE FOREIGN EXCHANGES AND THE INTERNATIONAL MOVEMENT
OF SECURITIES 215–221

Reduction of the gold flow to a minimum secured by exchange
operations of bankers and brokers, 215; by virtual pooling of the
foreign exchanges of all countries, 216; by maintenance of foreign
balances, 217; by international movements of securities, 218.
Short-time transfers of securities related to international investment operations. Movements of securities sometimes disturb
rather than smooth the fluctuations of exchange, 219. A continued lack of equilibrium between a country's debits and credits
must eventually result in an international redistribution of specie,
220. Importance of the time element, 221.

CHAPTER 19

CANADA 222–235

Borrowing from abroad the dominant factor in Canada's international trade, 1900–1913, 222. Excess of imports, inflow of
gold, and expansion of the demand liabilities of Canadian banks,
224. Secondary reserves; Canadian rates of exchange, 226.
Prices in Canada rose more than elsewhere. Prices of exported
goods rose less than domestic goods but more than prices of
imports, 227. Disappearance of many domestically produced
commodities from the list of exports, 229. Significance of the circumstance that the added imports come chiefly from the United
States, not from Great Britain, 231. Adjustment of trade
balances to international payments, 232. Experience of Canada
a striking verification of the essentials of the Ricardian theory.
Analogy of the outcome to that of an experiment, 233.

CHAPTER 20

GREAT BRITAIN, I 236–244

Recorded exports exceed imports until 1852; thereafter
imports exceed exports, 236. Increasing interest on foreign loans
and increased earnings from shipping account in large part for
the reversal, 237. Capital outflow, 238; its irregularity related
to the stages of the business cycle, 239. Some of the observed
phenomena before 1880 neither disprove nor confirm general
theory, 241.

CHAPTER 21

GREAT BRITAIN, II. THE TERMS OF TRADE, 1880–1914 . . 245–262

Decline in the import-excess after 1904 due to sudden increase
of capital exports, 245. Effect on the gross and net barter terms

of trade, 247. Gross terms of trade less favorable in 1890 and
1910 than in 1900, 251; net barter terms show similar trend,
252. Direction of the changes consonant with theory, 256.
Contrast with the case of Canada, 257; net and gross barter
terms of trade more favorable after 1900, 258. Relation of gold
flows, circulating medium, and prices more complex in Great
Britain than in Canada, 259. Closeness of the connection
between international payments and commodity movements
is perplexing, 260.

CHAPTER 22

THE FRANCO-GERMAN INDEMNITY OF 1871 263–278

Amount and character of the indemnity, 263. How the
funds for meeting it were raised in France. How they were
transferred to Germany, 265. Part played in the transfer by
French foreign investments, 266. The French experience in the
transfer of securities not applicable to heavy payments of a non-
political character. The German government's utilization of
the indemnity payments, 268. The economic effects; sustained
inflow of specie; expansion of circulating medium and sharp
rise in prices in Germany, 269. German part of the transaction
spread over many years, and its effects difficult to unravel, 272.
How does the mechanism of international payments function
when there are exceptionally heavy payments to be made? 273.
Adam Smith's explanation unsatisfactory, 274; Ricardian
explanation does not tell the story, 275. Explanation suggested
by German experience in the 70's, 276. A possible explanation
for the Napoleonic period, 277. Importance of the time element
in the processes of international payments again considered, 278.

CHAPTER 23

THE UNITED STATES, I. UNTIL 1900 280–291

The balance of trade before and after 1873, 280. Sudden
reversal with the crisis of that year, 282. Chaotic banking and
monetary systems before 1860 complicate the analysis, 284.
From 1860 to 1879 the mechanism contemplated in the Ricardian
theory could not operate, the case being one of trade under dislocated exchanges, 285. Even after return to the gold standard,
analysis is obscured by increasing domestic gold supply; by
crop alternations, 287; by silver issues, 289; by irregular movements of securities, 290.

CHAPTER 24   PAGES

THE UNITED STATES, II. 1900–1914 292–306

Situation after 1900. Astounding increase in volume of international trade coincident with great increase in gold supply, 292. An extraordinary excess of exports, 293. Its explanation, 294. Comparison of balance of payments with balance of trade reveals nothing out of accord with theoretical presumptions, 297. But the course of net and gross barter terms of trade displays no such trend as might be expected, 298. A possible explanation may be found in the effects of the protective tariff, 303.

CHAPTER 25

THE UNITED STATES, III. AFTER 1914 307–334

Crisis of 1914. Recovery by 1915, 307. Great increase in foreign demand for American products, followed by heavy imports of gold, 308. Borrowing by belligerents from investors in the United States as a means of paying for American exports, 309. Return of American securities to the United States, 310. Flow of gold into the United States in accord with usual analysis, but Ricardian reasoning as regards international trade not applicable; the sequence assumed in theory as to the relation of borrowing to exports reversed, 311. After the United States entered the war, loans to the Allies by the American Treasury, 313. Direct relation between the huge loans and the huge excess of exports, 314. The price inflation and the Federal Reserve System, 316. Post-war changes in the international balance of payments; in the non-merchandise elements, 318. United States becomes a large exporter of capital; rapidity of the transition from position of debtor to that of creditor, 325. Effect of post-war gold movements on United States monetary system not in accord with familiar doctrine, 329. How then explain equalization of imports and exports? 331. The problems of the future, 332.

PART III

INTERNATIONAL TRADE UNDER INCONVERTIBLE PAPER

CHAPTER 26

THE UNDERLYING PRINCIPLES 337–362

Mechanism of international readjustment thru price levels and money incomes necessarily different when compensatory movements of specie are lacking, 337. Use of certain terms : exchange, foreign exchange, paper exchange, specie exchange, paper conditions, specie conditions, dislocated exchanges, 338. Effects of inconvertible currency on international trade unduly simplified by followers of Ricardo, 339. Cassel's formulation of the purchasing-parity doctrine, 340. Analysis of international trade under the simplest conditions between countries having different monetary standards, 341. Effect of a sudden and large disturbing factor on the price of foreign exchange, 343. Price of foreign exchange may change independently of changes in the price level of either country. The theory of the *impact* of the respective volumes of remittances, 344. Changes in exchange rate may for a time act as a bounty on exports, 346. Is there a "normal" foreign exchange rate under dislocated exchanges? 348. Effect of fluctuation in exchange on domestic prices, export prices, and import prices, 349. Eventual results under dislocated exchanges the same as under specie, 352. Changes in the barter terms of trade, 355. Limits of fluctuations in the barter terms and in the rates of exchange, 356. Conclusion, 357.

APPENDIX

The analysis made in the body of the chapter illustrated by figures, 358.

CHAPTER 27

DISLOCATED EXCHANGES FURTHER CONSIDERED 363–373

Merchandise movements may be cause or effect of variations in the price of foreign exchange. Barter terms of trade modified by changes in demand, 363. Changes in demand usually gradual, and difficult to disentangle. Changes in supply are more often distinguishable, but as a rule the effects can be traced only thru the first stages, 366. Exchange between a country with a gold standard and one with a silver standard, 369. Trade between India and Great Britain, 370. Rates of exchange, like merchandise movements, may be either cause or effect of merchandise movements, 371. Changes in the gold price of silver, arising independently, are a complicating factor, 372.

CHAPTER 28

SPECULATION, PEGGING, THE GOLD EXCHANGE STANDARD . . 374–384

Short period movements of dislocated exchanges. Speculative dealings of much greater importance than under gold exchanges, 374. Does speculation diminish fluctuations? relation between

PAGES

speculation and the underlying forces, 375. Effects differ according as changes in underlying situation are sudden or gradual. Speculation does not affect the final outcome, 377. Pegging, its use and its influence, 378. Gold exchange standard virtually a pegging process, 380. Advantages of pegging. Difficulties arise when established rate of exchange ceases to correspond with relative prices and incomes, 381. Do changes in interest rates permanently modify fundamental factors? Do the advocates of gold exchange standards and of managed currencies neglect the long-run problems? 383.

CHAPTER 29

INFLUENCE OF CHANGES IN THE VOLUME OF PAPER MONEY . 385–392

Importance of distinction between progressive depreciation and stabilized depreciation, 385. Mere expansion of volume of paper money does not necessarily lead to a bounty on exports, 385. Situation under silver exchange, 386. Export bounty occurs in countries of paper money only when exchange rises more than prices, 387. But exchange may rise less than prices and thereby place a bounty on imports, 387. Duration of any bounty on exports dependent on conditions of supply for exported goods, 389. Very great issues of paper introduce a situation to which the reasoning proper for moderate expansions does not apply, 390. Depreciation of paper may bring about a flight of capital, and lead in itself to a bounty on exports, 391.

CHAPTER 30

SOME EXPERIENCES UNDER PAPER MONEY 393–408

Scarcity of pertinent inductive studies, 393. The United States for the period 1866–1879 presents a case adapted for verification, 393. Graham's analysis of price movements and international trade; the results in accord with theoretical prevision, 397. Danger of oversimplification in the interpretation of complicated phenomena, 399. No conclusions possible concerning ultimate effects, 400. Williams' analysis of Argentine trade in 1880–1900. Heavy borrowing was accompanied by movements of merchandise such as are in accord with theory, 401. Correspondence between quantity of paper and price of gold, 402. Low premium on gold a check to exports. Qualifications in interpreting the Argentine experience, 405.

APPENDIX 409–419
INDEX 421–425

PART I
THEORY

INTERNATIONAL TRADE

CHAPTER 1

THREE CASES

AT the outset I must ask the reader's patience, and a withholding of judgment on his part, till the close of a systematic and prolonged exposition. Some assumptions will be made in the earlier chapters that must appear quite out of accord with facts, and some extremely simple and apparently unreal situations will be considered. It will be assumed, for example, that countries or regions trade with each other by a process of barter, and that the people concerned weigh deliberately the advantages of barter. It will be assumed, again, that within each country commodities are exchanged, by those making them, on the basis of the quantities of labor given to their production. These commodities, too, will be assumed to be produced at constant cost — that is, tho the volume of output may change, each unit is always produced by the same quantity of labor. And so on thru a long list of provisional suppositions. As the subject is unfolded step by step, these will be qualified and supplemented, and verisimilitude will be attained, or at least some approach to verisimilitude. Many comments and criticisms that must arise in the reader's mind will be met, I trust, as he proceeds. He is asked to judge the analysis which follows as a whole, regardless of seeming inadequacy in any one part considered by itself.

We begin by distinguishing three sorts of cases. To these may be applied the terms: (1) absolute differences in cost; (2) equal differences in cost; (3) comparative differences in cost.

In the analysis and interpretation of these cases, "cost" will mean labor cost, measured in terms of time, — so many days. A given number of days' labor, supposed necessary for producing a given number of commodities, will constitute the cost of the commodities. It is not money cost or expenses that we start with, but labor and effort. Cost is low when little labor is needed to produce a given physical quantity, high when much is needed. It is inverse to the effectiveness of labor: the greater that effectiveness, the lower is cost.

I am aware that the point of departure thus chosen is open to criticism. It is that of Ricardo, Mill, and their successors; and the treatment of the subject at the hands of this school has always had a certain air of unreality, as if divorced from the actual conduct of trade. Instead of beginning with labor cost, as they did, we might first consider cost as understood in the everyday world — money cost, or supply price — and proceed thereupon to the labor cost. Either course is justifiable. The choice between them is one of methodology, or rather of the better method of exposition. In the chapters that follow the relation between the two kinds of cost, and their respective bearings on international trade, will receive careful consideration. The realities will not be neglected, even tho the first approach may seem far removed from the channels of actual trade. And the conclusions eventually reached would have been the same, and would have been reached by essentially the same reasoning if the starting point had been money cost, and if there had then been a working back to labor cost. The question, as just remarked, is one of procedure. I will not pretend that the plan of the present book is clearly the better. The reader is asked at this stage merely to bear it in mind.

For the present, then, we define cost in terms of quantity of labor, not in terms of money cost or of supply prices. On this basis we differentiate the three cases. Representative figures, of the kind which will be freely used in the ensuing pages, are as follows:

CASE I. ABSOLUTE DIFFERENCES

In the U. S. 10 days' labor produce 30 lbs. copper
" " U. S. 10 " " " 15 yds. linen
" Germany 10 " " " 15 lbs. copper
" Germany 10 " " " 30 yds. linen

In the United States the effectiveness of labor in producing copper is twice as great as is that of labor in producing copper in Germany; cost is one-half as great. In Germany, on the other hand, the effectiveness of labor in producing linen is twice as great as it is in the United States for that article; cost (of linen) again is one-half as great.

Each country has an absolute advantage over the other in the production of one of the commodities.

CASE II. EQUAL DIFFERENCES

In the U. S. 10 days' labor produce 30 lbs. copper
" " U. S. 10 " " " 15 yds. linen
" Germany 10 " " " 20 lbs. copper
" Germany 10 " " " 10 yds. linen

Here cost is lower in the United States than in Germany — the effectiveness of labor is greater — as regards both commodities, and in equal degree for both. The ten days produce 30 of copper in the United States, 20 in Germany. The ten days produce 15 of linen in the United States, 10 of linen in Germany. Labor is more effective in the United States all around by fifty per cent.

CASE III. COMPARATIVE DIFFERENCES

(a) In the U. S. 10 days' labor produce 30 lbs. copper
" " U. S. 10 " " " 15 yds. linen
" Germany 10 " " " 20 lbs. copper
" Germany 10 " " " 15 yds. linen

(b) In the U. S. 10 " " " 30 lbs. copper
" " U. S. 10 " " " 15 yds. linen
" Germany 10 " " " 15 lbs. copper
" Germany 10 " " " 10 yds. linen

Case III has two variants. In variant (a) the American effectiveness of labor is greater than the German in copper (30 to 20); whereas in linen there is no difference (15 in both countries). Considering the whole situation, the United States is the more fortunate country; but it is her better fortune in copper that alone makes the difference.

In variant (b), however, the United States has lower cost and greater effectiveness for both commodities, but not to the same degree for both. For copper the ten days in the United States produce 30, in Germany 15; the difference is as 2 to 1. For linen the ten days produce in the United States 15, in Germany 10; the difference is as 3 to 2. The United States has a greater advantage in copper than in linen. She may be said to have a comparative advantage in a more special sense.

In the chapters that follow we proceed to consider what are the possibilities of trade between the two countries in these three cases, and what the possible terms of trade. The situation will be analyzed first as if the conditions were the very simplest. Suppose the trade to be one of barter, the direct exchange of copper for linen. The two countries may be supposed to get together in mass meeting, so to speak, and to consider whether anything can be gained by an exchange of goods; much as we should consider what might be done by two collectivist communities which had no common medium of exchange.

CHAPTER 2

ABSOLUTE DIFFERENCES IN COST

WE begin with Case I. Consider first what would be the terms of trade within each country if both of the commodities were produced in each and were exchanged within each. Assume, that is, that the people of the two countries have nothing to do with each other. They go their own ways, quite without contact or trade between them. Assume further that the trade within each — this purely domestic trade — takes place as it would if the labor in each moved with complete freedom from occupation to occupation, from industry to industry. The two commodities then are exchanged, in the United States and also in Germany, in proportion to the amounts of labor needed to produce them. In other words, we proceed, as regards exchanges taking place within a country, on the basis of a labor theory of value. It will appear in due time how important is this assumption, and in what ways it needs to be revised and qualified. For the present, we simplify the case by supposing not only barter between the two countries, but also barter within each on terms settled by equalization of the returns to labor.

The figures for Case I, to repeat, are:

In the U. S. 10 days' labor produce 30 lbs. copper
" " U. S. 10 " " " 15 yds. linen
therefore in the United States 30 copper = 15 linen.

In Germany 10 days' labor produce 15 lbs. copper
" Germany 10 " " " 30 yds. linen
therefore in Germany 15 copper = 30 linen, or 7½ copper = 15 linen.

There is a wide diversity between the terms of trade that would obtain within the two countries. In the United States 15 of linen would exchange for 30 of copper; in Germany 15 of linen for 7½ of copper.

If now our supposed mass meetings took place and the possibility of trade between the two countries were contemplated, it is obvious that Germany would gain by sending 15 linen to the United States and getting anything more than $7\frac{1}{2}$ of copper in exchange. The 15 of linen are in Germany the product of 5 days of labor (30 linen for 10 days, hence 15 linen for 5 days). That same amount of labor in Germany (5 days) would produce $7\frac{1}{2}$ of copper. By shipping 15 of linen to the United States and getting *more* than $7\frac{1}{2}$ of copper in exchange, Germany gains. Conversely, the United States would gain by an exchange of 15 linen for anything *less* than 30 of copper. The ten days labor produce in the United States 30 of copper; any less quantity of copper (25 or 20) is the product of a correspondingly smaller amount of labor. But 10 days in the United States are needed to produce 15 linen. If the United States gets the 15 of German linen for as much as 27, 28, 29 of copper, she still gets the linen for less labor than would be needed to produce it at home.

The quantitative relation between these physical amounts — between pounds of copper and yards of linen — we designate as the "barter terms of trade." We are assuming, be it remembered, that no money is used and that the transactions are simply and solely the exchange of goods for goods. Much copper for little linen, or much linen for little copper — these are the possibilities of the barter terms of trade. What is the meaning of the phrase under this simple condition is obvious enough and is easily visualized.

But with the use of money and with sales and purchases in terms of money — under the complex conditions of the actual foreign commerce of the world — the facts which the phrase describes are by no means easy to visualize. Not only are they very difficult to keep in mind, but they are so disguised, so overlain by other more conspicuous and not less significant phenomena, that one is apt to forget that they exist at all. In the every-day talk about foreign trade their existence is completely ignored; one would not dream that there was such a thing. Even in the discussions of the economists they are often forgotten. Yet this is the important thing; it is here that we have the essence of international trade;

it is here that the fundamental problems appear. Let the reader attend to the phrase "barter terms of trade," prepare for its recurrence, bear in mind its meaning. A word of explanation on this matter of phraseology may be helpful. "Terms of trade" was suggested by Marshall.[1] "Terms of exchange," which at first may seem better, is confusing, for the reason that "exchange" is so constantly used in connection with the price of "bills of exchange" and the rates of "foreign exchange." Unfortunately there is nothing in the English tongue that corresponds to the German "Devisen." As in so many other problems of economics, we have retained the ways of common speech, and we designate by the same word — "exchange" — quite different things. The possibilities of misunderstanding will be lessened if we use the phrase "terms of trade" to designate the fundamental process of the traffic of goods for goods, and restrict the use of "exchange" as much as possible to bills of exchange and to dealings in them. To reduce still further the possibilities of misunderstanding, I have modified Marshall's phrase in the manner stated above, and shall speak of the "barter terms of trade."

Returning to our analysis, we simplify it by neglecting cost of transportation. The most obvious effect of cost of transportation is to narrow somewhat the range within which the terms of exchange are confined. If it costs one of copper to carry each batch of copper from the United States to Germany, and also costs one of copper to carry each batch of linen from Germany to the United States, the limits within which the exchange can take place will be 8½ and 29 of copper for 15 of linen, not 7½ and 30. At any figure above 8½ Germany will still gain; at any figure below 29 the United States will still gain. There are some further and less obvious complications from the introduction of cost of transportation, to which the older economists gave much attention and of which something will be said as we proceed.[2] All the complications from this factor, obvious or obscure, do not affect the essentials of

---

[1] Money Credit and Commerce, Book III, Ch. VI and *passim*.
[2] See below, p. 135.

the analysis, and for the present will be ignored. We shall assume that cost of transportation is so small an item that it may be neglected. Each commodity is supposed to exchange for the other on the same terms in both countries; which would not be the case if transportation costs were taken into consideration.

Each commodity then will be produced in one of the countries only. Copper will be produced in the United States only, being sent thence to Germany in exchange for linen. Linen will be produced in Germany only, being sent thence to the United States in exchange for copper. No linen will be produced in the United States, no copper in Germany.

If now we suppose the two regions are not separate countries whose inhabitants are kept apart by differences of language, custom, race, but are parts of a single homogeneous country — say New York and Pennsylvania, not Germany and the United States — our conclusions become different. They become different, that is, so far as concerns the possible barter terms of trade. The terms will then be settled at the fixed rate of 15 linen for 15 copper. The inhabitants of both regions will participate equally in the potential gains from the trade. But as regards trade between countries — to return to this case — under a rate more favorable to the United States, say of 15 linen for 8 copper, the total rewards of producers in that country, in quantities of linen and copper together, will be greater than in Germany. On the other hand, under a rate more favorable to Germany, say 15 linen for 29 copper, the total rewards will be greater in that country. If there be free movement of people between the two, such as takes place between different regions within a country, there will ensue equality of reward. That equality is reached under the rate of 15 linen for 15 copper.

The circumstance that gives to international trade its outstanding characteristics is the lack of free movement between the trading countries, and the consequent possibility of great divergencies between the returns to labor in them. The further significance of this factor, the causes of divergences between countries, the nature and effects of the divergences which still persist within a country, will be considered more at length as we proceed. The first and the main consequence in international trade is indicated in the simplest form by the figures just given. Barter terms of trade may emerge, and rewards to labor under which much more advantage accrues to one country than to another. And, to repeat, under the conditions here supposed, the *difference* in gain to the countries may be very great. The United States may gain a great deal from the trade and Germany but little; or Germany may gain a great deal and the United States but little. The barter terms may be highly favorable to Germany and but little favorable to the United States; or may be highly favorable to the United States and but little favorable to Germany.

We proceed now to modify the suppositions still further for Case I, in such way as to come a step nearer the realities. Countries do not exchange products for products thru mass meeting votes or any other process of conscious bargaining. Goods are sold for money. To quote Ricardo's phrase, "every transaction in commerce is an independent transaction." Linen will be sent from Germany to the United States only if it sells for a less price in Germany; and copper will be sent from the United States to Germany only if it in turn sells for a less price in the United States. Our next step is to introduce the mechanism of money and prices.

In doing so we still simplify the case. Suppose the circulating medium in the two countries to be the same, and to be gold. Assume that copper and linen are both sold for gold in the two countries, and that gold as well as the commodities moves freely from one country to the other.

Go further with the process of preliminary simplification. Assume not only that gold is the currency of both countries, but also that the greater or less plenty of gold money affects prices. More money means higher prices, less money lower prices. We shall assume, in other words, the validity of what is called the quantity theory of money. It is not material whether we accept also another proposition which goes with the quantity theory, namely that prices rise or fall in precise proportion to the increase or decrease of the monetary supply. It suffices for the present reasoning that they do rise when money becomes more plentiful, do fall when money becomes less plentiful. An inflow of gold from one country to another causes prices to fall in the first, to rise in the second. I would not be supposed to imply that so bare and simple a statement as this tells the whole story of the working of the monetary mechanism. As will appear later, some of the most troublesome complications of the subject arise precisely in connection with the working of that mechanism. The reader's patience is asked once more. Let the simpler aspects of the problem be first cleared up.

Suppose now money wages to be $1.50 a day in the United States and $1.00 a day in Germany. And suppose too that this is the sole expense involved in producing the commodities in the two countries. Ignore any return to capital; to that complication, as to others, attention will be given in due course. With regard to the supposed figures on wages, consider them for the present merely as a *status quo*. Accept them as existent. It will appear presently how they came to exist, and in what way such money rates of wages are related, in the last analysis, to the prices of the goods.

Then, still assuming that within each country there is free movement of labor and that goods sell on the basis of the labor involved in producing them, we have the following results:

	WAGES PER DAY	TOTAL WAGES	PRODUCE	DOMESTIC SUPPLY PRICE
In the U. S. 10 days' labor	$1.50	$15	30 copper	$0.50
” ” U. S. 10 ” ”	$1.50	$15	15 linen	$1.00
” Germany 10 ” ”	$1.00	$10	15 copper	$0.66⅔
” Germany 10 ” ”	$1.00	$10	30 linen	$0.33⅓

Observe the term "domestic supply price." By this is meant the price at which, under the given conditions of expenses of production, each article could be steadily brought to market and sold. It is the (simplified) money cost of production; the kind of "cost" which figures in most economic discussion and in all business discussion. Since we are here (and in almost all parts of this book) using "cost" in the other sense — that of labor cost — it will obviate misunderstanding and will conduce to clarity if we do not use the word at all when referring to the forces that act on money prices.   In considering these we shall therefore speak of domestic supply prices only ; or, for brevity, supply prices.   The German domestic supply price of copper is that at which copper would sell in Germany if there were no international trade at all, if copper were produced in Germany, and if its price were purely a domestic matter.   It is the price which the German producers must get in order to induce them to make that article.   Similarly the domestic supply price of linen in the United States is the price which would rule in the United States if there were no trade between the countries — the price which Americans must get in order to induce them to make linen at all.

A cursory inspection of the figures shows that the supply price of copper is lower in the United States ($0.50 there, $0.66⅔ in Germany) while that of linen is lower in Germany ($0.33⅓ against $1.00 in the United States).   The American producers of linen would be undersold by the German producers of linen ; the German producers of copper would in turn be undersold by the American producers of copper.   American copper would be sold in Germany, German linen in the United States.   The United States would produce no linen, Germany would produce no copper.

Suppose now the difference in money wages between the two countries to be the other way — higher in Germany.   Suppose German wages to be $1.50, American wages $1.00.   Then we have :

	WAGES PER DAY	TOTAL WAGES	PRODUCE	DOMESTIC SUPPLY PRICE
In the U. S. 10 days' labor	$1.00	$10	30 copper	$0.33⅓
" " U. S. 10 " "	$1.00	$10	15 linen	$0.66⅔
" Germany 10 " "	$1.50	$15	15 copper	$1.00
" Germany 10 " "	$1.50	$15	30 linen	$0.50

Here the same movement of goods takes place.   Copper is cheaper in the United States than it could be in Germany ($0.33⅓ there as against $1.00 in Germany) and will move thence to Germany.   Linen is similarly cheaper in Germany ($0.50 against $0.66⅔) and will move thence to the United States.

In other words, it is quite possible that money wages will be higher in the United States or that they will be higher in Germany. And evidently the gain from the exchange will be greater to that country which has the higher money wages. The price of each commodity, once the exchange has begun, will be the same in both countries. The German price for linen will be the ruling price in the United States as well as in Germany. The American price for copper will be the same in Germany as in the United States. But, with money wages higher in the United States and with the prices of the goods identical (both linen and copper), evidently the American purchasers will be better off. Conversely, if money wages be higher in Germany, as they quite possibly may be, the Germans will be better off.

The range of possible deviation in money wages between the two countries will be between $1.00 and $2.00. It is possible that money wages in the United States will be *nearly* double those in Germany; and money wages in Germany may be *nearly* double those in the United States. If, for example, money wages are $2.00 in the United States and $1.00 in Germany, we have:

	WAGES PER DAY	TOTAL WAGES	PRODUCE	DOMESTIC SUPPLY PRICE
In the U. S. 10 days' labor	$2.00	$20	30 copper	$0.66⅔
" " U. S. 10 " "	$2.00	$20	15 linen	$1.33⅓
" Germany 10 " "	$1.00	$10	15 copper	$0.66⅔
" Germany 10 " "	$1.00	$10	30 linen	$0.33⅓

Here the supply price of copper is the same in the two countries — $0.66⅔. But linen is very much cheaper in Germany — $0.33⅓ against $1.33 in the United States. No copper will move from the United States to Germany; but linen will move from Germany to the United States. As German linen is sold in the United States, gold will have to be remitted in order to pay for it. The outflow of gold from the United States will lower prices there, and will lower money wages also; while the inflow of gold into Germany will raise prices and money wages. Thereupon copper will begin to move in payment for linen. How great the movement will be and what the limits to it, need not at this stage be considered. It is enough to observe that as soon as money wages in the United States become less than $2.00 — less than double the German rate — the possibilities of sales of goods both ways will arise. And the converse applies, of course, to Germany. If German wages are twice as high as in the United States — $2.00 there against $1.00 here — the price of linen will be as low in the United States as in Germany, and copper alone will move between the two countries. With German wages less than $2.00 — less than twice as high — linen will move from Germany, and an exchange of goods for goods will begin.

In analyzing the possibilities of exchange under the supposition of barter, we have seen that the terms on which the barter of goods for goods will take place may vary between wide limits. It is easily shown that the same possibility of wide variation in these terms exists under a money régime also.

Let us suppose money wages to be higher in the United States than in Germany, but not as much higher as they might possibly be. Let wages in the United States be $1.50, wages in Germany $1.00: not twice as high, but 50 per cent higher. Then we have:

	WAGES PER DAY	TOTAL WAGES	PRODUCE	DOMESTIC SUPPLY PRICE
In the U. S. 10 days' labor	$1.50	$15	30 copper	$0.50
" " U. S. 10 " "	$1.50	$15	15 linen	$1.00
" Germany 10 " "	$1.00	$10	15 copper	$0.66⅔
" Germany 10 " "	$1.00	$10	30 linen	$0.33⅓

Linen is produced more cheaply (in money) in Germany, and flows thence to the United States; copper more cheaply in the United States, and flows thence to Germany; linen obviously being relatively the cheaper of the two.

The barter terms of trade are 15 of copper for 22½ of linen. At the price of copper which rules in both countries ($0.50) the sum of $7.50 will buy 15 of copper; while at the ruling price of $0.33⅓ for linen, that same sum will buy 22½ of linen. In other words, 15 of copper sent from the United States to Germany will procure 22½ of linen. And these barter terms of trade are, of course, in accord with the money wages in the two countries. Money wages in the United States are 150 per cent of those in Germany, and the product of ten days of American labor (30 of copper) exchanges for the product of 15 days of German labor (45 of linen).

The converse supposition — equally permissible under the given conditions — is that money wages are 50 per cent higher in Germany. Let them be $1.50 in Germany, $1.00 in the United States. Then we have:

	WAGES PER DAY	TOTAL WAGES	PRODUCE	DOMESTIC SUPPLY PRICE
In the U. S. 10 days' labor	$1.00	$10	30 copper	$0.33⅓
" " U. S. 10 " "	$1.00	$10	15 linen	$0.66⅔
" Germany 10 " "	$1.50	$15	15 copper	$1.00
" Germany 10 " "	$1.50	$15	30 linen	$0.50

As before, linen is produced more cheaply in Germany, and flows thence to the United States; copper more cheaply in the United States, and flows to Germany; but now with copper, not linen, relatively the cheaper of the two. The barter terms of trade are now 15 of copper for 10 of linen, or 22½ of copper for 15 of linen. At the price of copper which rules in both countries ($0.33⅓) the sum of $7.50 will buy 22½ of copper; while at the ruling price of linen ($0.50) that same sum will buy 15 of linen. The barter terms of trade have become more advantageous to Germany. And this betterment of Germany's gain is in accord with her higher money wages, now 50 per cent above those of the United States.

Suppose now that money wages are the same in the two countries. Let them be $1.50 alike in Germany and in the United States. Then we have:

	WAGES PER DAY	TOTAL WAGES	PRODUCE	DOMESTIC SUPPLY PRICE
In the U. S. 10 days' labor	$1.50	$15	30 copper	$0.50
" " U. S. 10 " "	$1.50	$15	15 linen	$1.00
" Germany 10 " "	$1.50	$15	15 copper	$1.00
" Germany 10 " "	$1.50	$15	30 linen	$0.50

Copper moves from the United States to Germany, and linen from Germany to the United States. Exchange of goods takes place, both countries gain, and both countries *gain alike*. The barter terms of trade are no more favorable to the one country than the other; they exchange their labor par for par, so to speak. Money wages being the same, the inhabitants of each country have the same degree of benefit from the trade between them.

This last supposition is in accord with what we should expect to find, and in the main do find, in trade within the bounds of a homogeneous country — in domestic trade. If we suppose the two regions to be, for example, New York and Pennsylvania, equality of money wages may be expected, and thereby equality of gain from the trade between them. Marked divergence from such equality would lead to a movement of population from one to the other, and eventually to an equal sharing of the gain. This result is dependent, it need hardly be said, on effective homogeneity between the peoples of the two regions; the inhabitants of both are able and willing to move as freely between the regions as within them, and can apply their labor as effectively in the one as in the other.

It is hardly necessary to point out that such an equal sharing of gain, with equality in money wages, does not imply an equal distribution of population between the two regions. New York or Pennsylvania might have very different numbers. That one of them which produced the commodities most in demand would have the larger population; the other would have the smaller. The volume of output both for copper (say) in Pennsylvania and for linen in New York would adjust itself to the conditions of demand for these articles in the two states, and the distribution of workers between them would adjust itself accordingly. The free movement between them which brought about the equality of wages would bring about (probably) an unequal distribution of population and a distribution shifting with changes in demand. It is the absence of free movement, and the consequent fixity of each population, that causes something *other* than equality of remuneration to determine the share which each region shall secure of the possible gain from trade. That other factor, as will appear in the sequel, is the state of demand in the two countries for their several products.

The type of international trade considered in this chapter — that in which there are absolute differences in cost — is found mainly in the trade between tropical and temperate countries. The tropical countries have an absolute advantage, because of climatic conditions,

in their several products; the countries of the temperate zone, and
especially those of European culture, have similarly an absolute
advantage, tho resting perhaps not so preponderantly on physical
causes.   That this is the sort of trade in which a gain accrues unmistakably to both sides has long been admitted.   So obvious, indeed,
is the gain that no attempt has ever been made, at least by the
peoples of the temperate regions, to hamper it by protective duties
or other restrictions.   But tho this much is readily perceived, few
understand that trade of this kind offers not merely a possibility of
clear gain, but a possibility of greatly varying apportionment of the
gain; that it might be carried on under conditions quite different
from those familiar to us, and still be to mutual advantage; and
that the key to the apportionment of advantage is found in the
money incomes of the people of the exchanging countries.   The
most striking concrete illustration is in the trade between Great
Britain and British India.   The trade is free (some recent restrictions thru import duties are so slight as to be negligible).   Money
incomes are high in Great Britain, low in India.   Those goods
which are exchanged between them — international goods — sell
at virtually the same prices in both.   Evidently the Englishman,
with his high money income, is in a better position as purchaser
of these international goods than is the East Indian with his low
money income.   But this is no necessary feature of the trade.   It
is quite conceivable, and quite consistent with the continuance
of the trade, that the situations should be reversed: that the East
Indian, not the Englishman, should have the higher money income
and the greater share of the possible gain.   And it is no less conceivable that money incomes in the two regions should be the same,
and the gain thus shared equally.   The existing situation is not at
all a necessary outcome from the given conditions, but only one
among several possibilities; and the significant indication of the
nature of the outcome which in fact has been reached is the difference of money incomes between the exchanging countries.

CHAPTER 3

EQUAL DIFFERENCES IN COST

THE figures representing Case II, it will be remembered, are :

        In the U. S. 10 days' labor produce 30 copper
        "   " U. S. 10   "   "   "   15 linen
        " Germany 10   "   "   "   20 copper
        " Germany 10   "   "   "   10 linen

Cost in terms of labor is lower in the United States for both articles; labor is more effective all around by 50 per cent. Then we have:

        In the U. S.   15 linen = 30 copper
        In Germany { 10 linen = 20 copper }
                   { 15 linen = 30 copper }

It is obvious that no gain can accrue to either country from a direct exchange of goods for goods. In both, linen and copper, if produced within their respective limits, would exchange on the same terms. The labor that would produce 15 linen in the United States would produce in that country 30 of copper. Precisely the same is the case in Germany. If Germany were to take the product of 10 days' labor in linen (10 of linen) and carry this amount to the United States, she would there get, at the American terms of trade, 20 of copper; and that amount of copper the same 10 days of labor will enable Germany to produce. Similarly, the United States could gain nothing by sending copper to Germany for exchange against linen.

It is further obvious that the people of Germany would presumably find it to their advantage to transfer themselves *en masse* to the United States. I say presumably; the advantage would not necessarily be realized. True, Germany is the less prosperous country; labor is less effective all around than in the United States;

19

and it would seem that her people have but to move to the better region in order to enjoy its better conditions. So it would be if the cause of advantage in the United States were merely of a physical sort — climate, land, or what not — and if the Germans were quite as capable of utilizing the natural conditions as the Americans. But if the differences in effectiveness do not rest purely on physical grounds; if they are due to aptitudes which the Americans possess but the Germans do not; if the Germans on moving to the United States could not there apply their labor with the same intelligence, ingenuity, vigor, as the Americans, — there would be no certainty of gain from the shift. As we shall see, causes of this kind do operate. Not physical causes alone — natural resource and the like — determine the current of international trade; the human factor counts heavily.

At this stage of our inquiry, however, we assume that the Germans remain in their own country. It is not material for what reason they do so. It may be that they are indifferent to a possible gain from transplanting themselves, being attached to their own country, familiar with its mode of life and ignorant of life abroad, immobile even tho they might prosper by moving. They are to be supposed, for the purposes of the present argument, to go their own way regardless of the American possibilities; the Americans also go their own way. And then the two groups will have no occasion for exchange of goods.

The same conclusion is readily reached under the supposition not of barter, but of money and prices: sales of goods and transactions between individuals.

We may make at the start any supposition whatever with regard to prices and wages; it will remain to be seen what figures represent the definitive conditions. Suppose that in the United States wages are $2.00 a day, in Germany $1.00 a day. Then we have:

	WAGES PER DAY	TOTAL WAGES	PRODUCE	DOMESTIC SUPPLY PRICE
In the U. S. 10 days' labor	$2.00	$20	30 copper	$0.66⅔
" " U. S. 10 " "	$2.00	$20	15 linen	$1.33⅓
" Germany 10 " "	$1.00	$10	20 copper	$0.50
" Germany 10 " "	$1.00	$10	10 linen	$1.00

The prices of both goods are lower in Germany than in the United States. Copper and linen alike would be exported from Germany. Specie would flow from the United States to Germany; prices would fall in the United States and would rise in Germany.

Suppose now that wages are still $2.00 in the United States, but are at the same rate in Germany — $2.00. Then we have prices in the United States as before. But now —

	WAGES PER DAY	TOTAL WAGES	PRODUCE	DOMESTIC SUPPLY PRICE
In Germany 10 days' labor	$2.00	$20	20 copper	$1.00
" Germany 10 " "	$2.00	$20	10 linen	$2.00

All prices now are higher in Germany than in the United States. Both copper and linen would be sent from the United States to Germany, specie would flow from Germany to the United States, prices would fall in Germany and rise in the United States.

Lastly, suppose wages in the United States to be $2.00, in Germany $1.33⅓. Then we have (for ready comparison the United States figures are presented again):

	WAGES PER DAY	TOTAL WAGES	PRODUCE	DOMESTIC SUPPLY PRICE
In the U. S. 10 days' labor	$2.00	$20	30 copper	$0.66⅔
" " U. S. 10 " "	$2.00	$20	15 linen	$1.33⅓
" Germany 10 " "	$1.33⅓	$13.33⅓	20 copper	$0.66⅔
" Germany 10 " "	$1.33⅓	$13.33⅓	10 linen	$1.33⅓

The price of each commodity is the same in the two countries. Copper sells for $0.66⅔ in the United States and in Germany too. Linen sells for $1.33⅓ in Germany and in the United States too. Neither article will move from one country to the other. There is no trade between them.

In other words, under the conditions of equal differences in cost, money wages will adjust themselves exactly to these differences. The effectiveness of labor in the United States is to that in Germany as 3 to 2; money wages in the United States are to those in Germany as 3 to 2. Prices of goods are the same in the two countries. The people of the United States, with their higher money wages, will be able to buy more goods for the wages of a given amount of labor — one day's or ten days' — than the Germans can buy with

their wages for the same amount of labor; this being the concrete
form in which the greater material prosperity of the United States
shows itself.   There is no gain to anyone from moving goods
between the two countries.   Labor might possibly move to advantage but goods cannot move.   And so each country goes its own
way, each with its own scale of money incomes, both with the same
scale of prices.

CHAPTER 4

COMPARATIVE COSTS

WE turn now to Case III, that of differences in comparative costs. For convenience in following the numerical illustrations, I shall use in the exposition that follows a different set of figures from those of the preceding chapters. The same principles are involved; the figures now used are selected for their greater simplicity.

Let us suppose that

```
In the U. S. 10 days' labor produce 20 wheat
 "   "  U. S. 10   "      "       "   20 linen
 " Germany 10   "      "       "   10 wheat
 " Germany 10   "      "       "   15 linen
```

Here the United States has an advantage in the production of both commodities. The effectiveness of her labor is greater both in wheat and in linen, but it is not greater to the same degree in both. In wheat it is as 20:10, while in linen it is as 20:15. The American effectiveness of labor in wheat is twice as great as that of Germany; in linen it is one-third greater. There is in the United States a comparative advantage in the production of wheat.

We might denote the situation by a different set of phrases. Instead of speaking of a comparative advantage, we might say that the United States has a *superior advantage* in wheat. She has an advantage in both commodities, but one greater in wheat than in linen. Germany, on the other hand, has an *inferior disadvantage* in linen. She is at a disadvantage in producing both commodities; but the disadvantage is less in the case of linen than in that of wheat. The outcome of an inferior disadvantage in trade between countries (or for that matter between individuals, or between groups within a country) is precisely the same as that of a superior advantage.

23

They are two forms of comparative advantage, each the complement of the other.

Looking again at the figures of our case, it is obvious that in the United States 10 wheat would exchange for 10 linen if both articles were produced within the United States. In Germany 10 wheat would exchange for 15 linen if both were produced in that country. At any rates between, both countries would gain from an exchange. At an exchange of 10 wheat for 14 linen the United States would gain 4 of linen, since the 5 days' labor entailed by producing the 10 of wheat would produce in the United States not 14 of linen, but only 10. At the rate of 14 linen for 10 wheat, Germany too would gain, but not so much; her gain would be 1 of linen. If on the other hand the terms of trade were 10 wheat for 11 linen, the United States would gain 1 linen and Germany 4 linen. At any rate of 10 wheat for more than 10 linen and less than 15 linen, both would gain. And at any such intermediate rate, each would confine itself to that commodity in which it had a comparative advantage. The United States would produce only wheat, and would get all her linen by sending wheat to Germany, exchanging it for linen; she would confine herself to the industry in which she had the superior advantage. Germany would produce only linen, and would get all her wheat by sending linen to the United States and getting wheat in exchange; she would confine herself to the industry in which she had the inferior disadvantage.

Turn now from this supposition to that of a money régime. Suppose that wages in the United States are $1.50 a day; wages in Germany are $1.00 a day. These figures, be it noted again, are merely illustrative; they do not stand for a necessary or definitive outcome. Assuming them for purposes of illustration, we have further:

	WAGES PER DAY	TOTAL WAGES	PRODUCE	DOMESTIC SUPPLY PRICE
In the U. S. 10 days' labor	$1.50	$15	20 wheat	$0.75
" " U. S. 10 " "	$1.50	$15	20 linen	$0.75
" Germany 10 " "	$1.00	$10	10 wheat	$1.00
" Germany 10 " "	$1.00	$10	15 linen	$0.66⅔

Observe that the prices of the goods are such that wheat moves from the United States to Germany, linen from Germany to the United States. Wheat, tho produced in the United States by labor receiving wages higher than those in Germany, yet sells for $0.75 in the United States. Wheat, if produced in Germany would sell there for $1.00; its domestic supply price — its cost of production in the business sense — is higher in Germany even tho it is produced by labor receiving wages lower than those in the United States. This sort of situation is apt to surprise most people: how can an article sell at a low price in a country where wages are high? The answer is simple enough: it can do so if the high paid labor is effective, as in this case with American labor for wheat. On the other hand, Germany can produce linen at a lower price than the United States, notwithstanding the fact that German labor is less effective in producing linen than American. The explanation again is simple: the labor, tho less effective, is paid at a money rate which is not only less, but is lower to an extent more than in proportion to the less effectiveness. Wheat is cheaper in the United States, tho produced with high-paid labor; linen is cheaper in Germany, tho produced with ineffective labor.

Come now a step still closer to reality. What quantities of goods might be expected to move between the two countries, and what total sums of money might they represent in the way of imports and exports?

Suppose — again for illustration —

The U. S. sends to Germany 8,000,000 bushels of wheat at $0.75 = $6,000,000.
Germany sends to the U. S. 9,000,000 yards of linen at $0.66⅔ = $6,000,000.

The money sums balance; the wheat sent from the United States exactly suffices to pay for the linen received from Germany. The transactions will be carried out thru the mechanism of the foreign exchanges, and the demands for bills of exchange would be exactly met by the offerings of exchange. Exchange would be at par, no specie would flow between the two countries; all is quiet.

With these transactions, 8,000,000 bushels wheat exchange for 9,000,000 yards linen. The barter terms of trade thus are 8 wheat = 9 linen; or, 10 wheat = 11¼ linen. That the trade takes place

on these terms is a matter of which no one in either country is
conscious, unless indeed it be some sophisticated economist.   All
that appears on the surface is that some Americans sell wheat in
Germany and some Germans sell linen in the United States; and
that the two amounts are equal in the only terms of which most
persons think — in money.   That money wages are higher in the
United States is also a circumstance of which they are aware; but
they take this as a matter of course, as a sort of God-given relation,
not to be further inquired into.   The fundamental fact, which
quite escapes their attention, is that in terms of physical quantity
the people of the United States get $11\frac{1}{4}$ of linen for every 10 of
wheat which they send to Germany.

Observe what will be the conditions of prosperity — the incomes
in terms of commodities — in the two countries.   Assume that
in both one-half of the money wages is expended on wheat, one-
half on linen.   Then,

$$\text{In the U. S. one day's labor} = \$1.50 = \begin{cases} 1 \text{ wheat} \\ 1\frac{1}{8} \text{ linen} \end{cases}$$
$$\text{In Germany one day's labor} = \$1.00 = \begin{cases} \frac{2}{3} \text{ wheat} \\ \frac{3}{4} \text{ linen} \end{cases}$$

The American is able to buy with his day's wages, in addition
to the one bushel of American wheat, $1\frac{1}{8}$ yards of German linen;
just $\frac{1}{8}$ more than he could buy if the linen were made in the United
States.   The German is able to buy, in addition to $\frac{3}{4}$ yard of German linen, $\frac{2}{3}$ bushel of American wheat, whereas he would have
been able to buy only $\frac{1}{2}$ bushel if the wheat had been of German
production.   The American gains $\frac{1}{8}$ yard of linen from the international exchange; the German gains $\frac{1}{6}$ bushel of wheat.

It is conceivable, however, as was indicated by the previous
analysis of barter conditions, that the people of the United States
might exchange with Germany on better terms.   They might
get — so it has been indicated — more than 11 linen for their 10
of wheat, up to a maximum of nearly 15 linen.   Under what circumstances will they get more?

The Germans, under the above conditions of equilibrium, have
been assumed to take 8,000,000 bushels wheat from the United

States at the price of $0.75. Suppose, however, that at this price they want more than 8,000,000; the German demand for wheat increases. More than the 8,000,000 bushels are bought in Germany, and more than $6,000,000 become payable by German purchasers to Americans. Foreign exchange no longer is at par. Exchange rises in Germany, falls in the United States. Specie flows from Germany to the United States. Prices tend to rise in the United States, to fall in Germany; and not only prices, but money wages also.

The nature of the outcome of these readjustments is indicated by such figures as the following:

Wages in the United States rise from $1.50 to $1.70.
Wages in Germany fall from $1.00 to $0.90.

At these rates of money wages:

	WAGES PER DAY	TOTAL WAGES	PRODUCE	DOMESTIC SUPPLY PRICE
In the U. S. 10 days' labor	$1.70	$17	20 wheat	$0.85
" " U. S. 10 " "	$1.70	$17	20 linen	$0.85
" Germany 10 " "	$0.90	$ 9	10 wheat	$0.90
" Germany 10 " "	$0.90	$ 9	15 linen	$0.60

Observe that, as before, the prices of both articles are such that they will move from country to country. Wheat in the United States at $0.85 still sells for a lower price than that at which it can be produced in Germany ($0.90). Linen at $0.60 in Germany still sells for a lower price than that at which it can be produced in the United States ($0.85). The range of difference between the domestic supply price and the import price is now less in wheat than in linen; but the differences are of the same kind as before.

The physical quantities moving between the countries also will be affected. More wheat will move from the United States to Germany, obedient to the greater German demand. But more linen will also move from Germany to the United States. Money incomes as well as prices rise in the United States, and the Americans will be tempted to buy more German linen. Since prices (as well as money incomes) fall in Germany, the price of linen will fall and Americans will be tempted still more to buy German linen. On the other hand, as American wheat prices rise, the German purchasers, tho still buying more wheat than before, will gradually slacken in their purchases of the American article.

The final outcome will be something like the following:

U. S. sends to Germany 10,500,000 bushels wheat at $0.85 = $9,000,000.[1]
Germany sends to U. S. 15,000,000 yards linen   at $0.60 = $9,000,000.

The money sums balance. Imports exactly pay for exports in each country. Foreign exchange is again at par; no specie flows.

The barter terms of trade have now become more favorable to the United States. In the physical quantities of the goods a different relation has developed. $10\frac{1}{2}$ million bushels of wheat now exchange for 15 million yards of linen; the terms of trade are $10\frac{1}{2}$ for 15, or 10 for (nearly) $14\frac{1}{4}$. Under the previous supposition the United States got $11\frac{1}{4}$ linen for every 10 bushels of wheat; now she gets $14\frac{1}{4}$ linen for every 10 bushels.

Continuing the analysis, we may examine what would be commodity wages ("real" wages) in the two countries. If, as before, the purchasers in both spent one-half of their incomes on each commodity, we should have:

In the U. S. wages $1.70 { one-half spent on wheat @ $0.85 = 1 wheat
  "   "   " linen @ $0.60 = $1\frac{5}{12}$ linen
In Germany wages $0.90 { "   "   " wheat @ $0.85 = $\frac{9}{17}$ wheat
  "   "   " linen @ $0.60 = $\frac{3}{4}$ linen

American wages have risen in terms of linen. Before, the day's commodity wages were 1 wheat plus $1\frac{1}{8}$ linen; now they are 1 wheat plus $1\frac{5}{12}$ linen. German wages will have fallen in terms of wheat; the day's commodity wages, which had been $\frac{3}{4}$ linen plus $\frac{2}{3}$ wheat, now are $\frac{3}{4}$ linen plus $\frac{9}{17}$ wheat. The less advantageous terms on which the trade takes place for Germany are reflected in lower commodity incomes for the Germans; and the more advantageous terms for the United States are reflected in higher commodity incomes for the Americans.

[1] The figures are not exact but may be accepted for purposes of illustration.

These last figures, however, call for correction. They have been worked out on the supposition that, as before, one-half of the wages in each country are spent on linen, one-half on wheat. But this supposition is not consistent with what has been assumed with regard to the conditions of demand; namely, that the demand of the Germans for wheat has increased. The Germans, under that assumption no longer spend one half of their wages on wheat. They have come to spend a *larger* proportion of their total income on wheat. The Americans, on the other hand, have been tempted by rising prices of wheat to send more of that commodity to Germany, and have been led to consume *less* of it themselves. And they have also been tempted by falling prices of linen to buy from the Germans more of that article; they have come to spend a larger proportion of their income on linen. We need to modify our figures accordingly.

Make the modification by supposing that under the changed conditions of demand $\frac{3}{5}$ of the Americans' income is spent on linen, $\frac{2}{5}$ of it on wheat; and that in Germany $\frac{1}{3}$ of the income is spent on linen, $\frac{2}{3}$ on wheat. Then we have:

In the U. S. wages $1.70 $\begin{cases} \frac{2}{5} \text{ or } \$0.68 \text{ spent on wheat @ } \$0.85 = \frac{8}{10} \text{ wheat} \\ \frac{3}{5} \text{ or } \$1.02 \quad '' \quad '' \text{ linen @ } \$0.60 = 1\frac{7}{10} \text{ linen} \end{cases}$

In Germany wages $0.90 $\begin{cases} \frac{2}{3} \text{ or } \$0.60 \quad '' \quad '' \text{ wheat @ } \$0.85 = \frac{14}{17} \text{ wheat} \\ \frac{1}{3} \text{ or } \$0.30 \quad '' \quad '' \text{ linen @ } \$0.60 = \frac{5}{10} \text{ linen} \end{cases}$

Compare now the figures with those arrived at on page 26, where the commodity wages were worked out under the first set of conditions, before the increase in German demand for wheat. Because of the increase in demand the nature of the changes in commodity wages is as follows:

	BEFORE	AFTER
In the U. S. commodity wages were	$\begin{cases} 1 \text{ wheat} \\ 1\frac{1}{8} \text{ linen} \end{cases}$	$\begin{cases} \frac{8}{10} \text{ wheat} \\ 1\frac{7}{10} \text{ linen} \end{cases}$
In Germany commodity wages were	$\begin{cases} \frac{2}{3} \text{ wheat} \\ \frac{3}{4} \text{ linen} \end{cases}$	$\begin{cases} 1\frac{4}{7} \text{ wheat} \\ \frac{5}{10} \text{ linen} \end{cases}$

Can it be held, under this revised (and consistent) statement, that commodity wages in the United States have unquestionably risen, those in Germany unquestionably fallen? True, the Americans get for the day's labor more linen than before — $1\frac{7}{10}$ linen instead of $1\frac{1}{2}$. But they also get less wheat — $\frac{8}{10}$ instead of 1. The gain in linen is considerable, the loss in wheat comparatively small. But are wheat and linen commensurable? And is it certain that the Americans secure a net gain from having more of linen when they also have less of wheat? The Germans, on the other hand, while they have less of linen — only $\frac{5}{10}$ linen instead of $\frac{3}{4}$ — have a bit more of wheat: they have $1\frac{2}{7}$ instead of $\frac{2}{3}$. For them, also, is it certain that the loss in linen over-balances the gain in wheat? Their loss in linen is considerable, the gain in wheat is slight; but the question for them, also, is how can these changes in the quantities of different commodities be reduced to common terms?

The only answer is that in terms of "utilities" (satisfactions, enjoyments, gratifications) *both* Germans and Americans have gained. In ultimate income, in terms of the psychological outcome, all are better off than before. This is shown by the simple fact of choice. As is assumed in the entire hedonistic calculus, it is choice between alternatives which alone shows whether we "like" or "enjoy" one source of satisfaction more than another. The Americans get less of wheat than they got before; but they have been led to accept that less amount because they have been tempted by the cheapness of linen. The fact that they give up some wheat in order to get more linen proves that the rearrangement suits them better, that their income in terms of satisfactions is greater than before. The Germans, too, while they have less linen than before, have more of wheat. Had it not been for their desire to have more wheat, they would not have parted with so much of their own product in order to get so small an addition of the American product. Given their changed demand, they are better off than before; they must like the present situation better than the earlier one or it would never have developed.[1]

The sense in which it can be said, then, that the new conditions

---

[1] This is no more than an illustration of the general principle that under complete freedom the terms on which the trading parties exchange can not alter unless there be an advantage to both sides from the altered terms.

of exchange are unfavorable to the Germans is simply that in physical units more of the German product is given for the American than before. In this sense, and in this only, are the barter terms of exchange less favorable to Germany than before.

Returning now to the main trend of the argument, we may state as follows the general conclusions which are indicated. The barter terms of trade between the countries depend on their states of demand; on the intensity and elasticity of Germany's demand for wheat, of America's demand for linen. The limits within which the terms of trade are confined depend on the range of difference in costs. In the case supposed, 10 of wheat can exchange for any amount of linen between 10 and 15. But the mere analysis of the differences in costs indicates nothing about the precise point between the limiting extremes at which the exchange will take place. That depends on the conditions of demand in the two countries. The greater the German demand for wheat, the more likely is it that the terms will be such as to yield Germany less wheat in exchange for her linen; the rate will be nearer 15 than 10. On the same reasoning, the less the elasticity of the German demand for wheat — the more her takings of wheat will persist with little abatement, notwithstanding a rising price of wheat — the more likely it is that the terms of trade will be disadvantageous to her. In the United States the moving forces are the same: the less her demand for linen, and the less easily that demand is stimulated by falling price, the more the terms will be to her advantage.[1] In the second case supposed above, where the German demand for wheat has increased, the Germans, as the price of wheat begins to rise, will gradually lessen their purchases. But the extent of the check to their purchases will depend on the elasticity of their demand. The more persistent is that demand, the less it is checked by rising price, the greater will be the alteration of the terms of trade to Germany's disadvantage. The flow of specie out of Germany will then continue longer than it would if demand were less persistent (i.e. less inelastic), and the fall in

---

[1] Stated in technical language, and in terms of diagrams, the two factors are the *position* of the demand curve and the *slope* of the demand curve.

German prices and in money incomes will go on until the eventual limit is approached when there is no longer any gain at all to Germany from the exchange. In the United States, on the other hand, the extent of the readjustment will be affected by the state of her demand for linen. If that demand is elastic — if her people buy more linen quickly as the price begins to fall — the movement of specie into the United States will be less great than it would be if the demand were inelastic. The rise in prices and in money incomes will be less, the alteration in the barter terms of trade less markedly to the American advantage.

Something must be added to this. It is not merely the character of the American demand for German goods that has to be considered. Regard must be had also to the demand schedules of the Americans for their own product, of the Germans for theirs. When German linen falls in price, the Americans, while tempted to buy more linen, must consider the fact that in order to do so they must dispense with some wheat which they have been consuming. And the Germans on their part, when American wheat rises in price, have to consider that their payment of an additional price for the wheat necessarily involves a diminution in the amount they can spend on their own linen.

In other words, the supposition of the preceding paragraphs tacitly included the assumption that the Germans did experience this sort of double change in their demand schedules. When the German demand for wheat increases, as was assumed above, that very change necessarily implies that the German demand for linen is less insistent than before. They care more for wheat and less for linen.

Analogous, tho not quite the same, is the position of the Americans. They are offered more of linen than before for a given quantity of wheat, and have to decide whether they will take more linen and consume less of their own wheat. The character or intensity of their demand for the two articles is not supposed to have altered. It is only that, with demand schedules unchanged, they are called on to use less of wheat and to buy more of linen. While the outcome depends in both countries on the double aspect of demand, — on the relation in each country between the conditions of demand both for the domestic product and for the foreign product — those conditions of relative demand have been supposed to alter in the one country, but not in the other.

In all this, be it noted, it is the changes in prices and in money incomes which serve to bring about the eventual results. Under the modified conditions brought about by an increase in the German demand for wheat, the concrete form in which advantage comes to the United States is that money incomes are higher, prices of imported goods (linen) are lower. And for the Germans the concrete form in which the disadvantage to them appears is that money incomes are lower, prices of imported goods (wheat) are higher. The quicker the flow of specie begins and the more prompt its influence on prices and incomes, the sooner will the readjustment work itself out. The whole chain of operations depends on monetary movements and monetary influences; a fact which cannot be too strongly emphasized when it comes to a testing or verification of the whole series of propositions presented in their simplest theoretic formulation.

CHAPTER 5

WAGES AND PRICES IN DIFFERENT COUNTRIES
DOMESTIC PRICES AND INTERNATIONAL PRICES

IN the preceding chapters the subject has been treated as if each and every commodity were within the range of international trade; or rather, as if there existed no other commodity than those within its range. Wheat and linen (or copper and linen) have alone been considered. Assuming that the conditions found for these are representative — that other commodities are in the same general situation as they — we reach the conclusion that some things, such as wheat, will be produced solely in the United States, while others, such as linen, will be produced solely in Germany. The price of each article will be the same thruout the trading areas (barring of course the differences that may result from cost of transportation). The purchasing power of money in terms of goods will be the same in the two countries. Money wages, however, will not be the same. In the case selected as illustrative they were found to be higher in the United States. The extent to which they may be higher — the maximum divergence — depends on the extent of the advantage possessed by the United States in the commodity which she exports. Within this maximum, the actual excess of American wages depends on the play of demand between the two bodies of consumers. The fundamental features of the situation, so far as its analysis has been carried hitherto, are that prices are the same in the two countries, while money wages vary.

But the supposition that all goods come within the range of international trade is not at all in accord with the facts. The scope of international trade is by no means all-embracing. So far from its being the case that each and every article is made solely

34

in one country and thence sent out to others — that all enter into foreign trade — it is more generally true that the goods made in a given country are sold and used in that country only. The conditions of international trade affect not the whole of a country's trade but only a minor part of it. We must distinguish between the *international* and the *domestic* goods: those, on the one hand, which are the objects of import and export trade and are the same in price thruout the international field; and those, on the other hand, which are not imported or exported at all, and do not necessarily have the same price in one country as in another. What can be said of the prices of the domestic commodities?

The essence of the answer to this question can be indicated by a simple illustration. Consider again the figures of the last case in the preceding chapter.

	Wages per Day	Total Wages	Produce	Domestic Supply Price
In the U. S. 10 days' labor	$1.50	$15	20 linen	$0.75
" " U. S. 10 " "	$1.50	$15	20 wheat	$0.75
" Germany 10 " "	$1.00	$10	15 linen	$0.66⅔
" Germany 10 " "	$1.00	$10	10 wheat	$1.00

Wheat and linen are international commodities, each produced solely in the country having the comparative advantage for it. Suppose now we have bricks, so bulky in proportion to value that cost of transportation is prohibitive. They cannot be shipped from country to country, but are produced in each country, and are sold in each quite independently. Wages being higher in the United States, most persons would say that bricks also must there be higher in price. But this is not at all certain to be the case; the converse is just as possible. Suppose that

	Wages per Day	Total Wages	Produce	Domestic Supply Price
In the U. S. 10 days' labor	$1.50	$15	2000 bricks	$0.75 per 100
" Germany 10 " "	$1.00	$10	1000 bricks	$1.00 per 100

We suppose, that is, the effectiveness of American labor in brickmaking to be high as compared with the effectiveness of German labor in that industry. The United States has the same advantage over Germany in brick-making as she has in her export industry (wheat); as regards both wheat and bricks the same labor produces twice as much in the United States as in Germany. The 10 days' labor produce 2000 bricks in the United States and but 1000 in Germany. Then, altho wages are higher in the United States, bricks are actually lower in price.

If now we change our supposition by assuming that the effectiveness of labor in the United States is not double that in Germany, but only one and one-half times as great, — if the 10 days' American labor produce 1500, — the American price of brick will be $1.00 per 100, identically the same as the German price. And if we change still further by assuming that the effectiveness of labor is the same in the two countries, — if in the United States as well as in Germany the 10 days produce 1000 bricks — the price will be higher in the United States; the American price will be $1.50 and the German $1.00.

In other words, the prices of domestic goods are not necessarily higher in a country of higher money wages. They will be higher only if the effectiveness of labor is *not* higher in the purely domestic field. If the effectiveness of labor is positively higher than it is for the same articles in foreign countries, domestic prices may be as low in those countries or may be lower. High wages and high prices do not go together, either as regards international commodities or domestic commodities.

We may proceed now to indicate summarily what determines the range of money wages in a given country and what determines that of commodity wages.

Money wages, it is seen, are high in a country which has advantageous terms of international trade, which carries on trade with other countries in such way as to secure large gains from the trade, — favorable barter terms of trade. The main factors on which these gains depend have been sufficiently indicated: an outstanding comparative advantage, and the play of demand in the terms of trade. High money wages and incomes are the indication of favorable terms of trade, and constitute the mechanism by which the gains are secured. The countries having these favorable conditions realize them concretely by buying with their larger

money incomes foreign commodities which are cheaper than they
would be if produced at home.

Regard, however, must be had also to what may be called the
absolute effectiveness of labor. On this something has already
been said, in our consideration of the nature and consequences of
absolute differences in cost; and more will be said when we come
to the competition of two (or more) countries when exporting the
same goods to a third country.[1] The bearing of absolute effectiveness can be readily indicated. Referring to our illustrative case,
we might modify the figures by supposing that in the United
States five days of labor, not ten, were required for producing the
stated quantities of linen and wheat. We should then have the
following:

	WAGES PER DAY	TOTAL WAGES	PRODUCE	DOMESTIC SUPPLY PRICE
In the U. S. 5 days' labor	$3.00	$15	20 linen	$0.75
" " U. S. 5 " "	$3.00	$15	20 wheat	$0.75
" Germany 10 " "	$1.00	$10	15 linen	$0.66⅔
" Germany 10 " "	$1.00	$10	10 wheat	$1.00

The United States here has the same comparative advantage
as before, but a greater absolute advantage in both commodities —
an even greater all-around effectiveness of labor than was before
assumed. Money wages in the United States are correspondingly
higher — twice as high as in the original supposition. But the
domestic supply prices remain as before; and so it is as regards
the sharing of gains ascribable to the barter terms of trade.

The general level of prices is not necessarily higher in the country
having the more effective labor, the more favorable terms, the
larger gains from international trade. True, prices of international
goods will be at the same level (still barring cost of transportation)
in the favored countries and in those not favored. But prices of
domestic goods obey laws of their own. Some of them may be
higher in price than abroad, some may be lower; and the general
level of domestic prices may therefore be higher or lower. So far
as the effectiveness of labor in producing domestic goods is great
(great, that is, in comparison with that of labor applied in other

---

[1] See Chapter 10.

countries to the same goods) they will tend to be lower in price. Conversely they will tend to be higher if the effectiveness of labor in producing them is small.

Concerning real wages also — wages in terms of commodities — no general rule can be laid down. Most persons would say that the people of the country where high wages prevail are more prosperous than those of countries with low wages. They may be or may not be. They are indeed better off as purchasers and consumers of international commodities; these being at the same prices everywhere. As regards domestic commodities, on which much the larger part of their money income is spent, they may be better off or may not be. It depends on the prices of these, which depend in turn, as we have just seen, on the effectiveness of labor in making them. The prices of domestic commodities may be higher than in other countries, and the people of the high-money-wages country, tho prosperous as purchasers of foreign goods, may be so much less prosperous in their domestic transactions that the net balance may be against them: their commodity wages may be less than in countries with low money wages.

I have just referred to the common but mistaken impression that a country of high money wages is necessarily more prosperous than one with low money wages. There are other common impressions even more widespread and more unqualifiedly wrong. Perhaps most familiar and most unfounded of all is the belief that complete freedom of trade would bring about an equalization of money wages the world over. It is a belief held especially in countries of high wages like the United States, and it goes with — indeed, is a part of — the most persuasive argument in favor of a policy of tariff protection. It seems plain as a pikestaff to the average person — to the average employer not less than to the average workman — that the country in which money wages are low can undersell the country paying high money wages; and that if the two compete without restriction, wages must become the same in both. The reasoning of the preceding chapters shows that there is no such tendency to equalization. Countries with high money wages trade with those of low money wages, to the advantage of both, and with permanent maintenance of the divergences in wages. The reasoning is simple enough. Stripped to the essentials, as it here has been, it can be followed with ease; and in the sequel it will be shown to be no less convincing when elaborated, qualified, illustrated, and verified from manifold facts in the world of affairs. Yet to most persons it seems perplexing and anomalous, and remains so even tho the main lines are followed and accepted on the first summary presentation. In the field of economics, as in every intellectual field, fundamental principles, however simple, are not really understood until they are applied, repeated, turned over, gradually worked into the full intellectual equipment of the recipient. Elaboration, manifold testing, verification, are necessary not only for the refinement and accuracy of the principles themselves, but also for their assimilation.

Another notion, equally erroneous, relates to international differences in commodity wages. With the belief that unfettered trade between nations must lead to an equalization of money wages goes naturally the belief that it will lead to an equalization of "the standard of living"; and more particularly will bring a lowering of the standard of the prosperous countries to that of the less prosperous. People do not often distinguish with any care between money wages and commodity wages; they are apt to apply the same impressions and fears to both without discrimination. So far as they do distinguish, they fear equalization and lowering quite as much with respect to the standard of living in terms of commodities as to wages in terms of money. After what has been said of domestic prices and commodity incomes, it is superfluous to dwell on the point. Differences in commodity incomes as well as differences in money incomes may persist under complete freedom of trade. The causes of the possible persistence of the differences, even with free exchange between countries, are no less clear than they are with regard to money wages.

In general, then, we may say that high wages and incomes on the one hand, and high prices of goods on the other, do not go together. They do not go together as regards international goods; those are the same in price between countries, while money wages vary. They do not go together as regards domestic goods; these vary from country to country, but do not necessarily vary in accord with money wages.

Nevertheless, there is a sense in which high wages and high prices do go together. Money wages and domestic prices run parallel; *changes* in money wages tend to accompany changes in domestic prices. If anything should occur which served to raise money wages — for example, altered and more favorable terms of international trade — a corresponding change would take place in domestic prices: they would rise to the same extent. Import prices, under the action of this factor, would not rise; they would fall. But domestic prices would adjust themselves to the higher level brought about by the new international conditions. Money wages would rise first in the export industries; the rise would then spread; eventually prices of goods and money wages in the purely domestic industries would be such as to render them as attractive as the export industries. This assumes, of course, that other things remain the same; that, for example, the technical methods of production remain unchanged — that no inventions or improvements are made which serve to increase the effectiveness of labor in the domestic industries. Such changes may operate to lower the price of a domestic article or series of articles at the same time in which international conditions are tending to raise them. We should then have the familiar case of interacting causes, in which the effect of the particular cause under inquiry is modified but not wiped out by others. Setting aside qualifications of this sort, which obviously do not affect the essentials of the conclusions, we may say that the relations of money wages and domestic prices, once they are established, remain the same. Domestic prices in the United States may be higher or lower than domestic prices in Germany; if higher, then a rise in United States money wages will carry them still higher; if lower, such a rise will make them less low.

It has already been intimated — to return to the main argument of this chapter — that the distinction between domestic and international commodities is an important one. How important it is, will appear more fully as we proceed.   It has been singularly neglected in the exposition of the theory of international trade and of its application.   Most writers have dealt with the subject as if wages and prices not only moved together, but were necessarily at similar levels : as if high prices all around must go with high wages, and low prices all around with low wages.   Commonly they speak as if advantageous terms of international trade must mean that the value of money is low all around, and prices high all around ; not only that there are high money wages, but that all domestic goods, all services, all lands, houses, and lodgings are correspondingly high.   Not so ;   the negative may be insisted on once more.   And since the domestic trade of every country quite outweighs its international trade, and the portion of its national dividend that comes from its purely domestic trade is the greater, it follows that the negative is no less important in its practical applications than in its theoretical significance.

Altho the present chapter, like all in Part I, is concerned mainly with a theoretical formulation, most matters of verification and illustration being postponed to Part II, a word may be said here on the extent to which practical application can be made of the distinction between domestic and international prices.   The needed statistical information too often is sadly lacking.   In but few cases have we price records which separate the goods that enter into foreign commerce from those that come on the domestic market only.   Most price data are prepared indiscriminately for any and all commodities, and most index numbers refer to one general (and for our purposes often confusing) price level.   Some of the most interesting and significant points in the theory of foreign trade are difficult to verify — cannot readily be subjected to the test of conformity to the facts of the case — because we do not possess the data in suitable arrangement and classification.

It is to be observed, however, that in one important respect we are not entirely bare of the information we need ; namely, on the rates of money wages.   Here there are, at least for some countries and for recent times, instructive figures.   They are more than instructive ; they bear on the heart of the matter.   The fundamental thing in the movement of domestic prices, as distinct from international, is the movement of money incomes; and among these, again, the basic are the wages of manual labor, such as are usually registered in the index numbers of wages. Here is the item that is most significant and most easy to interpret and follow. Changes in money wages, so far as peculiar to a given country — so far as due, that is, to causes affecting it alone, and not a reflex of a general movement appearing throughout the commercial world — are at once the chief indicator of changes in other domestic "prices", and also the effective mechanism through which the greater or less gain from international trade is transmitted to the several peoples. It is this which should especially be watched, and it is this, fortunately, which the statistical material, when available at all, is most likely to lay bare.

CHAPTER 6

WAGES NOT UNIFORM — NON-COMPETING GROUPS

In the present chapter, a qualification will be introduced. It is not so much a correction as an elaboration; another of the steps which are needed in order to bring the theoretic analysis more nearly into accord with the facts of trade. It is one, moreover, to which virtually no attention has been given in the literature of the subject.

In the reasoning of Ricardo and Mill, it was almost always assumed that within a country commodities exchanged in proportion to the quantities of labor necessary to produce them. Goods exchanged par for par in terms of labor. In our own very first suppositions — those of trade conducted under barter — it was assumed that if in the United States 10 days' labor produced 20 of wheat and 20 of linen, wheat and linen would of course exchange within the United States at the rate of 1 wheat for 1 linen. And in Germany, if 10 days produced 10 of wheat and 15 of linen, 1 of wheat would exchange for 1½ of linen. It was the very fact that within each country the relative values of goods depended on labor expended which led to the possibility of trade between the countries, and to the special problem of the terms on which they might barter their products. Similarly, when exchange thru the medium of money came to be taken up, the prices of goods within each country were supposed to depend on the labor given to making them — on their cost of production in the sense of labor applied. If 10 days' labor produced in the United States 20 wheat and 20 linen, wheat and linen would sell for the same price; with American wages at $1.50, each would sell for $0.75. If 10 days produced in Germany 10 wheat and 15 linen, wheat and linen would not sell for the same price; with German wages at

$1.00, wheat would sell for $1.00 and linen for $0.66⅔. In other words, wages were assumed to be not, indeed, on the same level in the two countries, but at one and the same level in all industries thruout the United States and at one and the same level in all industries thruout Germany.

The familiar fact, however, is that there is no uniformity of wages within any country. There are differences within each country as well as differences between countries. The workmen who produce wheat in Germany may receive lower wages than those producing linen in Germany; and the wheat laborers in the United States may be in a position of similar disadvantage. Obviously such differences could not persist if there were perfect freedom of movement from occupation to occupation within each country; just as the differences of commodity income and of substantial prosperity between countries could not persist if there were perfect international freedom of movement. To designate the actual situation within countries it will be convenient to use Cairnes's phrase "non-competing groups." The workers in the several occupations (or groups of occupations) may be said to be in groups which do not completely compete one with another. There are persistent obstacles to transfer from one group to another, and therefore persistent differences of wages, not smoothed out by the movement of men from the lower-paid groups to the higher.

Given this sort of situation, it follows that the prices of goods are not in accord with the quantities of labor devoted to producing them. Even tho wheat and linen be produced in the United States with the same amount of labor, the two articles will not sell for the same price if the wheat producers get lower wages. On the other hand, two articles may sell for the same price even tho produced with different amounts of labor. Wheat and linen may be produced by different amounts of labor in Germany; yet, if the rates of wages are inverse to the labor amounts — higher where the days of labor are few, lower where they are many— wheat and linen will sell for the same price. International trade, however, like domestic trade, is proximately a matter of money sale and purchase. Goods do not exchange directly for goods; they are sold for money and bought for money. The immediate actuating force is always that of the individual transaction — the sale of goods to advantage; and this means sale at a profit. How then can we have any assurance that such conclusions as were deduced in the preceding chapters concerning the influence of comparative labor costs have validity for the actual world? Goods are not bartered — wheat for linen — between countries. They are sold by individuals for cash. Their sale depends on prices; and prices are not necessarily, perhaps not usually, determined by quantities of labor given to producing the goods. How modify, adapt, reconcile our analysis of international trade to these plain facts?

Let us revert to the case considered in the preceding chapter. The figures with which we there began, it will be remembered, were as follows:

	WAGES PER DAY	TOTAL WAGES	PRODUCE	DOMESTIC SUPPLY PRICE
In the U. S. 10 days' labor	$1.50	$15	20 wheat	$0.75
" " U. S. 10 " "	$1.50	$15	20 linen	$0.75
" Germany 10 " "	$1.00	$10	10 wheat	$1.00
" Germany 10 " "	$1.00	$10	15 linen	$0.66⅔

The money cost of production of wheat is lower in the United States than in Germany; that of linen is lower in Germany. Trade takes place, the United States sending wheat, Germany sending linen. We still treat the wages outlay — that which the business world designates as "labor cost" — as if it were the sole item in supply price; return to capital is left for subsequent treatment.

Suppose now, that the German wheat laborers get as wages not $1.00 a day but only $0.66⅔. Suppose them to be, among the Germans, in a non-competing group, unfavorably situated, receiving less wages than obtained in other industries, but unable to betake themselves to the more prosperous group and therefore permanently in receipt of the lower pay. For the present, accept differences of this kind, whether in Germany or in the United States, as simply existent, disregarding the question how they come to exist, and how far they may be related to international trade, in the last analysis, as effects rather than as causes. These aspects of the problem will be considered at the close of the present chapter. Taking the modified wages figures, then, we have further modifications in the other figures thus:

	WAGES PER DAY	TOTAL WAGES	PRODUCE	DOMESTIC SUPPLY PRICE
In the U. S. 10 days' labor	$1.50	$15	20 wheat	$0.75
" " U. S. 10 " "	$1.50	$15	20 linen	$0.75
" Germany 10 " "	$0.66⅔	$ 6.66	10 wheat	$0.66⅔
" Germany 10 " "	$1.00	$10	15 linen	$0.66⅔

The supply price of wheat in Germany has fallen to $0.66⅔. The labor in that occupation is comparatively ineffective, yet its price to the employing capitalist is low. Wheat can be sold at a comparatively low price, even tho it requires comparatively much labor to produce.

Observe further that both wheat and linen are now lower in price in Germany than in the United States. Both will be sold indiscriminately in the United States by German exporters. On the other hand no commodity can move from the United States to Germany. Specie will flow to Germany and prices will rise there. Prices will fall in the United States. The rise in Germany and the fall in the United States will go on until both wheat and linen sell for the same prices in the two countries.

The resulting situation will be of the following sort:

	WAGES PER DAY	TOTAL WAGES	PRODUCE	DOMESTIC SUPPLY PRICE
In the U. S. 10 days' labor	$1.40	$14	20 wheat	$0.70
" " U. S. 10 " "	$1.40	$14	20 linen	$0.70
" Germany 10 " "	$0.70	$ 7	10 wheat	$0.70
" Germany 10 " "	$1.05	$10.50	15 linen	$0.70

The movement of specie will then cease, and all movement will cease. There will be no trade between the countries. Each will go its way regardless of the other. The case will be the same in its outcome as that of equal differences in costs.

What this signifies evidently is that the lower wages for German wheat growers have the same sort of effect as would a higher effectiveness of their labor. In terms of labor-cost, of effectiveness of labor, Germany has a comparative disadvantage in producing wheat. But this is offset, so far as the supply price of wheat is concerned, by the specially lower wages. In the market it is all one whether there be higher effectiveness of labor or lower rate of wages. Wheat would sell at a lower price ($0.66⅔) if the labor were as effective as German labor is in linen; it sells at that same lower price if the labor is obtainable at the lower rate of pay. International trade, to repeat, is governed proximately by prices; and the ruling prices, under this supposition of a non-competing group, are such that wheat is not sent from the United States to Germany even tho the United States has unmistakably a comparative advantage for producing it.

Now make a further supposition. Suppose that not only in Germany, but in the United States as well, the wheat laborers are in a low-lying group; that these Americans, like their German fellows, receive lower wages than obtain in other occupations, and therefore lower wages than the linen workers. Suppose that while wages in the United States are in general $1.50 a day, the wheat workers get no more than $1.00 a day. The German wheat workers, in their turn, receive only $0.66⅔ a day, as against a ruling German rate of $1.00 a day. Then our figures must be modified as follows:

	WAGES PER DAY	TOTAL WAGES	PRODUCE	DOMESTIC SUPPLY PRICE
In the U. S. 10 days' labor	$1.00	$10	20 wheat	$0.50
" " U. S. 10 " "	$1.50	$15	20 linen	$0.75
" Germany 10 " "	$0.66⅔	$ 6.66	10 wheat	$0.66⅔
" Germany 10 " "	$1.00	$10	15 linen	$0.66⅔

Prices are now such that commodities move both ways. The American supply price of wheat ($0.50) is now lower than the German supply price ($0.66⅔). Similarly German linen at $0.66⅔ is lower in supply price than American linen ($0.75). Trade between the two countries takes place as it would if the differences in wages within each of them did not exist — as if there were uniformity of wages in each and no non-competing groups at all.

The general conclusion thus indicated is that the existence of non-competing groups within a country affects international trade only so far as the situation thus engendered is peculiar to that country. If the groups are in the same relative positions in the exchanging countries as regards wages — if the hierarchy, so to speak, is arranged on the same plan in each — trade takes place exactly as if it were governed by the strict and simple principle of comparative costs. If the rate of wages in a given occupation is particularly low in one country, this circumstance will affect international trade exactly as would a high effectiveness of labor in that country. But if in other countries also the same occupation has a particularly low rate of wages, international trade will not be affected. The coefficient to be allowed for will be the same all around, and no special influence on trade between the countries will be felt. Trade will develop as it would if prices within each country were governed by labor costs alone.

For further illustration, let us turn to a variant of the previous case. Starting with a situation in which, so far as labor costs go, exchange cannot be expected to arise, introduce the complication of non-competing groups and observe how under the changed conditions exchange becomes possible and advantageous.

	Wages per Day	Total Wages	Produce	Domestic Supply Price
In the U. S. 10 days' labor	$2.00	$20	30 wheat	$0.66⅔
″ ″ U. S. 10 ″ ″	$2.00	$20	20 linen	$1.00
″ Germany 10 ″ ″	$1.00	$10	15 wheat	$0.66⅔
″ Germany 10 ″ ″	$1.00	$10	10 linen	$1.00

The case, it will be seen, is one of equal differences in cost. The effectiveness of labor in the United States is twice as great thruout as in Germany. Money wages in the United States are adjusted to this relation and are twice as high. Wheat is at the same price in the United States as in Germany; linen also at the same price in the two countries. Wages in each country are uniform — that is, are the same in wheat-growing as in linen-making. There are no non-competing groups. Prices are in accord with the respective quantities of labor. Germans and Americans go their way regardless of each others' doings.

Suppose now that German *linen* wages are not $1.00 but $0.75. The linen workers are in a low-lying non-competing group; their wages are less than prevail in other German industries. Our figures then are modified thus :

	WAGES PER DAY	TOTAL WAGES	PRODUCE	DOMESTIC SUPPLY PRICE
In the U. S. 10 days' labor	$2.00	$20	30 wheat	$0.66¾
" " U. S. 10 " "	$2.00	$20	20 linen	$1.00
" Germany 10 " "	$1.00	$10	15 wheat	$0.66¾
" Germany 10 " "	$0.75	$ 7.50	10 linen	$0.75

Wheat is still at the same price in both countries. But linen is now cheaper in Germany, and moves from Germany to the United States. At first specie alone moves from the United States to Germany. As prices fall in the United States and rise in Germany, wheat becomes cheaper in the former and dearer in the latter. Wages fall in the United States, rise in Germany. Equilibrium will be reached under conditions somewhat like these :

	WAGES PER DAY	TOTAL WAGES	PRODUCE	DOMESTIC SUPPLY PRICE
In the U. S. 10 days' labor	$1.80	$18	30 wheat	$0.60
" " U. S. 10 " "	$1.80	$18	20 linen	$0.90
" Germany 10 " "	$1.10	$11	15 wheat	$0.73⅓
" Germany 10 " "	$0.82½	$ 8.25	10 linen	$0.82½

This particular relation of prices and of money wages would be reached (wages in the United States $1.80, wages in Germany generally $1.10), as need not again be explained, if the demand for linen in the United States and the demand for wheat in Germany were such that the money value of the wheat sent from the United States exactly equalled the money value of the linen sent from Germany. The general outcome would plainly be that trade developed precisely as if the Germans had a comparative labor advantage — a comparative effectiveness of labor — in making linen. The conditions of labor cost are such that if these were the only governing factors, no trade between the two countries would develop. But the exceptionally low wages of the German linen workers cause Germany to have the equivalent of a comparative advantage. The case is the converse of that just considered.

Now push the matter a step still further. Tho we may conceive of non-competing groups as separate and distinct, it never happens

— virtually never — that a given commodity is produced solely by laborers of one group only. The usual situation, when once the division of labor has been considerably developed, is that a commodity is made by a combination of laborers belonging to different groups. The several laborers whose work serves to turn out linen, for example, will probably not be all in the same stratum; some will be well-paid, such as the mechanics who make and repair the machinery, others will be unskilled operatives who tend and operate it. The combinations are various in the different industries, various in different stages of industrial development, various in different countries. They are likely to be less heterogeneous (to refer again to the example of linen) where there is a household handicraft industry, such as long persisted in Germany, than where there is a highly developed factory system, such as alone is to be found in the American textile industries. The combinations are likely to be more heterogeneous and elaborate in manufactures than in agriculture; more so in countries industrially advanced like England or Switzerland than in those industrially backward like Spain or Portugal. But in every case, if account is taken of *all* the labor involved in producing a given article — of the labor given to the raw material, of that fashioning it, of that transporting and marketing it — some combination of different grades of labor will be found. The theory of international trade must be adjusted to this all-pervading heterogeneity.

For illustration of the working of this factor, return to a case of comparative costs such as was considered in the initial stages of our analysis.

In the U. S.	10	days'	labor	produce	20 wheat
" " U. S.	10	"	"	"	20 linen
" Germany	10	"	"	"	10 wheat
" Germany	10	"	"	"	15 linen

The case is one in which the United States has a comparative advantage in wheat — a superior advantage. Germany has a comparative advantage in linen — an inferior disadvantage. Under barter, the two would obviously find it advantageous to exchange American wheat for German linen. Under a money régime, with no non-competing groups and with prices adjusted in accord with labor costs in each country, the same result as obviously would ensue.

Suppose now something like the usual industrial situation : not merely non-competing groups, but also laborers from different groups combined in the making of any one article. Suppose that in the United States there are some groups whose established pay is $1.50 a day, others whose established pay is $1.00 a day. In Germany there are groups whose established pay is $1.00, others with $0.66⅔. In each country higher-paid and lower-paid laborers are joined in the making of linen, and are joined also in the making of wheat. For simplicity, suppose that in each industry one-half of the laborers thus combined are from the upper stratum, one-half are from the lower stratum. Then we have the following :

			Wages per Day	Total Wages	Produce	Domestic Supply Price
In the U. S. 10 days' labor {	5 days	@ $1.50 }		$12.50	20 wheat	$0.62½
	5 "	@ $1.00 }				
In the U. S. 10 days' labor {	5 "	@ $1.50 }		$12.50	20 linen	$0.62½
	5 "	@ $1.00 }				
In Germany 10 days' labor {	5 "	@ $1.00 }		$ 8.33	10 wheat	$0.83
	5 "	@ $0.66⅔ }				
In Germany 10 days' labor {	5 "	@ $1.00 }		$ 8.33	15 linen	$0.55½
	5 "	@ $0.66⅔ }				

Observe the domestic supply prices of the two articles. Wheat is cheaper in the United States, linen is cheaper in Germany. Wheat goes from the United States to Germany, linen from Germany to the United States. Precisely the same sort of trade takes place as would be found if there were no non-competing groups.

The general proposition to which this leads is simple enough, and indeed hardly needs to be brought out by figures. If the combinations of several sorts of labor, paid at varying rates, are *the same* in the two countries (the hierarchy of the groups being also the same), trade between them takes place exactly as if there were no internal differentiation at all — as it would if there were no non-competing groups. It is only a difference in the arrange-ment of the industrial hierarchy, not the hierarchy itself, that has effect on international trade. To change the simile, given the same industrial stratification thruout, the fact of stratification is of no consequence; the several layers are related to each other as if they were a pair of homogeneous structures

Such figures could be easily varied further, and the same principles further illustrated. We may suppose the relation between the rates of pay in different groups not to be the same in the two countries. That is, suppose non competing groups in each country, but with differences between the groups not the same in both. If the lower paid laborers in the United States (the unskilled, say) receive not only lower wages than those belonging to the higher groups, but wages farther down in the United States scale than is the case with corresponding sorts of laborers in Germany, then the commodities for whose production they are combined with the others will be affected in price exactly as if that sort of labor were especially effective in the United States. These commodities will be relatively cheap and will tend to be exported. Again, if it happens not only that a given group of laborers gets an unusual rate of pay, but also that a large proportion of this sort of labor is needed for producing a given commodity, the result will be accentuated. Assume, for example, that skilled workers of a given kind are to be had in Germany at a premium or differential over other workers which is not so high as the premium for the same skilled workers in the United States; assume further that the technical processes of an industry require a proportion of such workers larger than is needed in other industries; then the products of that industry will be particularly low in price in Germany, even tho not made with labor having any particular (comparative) effectiveness. They will tend to be exported; they may be exported even tho the labor lack something in comparative effectiveness.

There is more to be said, however. What causes the differences of wages within a country? What determines the relative positions of the non-competing groups? The underlying forces may be solely of domestic origin and effect; then they are to be conceived as operating on international trade as separate and independent factors. Or they may be themselves partly of international range; then the conditions of international trade themselves operate as cause, and the domestic and international factors become mutually dependent.

The underlying forces are solely domestic if social or industrial stratification within a country rests on deep-rooted differences in the standards of living of its several groups. This hypothesis has been stated with admirable precision by Marshall:

"Suppose that society is divided into a number of horizontal grades, each of which is recruited from the children of its own members; and each of which has its own standard of comfort, and increases in numbers rapidly when the earnings to be got in it rise above, and shrinks rapidly when they fall below that standard. Suppose, then, that parents can bring up their children to any trade in their own grade, but cannot easily raise them above it and will not consent to sink them below it.

"On these suppositions the normal wage in any trade is that which is sufficient to enable a labourer, who has normal regularity of employment, to support himself and a family of normal size according to the standard of comfort that is normal in the grade to which his trade belongs; it is not dependent on demand except to this extent, that if there were no demand for the labour of the trade at that wage the trade would not exist. In other words, the normal wage represents the expenses of production of the labour according to the ruling standard of comfort." [1]

In such case the relations of the several groups are settled by causes quite independent of international trade. They would persist if there were no such trade at all, and would be no more potent and no less if such trade took place on a great scale. The groups get their several rates of remuneration because of differences in the conditions of supply for the several kinds of labor and service, not because of the quasi-fortuitous impact of demand. They operate as causes of price (the price of a particular kind of labor); they are not the results of the price of goods. They are

[1] " Principles of Economics," 2d edition, pp. 557-8. I quote from the second edition because the statement there is more precise than in the later editions, where the same conception is to be found but in vaguer formulation.

purely domestic, in the sense that they rest on the standards of living in the groups, which are the outcome of historical and social forces in the given country.

But the causal sequence — still speaking of the domestic situation by itself — may not be so simple. It may be that the rates of pay in the several groups are settled by the mere conditions of demand; or, if not absolutely settled, affected or modified by those conditions for periods so long that they cannot be ignored even in inquiries that disregard short time phenomena. As is well known to the reader conversant with the history of doctrine on this topic, Cairnes treated the relations between noncompeting groups as dependent solely on demand. The principle of the play of reciprocal demand, to which Mill had turned for the explanation of the barter terms in international trade, was applied by Cairnes to the explanation of exchange between groups within a country. That group whose services (goods) were much wanted by other groups, and which itself wanted little of the services of other groups, was able to secure the greatest advantage from the exchange; it had the highest scale of earnings. Cairnes did not proceed to the apparently obvious corollary that *numbers* played a part in those relations. Any group whose numbers are small, confronted by another whose numbers are larger and exchanging products with that other, is likely to secure advantageous terms in the play of reciprocal demand. And the question of numbers raises that of the increase of numbers — the marriage-rate and birth-rate, and the standard of living. But this series of questions, to repeat, was never raised by Cairnes; the problem was treated by him as one solely of demand. And it may well be that we are not in a position to say much of the other side of the problem — the conditions of supply. The standard of living, as between different groups, can hardly be said to be well defined, still less to be well settled. Of necessity it acts very slowly in its effect on numbers. During the course of the period which must elapse before it can operate with effect — one or two generations — the impact of demand may shift. The relative rates of pay may shift accordingly, rising here, falling there; and the effects of a shift may endure so long that the standards themselves may change. There is as much evidence to show shift in the standards of living of different classes as there is to show fixity. It may fairly be maintained that when we pass beyond the forces of demand (which are in any case determinant only over many years) and try to examine the forces of supply, we do reach not a domain of fixity but one of constant flux.

If this be the just view, it follows that the impact of reciprocal international demand is not separate from that of reciprocal domestic demand, but merges with it and becomes part of one combined force. For example, we have supposed, in a previous illustrative case, that the linen makers of Germany are in a lower group, less well paid than other German workers. While German wages in wheat are $1.00, they are but $0.75 in linen. Why the difference? Is it due to settled standards of living in the several groups? To supply or to the play of demand? We may hesitate to go further than say that the numbers of persons in the other groups and the keenness of their demand for linen, compared to the number of the linen-workers and the keenness of their demand for the other products, have combined to bring about by a quasi-mechanical process the stated differences in the wages of the German exchanging groups. If this then be regarded as the initial situation — that established in Germany when isolated — and if we suppose her thereafter to be confronted with a demand for linen from the United States, this new demand for German linen is added to the former demand from the German workers themselves. The play of demand is altered to the advantage of the linen workers. The relations between the groups within Germany become different; the linen workers get higher prices for linen and higher wages for themselves.

How important in practice is the general train of reasoning followed in this chapter? Are we to conclude that the more simple analysis with which we started, resting on the assumptions of homogeneity in labor groups and uniformity in wages, becomes quite inapplicable where there are heterogeneous social and industrial conditions and wide diversities of wages in any one country?

The answer, as already indicated, depends not so much on the existence of non-competing groups in the several countries as on the similarity or dissimilarity of their make-up. Their bearing on international trade depends on whether they are of the same sort or of different sorts in the trading countries. Now, in the occidental countries — those of advanced civilization in the Western world — as a rule the stratification of industrial groups proceeds on the same lines. And it is between these countries that the principle of comparative costs is presumably of greatest importance. Since differences of climatic and physiographic character are less wide, divergences of absolute costs are less common and less great, and the limits within which the terms of exchange are confined not so far apart. And in the Western countries, to repeat, we find roughly the same social and industrial layers. The unskilled, by far the most numerous, get the lowest wages; the mechanics and well-trained stand distinctly higher; and so upward. This being the case, the differences in money costs *between* the countries are mainly determined by differences in labor costs; even tho *within* each country this factor may be profoundly modified.

Further: that combined influence which domestic and international demand may exercise on the position and prosperity of a given non-competing group is not of so great importance in practice as it is for the completeness and consistency of theoretic analysis. It is less important because the demand from abroad for any set of commodities, and thereby for the services of a particular grade of labor applied to making those commodities, is rarely so dominant as to change those relations between grades which would obtain within the country in any case. The lines of social and industrial stratification in a country are determined chiefly by the conditions that prevail within its own limits — by the numbers in the several groups and their demands for each others' services, and in some uncertain degree by their different standards of living. An added impact of demand from a foreign country will rarely change the relative rates of wages which have come about from the domestic factors. The social stratification that results from the domestic conditions is well established and seems to be deeply rooted; and it is not likely that international trade will impinge on it with such special effect on a particular grade as to warp it noticeably.

The case is somewhat different as regards the train of causation running the other way. While international trade is not likely to modify the alignment of grades within a country, peculiarities in that alignment may affect international trade. I will call attention to one or two instances in which this sort of influence seems to have appeared, departing for the moment from the general plan of this book, under which illustration and verification have been relegated to the later chapters.

The first illustration comes from the history and position of the chemical industry of Germany. I speak of the situation as it was before the war of 1914–18; what happened in Germany in the years immediately after the war is too confused for the illustration of the forces ordinarily at work in international trade. Before 1914, as is well known, chemical industries, and especially those yielding highly elaborated coal-tar products, were more successfully carried on in Germany than in any other country. Coal-tar dyes and drugs were supplied to England and the United States from Germany; the domestic output in these countries was negligible. Other countries also were supplied by German imports, tho not as preponderantly as the two English-speaking countries. The Germans evidently had some advantage in making these things. A comparative advantage? Certainly not one of a natural (physical) sort. It arose largely from the plenty and the especial cheapness of a particular kind of labor: that of chemists and of chemists' skilled assistants. Germany had a learned proletariat. The excellence and easy access of technological education, and the powerful social forces which attracted large numbers from the middle classes into the learned professions, brought about a large supply and a low remuneration of highly trained chemists. A similar excellence of intermediate education supplied to these officers a capable non-commissioned staff (to use a military analogy); there was a supply of exact, careful assistants and workmen, also paid at rates low in comparison to those of other countries. I will not say that this was the only factor that served to give Germany her unique position in the coal-tar industries. There were others, not least the marked faculty for elaborated organization which had developed during the latter years of the 19th century; a faculty that told with special effect in an industry like this — intricate, large in its scale of operation, yet not characterized by mass production. For the present purpose it is enough to note the influence of the labor situation. The special cheapness of the types of labor needed to an unusual degree in the industry served to give it a comparative advantage — that is, an advantage in the pecuniary terms which are decisive in the markets. And the advantage doubtless was not confined to the coal-tar and other chemical industries. It was probably generic. It appeared in scientific industries of other kinds, such as for example the making of optical instruments, surgical instruments, laboratory apparatus. Not one industry only, but a considerable number of German industries similar in character were given a place of their own in international trade because of the special position in Germany of the grade of labor needed for their products.

Quite a different illustration, derived from the situation of a group lying not in the upper line of workers but in the lower, is to be found in the United States during the same period. A marked peculiarity of the American labor situation during the generation preceding the Great War was the comparatively low rate of pay for the unskilled laborers. It was low, that is, in comparison with the pay of the upper stratum of the skilled laborers. While the pick and shovel man got more in the United States than in Europe, he did not get as much more above the European rate as did the American mechanic. The differential in favor of the mechanic was greater in the United States; the unskilled were relatively cheap, even tho not absolutely so, for the American employer. The cause is not far to seek. The enormous influx of immigrants maintained a great supply of unskilled labor and kept down its rate of pay. In the manufacturing industries of the

Southern States the utilization of a low-lying stratum of "poor whites" (not to mention the negroes) operated in the same way. The effect was to give an advantage to those industries, or those ways of conducting industries, in which the low-lying group of labor was used in large proportion. Industries of this type were accordingly in the same position in regard to international trade as if they had a comparative advantage; or if not so much as this, something to offset a lack of such advantage.

In the iron industry — that is, in the making of crude and half-finished iron and steel — the effect was of the former sort: the situation served to give a comparative advantage. The industry uses great masses of labor. The industry grew in the United States at an extraordinary pace between 1890 and 1915, and came to be an important industry of export. Here, too, the labor factor was not the only one; but it was an important one. It contributed to the remarkable overturn by which the United States, formerly an importer of iron and steel, became a great exporter of them.

In the textile industries an analogous development took place, but here not so much in the way of greater exports as of less imports; not so much the attainment of a clear comparative advantage as the elimination, in part or in whole, of a lack of superiority. The shift for the purposes of international trade was negative rather than positive. Those textile industries which could use unskilled labor for tending semi-automatic machinery for mass production found a plentiful and cheap supply at their command. Those for which still other conditions also were favorable, notably those manufacturing the cheap and medium grades of cotton fabrics, grew apace. Their position of indifference to foreign competition, almost if not quite attained even under the earlier conditions, was strengthened and consolidated by the cheapness of the routine labor. Textile industries of a different type, such as the silk and worsted manufactures, were enabled to attain a half-way position. For them the general conditions were less favorable; in order to hold their own against foreign competition, they needed a tariff prop much more than did the leading branches of the cotton manufacture. But the utilization of cheap common labor enabled them, not indeed to hold their own without protective duties, but to get on with a less barrier than would otherwise have been called for. The effect was the same in kind as that on the cotton industry, but not so marked in degree.

These peculiarities in the American labor situation did not rest on permanent causes. They were due, as has already been said, primarily to the great inflow of immigrants during the period in question. The restrictive legislation of 1916 brought a complete change, one whose effects will ramify far and in many directions, but in no way more than in a new adjustment of the relative wages of skilled and unskilled laborers. The differential will become less pronounced in favor of the skilled as against the unskilled. The industries which have adjusted themselves to a large and relatively cheap supply of the unskilled will have to readjust their ways. So far as they are subject to competition from foreign industries, they will be in a less advantageous position than before. The relations between the wages of the two groups will probably come to be in the United States not different from those in England, in Germany, and in Australia. This particular source of comparative advantage (or of an offset to a comparative disadvantage) will grow less and less, and probably will in the end disappear.[1]

[1] In these paragraphs I have sketched in bare outline the labor peculiarities of the American industrial situation as it stood before 1916, with regard only to their bearing on the particular phase of the theory of international trade here under consideration. As regards other aspects of the situation — the economic and technical development of the several industries, the tariff problems involved — I refer the reader to the extended discussion in my book on Some Aspects of the Tariff Question.

CHAPTER 7

CAPITAL AND INTEREST

STILL another factor, that of capital and interest on capital, will now be considered. We have seen that while the mere shift from cost in terms of labor to supply price in terms of money wages did not modify our conclusion, the consideration of differences in wages and of their influence on the money expenses of production did lead to significant modifications. So it will prove as regards interest on capital. Obviously this constitutes an item in the expenses of production; and it is one that has effects of its own. Yet these also are such as rather to modify the general conclusions reached on the simpler suppositions than to overturn them.

It is hardly necessary to remark that we need not consider separately such an item as the expense for materials — one that would bulk large in an accountant's schedule. It is familiar in economic doctrine that expense for raw materials may be resolved into previous expense for wages and interest. For the purposes both of international trade and of domestic trade we bring together in one sum total *all* the costs and expenses involved for a given article; not only those of the immediate producer, but those of the antecedent persons from whom he buys materials and supplies, and whom he recoups (with interest) for their expenses in the way of wages and still earlier materials. In the same way, when we considered the principle of comparative costs in its simplest aspect (disregarding money expenses and prices) we attended to *all* the labor involved in producing an article, not merely that of the last stages in its production. Raw materials, then, may be brushed aside, as involving an embodiment of previous labor and a recapitulation of previous wages and interest.

61

Rent, let it be briefly noted, is also to be brushed aside. In accord with the commonly accepted procedure in economics, we shall treat it as merely a differential element. It stands for the differences in the expenses of production under varying natural conditions, and serves to equalize them. Some relations between rent and international trade deserve attention and will receive it in the next chapter. For the present we shall disregard them.

We proceed then to consider the influence on international trade of an interest charge as one among the expenses of production. It will be convenient for this phase of the inquiry to revert to the second of the three original cases: that, namely, in which there are equal differences in cost and in which international trade will not arise. It appeared that trade could not be expected to arise, if regard were paid solely to labor and to wages — to quantity of labor and to the wages of labor. How if the additional factor of an interest charge is introduced?

Recall the former figures:

	WAGES PER DAY	TOTAL WAGES	PRODUCE	DOMESTIC SUPPLY PRICE
In the U. S. 10 days' labor	$2.00	$20	30 copper	$0.66⅔
" " U. S. 10 " "	$2.00	$20	15 linen	$1.33
" Germany 10 " "	$1.33	$13.33	20 copper	$0.66⅔
" Germany 10 " "	$1.33	$13.33	10 linen	$1.33

There are equal differences in cost; money wages are adjusted to those differences; the price of each article is the same in the two countries; no trade takes place.

If now we suppose a flat addition to be made, at the same rate, to the expenses of production all around, the possibilities of trade will be no greater. Add 10 per cent or 50 per cent (according as there is little expense, or much, in addition to the outlay for labor) to the wages bill in each case, to stand for interest. The figures then are all enhanced by the same amount, prices remain the same in the two countries, and no trade will arise. The mere circumstance that there is a return to capital leads to no modification of the analysis based on labor costs and wages alone.

Now change the situation by making the rates of interest not uniform thruout, but higher in one country than in the other.

Suppose the rate to be twice as high in the United States as in Germany. The interest charge (not the same thing, of course, as the rate of interest) to be added to the expenses of production then becomes twice as high. Suppose the interest charge be 50 per cent of the wages bill in the United States, 25 per cent in Germany; then we have:

	Days' Labor	Wages per Day	Total Wages	Interest Charge			Total Expenses	Produce	Domestic Supply Price
U. S.	10	$2.00	$20	50% on $20	=	$10	$30	30 copper	$1.00
U. S.	10	$2.00	$20	50% on $20	=	$10	$30	15 linen	$2.00
Germany	10	$1.33	$13.33	25% on $13.33	=	$ 3.33	$16.66	20 copper	$0.83
Germany	10	$1.33	$13.33	25% on $13.33	=	$ 3.33	$16.66	10 linen	$1.66

Both copper and linen are lower in price in Germany; both move to the United States; specie flows from the United States to Germany. Prices and money wages will fall in the United States, rise in Germany. Copper will rise in price in Germany until it is at the same price as in the United States; linen will rise similarly. After the redistribution of specie, the price of each article will be the same in the two countries, tho at a level somewhat higher all around than in the bare and simple situation first considered. Money wages will be readjusted, at rates somewhat lower than before in the United States, somewhat higher in Germany. The change in money wages signifies that with the higher interest charge in the United States the share of total national income which goes to the laborers is smaller there than in Germany. So far as concerns international trade, nothing happens except the temporary movement of goods one way and the redistribution of specie. Once this much is accomplished, the two countries have no trade connection; each goes its independent way. The mere fact that the interest charge is lower in the one than in the other does not cause the conditions for international trade to be different from what they were before.[1]

Now change the situation in still another way. Assume that one of the articles is produced with much capital, the other with little. Make the case extreme: suppose that one of them (copper)

---

[1] On the manner of constructing these figures, on some pertinent criticisms, and on the grounds for putting them together as is done in the text, see the note at the close of this chapter.

is produced with the aid of very much capital, the other (linen) with none at all. Suppose that the American capital investment for copper is $100, and that during the period over which $20 is paid for wages, 10 per cent on $100, or the sum of $10 in all, is payable to capital for interest. In Germany suppose the copper situation to be of the same sort. Then the German capital investment for copper will be $66.66, because the same quantity of labor applied to making that capital, paid at the German rate and having the German effectiveness, will bring the investment to that sum, as against $100 in the United States. The German interest charge for copper, at 10 per cent, will then be $6.66. For linen, be it remembered, there is no interest charge. Then we have:

	Days' Labor	Wages per Day	Total Wages	Interest Charge		Total Expenses	Produce	Domestic Supply Price
U. S.	10	$2.00	$20	10% on $100	= $10	$30	30 copper	$1.00
U. S.	10	$2.00	$20	nil		$20	15 linen	$1.33
Germany	10	$1.33	$13.33	10% on $66.66	= $6.66	$20	20 copper	$1.00
Germany	10	$1.33	$13.33	nil		$13.33	10 linen	$1.33

Both in the United States and in Germany copper is now higher in price than it was before the interest item was added. It was $0.66⅔ in both countries before the interest charge was added; it is now $1.00 in both. Being the same in both, copper moves neither way. The price of linen remains unchanged, still at the old figure and still the same in either country. Trade between the countries still will not arise.

Suppose now, however, that there is an interest charge for copper (and still for copper only — none for linen), but *not* at the same rate in the two countries. Suppose the rate to be 5 per cent in the United States, while it remains at 10 per cent in Germany. Then we have:

	Days' Labor	Wages per Day	Total Wages	Interest Charge		Total Expenses	Produce	Domestic Supply Price
U. S.	10	$2.00	$20	5% on $100	= $5.00	$25	30 copper	$0.83
U. S.	10	$2.00	$20	nil		$20	15 linen	$1.33
Germany	10	$1.33	$13.33	10% on $66.66	= $6.66	$20	20 copper	$1.00
Germany	10	$1.33	$13.33	nil		$13.33	10 linen	$1.33

The situation has changed. The price conditions are such that copper *will* move from the United States to Germany. Tho linen is still at the same price in both countries, copper has become cheaper in the United States, and can be profitably exported to Germany. Linen at the outset will not move from Germany; specie will be sent to pay for the American copper. As prices and money incomes rise in the United States and fall in Germany, linen will become dearer in the United States and cheaper in Germany, and will begin to move.

The extent of the consequent readjustment of prices depends, as need not again be explained, on the conditions of demand for copper in Germany, for linen in the United States. A possible outcome would be the following:

Days' Labor	Wages per Day	Total Wages	Interest Charge [1]	Total Expenses	Produce	Domestic Supply Price
U. S. 10	$2.10	$21	5% on $105 = $5.25	$26.25	30 copper	$0.87½
U. S. 10	$2.10	$21	nil	$21.00	15 linen	$1.40
Germany 10	$1.20	$12	10% on $60 = $6.00	$18.00	20 copper	$0.90
Germany 10	$1.20	$12	nil	$12.00	10 linen	$1.20

We now have the conditions under which both articles will move. Copper is cheaper in the United States, as before; but linen is now cheaper in Germany. International trade arises and rests on enduring conditions. It will go on indefinitely, to the advantage of both countries.

The general proposition to which this series of illustrative figures points is that interest on capital acts on international trade not in itself, but only in so far as it operates differently on different commodities. At the very start it is obvious that an interest charge, added uniformly to the expenses of production, brings no alteration in relative prices, since it acts equally on all commodities. Nor does an interest charge have an effect simply because it is at a different rate in the two countries — higher in one than in the other. If within each it acts uniformly thruout, it

---

[1] It will be noted that in calculating this interest charge, the capital amount has been made greater than before for the United States ($105 instead of $100), and less than before for Germany. This modification of the capital sum is in accord with the changes in money wages in the two countries and the consequent changes in domestic prices. As wages have risen by 5 per cent in the United States (from $2.00 to $2.10), the money value of the capital instruments will have risen by 5 per cent, or from $100 to $105. As wages have fallen by 10 per cent in Germany (from $1.33⅓ to $1.20), the money value of the capital instruments will have fallen by 10 per cent, or from $66.66 to $60.

leaves the relations between the countries undisturbed. Further: an interest charge does not alter conditions for trade, even tho it act on one commodity only, provided it acts on that commodity in the same way in both countries. The same is true (illustration in figures may be spared) if the interest charge, instead of being absent on one article while present on another, is merely greater on one than on another. If the difference is the same in both countries, international trade goes on in the same way as if this factor had not entered.

But the circumstance that the rate of interest is higher or lower in a country does have an effect when the needed capital equipment is greater for one commodity than for another. It bears *more* on those commodities which are made with much capital, making them relatively higher in price in the country where there is a higher rate of interest and a higher interest charge, lower in a country where there is a lower rate.

A low rate of return on capital, then, tends to give to a country a comparative advantage (*i.e.* the equivalent of one) for those goods which are made with much capital; these tend to be exported from it. A high rate of interest is correspondingly a handicap on the export of these same goods, a stimulus to their import. To put it in a more concrete way, a country in which capital has accumulated in large amounts and in which the investors are content with a low rate of return, tends to export articles which are made with much plant, and with raw materials which it takes *time* to produce and transport; whereas a country in which accumulation is smaller and the interest rate is higher, tends to import such articles. High or low interest does not in itself act as an independent factor; it exercises an influence of its own only so far as it enters to greater degree in one commodity than in another.

The conclusion is of essentially the same sort as that reached with regard to non-competing groups and differences of wages. So far as differences of wages are the same in two or more countries, and so far as goods are made in these countries with the same assortments (combinations) of different grades of labor, international trade remains as it would be in the absence of this complication. Only so far as there is a peculiarity in the position of a particular laboring group; or so far as a commodity is produced in one country with a different labor group or assortment of groups from that which is utilized in another — so far only does this factor exert a modifying influence of its own. The investment of capital and the payment of interest on capital are to be regarded in the same way. No essential modification of the original analysis is called for, unless this factor in turn leads to price phenomena which are different for one commodity in a given country from those for the same commodity in another country. A higher or lower rate of interest, so far as it operates on a particular commodity with *greater* effect in country A than in country B, has its influence in causing the price of that commodity to be different, relatively to other commodities, within the country; and thereby only does it have an influence of its own on international trade.

The quantitative importance of the capital charge factor in international trade is probably not great. As the whole tenor of the preceding exposition indicates, the range of its influence is restricted to a special set of circumstances. Within that range, its influence is further limited by the absence of wide inequalities in the rate of return on capital. Interest, while it does vary somewhat from country to country, does not vary widely between the leading countries of western civilization; and it is in the trade between these, and in the competition between them for trade with other countries, that the interest factor is most likely to enter with its independent and special effects.

The analogy to non-competing groups and laborers may again be applied. Capital may be regarded, if one pleases — of that I shall say a word presently — as an independent factor, competing with labor so far as concerns contribution to the output. But it does not compete with labor in the sense that there can be any equalization of sacrifice between capital and labor; the two sacrifices ("abstinence" and work) being in their nature incommensurable.[1] Marked differences in the rate of return on capital, persisting

[1] As was long ago remarked by Cairnes, Leading Principles, Part 2, Ch. 5, § 3.

indefinitely, are indeed quite conceivable, just as marked differences in the range between the wages of the several non-competing groups of laborers are quite conceivable; and there might be corresponding results of some quantitative moment in international trade. But since, as a matter of fact, the differences in the interest rate between countries are not considerable, we are justified in concluding that this element in the economic situation, like the element of persisting differences in wages to different workers, does not lead to a radical modification of our first conclusions.

There is more to be said, however, concerning the way in which the use of capital bears on international trade; there is another point of view. Tho the rate of return on capital may have no such marked influence as is often supposed, the fact that capital is used, and is used with far-reaching effects on the effectiveness of labor, has consequences in international trade which in turn are far-reaching.

Capital and labor are often referred to as agents which compete in production. This form of statement, useful for some purposes tho it is, does not describe with accuracy what happens when capital is made and used. Capital is itself made by labor; and the use of capital simply means the application of labor in another way — by an indirect and prolonged process. When a workman uses a tool in making a given article, the total labor given to produce the article includes not only what is done directly by the tool-user, but also a part of the labor of the tool-maker. If, for example, a tool is made by one man in a year, and lasts just a year; and if another man then works with that tool during its year of life; then the resulting articles are produced by the labor of two men each working one year, or of one man working two years. Similarly, if 100 men work with machinery made in a year by another 100 men; and if the machinery lasts 5 years; then in any one of the five years, the labor given to the resulting product is that of 120 men. This much is a commonplace in economic theory. It was clearly stated long ago by Ricardo,[1] and was explained, elaborated, insisted on, by Böhm-Bawerk.

[1] Ricardo's Principles, Ch. I., Sections 4, 5.

The concrete way in which the element of previous labor is reckoned by the business world is through the charge for depreciation in cost accounts. If machinery lasts 5 years, a considerable item must figure in the expenses of production to make up for its depreciation; if it lasts 20 years, the allowance is less, but is still there. Something must always be set down on this score; unless indeed the machinery last forever.

Now, in the illustrative figures used in the present chapter, no allowance at all was made for any such item. In other words it was tacitly assumed that capital (machinery or what not) did last forever. On that assumption the only new element brought into the account by the introduction of capital is the returns on it; past labor and depreciation need not be considered. In the actual world, however, it must always be considered. When making up the complete summation of the labor given to an article, we must put down something for the labor of the past which has been given to making the tools or machinery. It will be much or little, according as the capital instruments last a short time or a long; much or little, according as depreciation bulks large or small in the accounts.

Our total for the expenses of production (referring now to one of the previous illustrative examples), as modified by the introduction of capital, might then be stated in some such form as this:

WAGES PER DAY		TOTAL WAGES	INTEREST CHARGE AS BEFORE	TOTAL EXPENSES	PRODUCE	DOMESTIC SUPPLY PRICE
U. S. $2	10 days' current labor = $20 5 days' past labor = $10	$30	$10	$40	30 copper	$1.33

There is still more to be considered, however, than this revision of the method of figuring. The revised calculation (as the reader is likely to say) in itself adds nothing of moment. The number of days' labor for the given article, and the wages item in the expenses of production, became greater, and the figures are readjusted accordingly. What really signifies lies in quite another direction. The use of capital means not merely that an apportionment must be made (perhaps somewhat intricate) of the total labor given per unit of output. It means also that the effectiveness of the labor per unit is increased. The use of good tools and machines enables the same product to be got with much less of current labor. The illustrative figures just given would imply on their face that with the use of capital the total expense (the supply price) per unit becomes higher. For closer verisimilitude, they should look something like this: [1]

WAGES PER DAY		TOTAL WAGES	INTEREST CHARGE AS BEFORE	TOTAL EXPENSES	PRODUCE	DOMESTIC SUPPLY PRICE
U. S. $2	$\begin{cases} 3\frac{1}{2} \text{ days' current labor} = \$7 \\ 5 \text{ days' past labor } = \$10 \end{cases}$	$17	$10	$27	30 copper	$0.90

But further — and here we reach at last the point which is of importance for the theory of international trade — this reduction in the total labor applied, the increase in the effectiveness of labor, the lowering of cost in terms of labor and in terms of money, the whole train of modifications — is likely to take different shape in different countries. And different not only between countries, but between commodities. Some countries use tools and machines more readily and more effectively than others; some commodities are more amenable to the machine processes than others. Comparative advantages and disadvantages emerge.

These are advantages and disadvantages, be it remembered, arising from the relative effectiveness of the *totals* of the labor applied. They arise, not because the matter of return on capital is involved, but because a more complicated reckoning must be made of the effectiveness of labor. This fundamental fact is disguised by the business man's and the accountant's ways of reckon-

---

[1] Observe that the figures indicate a diminution in the amount of current labor as a consequence of the use of past labor (capital) ; and therefore a diminution in the total labor for the same output, in the total money expenses of production, in the supply price per unit. The amount of current labor, 10 days before, now is but $3\frac{1}{2}$ days; the total wages bill is $17, not $30; the total expenses of production are $27, not $40; the supply price per unit is lowered from $1.33 to $0.90.

No doubt, for still closer verisimilitude, it would be desirable to make the proportion of past labor to current labor smaller. As there is greater use of plant, the element of past labor (represented in accounting by the depreciation charge) tends to figure less and less per unit of product in comparison with current labor (the "labor cost" of accounting). The reader who is interested can easily work out further numerical illustrations.

ing. Depreciation is treated precisely as is the outlay for materials and supplies. Such items are treated in the accounts as if they were quite separate from the wages bill and the "labor cost." For the purposes of the economist, however, and not least for the theory of international trade, they must all be reckoned in the labor account. Their significance for our purposes lies in the fact that the economic analysis of capital outlays points to *differences* in labor cost; to variations in this essential regard from country to country and from commodity to commodity.

A country that makes large use of tools, machines, plants, and uses them *better* than another country, has a comparative advantage in the production of the commodities turned out with the abundant use of capital. Such in general is the situation between the countries of advanced capitalistic development, Western Europe and the United States, when compared with the tropical and backward countries. As between the Western countries themselves, there are similar differences. England had a marked advantage of this kind for a considerable period, from the early stages of the Industrial Revolution in the 18th century through the first third of the 19th, perhaps the first half. England continued during that period to have a comparative advantage in making those articles to which the machine-using processes could be applied with most effect; all countries applied them more or less, but England applied them better. The United States attained a development of a similar kind by the middle of that century, Germany and Switzerland before its close. Gradually all the Western countries learned to apply the new labor-saving processes. Yet they did not all learn to apply them with equal effect. Differences persisted, and these had their effects on international trade.

A curious contrast appeared in the latter part of the 19th century between the situation in England and that in the United States. It serves to bring into clear relief the distinction between the two ways in which the use of capital affects international trade, according as it operates on the one hand to introduce the element of return on capital or on the other hand to increase the effectiveness of labor. In both countries the use of well-devised tools and machines had been carried far — doubtless farther than in any other parts of the world. In both, the effectiveness of labor was made greater by the capital-using method of production. Probably the United States was somewhat in the van. Hence in those industries which were specially suitable for this method of production she had a comparative advantage. Doubtless she had in this regard an advantage in *all* industries, since her people thruout devised better tools than other peoples and used them better; but international trade was influenced only in so far as there was a peculiar — a comparative — advantage in some among her industries; that is, in so far as United States used capital better in some directions than in others. England also used tools and machines with large effect, even tho not with all-around effect as great as the United States. In England, however, the other side of the capital factor entered, giving a comparative advantage in certain directions; namely, the return which had to be paid in the way of interest on the needed capital was lower. So far as all of her industries shared in the lower interest rate alike, no influence of international trade could emerge. But so far as the technical development of a particular industry called for large capital — a large amount of previous labor allied with a moderate amount of current labor — the lower return on the capital embodying the previous labor gave that industry a comparative advantage. The iron industry was typical: larger plant, larger outlay for materials, comparatively small current-labor account. Here a low interest charge had a greater effect on prices, and thru prices a greater effect on international trade, than in industries where capital charge was a less important item. The United States, on the other hand, at this later stage, had an advantage in those industries where the use of tools and implements made the effectiveness of labor especially great. England had an advantage in those industries where much capital was used and where the lower interest rate enabled the commodities to be put on the market at a price especially low.

This contrast, noticeable in the last third of the 19th century, tended to diminish in the era which opened with the 20th century.

The difference in interest rates between England and the United States became less after 1900, and had less and less effect during the decade preceding the Great War. It ceased entirely during the war itself and the years immediately following. Whatever the future may bring — perhaps equality in interest rates between the two countries, perhaps a slight difference one way or the other — it is tolerably certain that this factor will no longer be of such weight as it was in the earlier period.

A similar contrast, and an illustration of a similar sort, can be found in the effects of railway transportation. The capital account is especially large in railways; the initial investment, the plant, figures to an immensely greater degree than in most industries. The interest charge is therefore an unusually large item in the expenses of production. As regards the labor item, the labor applied to the transportation of an article is as much a part of the total applied to producing it as is the labor of growing or of fashioning (manufacturing). When we envisage the total labor applied to an article produced in England or the United States, we must include the labor in the railway transport of raw materials to the places where they are fashioned and of the marketable goods to the places where they are sold. Now in the United States this labor has been applied with unusual effectiveness in long distance transportation. The United States thus has had a comparative advantage as regards commodities carried over great distances. On the other hand, as regards the interest charge entailed, the United States has been at a disadvantage compared to England. The interest charge, an unusually large item in railway expenses, was long at a higher rate in the United States, and hence had an effect in railway rates, for the same volume of capital, greater than in England. Hence in the United States there was an endeavor to get on with as small a capital-account as possible, and so to lessen the interest burden. But this mitigation of the interest charge, thru a minimizing of capital expenditure, was not at all the most important factor in maintaining for the United States a comparative advantage as regards the item of transportation. The important factor was that of the construction and operation of railways with marked effectiveness of labor; that is, the carrying of many ton miles per unit of labor expended. The great plant was economically laid out and effectively used. The net result was, and probably remains, that in articles which require long inland transportation before they can enter the realm of international trade, the United States had an advantage thruout the period in which the railway has come to be a factor of prime importance; and this notwithstanding the fact that thru much the larger part of the period, *i.e.* until the close of the 19th century, a higher interest charge on the heavy capital investment was in the nature of a handicap, serving to lessen in some degree the comparative advantage.

NOTE ON THE METHOD OF HANDLING CAPITAL AND INTEREST

Ricardo and his disciples, indeed any economist following the organon of Ricardo, would have criticized sharply the way in which the figures in the earlier part of this chapter are constructed. The basis of the criticism would be that the calculations imply a rise in the price of *all* goods in consequence of the introduction of interest (*i.e.* "profits"). The proper treatment is to regard the general level of prices as constant, and to analyze on that basis the connection between prices (values) and the return to capital (interest or "profits"). Then one would have to say that the rates of money wages which were originally set down under the simplest supposition (no capital involved) must be readjusted when capital enters. They must be readjusted downward; wages must be assumed to be lower. If, for example, 30 of copper, made by 10 men, sell for $20, the 10 men can *not* be getting as much as $20 in wages or $2 per man, since that would leave nothing at all for profit. Wages must be less than $2 a day. If profits are 25 per cent of the wages bill, the rate of wages will be $1.60 and profits will be $0.40; the two items making up the full expense ("cost") of production, equal to the supposed money yield of $20. A mere rise or fall in profits is to be treated as involving a corresponding fall or rise in wages, but not as leading to changes in the prices of goods. It is further to be pointed out, following the same analysis, that so far as profits enter to a different extent in one commodity than in another — so far as *more* capital is used per unit of current labor, or so far as the use of the same capital is spread over more time, — then a rise or fall in profits would affect the relative prices of goods. A rise or fall thus brought about in any one article would be offset, however, by a corresponding fall or rise in other directions. Changes in the prices of all goods the same way constitute merely a monetary phenomenon, and one not to be confounded with changes in the relative prices of different goods. The proper way to construct illustrative figures such as are used in this chapter is to treat the price level as constant; and the influence of capital should be shown by a process of discounting, as just indicated. So far as a discounting process operates differently on different commodities, there are possibilities of a modifying influence on international trade. And the nature of the modifications will be elicited clearly enough by this method of procedure.

I admit unhesitatingly that the discount method (Ricardo's) is sound. For some purposes, it is the only one that is sound. It is logically the only one tenable for the purposes which Ricardo had in mind when writing the chapter on Value in his Principles : that of analyzing the relations between wages and value, and in general the relations between distribution and value. But it does not seem to me necessarily imposed for the purpose of the present inquiry. It would simply lead to the same results, but by a more troublesome route. Illustrative figures such as I have worked out could be arrived at equally well by the discount method; and they would point to the same general conclusions. They are more easily calculated and more easily followed on the method which I have used, and are equally valid as regards the particular problem in hand; namely, that of showing in what way the item of interest has a modifying effect. True, they make the tacit assumption that advances in the prices of all goods take place as this item is introduced; the advances being greater or less according as the item counts more or less. In order to carry to its logical outcome this assumption of general price advances, it would be necessary to assume also equivalent changes in the monetary supply. For the completeness of the reasoning the reader who is intent on full logical consistency should bear in mind this additional assumption. For the purpose of tracing the effect on international trade — the sole object here in view — it has seemed to me easier and simpler to use the method of supplement, rather than the method of discount. If the object in hand were to consider each and every aspect of a theoretic analysis — monetary theory as well as the theory of distribution, domestic prices as they would be with and without a return to capital — the strict Ricardian procedure would alone be consistent and conclusive.

CHAPTER 8

VARYING COSTS; DIMINISHING RETURNS;
INCREASING RETURNS

THE reasoning of the preceding chapters has been based on the assumption that the cost of each and every article is uniform. Changes in the volume of output were supposed to have no effect on the cost per unit. But costs are not necessarily uniform; they are subject to variation according as the total product is large or small. It is incumbent on us to consider the influence on international trade of costs thus varying.

In analyzing this sort of situation I shall return to the highly simplified suppositions made at the start, neglecting the complications and qualifications which have been dealt with in the chapters immediately preceding. That is, labor cost in its simplest form will be considered, uniformity of wages assumed between the laborers (no non-competing groups), capital and a return to capital disregarded. These other factors — which we have seen not to be of such fundamental importance as that of effectiveness of labor — will serve to qualify the conclusions no more and no less than before.

Return once more to the illustrative case already used, showing differences in comparative cost, namely:

In the U. S. 10 days' labor produce 20 wheat
" " U. S. 10 " " " 20 linen
" Germany 10 " " " 10 wheat
" Germany 10 " " " 15 linen

The United States has a comparative advantage in the production of wheat; linen will move from Germany to the United States, wheat from the United States to Germany. The barter terms of trade between the two countries will be 10 of wheat for somewhere between 10 to 15 of linen — 11, 12, 13, 14 linen. The

76

greater the German demand for wheat and the less the American demand for linen, the more favorable to the United States will be the barter terms of trade; the rate between wheat and linen will be nearer to the figure of 15 linen for 10 of wheat. The less the German demand for wheat and the greater the United States demand for linen, the more favorable the terms will be to Germany — the nearer to the figure of 10 of wheat for 10 of linen.

The concrete way in which the conditions of exchange will work out will be thru the range of money incomes in the two countries. A rate advantageous to the United States will be attained by the people of that country thru their having higher money incomes, as well as higher domestic prices. American money incomes will be higher than German in any case; but the difference in favor of the United States will be greater or less according to the play of demand in the two countries for wheat and linen. They will gain as purchasers of import commodities, such as German linen. If on the other hand the conditions of demand should turn favorable to Germany, money incomes and domestic prices will be given an upward trend, and the Germans will secure a larger gain as purchasers of imports, such as American wheat. This is familiar matter; it is restated here by way of introduction to what follows.

Suppose now that in Germany all wheat is not produced under the same conditions. Suppose that while 10 days produce 10 of wheat on some lands, there are others on which the 10 days produce more. Grade the lands according as the product of this constant amount of labor is 11, 12, 13, 14, 15 of wheat. The price of wheat will be in accord with its cost on the poorest land in use, that on which the 10 days yield but 10 of wheat. The better lands will yield to their owners differential returns, or economic rent.

Under these conditions wheat growing will not cease in Germany after trade with the United States has set in. It would indeed cease if all the wheat were grown under the poorest conditions — were produced at the rate of 10 wheat for 10 days. Germany would then procure her entire supply from the United States in exchange for linen. But as there are varying conditions of supply within her own borders, she would always produce some wheat of her own. The very best German lands, those on which 10 days of labor yielded 15 of wheat, could always hold their own against American competition. Those on which the yield was less than 15 might or might not succumb under American competition. The continued cultivation of wheat on them would depend on the terms of exchange between the two countries. If the terms were 14 of wheat for 15 of linen (favorable to Germany), only those German lands which produced as much as 14 could continue in face of American competition; those on which the yield was less than 14 (13, 12, 11) would find themselves forced out. If, on the other hand, the terms of exchange were not favorable to Germany — if she got for her 15 of linen only 11 of wheat — a poorer grade of German land could continue the production of wheat. The more wheat the United States gives in exchange for linen, the more will Germany restrict her production of wheat to those lands on which her labor is least ineffective. That is, where it is least ineffective compared with American labor in wheat-raising; most effective, compared with other German labor in wheat. Barter terms of trade which are favorable to Germany will mean that the conditions are not favorable for the maintenance of her wheat production.

Obviously this means also that the rent of wheat lands in Germany depends on these same terms of trade. If the terms are unfavorable to Germany, — if she gets but 11 of American wheat in exchange for her 15 of linen — the wheat-growers on her poorer lands will remain in the market, and the differential advantage of the better lands will be little impaired. Their rent will be the excess of product over 11 of wheat, instead of the excess over 10; the margin of cultivation will move only from 10 to 11. But if the terms are favorable to Germany, — if she gets 14 of wheat for her 15 of linen — more of her wheat lands will be forced out of cultivation, and those which continue to grow wheat will afford less rent. The grade on which 14 wheat are produced for 10 days of labor will afford no rent at all; that on which 15 wheat are produced will afford a rent of only 1.

Under a régime of prices all these results will work themselves out as they would under a barter régime. If the terms of trade are

favorable to the United States, — if she gets 14 of linen for 10 of
wheat — money incomes are comparatively high in the United
States, comparatively low in Germany. Wheat then is comparatively high in price in the United States, and is at the same
comparatively high price in Germany.   Linen is at a comparatively
low price in Germany, and at the same low price in the United
States.   As consumers of linen, the Americans gain from their high
money incomes; as consumers of wheat, the Germans lose from
their low money incomes.   But as producers of wheat, the American wheat-growers are under a handicap in selling their wheat in
Germany.   They cannot sell so much, nor can they displace as
many German wheat-growers as they could if their money incomes
and their wheat prices were lower.   And the Germans as producers of wheat are not so hard pressed by American competition
as they would be if their (the German) money incomes were higher.
The low rates of money wages lessen their expenses of production,
and wheat lands which would go out if money wages were higher
are able to hold their own and maintain themselves in face of
American competition.

In the talk of the man on the street, and also, unfortunately, in
the reasonings of pretentious books on economics, consequences of
this kind are dealt with as if they indicated a disadvantage to the
United States and an advantage to Germany.   The American
wheat-growers find in higher money wages an obstacle to the cheap
production of wheat and to the extension of exports; this is bad for
the United States.   The German wheat growers find in lower
money wages an aid in meeting foreign competition; this is good
for Germany.   The man on the street almost invariably has the
mercantilist point of view: exports are to be promoted, but
domestic production is also to be safeguarded against competing
imports.   Not a few economists share these prepossessions, sometimes deliberately, more often thru a lack of sustained and consistent thinking.   True, no economist, and indeed no thinking
person, would deny that high money wages, combined with low
prices of goods, bring material prosperity; but, when faced by a
concrete situation, few accede readily to the conclusion that high

money wages, even tho they compel some domestic producers to lessen or abandon their output, are still the result and the indication of better conditions of the community at large.

Another problem, and one on which there is much more occasion for difference of opinion among the discerning, concerns the range of industries in which we may expect to find varying costs. Wheat has been selected for illustration, because it is a commonplace in economics that agricultural commodities are usually produced at varying costs. But are not other classes of articles also produced at varying costs? The more ample information yielded in recent times by statistical inquiry, and our greater familiarity with the actual conditions of industry, both point to the conclusion that in manufacturing industries also we find, at any given time, costs not uniform. Side by side there are effective and ineffective producers. Must we not assume for the entire range of industry conditions like those assumed for wheat? And is not the theory of international trade to be readjusted accordingly?

It would carry us far from the main topics of the present volume to consider this question in all its ramifications. The discussion involves moot points, and illustrates once more the impossibility of separating the theory of international trade from the general problems of economics. I content myself with a summary statement of the grounds for a negative answer; negative, that is, as regards any considerable modification of the theory of international trade.

Manufacturing industries do show varying costs. Uniform costs are never found. But the causes of variation are different from those found in the extractive industries; the persistence of the phenomenon is due to different causes; and the consequences are different, both as regards domestic trade and international trade.

The main cause of variation is in the personal element. Some managers of industry are more efficient than others, and cost of production at their hands is less. The explanations which usually figure in the discussions on this topic — better location of the low-cost establishments, better access to materials, better plant, better organization — are reducible to this one dominant element, the differences in managerial capacity.   The reason why some establishments, for example, are better located than others is at bottom the same as that why some are better organized than others: the managers are more shrewd and capable.   And these more capable managers get a differential return analogous to rent.   It is analogous to economic rent, that is, in industries where there is nothing which could in strictness be called a monopoly — where there is no control of supply in any single hand, but a free field for all who care to enter.

The phenomenon differs from that of economic rent, however, in that these powers of superior productiveness are *transferable*.   The abler business man is not bound to any industry or any field.   He roams at large, turning his faculties in whatever direction he finds they tell most profitably.   The case is otherwise with land and natural agents.   If a landowner finds his differential gain lessened, he must accept the situation once for all and submit to the loss.   To some extent he can indeed turn the land to one crop or another; but the possibilities of such shifts are limited, and they mean, not that loss is avoided, but only that it is perhaps made smaller.   The landowner cannot transfer the superior powers of his acres to other acres or to a manufacturing industry.   The superior business manager, however, if he finds that his powers are exercised with less effect in one industry than another, turns from the less profitable to the more profitable.

It is true that a superior business man may secure ordinary profits (*i.e.* non-superior profits) in an industry which would yield no profits at all to the non-superior business man.   Tho he engage in an industry which possesses no comparative advantage of the sort that has been illustrated and discussed in these pages, he may succeed, notwithstanding the absence of advantage, in making both ends meet and even in clearing a profit for himself.   But he cannot clear *as much* for himself as he could in industries adapted to the general industrial advantages of the country.   And the superior business man will not ordinarily turn to the ill-adapted industries.   One of the signs of superiority is the very fact that he has an eye for the more promising possibilities.   He sees better than most what is likely to be suited to profitable operation and what is not. It is true that accident, inheritance, early misjudgment, may start him in an industry which fails to give full scope to his abilities; and there are plenty of cases in which capable men, once started the wrong way, remain in the industry of first choice. But in the main it is otherwise. The business man of higher grade turns to operations that afford full scope to his abilities; and the more outstanding are those abilities, the less likely are they to be misapplied to unfruitful industries.

An excellent illustration of the consequences of this transferability, and of the general theorem here advanced, is found in the working of protective duties. Suppose an industry to be fostered by protection; for example, the linen industry in the United States operating under conditions of comparative disadvantage such as are shown in our figures. Suppose then that the protective duties are abolished; will the linen industry disappear from the country? It is entirely possible that an examination of the expenses of production of the several linen-making establishments will show them to be producing at varying money costs. Some among them will be found to be producing so cheaply that they can hold their own, and continue to make ordinary profits, even under free trade. But these will be the superior establishments, managed with superior ability; and their managers, even tho they meet their expenses of production and eke out a profit, will be getting a return less than in proportion to their powers. Sooner or later they will shift. The transfer to other industries will not take place easily or quickly, but in the end it will come. There may be in such a protected industry older men who, while capable, yet are too advanced in years for a complete change of base; and these will very probably remain where they are. But younger men of the same stamp will not be drawn to it; the industry will languish and in time will disappear.

Still another aspect of manufacturing industries must be considered. They are often said to present the conditions not of diminishing but of increasing returns. Is not our reasoning in need of elaboration and modification on this score? Just as there are special conclusions for the industries in which cost increases as output enlarges, so we might expect other special conclusions for commodities in which cost declines with enlarged output.

Two things must here be noted: first, what exactly is meant by a law or tendency to increasing returns; and second, what is the effect of this sort of tendency in international trade.

On the first topic some distinctions familiar in economic theory must be recalled. Any "law" of increasing returns means that *all* costs go down. The law is not at all the converse of that of diminishing returns in agriculture. In the latter, an increase of the output from a given plot or given area of land entails as a necessary corollary that, while the additional supplies are got at higher cost, the previous supplies continue to be got at cost unchanged. Therefore there are varying costs — some costs persistently higher than others. In the apparently opposite case of increasing returns, there are no persisting differences. True, there is lower cost with enlargement of output; but it is the entire supply which is produced at the lower cost. True, not all will be produced at lower cost immediately; but in the end it will. As has just been explained, there will probably be a transition period of varying costs. An improvement which lessens costs is almost invariably introduced gradually, first in one establishment, then in another. For a while costs will be lower in the forward than in the lagging industry. The ultimate effect will be a decline all around.

To come now to the main general conclusion which bears on the problems of international trade. Such a decline, when it has permeated the whole of an industry, may mean a change in its costs relatively to other industries. It may mean *a new alignment of comparative costs*, and accordingly may alter the conditions under which international trade is carried on. Such consequences, however, are not of a novel kind, and call for no new analysis. With the irregular progress of the arts, the conditions of comparative advantage are subject to constant modification; but these changes, while they lead to new conditions, involve merely the application of familiar reasoning to the changed situation.

Still a further remark, however, is to be made, one which illustrates once again the connection between the various parts of the structure of economic theory. Professor Marshall has taught us to distinguish between "internal" and "external" economies — between those improvements and lowered costs which arise primarily within each several establishment or industry and those which are the outcome chiefly of forces outside the establishment or industry. Concerning internal economies, such as mechanical inventions, scientific discoveries, better organization within the plant, little in the way of a trend or law can be made out. They come or do not come, as it so happens. But external economies have a trend which is predictable. They are in themselves the result of larger aggregate output. The mere fact that there is a larger total product of plows, motor cars, safety razors, tends to make each unit cheaper. Greater specialization and subdivision of labor become possible; there is a greater pervasive facility of industrial advance.

This is not the place for considering disputed matters relating to the general tendency. What concerns us is that it has some special consequences for the international trade of those countries which export manufactured articles. In agriculture, external economies are not indeed lacking in effect; larger aggregate output does bring into action some causes of decrease in cost (better roads, for example, or cheaper plows); but these are offset, in part or completely, by the tendency to diminishing returns in those operations which have to do with the direct culture of the soil. It is not easy to say under what conditions external economies may be so effective that agricultural costs on added yields from the same soil tend to increase or decrease as aggregate output enlarges. Something of this kind may happen for a while in a country which has intelligent and progressive population. But it would seem that with growth of numbers agricultural costs must increase *relatively;* that is, tho they fall, they will not fall as much as will the costs of manufactured articles. A country which is growing fast; whose industries are largely manufactures; whose exports of such goods are large; whose total output of them is increasing; whose costs per unit are therefore going down — such a country will not only have a comparative advantage in manufactured goods, but will probably have a growing comparative advantage. The more it produces of such goods, the greater may be its advantage for exporting them; and hence it will turn its labor cumulatively in this direction. While it will have costs which (in the long run) are uniform for each several article of export, its costs will tend also to decline for each several article. In that sense — considering successive stages, not any given stage — it will have varying costs.

This sort of advantage, even tho it generates itself and goes on crescendo, does not persist indefinitely. It rests primarily on human causes, not on those of the physical world without. It is subject to the vicissitudes of industry and in some degree to man's deliberate action. England seems to have had some cumulative advantage of this kind during the first half or two-thirds of the 19th century. As time went on, other countries entered on the same paths; and they were probably aided in doing so by protective duties on their manufactures, that is, by deliberate action. At all events the international division of labor, while still affected by England's matured position, was gradually controlled more and more by forces of a deeper and more permanent character, and this particular sort of advantage no longer played a part in shaping England's foreign trade. At a later period, during the closing years of the 19th century and the opening years of the 20th, the United States also experienced a burst of industrial advance, and with it an astonishing development of external economies; and with this again a re-alignment of the effectiveness of labor in the several branches of production. Here, too, while agriculture was affected somewhat, manufactures were affected more. The proportion of manufactured exports tended to increase; and what was no less significant, the proportion of manufactures among the imports tended to decrease. Here, too, the change, cumulative tho its moving forces were, was not likely to progress indefinitely. As in the case of England, it did leave its permanent impress on the international trade of the country, as well as on its domestic trade. But as time went on, other countries were likely to enter on similar paths; and then once more it became a question what were the long sustained currents in the movement of goods from country to country.

Mining industries present a peculiar case,[1] in international trade as well as in domestic. It is not easy to say whether they are to be regarded as analogous to agriculture or to manufactures. They are extractive industries, and therein like agriculture; but they are not subject to any "law" of diminishing return; at all events, to none of the same kind that bears on agriculture. It is true that in mining we find at any given period of time varying costs quite as sharply as in agriculture, and more sharply than in manufactures. But mining operations are not subject to the kind of pressure which appears when men cultivate the soil — when they use land as a means for yielding crops perennially. In mining there is a fixed store, not an instrument for transmuting matter. And the mines which are known and are in use at any one time, while they vary in richness, show no certain trend toward greater or less richness. All that we are sure of is that each and every single mine will sooner or later be exhausted; but it may continue to be unvarying in richness until it gives out. Still more uncertain is it whether new mines will be discovered, and whether they will prove worse or better than those previously worked. We have further to consider that while the variations between the costs at the several sources of supply are due to physical causes such as differences in richness and accessibility, their availability depends markedly on the same human factors which are outstanding in manufactures, the ability and venturesomeness of business leaders. All in all, it is doubtful whether we can speak in strictness of any tendency to constant returns or diminishing returns or increasing returns in mining.

For the theory of international trade we must be satisfied with some general empirical results. The tangled forces that act in the mineral industries — the mysteries of the earth's crust, unpredictable new finds, the progress of science, the progress of business management and industrial organization — bring it about that at

---

[1] As was long ago pointed out by Ricardo (Principles, Ch. 3).

one time this country, at another time that one, has special effectiveness, absolute or comparative, for copper, silver, tin, coal, iron. A *de facto* situation appears in the matter of comparative costs and comparative advantages, and international trade is shaped accordingly. Whether the trade is likely to continue for a given country on the same lines in the future as in the past or present, we have no means even of guessing. In the case of agricultural products we may expect, on grounds of general reasoning, that a change in demand or in supply will lead to certain permanent alterations in the positions and advantages of the several trading countries. But we can hardly apply such theorizing to the products of mines. We have simply to accept the situation as it happens to develop at the given time and place.

CHAPTER 9

Varying Advantages [1]

In the preceding chapters it has been assumed that there were but two commodities in the trade between the countries and one commodity exported from each. Any given country, however, exports not one article, but a number. This circumstance in itself would not necessarily point to modifications of the reasoning. If the several articles were all produced under the same conditions of advantage or disadvantage, they could be treated as one. But it is not to be assumed that all are alike in this regard — that there is in each and every industry of a given country the same trend in the effectiveness of its labor compared to effectiveness in other countries. It is almost certain that a country will have a greater superiority in some directions than in others. Once more we are compelled to modify our reasoning and amplify our deductions by introducing supplementary hypotheses; reshaping the conclusions reached on the simplest assumptions by introducing further assumptions such as to bring us closer to the realities.

Suppose that there are not two commodities but three; and suppose further that we find not the same relations of comparative effectiveness between the trading countries, but a graded situation. Let the three commodities be wheat, linen, and woolen cloth. The following figures will serve for illustration and for analysis.

In the U. S. 10 days' labor produce 20 wheat
" " U. S. 10 " " " 20 linen
" " U. S. 10 " " " 20 cloth
" Germany 10 " " " 10 wheat
" Germany 10 " " " 15 linen
" Germany 10 " " " 18 cloth

[1] For a compact and highly abstract analysis of the main trend of this chapter, see Appendix H of Marshall's Money, Credit, and Commerce, pp. 322–325. My own more elementary version had been made before Marshall's book appeared.

Observe that the effectiveness of labor in the United States is greater thruout than its effectiveness in Germany. The same amount of labor produces in the United States more of wheat than in Germany, more of linen, more of cloth. But the superiority is greatest in wheat; it is less in linen; it is least in cloth. What sort of trade will emerge?

Consider first the possibilities of barter; and begin by considering these possibilities separately for the three pairs of commodities; namely, wheat as against cloth, wheat as against linen, and cloth as against linen.

(1) Suppose the situation were wheat against cloth.

	DOMESTIC TERMS OF TRADE
In the U. S. 10 days' labor produce 20 wheat ⎱ " " U. S. 10 " " " 20 cloth ⎰	10 wheat = 10 cloth
" Germany 10 " " " 10 wheat ⎱ " Germany 10 " " " 18 cloth ⎰	10 wheat = 18 cloth

The United States and Germany would both gain at any barter terms of trade intermediate between 10 and 18 of German cloth for 10 of American wheat; the gain to the United States being greatest if nearly 18 of cloth were got for 10 of wheat, and that to Germany greatest if but little more than 10 of cloth were given for 10 of wheat.

(2) Suppose the situation were simply wheat against linen.

	DOMESTIC TERMS OF TRADE
In the U. S. 10 days' labor produce 20 wheat ⎱ " " U. S. 10 " " " 20 linen ⎰	10 wheat = 10 linen
" Germany 10 " " " 10 wheat ⎱ " Germany 10 " " " 15 linen ⎰	10 wheat = 15 linen

The United States and Germany would both gain at any barter terms of trade intermediate between 10 and 15 of German linen for 10 of American wheat. The nearer the terms were to 15 linen for 10 of wheat, the more the United States would gain; the nearer to 10 of linen for 10 of wheat, the more Germany would gain.

(3) Suppose finally that the situation were cloth against linen.

	DOMESTIC TERMS OF TRADE
In the U. S. 10 days' labor produce 20 cloth ⎱ " " U. S. 10 " " " 20 linen ⎰	10 cloth = 10 linen
" Germany 10 " " " 15 linen ⎱ " Germany 10 " " " 18 cloth ⎰	15 linen = 18 cloth *i.e.* 10 linen = 12 cloth

The United States and Germany would both gain if linen went from the United States to Germany. At any terms of trade between 10 and 12 of German cloth for 10 of American linen, both countries would gain.

Observe that in case (2) linen moves from Germany to the United States, to the gain of both countries. In case (3) linen moves the other way, from the United States to Germany, also to the gain of both countries. What determines whether one or the other sort of movement takes place?

The answer is: the outcome depends on the play of demand. The nature of the trade, and especially the movement of linen, will depend on the demand of the United States for her own wheat as compared with her demand for the two commodities which may conceivably be secured from Germany, cloth and linen; and on the demand of Germany for her own cloth as compared with her demand for the two commodities which may conceivably be secured from the United States. The barter terms of trade may be so favorable to the United States that she will find it advantageous to procure from Germany both linen and cloth. Or the terms may be so little favorable to the United States, and her margin of gain so narrow that, tho it remains advantageous to get from Germany that commodity (cloth) which Germany can supply most cheaply, it will *not* be advantageous to get from Germany the other commodity (linen) which Germany can supply less cheaply. It is in cloth that Germany has her greatest effectiveness of labor; it is here that she has the least of her inferior disadvantages; and cloth will move from Germany to the United States even tho the barter terms of trade are not favorable to the United States. Nay, as will be presently shown, those terms may be so unfavorable to the United States that she will gain by actually exporting linen to Germany. Linen may move either way, according as the barter terms of trade vary.

There are thus three possible cases:

I. Both cloth and linen may move from Germany to the United States. As regards the exchange between German cloth and American wheat, we have seen that both countries would gain if

American wheat were exchanged for German cloth at any figure between 18 and 10 of cloth against 10 of wheat. Suppose the barter terms of trade to be advantageous to the United States; that by sending 10 wheat to Germany she gets 15 of cloth. In Germany 15 of cloth are produced with the same labor as $12\frac{1}{2}$ of linen $(18:15::15:12\frac{1}{2})$, and it is immaterial to Germany whether she gives 15 of cloth or $12\frac{1}{2}$ of linen for the 10 of wheat. The United States gains by either act of exchange: if she gets 15 of cloth for 10 of wheat, she gains 5 of cloth; and if she gets $12\frac{1}{2}$ of linen for 10 of wheat, she gains $2\frac{1}{2}$ of linen. That particular combination or proportioning of the commodities (15 of German cloth and $12\frac{1}{2}$ of German linen for every 20 of American wheat) may precisely suit the mutual tastes or demands. Both countries will then gain if not cloth only, but linen also, moves from Germany to the United States.

II. Take now a situation toward the other extreme, one in which the barter terms of trade are favorable not to the United States but to Germany. Suppose the United States gets in exchange for 10 of wheat no more than 11 of cloth; the United States thus gaining from the operation only 1 of cloth. In Germany 11 of cloth are produced with the same labor as $9\frac{1}{6}$ of linen $(18:15::11:9\frac{1}{6})$, and the American wheat, which exchanges for 11 of cloth, would exchange at German rates for only $9\frac{1}{6}$ of linen. Obviously the Americans get more linen (10) for their 10 days of labor by producing it directly than by procuring it from Germany. But more. The United States now not only will find it worth while to produce her own linen; she will gain by exporting it to Germany and taking cloth in exchange. It is immaterial to the United States whether she sends 10 of wheat or 10 of linen to Germany — both are produced with the same labor. Within Germany, however, 12 of cloth exchange for 10 of linen, and therefore 11 of cloth exchange for $9\frac{1}{6}$ linen. The United States by sending $9\frac{1}{6}$ linen to Germany can get 11 of cloth in exchange. This particular combination or proportioning of commodities (10 of American wheat together with $9\frac{1}{6}$ of American linen in exchange for every 22 of German cloth) may again precisely suit the conditions of mutual demand; both wheat and linen then move from the United States to Germany.

III. Lastly, take an intermediate case — *the* intermediate case. Suppose the barter terms of trade to be 10 of wheat for 12 of cloth (less than 15 of cloth as in our first case, and more than 11 of cloth as in the second). Within Germany 12 of cloth are produced with the same labor as 10 of linen. The United States, sending 10 of wheat to Germany, and getting 12 of cloth in exchange, might indeed get also 10 of German linen in exchange. But 10 of linen are produced in the United States with the same labor as 10 of wheat; there is no gain to the United States. Germany might send 12 of cloth to the United States and would then receive in exchange 10 of linen. But 10 of linen and 12 of cloth are both produced in Germany with the same amount of labor ($6\frac{2}{3}$ days); and there would be no gain to Germany. Neither country would find it worth while to send linen to the other. The only gainful exchange is that of German cloth for American wheat. The case is, in a sense, the mid-way or balancing one, that in which one commodity (linen) remains where it is, while the others move to and fro.

This train of consequences from the play of varying demand is dependent on the *total* demand in each country for the products of the other. To speak more accurately, it is dependent on the state of demand among the inhabitants of the two countries for each and every one of the commodities which they might exchange. The Americans may care for cloth and linen so much, and for wheat so little, that they will offer wheat for the other two commodities on terms that make it worth while for the Germans to send both cloth and linen to the United States. Or, at the other extreme, the Americans may care for cloth and linen so little, and for their own wheat so much, that they will indeed take cloth in exchange for some wheat, but will take no linen; nay, may prefer to send some linen of their own make in exchange for cloth.

These possible relations may now be expressed in terms of prices and money incomes. Let it be remembered, in considering the figures which follow, that a relatively high rate of money wages in the United States — a considerable gap between American and German wages — signifies that the United States secures the larger share of the possible gain from the trade; whereas relatively lower rates in the United States — a smaller gap in money wages — signify that the United States secures the smaller share. For simplicity, the figures will be arranged on the basis of keeping money wages in the United States at a constant figure, namely $2.00 a day. The changes which serve to illustrate the different possibilities are here confined to Germany, where money wages become lower as the terms are less favorable to her, higher as they become more favorable.

Again we take the three possible cases.

(1) Suppose first a wide gap between German and American money wages. Let wages in the United States be $2.00, wages in Germany $1.20. We have then:

	Wages per Day	Total Wages	Produce	Domestic Supply Price
In the U. S. 10 days' labor	$2.00	$20	20 wheat	$1.00
" " U. S. 10 " "	$2.00	$20	20 linen	$1.00
" " U. S. 10 " "	$2.00	$20	20 cloth	$1.00
" Germany 10 " "	$1.20	$12	10 wheat	$1.20
" Germany 10 " "	$1.20	$12	15 linen	$0.80
" Germany 10 " "	$1.20	$12	18 cloth	$0.66⅔

Wheat is produced at lower money cost in the United States than in Germany and moves from the United States to Germany. Both linen and cloth are produced more cheaply in Germany and move thence to the United States. The United States, while gaining thru the importation of both, evidently gains more from the importation of cloth than from that of linen. She gets her cloth from Germany for $0.66⅔, whereas the price at which cloth can be made in the United States is $1.00. She gets her linen from Germany for $0.80; less than the American supply price of $1.00, but not as much below that price as in the case of cloth. Germany gains by a cheapening of wheat to the amount of $0.20. It would cost her $1.20 to produce wheat at home; she procures it from the United States at the price of $1.00.

Consider now the barter terms of trade which obtain under these circumstances. In both countries wheat sells for $1.00 and cloth for $0.66⅔, these being the "world prices." In terms of commodities, 10 of wheat exchange for 15 of cloth. The five days' labor which in the United States produce 10 of wheat would yield, if applied to cloth, 10 of cloth also; the United States, getting 15 of cloth for her 10 of wheat, gains 5 of cloth. Germany, on the other hand, gains 3 of cloth. With 10 days' labor she could produce 18 of cloth or 10 of wheat; with only 15 of cloth she gets 10 of wheat.

Linen sells for $0.80 in both countries; with wheat at $1.00 the terms of trade are 12½ of linen for 10 of wheat. The United States gets 12½ of linen for 10 of wheat, the product of 5 days' labor, whereas that labor would produce at home only 10 of linen. The gain is 2½ of linen for the United States. And Germany gains the same: the difference between 15 of linen and 12½.

(2) Next, assume barter terms of trade between the two countries which are more favorable to Germany; the evidence of the more favorable terms being higher money wages in that country. Suppose German wages to be not at a figure somewhat low ($1.20), but much higher, say $1.60. Wages in the United States we assume to remain at $2.00. Then we have:

	Wages per Day	Total Wages	Produce	Domestic Supply Price
In the U. S. 10 days' labor	$2.00	$20	20 wheat	$1.00
" " U. S. 10 " "	$2.00	$20	20 linen	$1.00
" " U. S. 10 " "	$2.00	$20	20 cloth	$1.00
" Germany 10 " "	$1.60	$16	10 wheat	$1.60
" Germany 10 " "	$1.60	$16	15 linen	$1.06¾
" Germany 10 " "	$1.60	$16	18 cloth	$0.89

Both wheat and linen are now cheaper in the United States than in Germany. The difference, of course, is greater for wheat, whose domestic supply price in Germany is $1.60, whereas it can be got from the United States for $1.00. Linen can be produced in Germany at a money cost of $1.06⅔; but it is obtainable from the United States at a slightly lower figure — $1.00. Cloth still moves from Germany to the United States, being put on the market in Germany at the price of $0.89 as against an American money cost of $1.00. The marked change from the previous situation is that linen, which before moved from Germany to the United States, now moves from the United States to Germany.

The barter terms of trade are, as between wheat and cloth, 10 of American wheat for 11.2 of German cloth; as between linen and cloth, 10 of American linen for 11.2 of German cloth. The United States thus gets for 10 of wheat only 11.2 of cloth, as against 15 of cloth under the previous conditions. Under those conditions she had such favorable terms for cloth as to lead her to confine her labor to wheat alone. Linen was then got more cheaply from Germany than by domestic production. Now the case for linen is reversed. It can no longer be got at lower price from Germany. On the contrary, it can be produced at so much lower money cost at home that it is actually exported to Germany. The explanation for this overturn, to repeat, is that the United States no longer gets the lion's share of the potential gain divisible between the two countries. She did get that preponderance of gain when her wheat was greatly in demand in Germany, and when on her part she did not readily take either cloth or linen in exchange. The relative states of demand have changed; the United States wants more cloth, Germany wants less wheat; to get what she wants, the United States finds it advantageous to send not only wheat, but linen also. The money wages and money prices constitute the mechanism by which those new conditions are transformed into actualities; but the fundamental cause of the change is the altered state of demand for the several articles in the two countries.

(3) Finally, the intermediate case. Let German wages be $1.50 a day — not so high as $1.60, not so low as $1.20. Then we have:

	WAGES PER DAY	TOTAL WAGES	PRODUCE	DOMESTIC SUPPLY PRICE
In the U. S. 10 days' labor	$2.00	$20	20 wheat	$1.00
" " U. S. 10 " "	$2.00	$20	20 linen	$1.00
" " U. S. 10 " "	$2.00	$20	20 cloth	$1.00
" Germany 10 " "	$1.50	$15	10 wheat	$1.50
" Germany 10 " "	$1.50	$15	15 linen	$1.00
" Germany 10 " "	$1.50	$15	18 cloth	$0.83⅓

The price situation is simple. Wheat is produced more cheaply in the United States than in Germany — $1.00 in the United States and $1.50 in Germany. Cloth is produced more cheaply in Germany — $0.83⅓ there as compared to $1.00 in the United States. Linen, however, has the same money cost of production in both countries; namely, $1.00. Wheat moves from the United States to Germany. Cloth moves from Germany to the United States. Linen moves neither way; each country produces for itself the linen that it consumes.

The barter terms of trade into which these prices ($1.00 for American wheat, $0.83⅓ for German cloth) resolve themselves, are 10 of wheat for 12 of cloth. On these terms, it is a matter of indifference to Germany whether for the 10 of American wheat she exchanges 10 of her linen or 12 of her cloth since in Germany 10 linen is equal to 12 cloth. For the United States, however, it is more advantageous to take the 12 German cloth in exchange for her own wheat inasmuch as in the United States 10 linen is equal to only 10 of cloth. In this case, therefore, the American situation would be decisive, and American wheat would flow to Germany and German cloth to the United States.[1]

---

[1] I have simplified these illustrations (as regards prices and money wages) by keeping the American figures unchanged thruout, and making the variations for German figures only. It is hardly necessary to say that the three cases, as here set forth, are not designed to show successive stages, the later of which develop from the earlier. If it were desired to illustrate the several stages by which the situation of Case 1 is transformed by a change of demand into Case 2, the procedure would be to trace the flow of specie from the United States to Germany, the rise in wages and domestic prices in Germany, the corresponding fall in the United States, and so on. The outcome would be a set of figures differing from those of the text, money wages becoming lower in the United States at the same time as they become higher in Germany. But the same *relations* between the two countries would be found. It has seemed to me superfluous to follow the suppositions thru in the more meticulous way. The reader who may be interested will readily do so for himself.

The equilibrium of international payments in all these cases will be reached when the *total* money sums due from the two countries to each other are the same. It is the amount which the Americans are ready to pay for cloth and linen, as compared with that which the Germans are ready to pay for wheat; or the amount which the Germans are ready to pay for wheat and linen as compared to what the Americans are ready to pay for cloth — these are the determinants of the character and the volume of the trade between them. It is superflous to present illustrative figures, since these would be no more than variants of illustrations already worked out in the preceding pages for similar situations.

CHAPTER 10

Two Countries Competing in a Third

Still another modifying circumstance is now to be introduced. So far the problems have been treated as if there were but two countries. We proceed to consider some changes or qualifications which appear when we have not a single country exchanging with one other, but several countries competing with each other in supplying another country. Here, as in the last chapter, the procedure will be that of considering labor costs alone, and these in their simplest aspects, the reader being assumed to bear in mind that other factors (such as non-competing groups among laborers, capital and the return on it, varying costs) complicate the situation and may modify the results. The analysis of the fundamental factor of labor costs, taken by itself, serves to bring out the essentials for the problem here in hand.

First, suppose a case in which there are two countries on the one side, a single country on the other. Let the two be the United States and Russia; the single one, England. Let the conditions be such that both the United States and Russia have a comparative advantage over England in wheat, England a comparative advantage over them in cloth. In figures, for example, thus:

In the U. S. 10 days' labor produce 20 wheat
" " U. S. 10 " " " 20 cloth
" England 10 " " " 10 wheat
" England 10 " " " 15 cloth
" Russia 10 " " " 10 wheat
" Russia 10 " " " 10 cloth

A glance shows that both the United States and Russia can trade to advantage with England, exporting wheat and getting cloth in exchange. Both have a comparative advantage over England in wheat, tho not of precisely the same kind. The United States has a superior advantage in wheat; Russia has an inferior disadvantage. Tho the United States produces both wheat and cloth with less labor than England, the effectiveness of her labor is particularly great in wheat. With the same labor, the output of wheat is twice as great as in England (20 to 10), while that of cloth is only one-third greater (20 to 15). Russia has no superiority over England in either commodity; but she has equal effectiveness in wheat (10 to 10), with a less effectiveness in cloth (10 to 15).

Russia and the United States, it is obvious, have no occasion to trade with each other. They present the simple case, already considered sufficiently, of equal differences in costs. The effectiveness of labor is twice as great all around in the United States as in Russia. Neither country would find it worth while to exchange with the other. The United States is the more prosperous, Russia the less prosperous. Were they alone, and England out of the case, neither would pay attention to the other; neither would be better off or worse off because of the presence of the other.

The terms of trade possible under these conditions would be 10 of wheat for anywhere between 11 and 14 of cloth. These terms, that is, would be possible in trade between the United States and England, and also in trade between Russia and England. England would exchange with each of the others on the same terms. So far as concerns the gain ascribable to international trade, both the United States and Russia would be on a footing of precise equality: their income in terms of the cloth secured from England would be enlarged to precisely the same extent over and above what that income would have been without the trade.

Express the same situation in prices and money incomes. As we have already seen, the double effectiveness of American labor as compared with Russian would cause money wages to be twice as high in the United States as in Russia; while the relations between the effectiveness of labor in England and in the other two countries would bring it about that money wages would be higher in England than in Russia, lower than in the United States. We may have, for example :

	WAGES PER DAY	TOTAL WAGES	PRODUCE	DOMESTIC SUPPLY PRICE
In the U. S. 10 days' labor	$2.00	$20.00	20 wheat	$1.00
" " U. S. 10 " "	$2.00	$20.00	20 cloth	$1.00
" England 10 " "	$1.25	$12.50	10 wheat	$1.25
" England 10 " "	$1.25	$12.50	15 cloth	$0.83⅓
" Russia 10 " "	$1.00	$10.00	10 wheat	$1.00
" Russia 10 " "	$1.00	$10.00	10 cloth	$1.00

The supply price of wheat is the same in the United States and Russia ($1.00), and wheat will sell at that price not only in these countries, but in England also. Russia cannot undersell the United States in wheat, even tho her wages are but half of American wages; since the effectiveness of her labor is also one-half. Cloth is produced at a cheaper price in England than in the other two countries; and English cloth will be exported to both, and will be sold in both at the same price — $0.83⅓. The American purchasers, tho they pay for the English cloth the same price as the Russians, have money incomes twice as large, and therefore are better off as purchasers. Their better situation, however, is obviously due to the same cause as the generally larger prosperity of the United States; it is the result of the greater effectiveness of labor in wheat. So far as concerns the terms on which the United States gets her cloth from England, she is on precisely the same footing as Russia.

Construct now an international balance of payments based on these price relations. Suppose that:

Russia and the United States (between them) buy from England
  15 million cloth at $0.83⅓ = $12,500,000
Russia and the United States (between them) sell to England
  12½ million wheat at $1.00 = $12,500,000

The two money totals are the same. An equilibrium of payments is established, foreign exchange is at par, no specie moves, the wheat and the cloth pay for each other. Wheat to the amount of 12½ million bushels is exchanged for cloth to the amount of 15 million yards. That is,

$$12\tfrac{1}{2} \text{ wheat} = 15 \text{ cloth, or } 10 \text{ wheat} = 12 \text{ cloth}$$

Of the possible terms of trade (10 wheat for anything more than

10 or less than 15 cloth) that at which the countries are bartering in fact is 12.

Suppose now a change in the conditions of demand. Assume that at the price of $0.83⅓ for cloth, *more* cloth than the 15 million yards can be sold in the United States and Russia. The increase in quantity demanded at that price may come from Russia alone, or from the United States alone, or partly from each of them. Whatever the region whence the increased demand appears, the result is that England sells more cloth. Her exports then exceed her imports in money value, and specie flows to her from the other countries. The consequences are familiar; prices and money wages rise in England, fall in the countries with which she is trading, and changes of this kind go on until a new equilibrium is established. The new states of wages and prices may be exemplified thus:

	Wages per Day	Total Wages	Produce	Domestic Supply Price
In the U. S. 10 days' labor	$1.90	$19.00	20 wheat	$0.95
" the U. S. 10 " "	$1.90	$19.00	20 cloth	$0.95
" England 10 " "	$1.35	$13.50	10 wheat	$1.35
" England 10 " "	$1.35	$13.50	15 cloth	$0.90
" Russia 10 " "	$0.95	$ 9.50	10 wheat	$0.95
" Russia 10 " "	$0.95	$ 9.50	10 cloth	$0.95

Money wages have fallen both in the United States and Russia; from $2.00 to $1.90 in the United States, from $1.00 to $0.95 in Russia. As purchasers of cloth, both Russians and Americans are worse off than before; their money incomes are lower, the price of cloth is higher. Money wages in England on the other hand have risen, and the English are better off as purchasers of wheat.

The readjusted equilibrium of international payments may then be exemplified thus:

Russia and the United States (between them) buy from England
    20 million cloth at $0.90 = $18,000,000
Russia and the United States (between them) sell to England
    19 million wheat at $0.95 = $18,000,000 [1]

It now appears that 19 million bushels of wheat are exchanged by Russia and the United States for 20 million yards of English cloth.

[1] To be exact, $18,050,000.

The barter terms of trade, that is, become 19 wheat for 20 cloth, or 10 wheat for $10\frac{10}{19}$ cloth — very nearly 10 for $10\frac{1}{2}$. Before the increase in demand for cloth set in, the barter terms of trade had been 10 wheat for 12 cloth; they are now 10 for $10\frac{1}{2}$. The English get the same quantity of wheat for a less quantity of cloth; they get a larger share than before of the possible gain from the trade.

It matters not, to repeat, whether the change in demand takes place solely in the United States, solely in Russia, or partly in one and partly in the other. An increase of Russian demand operates to make the terms less favorable to the Americans, even tho in the United States alone nothing has happened that would change the situation.

This sort of case, in the two possible phases here worked out, serves to illustrate a general proposition which played its part in the exposition of the classic doctrine. "There are two senses in which a country obtains its commodities cheaper by foreign trade; in the sense of value and in the sense of cost." [1] In the sense of cost, the United States thruout is getting its cloth cheaper than Russia. In the sense of value, both the United States and Russia get the English cloth on the same terms. Cheapness in the sense of costs depends on the amount of labor given to the exported commodities; this is less in the United States than in Russia. Cheapness in the sense of value depends on the barter terms of trade between the exports and the imports; at any one time this is the same for the United States and for Russia, but varies at different times according to the conditions of demand for wheat on the one hand, for cloth on the other.

Obviously it is more *probable* that the barter terms of trade will be favorable to England and that she will get her imports (wheat) cheaper in the sense of value, if there be not one country buying cloth from her but two or more. The greater the number of purchasers of her cloth, the larger the quantity that will be taken at a given price. If the other two countries, United States and Russia, have the same population and are alike in the demand of their peoples (in their demand schedules) for cloth, then the two of them

[1] Mill, Principles, Bk. 3, Ch. 18.

will take twice as much of cloth at the same price as either of them would take alone; and the barter terms of trade will become more favorable to England.

Turn now to a case of a different kind, and one more complicated. It is exemplified by the following figures:

DOMESTIC TERMS OF TRADE

In the U. S. 10 days' labor produce 20 wheat
10 ″   ″   ″   20 cloth } 10 wheat = 10 cloth

In England 10 ″   ″   ″   10 wheat
10 ″   ″   ″   15 cloth } 10 wheat = 15 cloth

In Germany 10 ″   ″   ″   10 wheat
10 ″   ″   ″   13 cloth } 10 wheat = 13 cloth

Here each of the countries has a situation as regards the relative costs of the two articles which is different from that of either of the others. The United States has a comparative advantage over both England and Germany in wheat, and might exchange wheat for cloth with either or with both. England has a comparative advantage in cloth not only as against the United States but as against Germany also; and she might send cloth to either in exchange for wheat. Germany might send cloth to the United States in exchange for wheat; but she might also send wheat to England in exchange for cloth. The limits within which the barter terms of trade thruout the trading area could establish themselves are 10 cloth for 10 wheat at the lowest, 15 cloth for 10 wheat at the highest. At any rate between these limits (*i.e.* wheat exchanging at the rates of 11, 12, 13, 14 for cloth) there will be trade. But which of these several possibilities will emerge?

The situation is essentially the same as that considered in the first part of this chapter; indeed, is no more than a variant. The answer again is that the outcome depends on the state of demand between the countries. As before, there are three possible cases.

(1) Suppose the barter terms of trade to be unfavorable to the United States — such as would exist if the demand of the United States for cloth were great, the demand of England and Germany for wheat small. Suppose it to be 10 wheat for 11 cloth. Both Germany and England would then send cloth to the United States,

and the United States would send wheat to both in exchange. England would gain more from the operation than Germany; she would gain the difference between 15 and 11. Ten days' labor in England yields 10 of wheat and 15 of cloth; if England gets 10 wheat for 11 of cloth, she gains the difference between 15 and 11. Ten days' labor in Germany yields 10 of wheat and 13 of cloth; if Germany gets 10 of wheat for 11 of cloth, she gains the difference between 13 and 11. The United States would gain the difference between 10 and 11.

(2) Next suppose that the terms of trade become distinctly favorable to the United States, — that she gets for 10 wheat as much as 14 cloth. Then England would send cloth to the United States and the United States wheat to England. But at these terms England and Germany would also exchange. Germany would gain by sending 10 wheat to England and getting 14 cloth in exchange. Since the given labor (10 days) would produce in Germany only 13 cloth, England would gain similarly; with 10 days' labor she could produce at home 10 wheat or 15 cloth; if she gets 10 wheat for *less* than 15 cloth, she gives her labor more advantageously to producing cloth only. At the rate of 14 cloth for 10 wheat, then, both the United States and Germany would send wheat to England, and England would send cloth to both; nor would any cloth be made either in Germany or the United States. No trade would take place between the United States and Germany, notwithstanding the fact that trade between them would develop if England were out of the way and they were confronted merely with each other.

(3) Suppose now the intermediate stage, that at which the terms of trade are exactly 10 wheat for 13 cloth. England then will send cloth to the United States and the United States will send wheat in exchange. But for Germany the situation would be one of indifference. If she were to send 13 cloth to the United States she would secure (at the rate established between England and the United States) 10 of wheat, or precisely the same amount of wheat as she could produce at home with the labor given to producing the 13 of cloth. The trade would be between the United States and

England only. Any deviation from these terms (13 cloth for 10 wheat) would cause Germany to enter. If the cloth given in exchange for 10 wheat were more than 13 cloth, Germany would turn from cloth to wheat and would send wheat to England. If it were less than 13 cloth, Germany would turn from wheat to cloth, and would send cloth to the United States. At the precise figure of 13 cloth she would have no inducement for concerning herself with the other countries at all, and would go her way, producing for herself both cloth and wheat. The only trade would be between the United States and England.

These suppositions, like the various others which have been considered in the preceding pages, can be put in terms of money prices and money incomes. At the risk of wearying the reader, I will indicate how money wages and money prices might shape themselves in the three countries in the several cases just described.

(1) Suppose that money wages and domestic supply prices in the countries are as follows:

	WAGES PER DAY	TOTAL WAGES	PRODUCE	DOMESTIC SUPPLY PRICE
In the U. S. 10 days' labor	$2.00	$20	20 wheat	$1.00
" " U. S. 10 " "	$2.00	$20	20 cloth	$1.00
" England 10 " "	$1.40	$14	10 wheat	$1.40
" England 10 " "	$1.40	$14	15 cloth	$0.93
" Germany 10 " "	$1.21	$12.10	10 wheat	$1.21
" Germany 10 " "	$1.21	$12.10	13 cloth	$0.93

The domestic supply price of cloth is the same in England and in Germany — $0.93. It is lower than the domestic supply price of cloth in the United States; and both German and English cloth will be sold in the United States at a price which no American cloth maker could meet. The Americans would get their cloth for $0.93 by importation, instead of paying $1.00 for it, as they would if it were made at home. Both Germany and England would get American wheat for $1.00. Wheat, if grown in England, would entail a money cost of $1.40; if grown in Germany, would entail a money cost of $1.21. In other words, England would gain the difference between $1.40 and $1.00, and Germany the difference between $1.21 and $1.00. Both gain, but England gains more.

The barter terms of trade would obviously be 10 wheat = 10.7+ of cloth; this being the ratio in terms of physical units of the price relations — $0.93 for cloth and $1.00 for wheat. That is, 10 wheat exchange for *less* than 13 cloth. Trade on this basis, as we have seen, gives a large share of the possible gain to England and Germany; a comparatively small one to the United States, even tho one sufficient to make the exchange of some advantage to her.

(2) Let the figures now be shifted in such manner as to conform to terms of trade under which 10 wheat exchange for more than 13 of cloth. For simplicity, we keep the United States figures as they were before, as regards money wages and the domestic supply prices of goods, confining the readjustments to the other countries.

	WAGES PER DAY	TOTAL WAGES	PRODUCE	DOMESTIC SUPPLY PRICE
In the U. S. 10 days' labor	$2.00	$20	20 wheat	$1.00
" " U. S. 10 " "	$2.00	$20	20 cloth	$1.00
" England 10 " "	$1.10	$11	10 wheat	$1.10
" England 10 " "	$1.10	$11	15 cloth	$0.73
" Germany 10 " "	$1.00	$10	10 wheat	$1.00
" Germany 10 " "	$1.00	$10	13 cloth	$0.77

Wages have now fallen in England from $1.40 to $1.10, and in Germany from $1.21 to $1.00. The supply prices of English and German goods have fallen correspondingly. Such is the nature of the results to be expected if a change in demand sets in which causes the barter terms of trade to be more favorable to the United States — if more wheat were demanded by England and Germany under the price conditions of Case 1 than was equal in money value to the cloth demanded under those conditions by the United States. Wages and the supply prices of goods are lower in England and Germany than they were before. The domestic supply price of wheat is now the same ($1.00) in Germany as it is in the United States, and wheat would not move between the two. But the price of wheat is lower than its domestic supply price in England ($1.10) and England would import wheat from both Germany and the United States. The domestic supply price of cloth, on the other hand, is lower in England ($0.73) than it is in either Germany ($0.77) or the United States ($1.00), and cloth would move from

England to both. The price of wheat thruout the trading area would be $1.00, the price of cloth $0.73. The terms of trade in physical units would be the ratio of those figures, that is 10 of wheat for 13.7 of cloth — *more* than 13 of cloth for 10 of wheat. And Germany would no longer be an exporter of cloth to the United States, but an exporter of wheat to England.[1]

(3) Readjust finally in such way that the money wages and the supply prices correspond to barter terms of 10 wheat for 13 cloth. We still keep wages and prices in the United States at the original figures, confining the shifts to the other countries.

	WAGES PER DAY	TOTAL WAGES	PRODUCE	DOMESTIC SUPPLY PRICE
In the U. S. 10 days' labor	$2.00	$20	20 wheat	$1.00
" " U. S. 10 " "	$2.00	$20	20 cloth	$1.00
" England 10 " "	$1.15	$11.50	10 wheat	$1.15
" England 10 " "	$1.15	$11.50	15 cloth	$0.77
" Germany 10 " "	$1.00	$10	10 wheat	$1.00
" Germany 10 " "	$1.00	$10	13 cloth	$0.77

Under these conditions England and the United States exchange wheat and cloth; since the supply price of wheat in the United States ($1.00) is lower than that of wheat in England ($1.15), while the supply price of cloth in England ($0.77) is lower than that of cloth in the United States ($1.00). English cloth will be sold in the United States and England at $0.77, and American wheat will be sold in both at $1.00. The barter terms of trade will be 10 wheat for 13 of cloth (the ratio in physical units of the price relations $0.77 and $1.00).

Germany, however, can find no advantage from participation in trade on these terms. If indeed Germany and the United States alone were confronted with each other, trade would arise between them. Tho wheat is at the same price in both ($1.00), cloth is at $0.77 in Germany and at $1.00 in the United States; cloth would

[1] It will be observed that in Case 2 the wages relations of the countries are different from what they were in Case 1. In that earlier case, wages in England were $1.40, in Germany $1.21; that is, in the ratio of 15 to 13, which is the ratio of the effectiveness of labor in the two countries for the article exported (15 cloth for 10 days' labor in England, 13 cloth in Germany). In Case 2 wages in the United States are $2.00, in Germany $1.00, that being again the ratio of the effectiveness of labor in the exported article (20 wheat for 10 days' labor in the United States, 10 wheat in Germany).

move from Germany to the United States, specie at first move from the United States to Germany; in the end Germany would exchange cloth for American wheat.   But English cloth already sells in the United States for $0.77, and Germany's supply price is that same figure — $0.77.   Germany can gain nothing by the export of cloth to the United States, and the United States can gain nothing by the export of wheat to Germany.   The barter terms of trade between England and the United States are 10 wheat for 13 cloth.   This is precisely the domestic term of trade within Germany between wheat and cloth; domestic supply prices in Germany are adjusted to this situation.   England and the United States find it advantageous to trade on these terms; and so long as they do so on these precise terms, Germany has nothing to do with either of them.[1]

[1] The reader will note that in arranging these figures of wages and prices I have followed the same plan of simplification as in the preceding chapter (Ch. IX); namely, that of keeping the American figures the same and making the changes in the German and English figures only.   It is not to be supposed here, any more than it was to be supposed for the earlier figures, that the several cases represent successive stages, of which the later might develop from the earlier.   Worked out for such successive stages, the figures would be different; but the principles elucidated and illustrated remain the same.

CHAPTER 11

NON-MERCHANDISE TRANSACTIONS
TRIBUTES, INDEMNITIES, TOURIST EXPENSES

So far those transactions only have been considered which arise out of sales and purchases of merchandise. Imports and exports of goods have been treated as if they constituted the sole operations in international trade and as if they alone gave occasion for international payments and the transfer of money. As is familiar enough, there are other operations of large consequence. Payments arising from international indebtedness — the making of loans and the payment of interest on loans — are perhaps the most important among them; most important because, for several generations at least, they have played a considerable part in the trade of many countries and over long stretches of time. Other payments also, for expenses of tourists, for charitable or family aid, indemnities payable after defeat in a war, have been important; and tho less constantly in evidence than the items arising from indebtedness, they have at times risen to a commanding position. Charges for freight and passengers carried in the vessels of another country, and banking and insurance charges, are also substantial in amount.

These various transactions have come to be of increasing importance since the early part of the 19th century. It is true that all of them taken together have never been as large as the transactions on merchandise account. In no country and at no time — so far as I know — have they been equal (measured in terms of the sums of money involved) to the sales of goods between countries. But they have become large and have tended to constitute a growing proportion of the total. We may proceed to consider the principles applicable to them and the modifications of our main

108

conclusions which they suggest. The reader will bear in mind that it is the principles alone which are here to be considered. The actual operations will be described and discussed at some length in the second part of this book, and will give occasion for considerable qualifications, perhaps modifications, of the principles.

"Invisible" is the adjective commonly used to describe these items. They are invisible simply in the sense that they are not recorded as publicly as the imports and exports of merchandise, and on the whole are not so accurately known. The term is convenient when one wishes to speak of the whole series of items and to compare them with the goods transactions.

Begin with the simplest case of all : a remittance that has to be made from one country to another, with no *quid pro quo* obtained or to be obtained from the country receiving the payment. Such, for example, would be the remittance of income to absentee landlords ; more strikingly, a war indemnity payment, or a mere tribute. When there is, immediately or ultimately, directly or indirectly, a return of some sort by the receiving country — as with freight charges, tourist expenses, loans — the situation is different in some essential particulars. Eliminate this perhaps complicating element by taking a case in which there is no *quid pro quo* of any kind : something in the nature of a tribute.

Suppose further that a stated payment is to be made regularly year after year. Sporadic payments are commonly effected, under the modern organization of money and credit, by methods which disturb the ordinary course of trade to a surprisingly small extent ; and very heavy payments of this kind are often settled with great smoothness. Steadily continuing payments, however, even tho moderate in amount, are not wound up without affecting the main current of international trade — the movement of goods from country to country.

Recall the figures already considered. Suppose :

```
In the U. S. 10 days' labor produce 20 wheat
 "   "  U. S. 10   "       "        "    20 linen
 " Germany 10   "       "        "    10 wheat
 " Germany 10   "       "        "    15 linen
```

The United States has a comparative advantage in producing wheat, and will import linen from Germany even tho her labor is more effective in producing linen than is German labor. The barter terms of trade will be 10 of American wheat for anything between 10 and 15 of German linen. The nearer it is to 15 linen — the more linen Germany gives for 10 of wheat — the more the United States will gain; the nearer it is to 10 linen — the less linen Germany gives for 10 of wheat — the more Germany will gain.

Carry the case out in terms of prices and money wages. I select, as the starting point in the present set of illustrative figures, a situation in which the barter terms of trade are 12½ of linen for 10 of wheat — that in which the gain from the trade is equally divided between the two countries.

	WAGES PER DAY	TOTAL WAGES	PRODUCE	DOMESTIC SUPPLY PRICE
In the U. S. 10 days' labor	$1.70	$17	20 wheat	$0.85
" " U. S. 10 " "	$1.70	$17	20 linen	$0.85
" Germany 10 " "	$1.02	$10.20	10 wheat	$1.02
" Germany 10 " "	$1.02	$10.20	15 linen	$0.68

The money cost of wheat is less in the United States than in Germany, and wheat moves from the United States. The money cost of linen is less in Germany, and linen moves thence to the United States.

Suppose, lastly, that at the prices stated ($0.85 for wheat and $0.68 for linen), the quantities of the two commodities that move are:

    10,000,000 wheat exported from the U. S. at $0.85 = $8,500,000
    12,500,000 linen exported from Germany at $0.68 = $8,500,000

The money amounts balance. Foreign exchange is at par; no specie flows. 10 millions of wheat exchange for 12½ millions of linen; the barter terms of trade thus are 10 wheat for 12½ linen.

Suppose now that the United States has to remit to Germany a million dollars annually — a tribute, or the like. The total money sum payable by people in the United States to those in Germany is now nine and a half millions — eight and a half millions for the linen bought, and the tribute of one million. Foreign exchange is no longer at par; the American exports of wheat no longer yield bills on Germany in amounts sufficient to supply the needs of those who have to remit to Germany. Exchange on Germany rises to a premium in the United States; specie flows to Germany. Prices and money wages fall in the United States, rise in Germany. These changes will go on until a stage of equilibrium is reached, which may be exemplified as follows:

	WAGES PER DAY	TOTAL WAGES	PRODUCE	DOMESTIC SUPPLY PRICE
In the U. S. 10 days' labor	$1.60	$16	20 wheat	$0.80
" " U. S. 10 " "	$1.60	$16	20 linen	$0.80
" Germany 10 " "	$1.15	$11.50	10 wheat	$1.15
" Germany 10 " "	$1.15	$11.50	15 linen	$0.76⅔

Wages have fallen in the United States from $1.70 to $1.60; they have risen in Germany from $1.02 to $1.15. The money cost of wheat has fallen in the United States from $0.85 to $0.80 and is now considerably lower than the German money cost of wheat; the money cost of linen in Germany has risen to $0.76⅔ and is now not much lower than the American money cost of linen.

At these prices suppose the movement of goods to be:

10¼ millions of wheat at $0.80 exported from the United States = $8,200,000
9.4 millions of linen at $0.76⅔ exported from Germany   = $7,200,000

The exports of wheat from the United States exceed in money value the exports of linen from Germany. The difference is a million dollars, precisely the sum which has to be remitted to Germany; that is, it suffices to yield the volume of bills in Germany which are wanted by those persons (private individuals or public officials) having the remittance in charge. The demand for bills is just met by the supply; foreign exchange is at par; equilibrium has been reached.

The equilibrium, it is to be noticed, is one in the "balance of payments," not one in the "balance of trade." The payments to be made by the United States to Germany are completely met. But the balance of trade — the balance of merchandise operations — is "favorable" to the United States; her exports of goods exceed her imports in money value. The balance of trade is "unfavorable" to Germany; her imports of goods exceed in money value her exports. These expressions "favorable" and "unfavorable" balance, with their implication that a country secures a gain in the one case and suffers a loss in the other, are so commonly used in the ordinary talk about international trade that it is difficult to keep away from them entirely. They rest on the obvious fact that *if* there be no other than merchandise transactions, an excess of exports over imports will cause a flow of specie into a country; and they rest further on the persistent mercantilist notion that there is something advantageous or "favorable" to a country in a relation of exports to imports which, *if* it stood by itself, would cause specie to flow in. The qualifying *if* has become of more and more importance in modern times, and consequently the mercantilist terminology, misleading in any case, has lost its significance even as a description of the forces on which depends the movement of specie. Non-merchandise transactions have become so large, and affect so steadily the trade of each and every country, that the relations of imports and exports in themselves give a very uncertain clue to that which in reality determines the specie flow. It is the balance of international payments which determines this flow. In our supposed case the balance of payments is precisely settled; the balance of trade, even tho it be called "favorable" to the United States and "unfavorable" to Germany, leads to no movement of specie either way.

In the important sense, the situation has become less favorable to the United States; and this in two ways. Not only do the people of the United States part with a considerable volume of tangible goods (wheat) in order to make the required payment to Germany, but in order to carry out the transaction and at the same time pay for the linen which they continue to buy, they have to barter their wheat for linen on less advantageous terms.

Consider the figures. Before the tribute became payable, the United States sent 10 millions of wheat to Germany, and got in exchange 12½ millions of linen; for each ten of wheat 12½ of linen were got. When the new equilibrium is attained and the annual payment of the tribute is effected, the United States sends 10¼ millions of wheat and gets but 9.4 millions of linen. She sends more wheat and gets less linen; she exchanges 10¼ of wheat for 9.4 of linen, *i.e.* 10 of wheat for 9.2 of linen. The barter terms of trade are much less favorable to the United States, much more favorable to Germany.

These figures, however, call for further consideration. The wheat sent from the United States is to be regarded as making two payments: one to meet the obligatory remittance, the other for the German linen. The two may be separated in this fashion:

$$1,250,000 \text{ wheat at } \$0.80 \text{ for remittance} = \$1,000,000$$
$$9,000,000 \text{ wheat at } \$0.80 \text{ for linen} = \$7,200,000$$

The wheat that serves to pay for the linen amounts to 9,000,000 bushels. It is this quantity — less than the total sent — which can be said with accuracy to be exchanged for the 9,400,000 linen. The barter terms of trade, so considered, are 9 of wheat for 9.4 of linen, *i.e.* 10 wheat for 10.4 linen. This is not so unfavorable to the United States as the relation just mentioned — 10 for 9.2. But it remains much less favorable than the ratio of 10 to 12½ which prevailed at the outset. To repeat, the people of the United States suffer loss in two ways. They send wheat to pay the tribute; and, in order to get the linen they want, they must give more wheat for each unit of linen which they continue to buy.

There are thus two ways of looking at the barter terms of trade. One may be indicated by the phrase "gross barter terms of trade"; the other by "net barter terms of trade." The first regards the whole volume of goods, both imports and exports. The second regards those goods only which pay for goods; it demarcates any movement of goods which serves for other payments. (I neglect services, for reasons presently to be explained.)

The gross barter terms in the present illustration are 10 wheat for 9.2 of linen; the net barter terms are 10 wheat for 10.4 linen. For some purposes the first is the important one, for other purposes the second. As regards the limiting figures — the range within which trade is possible — the net terms are alone important,

and indeed are alone to be considered. The net terms cannot be
such that the United States gets for her 10 of wheat *less* than 10 of
linen. But the gross terms may be disadvantageous to this drastic
extent. The United States in the present case actually gets only
9.2 linen for every 10 of wheat she sends to Germany. True, she
gets as much as 10.4 of linen for the money that is paid for every 10
of wheat she exports.[1] But she sends additional wheat to Germany,
which serves for the tribute remittance and brings it about that
on the total transactions she gets only the 9.2 linen for every 10 of
wheat. And it is these total transactions which are really of
significance for her welfare. Germany has no substantive concern
in the manner in which the money account is drawn up and the
balance of payments is reckoned, in analyzing how much of wheat is
to be regarded as paying for linen and how much is to be set down
for the other remittance. What actually happens is that the
United States parts with 10¼ millions of wheat and receives no more
than 9.4 millions of linen. Germany gets much wheat, gives little
linen. And this situation persists indefinitely. Year after year
— so long as the tribute continues and no other items enter — the
United States sends to Germany a large slice of the product of her
labor and receives a small slice of the product of German labor.

The *degree* to which the barter terms of trade, both net and gross,
are altered to the disadvantage of the United States depends on the
conditions of demand. The particular figures just chosen to illustrate the consequences of a tribute payment were such as would
result from a play of demand unfavorable to the United States.
They are conditions of inelastic demand in Germany for wheat and
of elastic demand for linen in the United States; in more precise
terms, conditions in which the elasticity of demand is less than
unity in Germany and more than unity in the United States. Tho
the price of wheat falls from $0.85 to $0.80, Germany buys but
very little more wheat; and she spends on wheat a total sum less
than she spent before — $8,200,000 now, $8,500,000 before. In

---

[1] The terms of 10 wheat for 10.4 for linen, it will be noticed, are those which conform to the prices of wheat and linen in the supposed trade. The price of wheat is
$0.80, that of linen is $0.76⅔; the corresponding figures for the barter terms are 10
and 10.4.

the United States, on the other hand, the amount of linen bought shrinks greatly in consequence of the rise in linen price (from $0.68 to $0.76⅔); and the total amount which she spends on linen falls substantially, from $8,500,000 to $7,200,000. If the German conditions of demand were the opposite from these — elastic for wheat — there would be a mitigation of the American loss in the barter terms. The United States would still find that she exchanged wheat for linen on terms less favorable than before, but not so much less favorable as in these illustrative figures.

It need hardly be pointed out that in all such cases the figures of relative money wages are in the last analysis the *results* of the prices of the goods. They have been stated, for convenience of exposition, as if the wages determined the prices; the wages being the "supply prices." But it is the goods, of course, which first feel the impact of the play of international demand, and it is the prices of the goods which determine the money incomes. Wheat and linen rise or fall in price as changes take place in international payments; thence are derived the rates of wages; these wages then appear as the money costs, the supply prices, of the goods.

The reader who is not wearied by the details of such figures may follow them as they can be worked out for still one other sort of case, illustrative of a situation in which the play of demand is more favorable to the United States — that is, one in which the German demand for wheat is elastic (greater than unity) and the American demand for linen is also elastic.[1]

Reverting to the figures with which we started (p. 110), suppose once more an initial flow of specie, caused by a payment for tribute, and the consequent changes in prices and money incomes. Assume the following stage to have been reached :

	Wages per Day	Total Wages	Produce	Domestic Supply Price
In the U. S. 10 days' labor	$1.65	$16.50	20 wheat	$0.82½
" " U. S. 10 " "	$1.65	$16.50	20 linen	$0.82½
" Germany 10 " "	$1.05	$10.50	10 wheat	$1.05
" Germany 10 " "	$1.05	$10.50	15 linen	$0.70

[1] The following pages deal with some refinements which the reader may skip without break in continuity, passing to page 117.

It will be observed that wages in the United States have fallen, but have fallen less than in the case just discussed: they have fallen from $1.70 (the figure at the original equilibrium) to $1.65, but not as low as $1.60. German wages on the other hand have risen, but not so much; they have risen from $1.02 to $1.05, not to $1.15.

At the prices thus figured out, suppose:

U. S. exports to Germany 11 million wheat @ $0.82½ = $9,050,000 [1]
Germany exports to U. S. 11.5 million linen @ $0.70 = $8,050,000

At the new price of $0.82½ for wheat (lower than $0.85) Germany takes a greater quantity — 11 million bushels instead of 10 million; and her total payment to the United States for wheat rises from $8,500,000 to $9,050,000. At the new price of $0.70 for linen (higher than $0.68) the United States takes a less quantity of linen from Germany — 11.5 million yards of linen instead of 12.5 million; and her total payment to Germany falls from $8,500,000 to $8,050,000.[2] The new gross barter terms of trade, *i.e.* the relation of *all* the United States wheat to the German linen, then become 11 wheat = 11½ linen, or 10 wheat = 10.45 linen.

Of the total export of wheat from the United States, however, a part only serves to pay the tribute of $1,000,000; the rest pays for the German linen. The apportionment of the wheat exports for the two purposes is:

1.2 million wheat at $0.82½ for tribute = $1,000,000
9.8 million wheat at $0.82½ for linen = $8,050,000
                                         $9,050,000

The net barter terms of trade are then:

9.8 wheat = 11½ linen, or 10 wheat = 11.8 linen

Under the previous supposition, the net terms had been:

10 wheat = 10.4 linen

The United States now gets terms more favorable than before — 11.8 of linen instead of 10.4 linen.

---

[1] Approximately.

[2] It will be borne in mind that an elastic demand means that at a lower price a greater sum total will be given, and conversely at a higher price a less sum total.

Obviously, however, the United States gets terms which still remain less favorable than they were at the outset. We started, it will be remembered, with barter terms of trade such as to divide equally between the two countries the possible gain from the trade — 10 wheat for 12½ linen. The new terms just worked out, tho more favorable to the United States, are still not so favorable as those from which we began: the United States still gains less than at the outset.

The terms will be again shifted, and in the same direction, if we suppose the German demand for wheat to be still more elastic, and the American demand for linen still more elastic. All the figures will then be correspondingly modified — higher price of wheat, lower price of linen, higher money rates of wages in the United States, lower money rates of wages in Germany. But the rates of wages in the United States will always be lower than they were before the tribute payment set in, the German rates always higher. The barter terms of trade, again, might be but little less advantageous to the United States than before; they might be almost as much as 12½ linen got for 10 wheat; but they would never be quite so much. The barter terms might be 12.2 or 12.4 linen for 10 of wheat, but so long as the annual remittance of $1,000,000 was necessary and no other new factor intervened, could never be 12.5. The United States always would have not only to pay the tribute, but would have to exchange its exports for its imports on less favorable terms.

"Less favorable terms." A distinction is to be drawn with regard to the significance of this designation according as it is applied to the sort of situation here analyzed, or to that arising from a mere change in demand. The latter case, that of a change in demand, was considered in a previous chapter.[1] It was there pointed out that a change in demand is a voluntary act, or rather change of attitude, on the part of one or both of the exchangers. When the demand schedule, for example, shifts in such manner that at the same price more of a commodity is bought than before — if the demand curve moves to the right — the change means that people

[1] See Ch. 4, pp. 26–33.

are ready to pay a higher price for a given quantity, simply because they get greater satisfaction from that same quantity than they got before. True, they give more of their income for each unit of the commodity than they gave before, and in that sense may be said to buy it on less favorable terms. But there is no hedonistic loss; merely the registration of a different state of mind. And similarly when the people of one country choose to give more of their own goods in exchange for those of another country, the barter terms, stated as physical equivalents, become less favorable; but they do so merely because wants have changed and are now satisfied in a different way.

The case of a tribute is different. Tho the demand schedule in the tribute-paying country remains unaltered (as was assumed in the first part of this chapter) the barter terms become less favorable. Whether we look at the gross or the net terms, the tribute causes it to give more of its own goods, unit for unit, in the exchange for the goods of the other country. It can not console itself, as in the other case, by the reflection that after all this is precisely what its own changed state of mind has brought about. The only consolation is that it still gains from the trade. The goods which it sends out in payment for its imports still cost it less labor than would be needed for producing the imported goods at home. True, less of the imports are got in this exchange than would have been got if there were not the extra payment. But to continue the trade is the best way out of a bad business.

The case of a tribute is extreme; and for that very reason it has here been examined. It stands for a pure payment without *quid pro quo*. At the opposite extreme are payments, also standing for "invisible" items, where the country to which the payments are made and to which the additional goods flow does give in exchange something, even tho not visible goods; where there *is* clearly a *quid pro quo*. Commonly enough, in the discussion of this aspect of international trade, all the invisible items are lumped together, as if all had the same meaning and the same effects. Not so; they differ. To take a case analogous to a tribute, and nowadays familiar, reparation or indemnity payments stand for one sort of effect; whereas payments which arise from the expenditure of tourists in foreign countries stand for quite another. Payments connected with foreign loans stand midway; and this whether we consider the initial lending of the principal amount by the creditor country or the subsequent payment of interest by the debtor country. I shall say something of loan and interest payments in another connection.[1] For the present, by way of elucidating the essential differences between the several sorts of cases, we may consider a case which stands at the opposite extreme from tributes or indemnities — that of tourist expenditures.

The expenses of Americans who travel abroad form a large item in the balance of payments of the United States. They give occasion to remittances to foreign countries, and, thru the process just explained, tend to cause merchandise exports to exceed imports.[2] This item, if it were the only transaction other than sales of goods — the only invisible item — would bring about a balance of trade "favorable" to the United States. As regards the physical goods exported and imported, the situation of course would *not* be favorable to the United States; the relation of American incomes to foreign incomes, and the barter terms of trade would become less advantageous to the United States than before. So far the case is the same as with a tribute.

Obviously, however, there are differences. In return for the additional commodities exported — the excess of exports — the Americans get not indeed imported goods, but the pleasures of travel. Taken as a body, they prefer these pleasures to the enjoyments which would have been yielded by the exported goods, or by their equivalents, if consumed at home. To state the same thing in another way, the American tourists, by spending abroad, cause American labor to be turned to making exported commodities, rather than to making such commodities as the travellers would have purchased if they had remained at home. There can be here no question of a loss, such as a tribute would entail; it is merely a

---

[1] See below, Ch. 21, pp. 254–262.

[2] See below, Ch. 24, p. 295, for a consideration of the part which this item plays in the international trade of the United States.

matter whether expenditure in one direction is preferred to expenditure in another. The American demand schedule has shifted. Regarding the tourists as one among the various groups of Americans who find foreign products to their liking, the American people as a whole now want more of foreign things than before. A readjustment of the barter terms of trade is necessarily involved; but it no more involves a real loss, in the hedonistic calculus, than any case of change in demand. It is a matter of what people prefer.

Another point may be raised: the relation of such remittances to the distribution of wealth within a country. In the preceding paragraphs it has been tacitly assumed, for simplification of the problem, that the Americans, travellers and stay-at-homes, are a homogeneous set of persons. We have neglected what is suggested by the familiar conditions of travel — that, so far from there being homogeneity, the travellers are the rich, while the bulk of the Americans and the main consumers of imports are those of slender means. We have supposed, then, that the American travellers are a sample of the Americans as a whole; or, what amounts to the same thing for the purpose in hand, that the set that travels is the identical set that is buying the imports. Applying this supposition to our illustrative case, the American travellers and the American purchasers of German linens may be regarded as the same group. Then these travellers not only have to meet their expenditures abroad, but have also to face the fact that their German linen bought in the United States is more expensive than before, while their money incomes (derived from domestic sources) are smaller than before. If they nevertheless continue to travel, it must be because the attractions are so great as to outweigh all the drawbacks, increased expense of linen included. The net gain in satisfactions or gratifications remains; otherwise this particular choice would not be made.

It is to be granted, of course, that the supposed homogeneity of purchasers is not necessarily, perhaps not generally, in accord with fact. The American tourists may be quite a different set of persons from those who buy the goods imported. But this consideration introduces an extraneous set of factors — the distribution of income in the United States, its inequality between classes or geographical sections, its possible disturbance and readjustment under new conditions. *Any* changes in the direction of consumption may have effects not only on the direction of production but on the distribution of income also. This problem involves reasoning which is in part similar to that on international trade, but leads to nothing inconsistent with its conclusions or serving to modify the essentials of the conclusions.

A somewhat special case is that of gifts or charitable contributions. It is like that of a tribute, and also unlike. As with a tribute, nothing in the way of commodities or services is received by the country which makes the payments: there is no *quid pro quo*. But they are made voluntarily, not under compulsion. Very heavy remittances of this sort were made from the United States to foreign countries during the last generation, say from 1895 to the present time (1925); some details will be considered in a later chapter.[1] Such operations affect the course of international trade in commodities — the exports and imports of goods — in the same way as tributes or travellers' expenditures. Their tendency is to bring about an excess of merchandise exports, a "favorable" balance of trade, lowered money incomes and domestic prices in the remitting country, higher incomes and prices in the receiving country. They lead also to barter terms of trade less favorable to the remitting country. The people of that country not only export *gratis* the tangible goods which serve to meet the charitable remittances; they lose also thru the circumstance that they get less imported goods in exchange for the exports which are the commercial items in the account. The remittances thus may be said to cost the donors more than they reckoned on, more than they are aware of. But the contributions continue to flow, even tho the people who make them find that their money incomes tend to fall, while imported goods tend to rise in price. They have the satisfaction, approved by the moralist, of doing a merciful deed; and that satisfaction is not dimmed because the doing entails more of material curtailment than was resolved on at the start. On the

[1] Chapter 24, p. 294; Chapter 25, p. 322.

principles of a higher or sublimated utilitarianism, they suffer no loss, nay, reap the highest gains, thru the whole gamut of the performance.[1]

[1] It may be remarked that, so far as concerns ulterior effects on classes *within* the United States, this case is probably different from that of travellers' remittances. The persons by whom funds were sent abroad on donation account (in the U. S. since 1895) were predominantly the poor rather than the rich. The buyers of the imported goods, on the other hand, were the rich quite as much as the poor ; tho it is to be confessed that this statement rests on general observation, and can be substantiated by no specific proof. At all events the probabilities (or possibilities) in this direction indicate again that the repercussion of international advantages or disadvantages on the several classes and sections within a country is quite an independent matter, not to be taken up as part of the theory of international trade proper.

CHAPTER 12

Non-Merchandise Transactions Further Considered
Loans and Interest Payments, Freight Charges

Loans made by the people of one country to those of another, and interest payment on such loans, have already been mentioned as among the most important of the non-merchandise items in international trade. They also, while having effects similar in the main to those of other invisible items, present some problems of their own.

For illustration we may suppose that loans are made by British to Americans. For brevity, we commonly speak of such loans as made by Great Britain to the United States; as if one government made them to the other, or the British as one body or entity made them to the Americans as another. In fact, the transactions are commonly between individuals, or (what comes to the same thing for our purpose) between individuals on one side and political bodies on the other. Loans are indeed sometimes deliberately made by one state to another; such operations played a large part in the Great War of 1914–18, and were not unknown in earlier periods. They are the results of political or military exigencies, and while involving no principles different from those applicable to the transactions between individuals, are yet likely to have a range and scope quite beyond those of ordinary commerce. For this reason they will be considered separately in later chapters. Here we confine attention to loans by individuals, not of an emergency or catastrophic sort, made for profit, exercising their effects gradually and as a rule quietly on the every-day phenomena of international trade.

Such loans by the one party, borrowings by the other, must result in a flow of specie from Great Britain to the United States. "Must result" — this puts the case too strongly. The flow will not necessarily take place; possibly there will be none at all. And such flow as does take place is not likely to be equal in volume, either in the very first stage or later, to the amount of the loan. And yet it can be said almost with certainty that some specie movement there will be.

The possible but improbable case where there will be no movement of specie at all is when the borrowers use the entire amount of the funds put at their disposal by the lenders, in buying commodities in the lenders' country. And further: the borrowers not only make purchases in the lenders' country, but these purchases are additional to what would have been made in any event. Suppose the lenders, for example, to be British, the borrowers Americans — the sort of relation which existed between these two peoples thru the 19th century. Suppose the Americans are railway promoters who use the entire proceeds of the loan in Great Britain for buying rails, locomotives, bridge material, and the like. Other American purchases go on as before, and other goods continue to move from Great Britain to the United States as before. The new purchases and new exports exactly absorb the funds which British lenders have put at the disposal of American investors. No remittances at all will be made from Great Britain to the United States. English commodities will go to the United States as the direct result of the loan.

This sort of consequence — an immediate export of goods from the lending country, and for the time being no further change — may ensue as the result either of the ordinary economic forces, or of a set policy in which there is deliberate or conscious diversion of international trade. In the period since 1890 there has been much endeavor of the second kind. This was often the case in France and Germany during the generation preceding the Great War of 1914–18. It was the undisguised policy of the governments in both countries, and of the financial promoters and institutions which were in close touch with the governments, to arrange the terms of foreign loans in such way that the borrowers should spend the entire proceeds in France or Germany. Virtually the same sort of thing appeared in the huge loans which were made from the United States to the Allies during the Great War itself; tho here, as will be shown in a later chapter, the conditions were quite exceptional and the consequences unusual. It appeared again, and under conditions not so exceptional, in the American loans of the post-war years. It may continue to play a considerable part in the future. The bankers who float loans are often representatives of manufacturing enterprises for whose output they wish to secure a market. Governments and the business public are fairly obsessed with a determination to promote exports in every possible way — the ineradicable spirit of mercantilism. And where the loans are made not merely for industrial purposes, but for military or naval equipment, the combination of political and economic motives acts even more strongly to link foreign loans directly with commodity exports.

It is the other sort of interlinking, however, that not deliberately designed, which has played the larger part in the past and may be expected on the whole to do so in the future. During the greater part of the 19th century loans were made without express stipulation of the kind just described. Great Britain was then the main lending country. Great Britain was also the cheapest place in which to buy industrial equipment. Borrowers laid out a portion of the borrowed funds, tho not often the whole, in buying British goods; they did so merely because they found it to their own advantage to do so. The same has been the situation with most of the loans made by the United States to foreign countries in the post-war period, or at least after 1920. The borrowers are free to do as they please with the proceeds of the loans, and it is not to be foreseen whether they will use them in any part for purchases in the United States.

In all these cases, whether there be express stipulation concerning the purposes to which the loans shall be devoted, or a purely commercial use of the funds in the lending country, the effect of the borrowing on the substantive course of international trade becomes direct. The merchandise movements and the merchandise balance of trade are affected at once. Merchandise exports from the lending country exceed merchandise imports, without any intermediate stage of disturbance of the foreign exchanges, flow of specie, and so on. The balance of trade becomes at once "favorable" to the lending country, and "unfavorable" for the borrowing country. There is no disturbance of foreign exchange, no flow of specie, nothing to modify the level of prices or wages either in the lending or in the borrowing country.

It is extremely rare, however, that the purchases of goods in the lending countries by the selfsame foreigners who contracted the loans take place to such an extent as to obviate the flow of specie completely. Not the entire proceeds of loans are likely to be spent in this way, only some fraction. Even if railway promoters from the United States or Canada or Argentina, who borrow in England, also buy railway material in England, they are likely to use in this way only a part of the funds. Some part they will spend at home, for labor, for miscellaneous supplies, divers expenses. It is conceivable, nay probable, that they will raise some portion of their capital at home, and only the residue abroad. And it is then conceivable that they will use for domestic expenditures the funds raised at home, and will use the proceeds of foreign loans entirely for purchase abroad. But it is most improbable, even when there is a division between foreign and domestic financing, that an exact balance of this sort will be struck. In the majority of cases a part of the foreign funds, and usually a considerable part, will be wanted for expenditure in the borrowing country itself. Then, to repeat, the outcome must be a flow of specie from the lending to the borrowing country. Remittances will have to be made, in our illustrative situation, from London to New York. Specie will flow; the consequences become the same as those which ensue when remittances have to be made for any other invisible item.

These consequences will of course ensue quite without modification if there be no immediate purchases of goods at all in the lending country. Such was doubtless the case with a large proportion of the British loans both of earlier and later date. It was so with the continuous stream of loans by the French in those earlier loans of the second and third quarters of the 19th century, made when neo-mercantilism was not yet rampant. The transactions were such as to involve at the outset nothing more than the obligation to put funds at the disposal of the borrowers; while the borrowers themselves transferred these funds, except for the possible use of some fraction forthwith in the lending country, to their own country. All in all, we are justified in treating this as the normal and ordinary course of events. International loans disturb the existing balance of payments; remittances are made to the borrowing country; specie flows thither from the lending country.

The further course which events may then be expected to take is sufficiently familiar, and need not again be analyzed in detail. The loan being made (in our assumed case) by British to Americans, prices and incomes fall in Great Britain, rise in the United States. An excess of exports develops in Great Britain; not immediately, but by a gradual process. She comes to have a "favorable" balance of trade. In the United States an excess of imports gradually appears — an " unfavorable " balance of trade. The people of Great Britain send merchandise to the United States, and add to the tangible equipment of the Americans, or to their consumable goods, giving up for the time being some of their own possessions and adding to those of the Americans. But not only do they give up something in this way — make a sacrifice, incur a loss, for the time being — but they incur a further loss in that the barter terms of trade become less advantageous to them. The imports which they continue to buy from the United States are got on less favorable terms than before. Conversely, the people of the United States have a double gain; not only do they get an extra supply of imported goods, but *all* the imports, the goods plainly and simply bartered as well as the extra goods that represent the loans, are got on better terms than before.

The ulterior consequences on the barter terms of trade, let it be repeated, will not appear so far as the borrowers make direct purchases of goods in the lenders' country. And if the borrowed funds are used *in toto* for such purchases, the ulterior effect will not ensue at all. If part is so used, the effects will be mitigated. The actuating machinery for these effects is the flow of specie, which is eliminated so far as there are the direct purchases.

Proceed now a step further. Assume again a simple case, for elucidation of the principles. Suppose that loans go on year after year, the same amount annually. Each year Englishmen lend to Americans a given sum, say 10 millions. Assume also, for simplicity, that there are no direct purchases by the borrowers, but always — in the first instance, that is — a flow of specie into the borrowing country. In due time, the length of the interval depending on the sensitiveness of prices to the increase or decrease of specie, a continuing "favorable" balance of trade appears in Great Britain and the reverse appears in the United States. The lending country has a steady excess of exports, the borrowing country a steady excess of imports. Specie no longer flows; the continuing loans are made thru the mechanism of merchandise movements.

At an early stage in the operations, however, another factor begins to enter. Each year the borrowing country has to pay interest on the loans contracted so far; and to that extent the amount which the lending country has to remit on capital account is reduced, as regards the net balance of the international account. The interest charge to be paid by the borrowing country grows with every year. The capital sum from the lending country remains (under our supposition) the same from year to year. The accumulating interest charge will grow, and in time will be equal to the constant capital sum. Eventually, it will be greater. At the outset the transactions lead the lending country to make remittances to the borrowing; in the end it is the borrowing country which has to remit.

These shifts in the relations between creditor and debtor country will manifest themselves in the flow of specie between them and in their merchandise transactions. The initial flow from the lending country is destined to be checked in any case by the changes in prices. But it will be checked the more quickly by the accruing interest charge. The accommodation of the merchandise balance (the balance of trade) to the balance of payments will therefore take place more promptly than in the case of other invisible items, such as tourist expenditures. And eventually there will be a reversal of the initial features. Specie will flow back to the lending country; its prices and money incomes will rise; the borrowing country will have falling prices and incomes; the lending country will come to have an excess of merchandise imports and the borrowing country an excess of merchandise exports. A cycle of operations is set in motion by a steady succession of international loans. Their effects on international trade and international payments are different according as the transactions are in the initial stage, the midway stage, the final stage.

In popular talk on these matters it is commonly assumed that a creditor country *ipso facto* has an excess of merchandise imports, and a debtor country an excess of exports. The creditor country — so people imply in their everyday talk — has payments to receive, the debtor country has payments to make; the former is expected to show a net credit in its accounts, the latter a net charge or net outgo. Not at all. The state of the merchandise account, the balance of the money values of imports and exports, may run either way, for either debtor country or creditor country. It depends on the stage which the credit operations have reached. And, similarly, there is a common erroneous notion that the flow of specie tends to be toward the creditor country; that the course of the foreign exchanges is naturally such as to cause specie to move to it, or at least such as to bring some pressure that way. Again not at all. The movement of specie may tend to be in one direction or the other, according to the stage of the cycle.

It is to be remarked, however, that the transactions rarely show such regularity as the preceding analysis has implied. On the contrary, they usually take place with marked irregularities. And not only are they irregular; they are subject to abrupt stoppages. They frequently entail spasmodic changes in international payments and in the movement of goods.

These irregularities, of which abundant illustrations will be given in later chapters, deserve some further consideration even at this point. *If* loans on capital account were continued regularly at the same amount year after year, the accumulating interest payments would bring about, at the date when reversal of the relations began to set in, a slow and gradual readjustment, not a sudden overturn. The borrowing country would almost imperceptibly accommodate itself to a new situation, in which specie would seep out, prices gradually fall, merchandise exports rise and imports fall. A "favorable" balance would become in time a settled feature of its international trade. In fact, however, the loans from the creditor country, so far from being made at the same rate year by year, begin with modest amounts, then increase, and proceed *crescendo*. They are likely to be made in exceptionally larger amounts toward the culminating stage of a period of activity and speculative upswing, and during that stage become larger from month to month so long as the upswing continues. With the advent of a crisis, they are at once cut down sharply, even cease entirely. The interest payments on the old loans thereupon are no longer offset by any new loans; they become instantly a net charge to be met by the borrowing country. A sudden reversal takes place in the debtor country's international balance sheet; it feels the consequences abruptly, in an immediate need of increased remittances to the creditor country, in a strain on its banks, high rates of discount, falling prices. And this train of events may ensue not once only, but two or three times in succession. After the first crisis and the first overturn, the debtor country is likely to recover. Within a few years loans from the creditor country may be resumed, another period of activity and speculative investment set in, the old round repeated, until finally another crisis comes and another sudden overturn in the balance of international payments. The final outcome, when this long period of irregular movements has run its course, is that the debtor country has more to remit on interest account than to receive on principal account, and that the remittance is effected by an excess of merchandise exports over imports. The history of the United States and of Argentina, both of which were typical borrowing countries at similar stages in their economic development, shows these successive waves of international borrowings, repeated crises, deviations from the simplified process set forth in the preceding pages.

On the whole and in the long run, the actual course of events conforms to the theoretic analysis. The consequences indicated by that analysis, so far from being completely obliterated by the irregularities, rather become accentuated and more conspicuous. The unmistakable fact of experience is that a country which is in the early stages of lending to others has an excess of merchandise exports; it has a "favorable" balance of trade. On the other hand, a country in the early stages of borrowing has an excess of imports — an "unfavorable" balance. At the further end of the international credit cycle, a country which for decades and generations has been making foreign investments, and to which, therefore, interest payments have been steadily accumulating, has an excess of merchandise imports, an "unfavorable" balance. Conversely, a country which is in the early stages of borrowing does in fact have an excess of imports; but when it has been a borrower over a long period, it has an excess of exports. If the borrowing process has ceased, or has greatly declined, this stage is the more pronounced. It is reached, if its borrowing operations have already gone on for decades and generations, even in the face of continuing large loans. With all the irregularities in the steps by which the successive stages are traversed, the stages themselves are in almost every case to be discerned; and they follow one upon another in the order which general reasoning leads us to expect.

Reverting now to that part of the theoretical analysis which relates to the barter terms of trade, the reader will observe that while these terms tend to be made more favorable to the borrowing country during the earlier phase of the cycle, they become in the later phase less favorable to the borrowing country and more favorable to the lending. What the lenders as a people lose at the start, they are likely to regain at the end. Obviously, the balancing of loss and gain is not likely to be precise; least of all is any such offsetting to be clearly discerned or measurable. Whether there proves to be in the end a final surplus of gain one way or the other will depend on the demand for the commodities of each country by the people of the other. Both as regards the commodities exchanged and their demand schedules, there may easily be changes during the long period — a generation, a half-century —

over which the whole series of operations extends. All that can
be said is that there is a general off-setting tendency between the
earlier and the later stages, and a presumption that in the entire
balance of this account neither country is likely to have any considerable net gain.[1]

Freight charges and passenger fares constitute another important
item. Of the two, freight charges are the larger, and while in the
main they raise no new questions, some aspects deserve separate
attention.

The item of freight charges appears more particularly in the
trade between countries separated by large stretches of ocean.
Here there is a considerable gap between the place where the goods
leave one country and that where they enter another; and a charge
arises which does not necessarily form a part of the expenses of
production within either. It is this circumstance — that the
expenses may be incurred by residents of either country and that
payments therefore may become due either way — which is peculiar to the item of freight charges. In other respects they present
no peculiar features. They constitute a payment for service rendered; and so far as the service is rendered to persons in one country by persons living in another, payments must be made to the
foreigner. The item figures in the international balance sheet like
any other, with the same effects as a payment for goods. It is
invisible, too, in the same sense as tourist expenses are; that is,
no official record is made and the amounts that must be remitted
are often not easily ascertained.

There is a distinction, however, between the sum which the
individual purchaser of foreign goods must pay for them, and the
amounts which must be remitted to the foreign countries in payment
for the goods. The individual purchasers must pay the foreign

---

[1] If indeed the principal sum is *never* repaid — if the interest payments by the
debtor go on indefinitely — there is some likelihood that the barter terms, being
thus permanently affected to the disadvantage of the borrowing country, will
cause more loss to it than had been gained in the period (which could hardly be
permanent) where the new loans had caused the terms to be advantageous.   I leave
the reader to judge, especially after he has considered the qualifying and explana-
tory chapters that are to come later, whether a consideration of this sort is worth
mentioning at all.

price (*i.e.*, the price at the place of export) plus freight charges. But this is not necessarily the amount which the people of the importing country have to remit to the exporting country, say Great Britain. If the goods are carried from Great Britain in vessels of the United States, the freight charges are paid by one set of Americans to another set of Americans. The freight item then is purely domestic; no remittance to Britain must be made. The British goods alone need to be paid for. But if the goods are carried in British vessels, some British persons must be paid for the further service of bringing them over. It is immaterial to the individual Americans who happen to buy the goods whether this additional payment goes to their own countrymen or to the British. But it is material for the balance of international payments; an item arises in the latter case which must take its place in the adjustment of that balance.

The same distinction of course must be made at the other end — that is, as regards a country's exports. American sellers of goods, when they export them to Great Britain, get only the price of goods at the place of export. The British purchasers pay as individuals that price plus cost of ocean transportation. If the goods are carried in American vessels, the freight charges become an additional item, also payable to Americans, even tho (in modern times) presumably a different set of individuals from those that have sold the goods. Should the goods be carried in British vessels, the freight charges become a payment made by one set of the British to another set, not made by the British to the Americans; and then it does not figure in the international balance sheet.

If, now, the business is halved — if half of the carriage is done by British vessels, half by American — the items offset each other in the international account. As much is due one way as the other. The total volume of international payments is greater than it would be if the countries were contiguous, but the balance of payments is not affected. If, however, all the carriage takes place in the vessels of one of the countries, say Great Britain, a balance becomes due to that country. Supposing the other transactions between the countries to balance — imports and exports, and whatever further items there may be — the additional sum due to Great Britain will be provided in the same way as in other cases of unsettled balance of payments. The theoretical solution is familiar. If payment had balanced before this item was present — if we suppose this to appear as a new item — specie flows to Great Britain; a double set of price changes sets in, upward in Great Britain, downward in the United States; imports and exports are modified; finally Great Britain has an excess of merchandise imports, the United States an excess of merchandise exports. And this series of changes brings the familiar consequences for the barter terms of trade; they become less favorable to the United States, more so to Great Britain. The people of the United States get their imported goods on less favorable terms than before; those of Great Britain get theirs on more favorable terms.

Shipping charges and shipping earnings thus have a place in international trade precisely like that of tourist expenditures. They take their place in the balance of payments, and they affect the net barter terms of trade — these only, not the gross terms. The Americans (say) pay the freight charges to the British, and get the freight service; they get their *quid pro quo* at once. They pay others for doing the work of carriage, rather than do it themselves; and the reason why they make the payment, in the last analysis, is that the others can do the work of carriage cheaply, while they themselves can apply their labor more effectively in other ways. It is quite superfluous to explain, to those who follow the general reasoning of the theory of international trade, that there is no net loss to the Americans from their payment of shipping charges. The case is similar to that of tourist expenditures and dissimilar to some of the other transactions considered in the preceding pages, in that there is an *immediate* service, for which payment is made at once. At once, that is, in the sense in which it can be said that the entire balance of international payments is settled at once; it is a balance settled very promptly, within a few months or a year. Of the temporary extensions and adjustments of "unfunded" balances more will be said elsewhere; they cause no modification of the general principles here under consideration. Freight charges, to repeat, constitute items in the international account, essentially like the purchases and sales of merchandise, and are settled as promptly as these. The mere payment of them no more constitutes a source of loss to the paying country than does its payment for imported goods.

The possible effects of transportation charges on the barter terms of trade was the occasion for discussions and distinctions which held a considerable place in the older literature of the subject and may be briefly mentioned. There is an obvious gap (as has been noted) between the sum which the exporter receives for his goods, and that which the importer pays for those same goods: the gap standing for the transportation or freight charge. The price which the importer pays, and which he then charges to the consumer, is higher than it would be if there were no freight charge at all. Consequently the amount which the consumer purchases will be different from what it would have been if the price had not been so raised. This reaction of price on quantity demanded takes place on both sides; in our supposed case, it takes place among the purchasers both in Great Britain and the United States. The British buy less than they would have bought if there were no expense of transport; the Americans likewise buy less. But the effect on demand will not necessarily or probably be the same on both sides. It is not likely that the elasticity of demand for imported goods is the same in the United States for British goods as it is in Great Britain for American goods. The barter terms of trade, then, under the interplay of mutual demands, will be different from what they would have been in the absence of transportation charges — different from what they would have been between quite contiguous countries. In this sense, and in this sense only, it can be said that freight charges do not necessarily constitute an unalloyed burden on the receiving (importing) country, but may be borne in part by the despatching (exporting) country; indeed, conceivably borne by this country in whole. The price of every imported article is higher to the purchaser in the importing country by the amount of the transportation charge; in this direct and obvious sense the charge is borne by the importing country, not by the exporting. But in general price levels and income levels, and thereby in the barter terms of trade, there may ensue conditions different from what would have been in the absence of such a charge. In consequence the net gain from the exchange of commodities may be quite as great to one of the trading countries, or nearly as great, as if they had been contiguous; nay, it is conceivable, even greater than if they had been contiguous.

These, however, are recondite possibilities, quite beyond the ken of the individual buyers and sellers, and of interest only to the speculative economist. Even for him they constitute an intellectual plaything rather than a matter of substantive importance. They are no more than ramifications of the abstract theory, and belong among the phases of the theory which it is impossible to verify or illustrate from the actual course of events.[1]

Of some substantive importance, on the other hand, is a complication which the item of freight charges entails in the interpretation of import and export statistics.[2]

The common practice in the compilation of official statistics on the movement of merchandise is not the same for exports as for imports. To put the difference in commercial terms, exports are usually figured f.o.b. (free on board), imports usually c.i.f. (cost plus insurance and freight). The exports, that is, are recorded in terms of the value of the goods as put on board at the place of departure; the imports are recorded in terms of the value of the goods as received at the place of arrival. When valuing exports, cost of transportation is ignored; when valuing imports, it is included. The consequence is that recorded imports tend to be over-stated to the extent of that item, while recorded exports tend to be understated.

The statistical puzzles to which the practice leads can be best illustrated by analyzing some possible cases. Simplifying the analysis, as has been done for other problems, we may take

---

[1] See the well known passage on the subject in Mill, Book 3, Ch. 18, Sec. 3.

[2] The passages which follow have no necessary relation to the preceding parts of this chapter. They are inserted here as the most convenient place for dealing with a somewhat intricate problem of statistical interpretation; and they may be skipped by those who wish to follow without digression the main course of the exposition.

the trade of two countries only. Suppose that between these two the shipping trade is equally divided, the goods being carried half in the vessels of one of them, half in the vessels of the other. The charges for shipping thus cancel each other in the balance of international payments, and in any calculation of what may be due from one country to the other they may be disregarded. Suppose now that the merchandise exports and imports also balance, and that there is thus a settled equilibrium in the total account. Nevertheless, under the usual practice, each country would show in its official statistics an excess of imports; each would apparently have to make a remittance to the other in order to balance the international account. The shipping charges are ignored in the statistics of both as regards carriage one way; but as they are equally divided between the countries, the omissions cancel. An international trade account which on its face seems to be doubly unstable, indeed incomprehensible, is in fact stable and simple.

Now suppose not that the shipping trade is equally divided between the two countries, but that all the carriage is done in vessels of one of them. Take for example Great Britain and Australia. Both keep their statistics in the usual way, but the carrying is all done in British vessels. The actual position of Australia in the international account will then be in accord with that shown by her trade statistics; but the actual position of Great Britain will not. Australia in fact has to pay Great Britain not only for the British goods imported, but for those goods as delivered in Australian ports, *i.e.* plus freight. She receives from Great Britain only the value of her own export f.o.b. (*not* including freight). If then her official statistics show an excess of imports (as in the case considered in the preceding paragraph), this indicates that in fact a balance must be paid to Great Britain, and specie must be sent in settlement. If, however, her exports as recorded, so far from being less than the imports, appear to equal them, there will be an established equilibrium. Only when the exports f.o.b. equal the imports c.i.f. will there be a settled balance of payments for a country which does no shipping of its own and keeps its official statistics on the usual plan.

Great Britain, on the other hand, must show under these conditions (the carrying all done in British vessels) an accentuated excess of imports — a *greater* excess of imports than would appear on her records if the carrying trade were equally divided. She must have a real excess of imports of merchandise, not merely the nominal excess which the statistical practice of itself tends to show. Her recorded imports are doubly swelled; first by the practice of valuing them c.i.f., and second by the substantial fact that she has payments to receive for the carriage of her exports.

Not all countries, however, follow the practice of valuing exports one way, imports the other; and here the complication becomes different. The United States, for example, instead of valuing imports on the c.i.f. basis, values them as the exports are valued in most other countries; that is, on the f.o.b. basis. Her statistics give the values of imports at the time and place of exportation from the foreign country, not their values on arrival at the United States ports.[1] Cost of carriage is ignored in the official records of imports as well as of exports.

Here again we may consider the same two representative cases: one in which the shipping trade is equally divided, the other in which it is all in the hands of one country. Take the United States and Great Britain, again, as Australia and Great Britain were taken before. If, first, the carrying trade is equally divided between the United States and Great Britain, and the charges on this account just balance each other, the official statistics will show, as regards exports and imports, an excess of imports for Great Britain but for the United States imports just equal to the exports — no difference either way. For the United States the official showing will be in accord with the facts — a settled equilibrium. But for Great Britain an excess of imports will be shown; and that excess, so far from indicating an unsettled balance, will be but nominal. Great Britain will not in fact have any payment to make to the United States; her imports will only *seem* to exceed her exports.

[1] This was the case, at least, for many generations. The tariff act of 1922, with its novel provisions for a possible "United States" valuation, brought about a change for some portion (not considerable) of the imports.

If now the shipping is all done in British vessels (this of course was the sort of situation that prevailed as between these two countries for a generation preceding the war of 1914–18), the actual relations become different. The official statistics will again reflect the change; but again with figures not indicative of the real situation. If the merchandise imports and exports of the United States, as recorded by the United States, are the same in money value — that is, if the imports f.o.b. just equal the exports f.o.b. — the United States has nothing left with which to pay the freight charges due to British vessel owners. In due time the relation of imports to exports will become such as to bring about payment for this extra item; the exports recorded f.o.b. must exceed the imports recorded f.o.b. by the amount of the freight charges. An equilibrium of international payments will be reached only when the United States statistics regularly show an excess of exports. And this will indicate the real situation : the United States will be paying for the shipping services by sending merchandise to Great Britain. On the other hand, Great Britain, whose records would show an excess of imports in any case, because of her statistical practice, will again show — as in the case of trade with Australia — a *greater* excess of imports than would be shown if the shipping trade were equally divided. Part of her import excess will be nominal, but part will be real.

In sum, the usual statistical practice — that of valuing imports c.i.f. and exports f.o.b. — makes the imports of most countries appear large in relation to their exports. If all countries kept their records in this way, all would tend to show an excess of imports. That is, to state it more carefully, if merchandise exports and imports were such as exactly to pay for each other — if this, the simplest situation in international trade, were established, and if shipping trade were equally divided, so that nothing from this factor intervened to disturb the simplicity of the situation — nevertheless the statistics would show for each and every country an excess of merchandise imports. And therefore if the shipping trade is *not* equally divided, allowance has to be made for this continuing deceptive circumstance; a discount, so to speak, has to be made from the recorded imports. Where still other invisible items than freight enter in the international account, such as loans, interest, tourist expenses, and the like, this continuing deceptive circumstance must still be allowed for. The imports always appear too large, and some discount must be made. When, on the other hand, the usual practice is departed from, as in the United States, a qualification must be made as regards the allowance: the discount is to be applied to foreign nations as regards their recorded trade, but not to the United States as regards her recorded trade.

CHAPTER 13

DUTIES ON IMPORTS AND THE BARTER TERMS OF TRADE

IT would be possible to carry much further the sort of analysis which has been undertaken in the preceding chapters. The fact that each country deals not with one other only, but with many, would lead to modifications or elaborations over and above those already considered. The competition of various countries as buyers and sellers obviously has the effect of limiting more narrowly the range within which the barter terms of trade may vary; the terms of trade become dependent not on the demand schedules of any pair or trio of countries, but on those of all the trading countries combined. So much goes without saying.

More intricate are the possibilities in another direction. The imposition of taxes on imports and exports may affect the barter terms of trade — almost surely will do so. A tax on imports is equivalent to a deliberate lessening by the taxing country of its demand for foreign products. A tax on exports is equivalent to calling on other countries to decide whether they will continue to lay out as much as before on the taxing country's products. These may be described as intentional deflections of the play of demand; and they may be analyzed as having different effects according to the way in which they are levied — whether as taxes in kind, or (of course the only way that signifies in practice) as taxes in money. The effects which taxes may have on the volume of international trade and on the barter terms of trade have been the occasion of some of the most ingenious and intricate theoretical reasoning, and some most remarkable manifestations of casuistic ability.

I shall not attempt to refine further in the theoretical analysis. In doing so, there is always danger of lapsing into intellectual gymnastics. The suppositions made are sometimes improbable

141

to the point of unreality (as, for example, that of taxes in kind). More commonly, the deduced conclusions, even if resting on probable assumptions, are such as cannot be specifically discerned or verified in the actual course of events. And, as I need hardly confess again, the mathematical processes by which alone some of these conclusions can be deduced are beyond my competence; I could make no pretense of contributing anything new either in substance or in the way of exposition.

Neither is it within the scope of the present volume to enter on the controversy regarding free trade and protection. This in its main outlines is simple; simple at all events as compared with the topics taken up in the preceding pages. In a later chapter I have summarized those results of my inquiries on the effects of tariff legislation which have some direct bearing on the principles with which the present volume deals.

There is, however, one possible effect of taxes, and one phase of the protective controversy, on which something may here be said. I direct attention to this particular point of theory because of its connection with certain concrete problems of verification or interpretation which arise in connection with the international trade of the United States. The point is not of an essentially new or intricate kind. It relates to the effects which taxes on imports, and especially taxes which are protective, may have on the barter terms of trade.

Suppose, first, that a country imposes duties on imports which are purely of a revenue character. The proximate effect is to raise within the country the price of the dutiable article or articles (hereafter we may speak for simplicity of but a single article). True, in the case of a commodity produced under monopoly conditions, and having an extraordinarily elastic demand schedule, the price might remain unaffected. But this is a negligible case; under almost every imaginable condition there will be some rise in price. Assuming then, as we may, that price rises, less of the commodity will be bought. Only if demand were absolutely inelastic would the quantity bought remain the same. Demand being always in some degree elastic, less will be bought, and imports will decline.

Observe that while price rises to the consumer, the total sum which is paid to the foreign producer will not rise. The quantity bought from the foreigner — the number of units of the commodity which are purchased from him — becomes less, while the price per unit paid *to him* will not rise. True, because of the duty the consumer will pay a higher price. But the addition to the price goes to the government; it has nothing to do with the price received by the foreign exporter. Imports will decline, not because a larger price has to be paid to the foreigner for the goods but because an addition to the foreigner's price must be paid in order to meet the tax imposed at home.

The extent to which imports then decline will depend on the degree in which the demand for the commodity is elastic — whether the elasticity of demand is less or greater than unity. If demand be inelastic, the consumer will continue to buy nearly the same quantity as before. Imports will decline but little. The total sum spent for the article by the consumers will be greater than before, and the government will secure a large revenue from the tax. If on the other hand demand be elastic, the consumer will be led to lessen his purchases of the article very considerably, and the total sum spent for it will shrink. Then imports decline heavily, and the revenue which the tax yields to the government becomes correspondingly less.

But, to repeat, in any event imports will decline somewhat. And that decline at once sets in motion a train of forces which diminish the volume of international trade and at the same time cause the barter terms of trade to be more favorable to the country imposing the duties. Suppose the tax-imposing country to be the United States. That country's imports for the time become less. Exports, however, remain as great as before. Specie flows in, prices and money incomes rise. In foreign countries the opposite consequences ensue. Specie flows out, prices and money incomes fall. The reader will readily follow the further consequences. As money incomes rise in the United States, consumers will be led to spend more on imported goods. They will buy more of other imports (those which are not taxed) since these become cheaper as prices abroad decline; and they will soon begin to buy somewhat more of the taxed goods themselves, as these show a decline from the enhanced price which appeared on the first imposition of the duty. On the other hand, consumers abroad will buy less of American articles than before. Their money incomes have been lowered, while they are faced by higher prices of the American goods. Exports from the United States will decline from the volume at which they stood at the outset. The movement of specie, and the consequent changes in prices and money incomes, will go on until the money value of the total imports again equals the money value of the total exports. Then new conditions of international trade will have been established; and these new conditions will become definitive; that is, will persist, other things remaining the same, as long as the duties persist.

Eventually, then, equilibrium will be restored. American imports will be less, exports also less; the total volume of international trade will be diminished. But when the new equilibrium is reached, the terms of trade will have been altered to the advantage of the United States. Her people will have higher money incomes, and will be buying foreign goods which are lower in prices. Conversely, the people of foreign countries will have lower money incomes, and will be buying American goods which have risen in price. The Americans will be the gainers under the new terms of trade, the others the losers. For a given physical quantity of exports the Americans will be receiving a larger physical quantity of imports. The barter terms of trade will be changed to their advantage.

Needless to say, the *tax* which the American consumers pay, in the form of enhanced prices of the dutiable imports, is not to be regarded as a loss, not as something which offsets the gain to them from the better terms of trade. The proceeds of the tax serve to pay public expenses. Had it not been for them, some other levy would presumably have to be made. If it be suggested that the tax may lead to public extravagance, to expenditures that are wastefully made or bring no substantial gain to the community, it is sufficient to remark that this may happen under any and every tax. The consideration of such possibilities is not germane to the matter in hand. A tax of this kind, or any particular tax, has in itself no tendency to promote misapplication of the public funds. It is the general state of a country's government that determines whether its tax revenue shall be well or ill used. So far as concerns the effects of international trade, it matters not what the government does with the proceeds of the tax; we may assume they are as well applied as the proceeds of other taxes.

Proceed now to a further set of possible consequences. So far it has been tacitly assumed that the duty is imposed for revenue purposes only. Suppose now that the duty is not merely for revenue, but is for protection. Its object then is to promote the production within the country of a part or the whole of the goods previously imported. In so far as it achieves this object, the results just indicated still ensue, and will be accentuated. Imports are cut down, not only because price rises and consumption becomes less, but because articles which before had been imported are made within the country. Specie flows into the country to a greater degree than under a revenue duty. Prices and money incomes rise more within its borders, and the barter terms of trade come to be altered even more to its advantage. Such imports as continue to come in — and, as will presently be explained, by no means all are likely to be shut out — will be procured at better terms.

In the case of protective duties, however, something more happens. There arises a real offset to the gain from better terms of trade. In so far as the taxed goods are produced within the country, there is loss, not gain. The price of these goods also is raised to consumers by the amount of the duty; that is, they are higher in price within the country than without. The enhancement of price, tho a tax in precisely the same sense as in the case of articles which continue to be imported, brings no revenue to the government. It goes to the domestic producers. And to them it represents no gain — that is, no special gain. It is in the nature of a bonus which makes it possible for them to conduct an industry in which the country has no sufficient ad-

vantage. The returns to labor and capital in the newly stimulated industry are not higher than those current in the country
at large. They may indeed be unusually large for a time after
the first imposition of the duty; but if the industry be open to
competition, they will come to the same level as elsewhere. That
level, however, cannot be maintained unless prices of the goods
are higher than they would be if imported; and to the community
at large this difference in price represents pure loss.

In the case of a protective duty, then, there is a balancing of
loss against gain; a loss which is overt and obvious, in the higher
price of the goods whose domestic production is stimulated by the
duty, and a gain, much less obvious, thru the more favorable
terms of trade. There is no way of ascertaining which is the
greater — whether the net result is positive or negative. Eventually the outcome would be affected on the one hand by the extent
to which a disadvantageous domestic industry is brought into
existence, on the other hand by those conditions of demand which
determine the barter terms of trade in general.

In the exposition of this subject at the hands of the younger
Mill, it was said that no gain at all accrues to a country from protective duties; these being believed to be "purely mischievous,
both to the country imposing them and to those with whom it
trades." [1] This seems to be an error. If indeed *all* taxes on imports were protective, and if all were pushed so high as to attain
unflinchingly the object of protection — domestic production of
everything, all imports completely shut out — there would obviously be no gain from international trade, since the trade would
cease once for all. But protection is never carried so far. As
regards a particular article or group of articles, importation may
indeed be entirely stopped. But other articles continue to come
in, perhaps in large volume. There are many goods, such as the
tropical products extensively used by the people of temperate
zones, which it is so difficult to produce at home that an application of the protective policy to them is admittedly preposterous.

---

[1] See Mill's Essays on Some Unsettled Questions, pp. 21 seq., and his Political
Economy, Book 5, Ch. 4, section 6.

They continue to come in free; and as regards them, the barter terms of trade become more advantageous in consequence of the exclusion of the protected goods.   And even as regards the latter, the same result may endure in part; that is, so far as the goods continue to be imported.   The duty may be so nicely adjusted to the difference in money cost between domestic and foreign producers that domestic production is stimulated, while some imports nevertheless continue.   A result of this kind is aimed at by persons who contend for a "competitive tariff" — one which shall leave a precise balance between domestic producers and their foreign competitors.   A division between imported and domestic supplies also takes place, as has been elsewhere indicated, where the domestic industry is carried on under the conditions of diminishing returns.[1]   All in all, a rigorous and effective system of protection may yet permit a large volume of goods to come in from foreign countries.   Those goods which continue to be imported are then obtained on the better terms of trade.   There does exist this gain, to be reckoned as offsetting the direct loss caused by the protective duties.

A different ground for questioning whether in the end the attainment of any gain whatever will persist is that every country can play the same game.   If the United States can get better barter terms of trade by imposing duties on goods coming from foreign countries, those other foreign countries can do the same by duties on goods coming from the United States.   The application of the process on both sides not only increases the loss arising from the protective duties in themselves, but lessens the total gain from the division of labor that continues between the two sets of countries. True, some among them may perhaps retain a larger share of the remaining gain than others.   But this preferential position, depending as it must on the elusive conditions of reciprocal demand, is neither easy to make sure nor easy to keep if once attained. Considering the trading world as a whole, and having in mind all the possibilities of retaliation, the quest of this sort of gain must be admitted to be highly hazardous.   And if one finds the ordinary

[1] See Chapter 8, p. 87.

arguments for protection untenable, nay intellectually repellent, and those for international coöperation and concord strong and appealing, there remains no inclination to commend this particular method of trying to capture a greater share of the total gain from trade between nations.

As a dry matter of analysis, however, it is to be said that, in this matter of import duties and the barter terms of trade, the position of the United States was long a comparatively advantageous one. The country's exports were chiefly foodstuffs and raw materials. Raw cotton bulked large among them; an article so much wanted by other countries that they never impose duties on it. Foodstuffs, again, were never subjected to duties by Great Britain, to which they went so largely; and the duties put on them by the countries of the Continent did not seriously check the imports that way. The countries to which the American exports mainly went were thus unwilling or unable to play the game of retaliation with much prospect of success. The protective duties imposed by the United States, however, did have the effect of checking some imports heavily and of stimulating domestic production to a corresponding extent; while yet other imports continued to come in. These other imports were in part goods of the protected class which came in over the barrier of the duties, such as wool, sugar, and sundry manufactured goods. In much larger part they were tropical or semi-tropical goods which were admitted free. It was the latter which came to predominate more and more largely in the import trade of the United States. As regards these, the barter terms of trade quite possibly become more advantageous, without any such offset as must be reckoned in respect of the protected goods.

So much as regards the general reasoning and some possibilities of its application. What bearing it may conceivably have on the actual course of the international trade of the United States will be considered in another connection.[1]

---

[1] See below, Ch. 24, pp. 299–306.

PART II

PROBLEMS OF VERIFICATION

CHAPTER 14

INTRODUCTORY

THE preceding chapters have been almost without exception heroically abstract. They have dealt with the "pure theory" of international trade. To many a reader the assumptions and conclusions will have seemed to be no more than intellectual playthings. These calculations of the possibilities of gain from exchange of goods between the trading countries, these figures on the barter terms of trade and their limits, this analysis of the forces that determine the precise figure at which the terms settle themselves — all have an air of unreality. They resemble those calculations of barter rates between individual exchangers which appear in the books on pure economics, and the calculations which analyze utility, marginal utility, marginal pairs, the familiar A's and B's, the Primus, Secundus and Tertius of economic lore. Thruout we seem to be dealing not with living human beings but with puppets moved by the economist's sleight of hand.

A similar air of unreality pervades our calculations on the flow of specie from country to country, and the consequent changes in prices and money incomes. True, these are not quite so abstract as the calculations on the barter terms of trade. They seem to come nearer to the actual world; and it is precisely because they have at least the appearance of a closer approach to reality that the figures on prices and money wages have here been worked out more elaborately than has been the practice in previous expositions of the subject. Yet even so, the results have a smoothness, a neatness, a specious conclusiveness, that must lead the man of affairs and the economic realist to pause. Can things work out quite so easily and automatically? Do the conditions of production and exchange respond to changing prices in accord with this harmonious and self-adjusting scheme? In the actual conduct of international trade do commodities thus move now one way, now the other?

In answer to questions of this kind it must be admitted at once that all abstract economic theory, and especially economic theory of the type illustrated in the preceding chapters, provides nothing more than working hypotheses. The process is no more than a preliminary approach toward principles and established conclusions. I would not belittle the importance of these first steps. Procedure such as they typify is indispensable in all scientific investigation. But they are no more than first steps. What we are concerned with at the end is the understanding of the phenomena of the actual world. Until we test and verify the hypotheses, we have no theory of international trade; we have no more than prolegomena to a theory. The task of verification has been too much neglected, not only as regards international trade, but as regards all the problems of exchange and distribution. The neglect is explicable on various grounds; partly the intellectual neatness and apparent conclusiveness of the deduced conclusions, largely the lack of descriptive and statistical material of a kind serviceable for the purposes of verification. The available material, however, is becoming steadily more abundant and more serviceable. Tho far from fully adequate, it is certain to be greatly enriched with the progress of descriptive economics and of statistical science. Even as it stands, not a little can be done; enough to clothe the dry bones with some flesh and blood, to give some indication of the degree of validity which appears when the deduced formulae are compared with the concrete phenomena of trade between nations. The present Book will be devoted to such comparisons — to problems of verification.

Some sort of verification is supplied by attentive observation of familiar phenomena. Most patent of all is that derived from the relation of imports and exports; the tendency to an equality of money values between them; the mechanism of the foreign exchanges, the comparatively small flow of specie which in fact takes place, the conduct of international trade by a process which is substantially barter. These are matters familiar to economic students. The part played by the foreign exchanges, where the trading countries have the same standard (gold), is one of the topics best understood and most adequately discussed in the subject matter of economic science. The man on the street, knowing that international transactions are conducted in terms of money, thinks commonly, or at least commonly speaks and writes as if they were settled in actual cash; he imagines money to go out in payment of imports and to come in for the exports. The economist, indeed any attentive observer, sees in these transactions a typical case of trade carried on in terms of money but with little intervention of money. All this, to repeat, is familiar; it is quite in accord with theoretic reasoning; and so far verification is simple and easy. In the present volume it needs no further attention.

The more complicated relations between imports and exports which arise when there are non-merchandise transactions serve almost as well among the simpler verifications of the theory of international trade. The well-known discrepancies between the money values of imports and exports — an excess of imports here, an excess of exports there — are quite in accord with the theoretic analysis. They will be considered at some length in the following pages. I may remark at once that, while the general character of the phenomena is in accord with the hypothetical deductions, some features can be explained only by the introduction of variants in the assumptions. Some, too, prove in the end not easily reconcilable with the generalizations of pure theory either in its original or in a modified form. The more detailed consideration of certain cases of non-merchandise transactions will be among the most instructive in our attempts at verification.

A different phase of that verification which is derived from the attentive consideration of these familiar phenomena appears when we observe prices and money wages in different countries. It is a common impression that there is a tendency to world-wide equalization of prices and wages; that, given free trade, the same rates of wages and the same range of prices must prevail in all countries; that the flow of gold tends to make them uniform thruout the world.

Another impression or belief, closely related to this, is that not only prices and money wages, but real incomes and the standards of living would be brought to one uniform level everywhere by unfettered international trade and international competition. Hence the uneasiness, even terror, about the "yellow peril": a supposed danger that the teeming millions of the East will compete with the peoples of the West and reduce the economic conditions of all to a common low level.

Yet it is elementary knowledge that countries trade with each other and that wide differences in wages and prices persist none the less. The most striking illustration is in the relations between Great Britain and British India. Here exchange between two large populations has been carried on for several generations in great volume, with rapid and cheap transportation and with complete free trade. Yet money wages have remained very much higher in Great Britain, and the general monetary scale has remained very much higher. Commodity wages, too, have been vastly higher. The same phenomenon, less striking as regards the differences in real and money wages, but more striking as regards the closeness of the contact, appears on a comparison between Great Britain and Continental Europe in the period that followed the adoption of free trade in Great Britain — a period of about fifty years in the latter half of the 19th century. The relaxation of duties, to a point almost negligible so far as concerns the present discussion, which took place in Great Britain about 1840, was followed twenty years later by a similar relaxation on the Continent. The Anglo-French Treaty of 1860 (the Cobden-Chevalier Treaty) led to a network of conventional arrangements between the important European countries, and brought about not, indeed, complete free trade, but a range of import duties so low that it could have been no appreciable factor in maintaining differences in wages and prices. Yet these differences persisted.

Great Britain continued to be the country of high wages and high expenses. The habitual standard of expenditure, the "cost of living" and what not, remained decade after decade higher than on the Continent.

It is part of the same set of phenomena that neither high money wages nor low money wages, neither a high monetary scale nor a low one, count as factors in promoting international trade or in retarding it. An impression as common as the one just mentioned (that free trade must lead to an equalization of wages and prices) is that a country where wages and prices are high finds it difficult to export, while one where they are low finds it easy to export; and that, conversely, imports tend to flow especially from the countries with a low monetary scale toward those with a high scale. The plain facts known to everyone are quite out of accord with any such notion. The surprising thing is that, plain and well-known as the facts are, the notion is so persistent. Goods move from the dear countries to the cheap countries, from those with high wages and great prosperity to those with low wages and hard conditions, quite as much as the other way. The money values of the goods that move the two ways are on the whole equal, the discrepancies being of minor moment and easily explicable in connection with the invisible items of international trade. The goods continue to be exchanged on the basis of an equalization of money values, decade after decade and generation after generation, without check to their exportation from the dear countries or increase of their exportation from the cheap ones.

Many familiar facts are thus quite in accord with the deduced theory; they stand as obvious verifications. Not only this: no other explanation of the facts has ever been offered. Commonly enough, even in pretentious books on economics, the variations in prices and money incomes between different countries are referred to as if they were ultimate data — a situation which the economist finds once for all, which he need not try to explain, and for which his only concern is with the conclusions or corollaries it suggests. Most German writers on international trade speak as if these phenomena were determined by inscrutable forces;

as if they were the acts of God, so to speak, concerning which it is beyond human ken to find explanation. Sometimes they are referred to as if simply the result of historical circumstances. They happened so, came to be so; it is otiose to inquire whether they might have been otherwise. One outstanding merit of the abstract theory is that it does consider why the facts are so and not otherwise. It gives a reasoned explanation of the differences in money incomes between different countries, of the causes which make wages and prices higher in some than in others, of the bearing of the differences on the material prosperity of the exchanging regions. The theory may not be a complete one; it may not be even a sound one. But it does grapple with the problems, and is the only one that has ever done so. What has been propounded in opposition by critics has evaded the problems, constructed nothing.[1]

These general remarks may be supplemented by some consideration, again very general, of the case in which differences of wages and prices are most conspicuous — the relations between Western Europe and the Orient. How far can it be said that these marked contrasts conform to the deductions of theory? How far do they serve as verification, how far suggest problems still to be solved?

Recall the general lines of the theoretical analysis. The case would appear to be one of absolute differences in costs; this much seems to be indicated by the great disparity between the money incomes and monetary standards of the two regions. India — taking this country as the largest of the tropical countries, and for so long a period the most important — has an absolute advantage

---

[1] It is surprising that, in the very latest German systematic compendium, so keen and well-equipped an economist as Wieser should fall into errors of the kind noted in this and the preceding paragraphs. He imputes it as a defect of the "classical quantity theory" that "the value of money is supposed to equalize itself internationally by an automatic process. Gold, like every other commodity, seeks the places where it has the highest value and flows thither from the places of lower value." And a further error is said to be that abstraction is made of the historical restriction to which individuals are subject — restrictions which above all affect human beings themselves and stand in the way of "an equalization of their culture in kind and in extent." Grundriss der Sozialökonomik, Vol. I, Theorie der Gesellschaftlichen Wirtschaft, p. 433 (1914). Such versions of the doctrines of the Ricardian school are the exact opposites of their real content.

in the production of its own special commodities; it produces them with less labor than they would entail in Great Britain. And Great Britain — taking this in turn as the representative European country — produces its manufactures with less labor than would be needed to produce them in India. The relation is one in which an exchange of goods is obviously advantageous to both countries, but also — what is less often seen — one in which there is a wide range within which the barter terms of trade may vary. Those terms might bring to England the lion's share of the possible gain, or might bring it to India. It is the relation of money incomes in the two countries that gives the indication — constitutes the mechanism — of the more or less advantageous positions of the parties. The country which has the higher range of money incomes gains most from the trade; that having the lower range gains least. In the actual case evidently England (Europe) has the greater gain, while India (the Orient) is in the less advantageous position.

Presumably this difference in favor of England, to continue the explanation suggested by theory, is due to the play of international demand. The Orient wants the goods of Europe more than Europe wants those of the Orient. To put the same thing in more technical terms, the make-up of the demand schedules in the two countries, reflecting the elasticity of demand for the several commodities, is such as to bring about terms of exchange under which much of Oriental goods is exchanged for a given quantum of European goods. And this result is in turn brought about by the distribution of specie. The higher range of European wages, prices, monetary standards, it is to be supposed, results from a steady tendency of specie to be gathered there. As changes take place in the total of specie that constitutes the medium of change thru the world at large, it is to be expected that a larger proportion will make its way to the countries of the West. The general tendency of the flow of specie might then be expected to be away from the East and toward the West.

This generalization from the theoretic reasoning may well cause the reader to pause. The actual flow of specie, as we all know, is quite different from what could be thus deduced. For centuries, indeed from the earliest stages of trade with the Orient down to the very most recent times, the movement has been exactly the other way. Gold and silver have moved into the Orient, not out of the Orient. Whatever conformity to theory there may seem to be in the relative wages and prices of the two regions, the familiar fact of the sustained drain of specie to the East is quite out of accord with the theoretical presumption. The skeptic who finds in our elaborate and intricate structure no more than an intellectual plaything is likely to be confirmed in his doubts. Here is no substantiation of the theory; rather, the reverse.

In truth, the case is troublesome. I am not at all sure that it can be reconciled with the hypotheses and conclusions which have been set down in the preceding chapters. Yet there are aspects, again familiar, which make it less anomalous than appears at first sight, and less inexplicable on the orthodox lines, perhaps on the whole consonant with them.

First, the flow of specie from the West to the East is not in the main a flow of money; it is a flow of the precious metals as commodities. That is, the silver and gold, tho their export serves to lessen the monetary stocks of the West, do not add to those of the East, or at least do not add in the East by any means as much as they take away from the West. They are used in the East chiefly for ornament and for hoards; they do not enter into active circulation. To use Jevons's phrase, India is a sink for the precious metals; they flow into that great region, almost disappear from view, and cease to function as money. They are in fact *commodities* sent by the West to the East, and commodities for which the demand is increasing and probably elastic.

Further, the specie supply in the West, from which was derived the portion sent to the East, was not stationary, but steadily augmenting. In our theoretic analysis it has been assumed — this being the first and simplest approximation — that the total international supply of specie is a given amount, and that the play of international demand merely determines the distribution among the several trading units of that fixed stock. The historic case is quite different. The world's supply, so far from being stationary, has been enormously increased; and the constantly inflowing product of the mines has gone first to the West. However much the wealth of Ormuz and of Ind may shine in tradition, the East has never been a considerable producer of the precious metals. Certainly it has produced nothing of moment during the period since the 16th century, when the trade with Europe began to reach considerable volume, and when, too, our information begins to be somewhat exact. The great increases in the supply of the precious metals have taken place in quarters far from the Orient; not only the famed American influx of 1550–1650, but the Australian and Californian flood of the mid-nineteenth century, and the vast amount, first of silver then of gold, which poured in steadily after 1870. Thruout, what happened between West and East was not a process of distributive changes in an existing fixed stock, but a parcelling out among different regions of a constantly augmenting supply. True, a considerable part of the continuing product of the mines went to the East. But much the larger part of that disappeared in the sink. What then constituted an addition to the circulating medium of the East was vastly less than what was retained in the West and there functioned actively as money. Of the total increase in the world's monetary stock a much larger part went into circulation in Western Europe than in Asia, the disparity being the greater if reckoned not in terms of aggregate quantities but in amounts per head of population.

These elements of the situation became more pronounced after the middle of the 19th century. Then both the volume of the trade in commodities and the volume of the specie flow reached dimensions never before dreamed of, as indeed all economic phenomena have become unexampled in magnitude. And with the extraordinary increase in quantities, there came an accentuation of the particular international relations which we are now considering. Money incomes and money standards in the Western countries rose almost steadily — sometimes indeed with a standstill or a brief retrogression, but with upward movements after every period of hesitancy, and in the end with great definitive advances. Money incomes and monetary standards in India and the East rose also, but not at all in proportion to the changes in the West. The advantageous position of the Occident in its trade with the Orient was maintained and became even more advantageous. The people of the West have had higher money incomes, and thereby have been enabled to buy more easily the products of the East, which, tho rising in price, have not risen as much as have Western incomes. The converse has taken place in the East.

This general situation, favorable to the West in the way to which the reader's attention was called at the outset, no doubt developed with some marked complications, and perhaps with the concurrence of processes not contemplated in the simple theoretical formulation. The variants and modifications are not necessarily inconsistent with the theoretical analysis. But I would not be supposed to maintain or even suggest that the trade between Europe and the East furnishes a ready verification of the theory of international trade. The subject is one (among many such) for which we need laborious examination of the historical course of events and careful scrutiny of the statistical material. Without research of this kind no verdict for or against the presumptions of theory can be reached.

It may be doubted, indeed, whether we shall ever have at our disposal the data needed for any clear conclusions on this phase of the history of commerce. What has been said in the preceding paragraphs rests on the most general and familiar information. A detailed investigation, if such prove feasible, proceeding from the same points of view, would doubtless bring out aspects of the case not here touched at all. Such an investigation might confirm the interpretations suggested, might run counter to them, might suggest new or modified hypotheses for the explanation of unexpected phenomena. After all was done, the trade between the Orient and the Occident would probably be found to present not so much a verification of theory as an example of the complexities of the problems of verification.

CHAPTER 15

DIFFERENCES IN LABOR COSTS [1]

THE principle of comparative advantage or comparative costs has bulked large in our theoretical analysis. What confirmation or verification of its significance is supplied by the facts?

In one respect we are much hampered in the search for pertinent facts. The data on costs which are most abundant are quite inapplicable. They are accountant's figures; that is, figures on money costs, on expenses of production, supply prices. The principle of comparative advantage or comparative costs, however, has regard to the quantities of labor needed for a given physical output. Labor cost in this sense is a matter of no concern at all to the accountant, and ordinarily of equally small concern in the business man's reckoning of profit and loss. It is "labor cost" in quite a different sense from that which is sought in business figuring. What the business man and his accountants mean by labor cost would be better described for our purposes by such a term as "wages expense" — the amount of money paid out in wages for a given unit of product.

The labor costs of the accountant and business man (wages expenses), it is true, might conceivably be converted into labor costs of the kind significant for the present inquiries. They could be so converted by reckoning also the money rates of wages per hour or per day. If these money rates of wages are known, the conversion would seem to be no troublesome matter. Yet in fact it is troublesome. The instances are rare in which the two sets of figures needed — wages expenses per unit of product on the one hand, wages paid per unit of labor (hour or day) on the other

[1] The substance of this chapter appeared as an article in the Quarterly Journal of Economics for November, 1924 (Vol. 39).

hand — are both available for a given product. Even when thus
available, the data involve inference, and may call for qualification and explanation. They are after all indirect, not direct,
and are less conclusive than observations or measurements which
have in view an immediate comparison of the quantities of labor
exerted for a given output. At all events, whether likely to be
satisfactory or not, evidence of this indirect sort is not forthcoming.
I may remark, by way of anticipation, that other evidence of the
indirect type, indubitably significant, is available in abundance; to
this attention will be given in the next chapter.

So far as concerns direct data, we are compelled to turn to
scattered instances in which for one purpose or another information
has been secured on the quantities of labor needed for producing
given units of goods. To be pertinent for our inquiry, the information should relate, of course, not to one country alone, but to
two or more; that is, to one and the same commodity in the several
countries. Such sporadic figures of this type as are available have
usually been gathered for other problems than those of international
trade. I proceed to adduce some data which have come to my
attention.

The Bureau of Mines of the United States Department of the
Interior has been engaged for many years in an endeavor to check
accidents in coal mines. This country has had a disgraceful position in this regard, standing lowest among all the advanced countries in its record of accidents and fatalities. The Bureau of Mines,
in the endeavor to bring out the large proportion of fatalities
both to men employed and to tonnage mined, has collected
figures of both kinds for various countries. It has thus enabled a
comparison to be made of the relation between man power and
physical output — the tons produced per year for each man
employed. Figures are available showing how many tons of coal
were brought to the pit's mouth for each miner; and also how
many tons for each worker of every kind (not only the underground
men, but all employed about the mines). I give the figures for
selected years:

COAL

Tons of Coal Produced per Year

	1911		1914		1918	
	Per Underground Worker	Per Worker of Every Kind	Per Underground Worker	Per Worker of Every Kind	Per Underground Worker	Per Worker of Every Kind
United States	819	681	803	673	1134	890
Great Britain	371	300	341	275	337	265
Prussia	381	285	389	284	409	—
Belgium	244	176	200	143	207	138
France	300	216	—	—	—	—
Nova Scotia	696	555	657	536	718	460
New South Wales	763	560	770	589	824	605
India	196	127	200	128	203	126

The effectiveness of labor in the United States is greater than in any other country. It is more than double that of Great Britain or of pre-war Prussia, at least thrice that of Belgium, five times as great as that of British India. It is markedly greater than that of the nearest rivals, New South Wales and Nova Scotia.[1]

The figures may be put in another way: in terms of the daily output per person. Since the number of days of work in the year is not the same in the several countries, such figures do not show precisely the same relations as those of annual output. In the

[1] The contrast would have been still greater had account been taken in the United States of bituminous coal alone ; and it is this which would afford the better basis of comparison with other countries. I append figures showing the annual product per year in the United States (all workers included), separately for the two kinds of coal over a series of years :

	Bituminous Tons per Head	Anthracite Tons per Head	Coal of Both Kinds Tons per Head
1914	724	505	673
1915	794	504	724
1916	896	548	818
1917	915	646	860
1918	942	672	890

United States the year has less working days for coal miners than in most countries. But this circumstance does not affect appreciably the comparisons. Put in terms of daily output per worker, we have:

TONS OF COAL PRODUCED PER DAY PER UNDERGROUND WORKER

	1911	1914	1918	1922
United States				
bituminous	4.01	4.28	4.68	5.10
anthracite	2.91	2.78	3.31	3.18
Great Britain	1.36	1.25	1.19	1.17
Prussia	1.29	1.26	1.40	—
Belgium	0.82	0.76	0.72	0.75
France	1.06	1.07 [1]	0.91	0.84

The explanation of the American effectiveness of labor in coal-mining is to be found partly in the human factors, partly in those of nature. The seams in the United States are thicker than in most countries, and in general are more accessible. But coal-cutting machines are used more widely than in other countries; and this, even when the comparison is made with countries having seams quite thick enough for machine mining. In the United States (1918), 56 per cent of the coal was machine-mined; in Nova Scotia (1916), 44 per cent; in New South Wales (1918), 25 per cent; in Great Britain (1918), 11 per cent. In the three last-named there is nothing in the quality of the seams which stands in the way of mining by machine.

Similar in character is a comparison made by a well-known German economist [2] for another bulky and homogeneous commodity — brick. The regions compared were Germany and the United States; and for the United States, the State of New York separately, as well as the country at large. In the United States, for the year 1905, the output of bricks per person employed was 141,000; for the State of New York alone, the output was 180,000. In Germany, for 1904, the output per head was only 40,000. The

[1] First half of the year.
[2] K. Ballod, in the Jahrbuch für Gesetzgebung, 1910, p. 294.

German brick, however, is larger than the American in the proportion of 3 to 2; making allowance for this difference, the German output, for comparison with the American, may be reckoned at 60,000. The discrepancy in favor of the United States remains very great. The effectiveness of American labor in brickmaking, for the country at large, is over twice as great; and for the State of New York alone it is thrice that of German labor.[1]

Coal and brick belong in the class of domestic commodities. So great is their cost of transportation that in the main they do not come within the domain of international trade. True, this is less unreservedly the case with coal than with brick. Coal moves over greater distances than brick, and sometimes moves from country to country. England exports much coal, partly because the mines are near tidewater, and partly because freight rates are specially low on outward-bound shipping. German coal moves across the border to nearby regions of the Continent. Nevertheless, in the main both commodities belong in the domestic class. The advantage which the United States has in producing them hence shows its consequences rather within the country than in its exchange with other countries. Tho the money rates of wages in the United States were double those in Germany (I speak of the pre-war period), the effectiveness of American labor in brick-making was more than double; bricks might therefore be expected to be cheaper, at the works or near by, than in Germany. So as regards coal. Money wages were higher in the United States than in England and in Germany; they were a little higher in England than in Germany, but the difference was not great enough to affect materially a comparison between the United States and the other two. The effectiveness of labor in coal-mining was greater in the United States than in either of them, and

---

[1] I cite a further bit of evidence on this same commodity. "I was in a brickyard at Singapore, where I calculated the product of the men. Their rate of pay was 35 cents per day in our money. I happened to have in my pocket a very accurate cost statement of a brickmaking company in one of our Eastern cities, signed by its president, and when the superintendent of the Singapore yard and I figured his labor (i.e. wages expense) together, they were precisely the same." Redfield, The New Industrial Day, p. 121.

more so than in proportion to the money rates of wages. That is, coal would be expected to be cheaper in the United States, at the pit's mouth or nearby. And such, as is familiar knowledge, has been the case.[1]

In both commodities the United States seems to have a comparative advantage, which, however, is prevented from having an effect in international trade by the high cost of transportation. The American coal mines, unlike those of England and Germany, are situated far from the border and far from tidewater. Only as regards Canada is there a possibility of transportation across the political border; and as regards Canada, it may be remarked, the phenomena are those of domestic rather than of international trade. Were it not for the inhibition arising from cost of transportation — the fact that brick and coal cannot be carried across land and ocean as, for example, cotton can be — we should expect coal to move from the United States to Great Britain, and both coal and brick to Germany.

A comparison is made by Dr. Ballod for another commodity which is chiefly domestic, even tho, like coal, it passes occasionally into the international field. In breweries, he finds that in Germany there were turned out in 1907, 614 hectolitres of beer per workman; in the United States (1900) very nearly 1000 hectolitres per workman.[2] The physical output was thus as 2 to 3. I would not undertake a judgment on the delicate question of the allowance to be made for a difference in quality between the Amer-

[1] By way of example, I give the following figures for the year 1913. The prices are average (or rather representative) prices for that year as a whole. While they can not pretend to any refined statistical accuracy as averages, they are quite sufficiently accurate to indicate the relations between prices in the three countries at that time. I have summarized them from figures much more detailed, which were kindly supplied to me by Professor J. E. Orchard of Columbia University.

COAL PRICE F.O.B. AT MINE, 1913

	UNITED STATES (Pittsburgh)	GREAT BRITAIN (Durham)	GERMANY (Ruhr)
Coking Coal	$1.65	$2.75 @ $3.30	$3.06 @ $3.50
Gas Coal	1.65	3.12	3.40 @ 3.75
Best Steam Coal	2.50	4.00	3.50

[2] Jahrbuch für Gesetzgebung, 1910, p. 283.

ican and the German beverage. Merely on the basis of quantity, it would seem that Germany had a comparative advantage in beer over brick and coal; that is, in the phraseology suggested elsewhere in these pages, she had an inferior disadvantage. The productivity of her labor was less than that in the United States for both groups of commodities — beer on the one hand, coal and brick on the other — but the disadvantage was less marked in the first-named group. Perhaps, in the land of Gambrinus, a better quality of the product makes the disadvantage even smaller, the comparative advantage more marked.

Between the United States and Great Britain (*i.e.* the United Kingdom) some most interesting comparisons of wide sweep have been worked out by Mr. A. W. Flux. That able economist and statistician has used for the purpose the census returns of production for the year 1907 in Great Britain (the first returns of the kind gathered in that country) and those for the year 1909 in the United States. Here, as with the coal figures, what concerns us is the product per man for each several commodity in the two countries, the total physical output in each of the selected industries being divided by the total number of men employed. Simple tho this may seem, it is by no means easy to arrive at usable results. In order to render the figures for the two countries comparable, it was necessary to make sure that the demarcation of each industry was the same in both — that there was no divergence of classification and scope. Allowance had further to be made for the difference of two years between the census dates (1907 and 1909) and for differences in the activity of trade and industry which might affect the output. The last-named factor was most carefully considered by Mr. Flux, but, as it happened, proved not to be of much moment for the inquiry. More important was the need of confining the inquiry to industries turning out the same homogeneous product in both countries. Differences in quality might obviously restrict comparisons. Mass products, the same the world over, turned out in such large amounts that the census authorities can scan them with ease and that minor errors are likely to offset each other — these offer the best possibilities for such comparisons; and it is for these that Mr. Flux worked out the results.[1]

First, pig iron. The output per person employed was 39 tons in Great Britain in 1907; it was 84.5 tons per person employed in the United States in 1909. That is, for each person employed the output was more than twice as great in the United States.[2] For steel products the difference was even greater. The output per head was 25 tons in Great Britain, 77 tons in the United States; nor was the difference any more to be explained in this case than in that of pig iron on the ground of discrepancy in the character of the article (heavy steel, say, against more finished forms).

Some further figures on the steel industry of the two countries are suggestive. They relate to steel works of all kinds, and (I judge) do not cover precisely the same ground as those for "steel products" just given. They are stated in proportions; they show merely relations between conditions in the two countries.

	PROPORTION OF UNITED STATES TO GREAT BRITAIN	
Total Tonnage	4	1
Numbers of workers	7	6
Horsepower per worker	10¾	5¼

Tho the number of workers in the United States is not markedly greater than in Great Britain, the tonnage produced is four times as great. But the equipment of the workers, as indicated by the horsepower of the machinery employed, is twice as great. No

[1] Mr. Flux put his figures at my disposal in manuscript form many years ago (before the Great War), but was unwilling to publish them, tho urged to do so. He has most kindly permitted me to use them here. Some among them he has used in his paper on the Census of Production in the Journal of the Royal Statistical Society for May, 1924. In that paper he has also made most interesting comparisons between the pecuniary yield per workman in various British and American industries, and between the wages rates in the two countries.

[2] These figures refer to manufacturing operations in the strict sense — to those included in accountants' reckoning of conversion cost. They are the costs *above* ore, coal, limestone. Dr. Ballod, in the article in the Jahrbuch für Gesetzgebung already referred to, gives figures of pre-war product for the United States and Germany on a different basis, including all the labor for ore, coal, etc., as well as for labor at the furnace. He arrives at 295 tons per workman in Germany for 1906, 424 tons for Pennsylvania in 1900. I can not be sure of the comparability of these figures.

doubt, in a strictly accurate accounting, the machinery employed should also be reckoned in terms of labor. That is, there should be reckoned, in addition to the labor currently applied by the workers of the year, some part of the labor given in previous years to making the machinery — so large a part as corresponds to the depreciation of the machinery during this one year. Thus revised, the figures would show not quite so great a superiority in effectiveness for the United States. None the less a marked superiority would remain. And the explanation of that superiority, it is to be observed, is the very fact that more horsepower, more machinery was used. In the language of everyday life, it was the greater use of power and machinery that most contributed to making American labor effective and productive. In the language of economic theory, it was the use of previous or ancillary labor, given to making the machines, which — combined with the necessary waiting — served toward making *all* the labor more effective.

The reader will bear in mind that in this chapter we are concerned solely with the fact of differences in physical output. The causes of the differences are another matter, to which attention will be directed in the next ensuing chapter. But certain other figures, which have at least a possible bearing on the causes (the explanation) of the differences, may be of interest. It appeared that for each ton of pig iron produced there were used in Great Britain 2.48 tons of ore and cinder (lime-stone); in the United States, 1.96 tons. In this regard, the effectiveness of labor was somewhat greater, tho not strikingly greater in the United States. The advantage was presumably due to a simple physical cause, the greater richness of the American ore; and not to any human cause, such as greater use of power and machinery, or more effective exertions by the workmen. As regards coal consumption, there was a similar difference. For each ton of pig iron produced, 2.09 tons of coal were used in Great Britain, 1.74 in the United States. Here also the main explanation is probably to be found in the better quality of the American coal used in the blast-furnaces. I know of no evidence to indicate that there was better handling or utilization of the coal.

A difference equally striking appeared in the case of tin-plate. The weight of tin-plate produced was approximately the same in the two countries: 529,000 tons in Great Britain, 587,000 tons in the United States. The number of persons employed was, however, vastly greater in Great Britain: 20,628 against only 5846 in the United States. In terms of physical output per person employed, the figures were 25.6 tons per head in Great Britain and 100.4 tons per head in the United States. As Mr. Flux remarks, "while the quality of goods was not necessarily equal, the divergence in the net output (in terms of money) appears to be related rather to the volume of output than to the price obtained per unit of quantity."[1]

In sugar refining, the number of tons refined per year was 87 in Great Britain, somewhere between 150 and 180 tons in the United States. The figure for the United States was somewhat uncertain, because the statistics did not make it clear that all the American sugar consumed went thru the refineries; some fraction certainly did not; the maximum figure (180 tons) was computed on the supposition that the whole supply was refined. Even taking the lowest figure (150) the contrast with the British figure (87 tons) is marked. In flour milling the contrast, even tho less great, is also marked. The output in Great Britain was 153 million cwt., against 429 million in the United States; the number of persons employed was 36,177 against 66,054. This works out, in round numbers, 4250 cwt. per head in Great Britain, compared with 6500 per head in the United States. And here too the figures of horsepower in the industry point to human factors as most important among the causes of the difference. The horsepower per employee in the flour mills of Great Britain was 5, in the United States 13. The indication is that capital, plant, machinery, played a larger part in the latter country.

In other industries, where direct statements of physical output were not available, it was none the less possible to make significant comparisons. This was the case where the output in money

---

[1] The price obtained (average value) was £14 per ton in Great Britain, £11 per ton in the United States.

terms (stated values) was known, and where it was also known
that the prices and qualities of the products were virtually the
same. For butter, *e.g.* the net output in Great Britain was found
to be, in money terms, £125 per head, in the United States £242
per head. Differences in price for the article between the two
countries were negligible. It follows that physical output was in
the ratio of the value output, that is, nearly 1 to 2. So in the
case of ice. The value output was £212 per head in Great Britain,
£307 in the United States; the prices of ice in the two countries
were, as it happened, identical. The physical output per head was
therefore in the ratio roughly of 2 to 3.

For another commodity, window glass, figures are available
from a different quarter, and comparisons of a similar sort can be
made; in this case for the United States, Belgium, and Sweden.
The figures were put together by the Tariff Commission of Sweden,
being computed as part of an investigation of the relation between
costs of production in that country and costs in the important
competing countries.[1] They are of special interest because for the
United States they give two sets of data, one for the hand-blown
glass, the other for the glass made by machine. The industry
in the United States has been revolutionized in recent times by the
invention and successful operation of elaborate machinery.[2] The
new process — one further phase of the conquering march of the
machine processes — has largely displaced in this country the glass
blower who dominated in the older handicraft stage of the industry.
During the Great War, as it happened, there was a pause in this
process of displacement. Various neutral countries turned to the
United States for supplies, since Belgium (which had been the
most important country of export) was in chains. Consequently

[1] I am indebted for these figures to Professor B. Ohlin, of the University of
Copenhagen, who called my attention to them during his sojourn in the United
States in 1923.

[2] On this striking industrial development see an excellent publication of the
United States Department of Commerce, Miscellaneous Series No. 60 (1917):
The Glass Industry, Report on the Cost of Production of Glass in the United
States. — The machines are blowing devices: an intricate apparatus for doing with
compressed air what the hand blower did with his lungs.

the American hand factories of the older type, and the glass blowers working in them, experienced for some years a revival of activity and prosperity. This was no more than a temporary interruption of the main trend; the machine process was triumphing in the United States, and indeed seems destined to rule soon in other countries also. During the stage of transition, thus prolonged in the United States by the war conditions, machine and handicraft processes were applied side by side. Hence comparisons were made by the Swedish investigators not only between the European countries and the United States, but between the two methods of production in the latter country alone.

The figures follow. They give the output per worker, in terms of square meters.

WINDOW-GLASS OUTPUT (SQ. METERS PER WORKER)

	YEAR	MONTH	DAY
Sweden (1913)	2890	260	10
Belgium (1906)	3400	310	11
United States (hand-blown, 1915)	2800	400	16
United States (machine-blown, 1915)	5250	650	21

In considering the figures, regard must be had to differences in working arrangements. The season in the United States is but seven months in the hand factories, eight months in the machine factories; during the hot summer months the works are shut down. In Sweden and Belgium the operations run thru ten to eleven months, and in Belgium work goes on thru the Sundays. Apparent discrepancies between the figures for year, month, and day are thus accounted for.

It appears that, for the hand factories, there are no marked differences in the annual output per head for the three countries. Per day, the effectiveness of labor is greater in the United States (16 as against 11 in Belgium and 10 in Sweden); but for the year, the United States ranks lowest. Belgium ranks highest for the year, but this is the result mainly of prolongation of labor thru a larger portion of the year.

When comparison is made, however, between the machine

factories of the United States and the hand factories in all three countries, the case is quite different. The superiority of the United States is marked. The output per day is more than twice as great for each workman in the United States as in the two other countries. Per year the difference is not quite so great, because of the less number of operating days. The machine processes, however, are carried on in the United States over a larger number of days than are the hand processes in that country; hence, while the superiority of the machine is not so marked in the daily output (21 to 16), it becomes so as regards the annual output (5250 against 2800). Anyone who has seen both processes at work, as I have, will readily understand that the machine operator can keep at his task thru more days and thru hotter days than can the hand blower.

It is instructive to contrast these figures of labor cost — that is, of labor bestowed — with cost figures of the ordinary sort. The same investigation brought together the money costs, the "expenses of production," in the three countries, and, among these money costs, itemized separately the wages expenses. The results confirm what was said in an earlier chapter [1] on wages and prices in relation to international and domestic commodities, and they bear also on the further elucidation of the same general subject which will be found in the next chapter. The figures are as follows:

MONEY COSTS OF PRODUCTION PER BOX OF 100 SQ. FT. WINDOW GLASS

	Hand-blown			Machine-blown
	BELGIUM 1912	SWEDEN 1912	UNITED STATES 1915	UNITED STATES 1915
	¢	¢	¢	¢
Raw material	19.6	43.9	32.7	29.7
Fuel and Power	53.3	103.4	31.6	26.3
Packing	30.0	13.0	27.1	22.2
Wages	105.6	97.8	222.2	134.5
Miscellaneous Expenses	32.2	45.0	55.2	63.8
Total	$2.41	$3.03	$3.69	$2.77

[1] See Chapter 5.

Money cost is much higher in the United States for the hand factories. But when the American machine product is compared with the hand product of Belgium and Sweden, the money cost is about the same — a little lower than in Sweden, a little higher than in Belgium. The main factor in all cases is the wages expense. For the hand factories, this item is more than twice as high in the United States. The money wages for the workmen, and especially for the blowers, are higher than in the two European countries, in accord with the higher pecuniary standards prevailing in American industry at large; but the effectiveness of the labor is no greater; the wages cost per unit of product is therefore higher. In the machine factories, the American money rate of wages is also high; but the effectiveness of the labor which operates the machines is greater; therefore the wages cost per unit, while somewhat higher than in Belgium and Sweden, is by no means higher to the same degree as under the hand process. For both processes, the United States has lower money costs for fuel and power, a natural concomitant of the effectiveness of its labor in producing coal (as shown in the earlier pages of this chapter). In sum, the United States has greater effectiveness in producing window glass by the machine process, but no superiority at all in producing by the hand process; in other words, a comparative advantage in the former.

For Japan and the United States I am able to cite data in which again money cost can be contrasted with labor cost, or at least with indicia of labor cost. The United States Tariff Commission caused inquiries to be made in 1921 on competition between the United States and Japan.[1] Among the industries examined was the cotton manufacture; and in that industry, attention was given to certain staple products — yarns and plain woven goods — of such character that comparisons could readily be made between the conditions of production for the same articles in the two countries. It should be remarked, however, that the homo-

[1] The Japanese Cotton Industry and Trade; Report by the United States Tariff Commission, 1921. The date to which the statements refer is 1920. The passages referred to in the text are at pp. 100, 114–117.

geneity is by no means complete. Japanese yarn, for example, tho it be of the same count as the American, is inferior in quality. The inferiority, as it happens, is not a handicap to the Japanese yarn in China, the chief market to which it is exported; tho it would very much affect the sale if exports were made to the United States or to a European country. The same inferiority appears in the woven cloths. The differences in quality serve to render even more striking the comparisons which follow, since these make no allowance for the poorer quality of the Japanese product.

The outstanding fact is that the output per laborer employed is four times as great in the United States as in Japan. The output of yarn (number 20, *i.e.* medium yarns) per spinner is 104 pounds per day in Japan, 414 per day in the United States. The output per weaver is 145 yards daily in Japan; it is 450 yards per day in the United States on plain looms, 1100 yards on automatic looms. Plain looms in the United States are obsolescent for fabrics of the kind selected for this comparison. Only older mills still use them; the automatic loom is the representative apparatus. Both for spinning and weaving, some qualification needs to be attached to the comparisons. The American spinner has the aid of a doffer boy or girl; the American weaver on automatic looms has the aid of a similar attendant who supplies fresh bobbins. But the inclusion of this additional American labor would affect the final figures but little. Nor would they be much affected by the inclusion of still another item; namely, the higher capital cost of the automatic loom. I have already indicated in what way this circumstance should be taken into account;[1] it can be of but slight effect on the total of labor involved per unit of output.

The same contrast appears, and no less strikingly, when it is presented in the inverse way. We may ask what is the number of workmen employed per unit of machinery, thus envisaging not the number of units produced per workman but the number of workmen per unit of product. "A Japanese cotton mill requires approximately four times as many employees for the same amount of machinery as does a similar American mill. . . . On a standard

[1] Chapter 7, pp. 68 *et seq.*

count of yarn the average Japanese spinner tends about 240 spindles while spinners in an American mill, with some assistance from a doffer, tend at least 1,000 spindles and frequently more. Similarly, in weaving staple cotton sheetings, the Japanese weaver seldom operates more than two plain looms, while the American weaver, with perhaps some assistance in supplying fresh bobbins, normally tends from eight to ten plain looms, and on looms equipped with automatic filling batteries, 20 looms per weaver is normal, and 24 or 26 is not uncommon." [1] It is true, of course, that the product for a given outfit of machinery is not necessarily the same in the two countries. What difference there is, however, would be in favor of the American mill; its machinery, we may safely assume, runs faster and more continuously, turns out more per hour and per day, than the Japanese. Not only as regards the specific operations of spinning and weaving, but for all the mill labor and for the mill product in its completed form, the physical product would doubtless be found at least four times as great in the American mill.

The figures on money cost — accountant's cost — for the two countries reflect the same situation and substantiate the conclusions. Money wages in Japan are much lower. Japanese weavers, for example, get one-fifth to one-sixth of what American weavers get. But so much greater is the effectiveness of weavers in the United States that the weaving cost (money expense) per yard of cloth is three-eighths of a cent ($0.00375) in a Japanese mill and about one-fourth of a cent ($0.00270) in an American mill working with automatic looms. In spinning, with the same differences in money wages, the manufacturing ("conversion") cost of a pound of number 20 yarn was $0.087 in Japan, $0.112 in the United States. The final figure in this case is higher for the United States, wages being lower in Japan *more* than in proportion to the lower effectiveness of labor. If account were taken of the poorer quality of Japanese yarn, the effective money price,

---

[1] I may add that since the time when this was written (1921), the number of automatic looms tended by an American weaver has still further increased, and in some mills was in 1924 double the number stated in the text.

the competitive position in the market, would be the same for the two products.

In thus considering competitive conditions, however, we are passing the limits of the present chapter. We have been concerned with the direct and simple fact of differences in labor cost for the same commodity. A consideration of money costs, prices, the possibilities of the sale of a commodity in the markets of another country leads to the indirect evidence of differences in cost. To this attention will be given in the next chapter.

CHAPTER 16

COMPARATIVE ADVANTAGE AND PROTECTION IN THE UNITED STATES

WE proceed now to the consideration of some indirect evidence on differences in comparative costs; evidence which, as remarked in the preceding chapter, is more abundant than that of the direct sort. It is derived from the observation and analysis of some patent economic facts, and above all from observation of the effects of protective tariffs. An examination of the concrete effects of protective legislation brings out a wide range of phenomena which can be explained only in the light of the doctrine of comparative advantage, and which in turn serve to give support to that doctrine. For my own part, it is prolonged inquiry on the working of protective duties in the United States which has confirmed my conviction that the actual course of industrial development and of trade between nations affords a striking verification of essential features in the theory of international trade; and it is this conviction which in turn has led me to reflect on the importance of the general problem of verification, and to search for possibilities of similar verification in other directions also.

The evidence furnished by the development of American industries under the influence of tariff legislation is most striking in the contrast between the extraordinary growth of some protected industries and the marked failure of others to show a growth at all corresponding. We have here a set of phenomena which, tho commonly discussed quite without regard to the general principles of international trade, are in fact clearly related to those principles — confirm them in the main, suggest modifications or qualifications in some directions, serve on the whole to illuminate and clarify the theoretical analysis. And it is no less true that most

178

of the arguments commonly heard in the popular controversy, and particularly those on the supposed effect of protection in raising wages or keeping them high, can be understood and weighed only in the light of the doctrine of comparative advantage.[1]

The principle of comparative advantage applies more fully and unequivocally to the United States than to any country whose conditions are known to me. The difference in money wages between the United States and European countries is marked; the difference in commodity wages, tho not so great, is none the less also marked. Notwithstanding the high wages, constituting an apparent obstacle or handicap for the domestic producer, the United States steadily exports all sorts of commodities, not only agricultural products, but manufactures of various kinds. Evidently they could not be exported unless they were sold abroad as cheaply as foreign goods of the same sort are there sold; and that these, the products of highly paid labor, are exported and are sold cheap, is proof that American industry has in them a comparative advantage. There are other goods which, tho not exported, are not imported; goods where the balance of advantage is even, so to speak. They are not such as are ruled out of the sphere of international trade once for all, because of great bulk or necessity of production *in situ;* they might conceivably be imported; yet in fact they are not imported. These are the products of industries in which American labor is effective, yet not effective to the highest pitch; effective in proportion to the higher range of money wages in the country, but barely in that proportion, or less than in that proportion. The explanation of their continued importation lies in the fact that the terms of trade are so favorable to the United States that this country gets the best

[1] In the pages which follow I have made free use of passages from books which I have already published. Most of the matter thus used for the second time is from the book on Some Aspects of the Tariff Question. The rest is from the essay on Wages and Prices in Relation to International Trade, contained in the volume of collected papers entitled Free Trade, the Tariff, and Reciprocity. I have repeated in part the same language, since it seemed not worth while to put in other words what had already been expressed as well as lay in my power. The reader who may wish for a more detailed exposition, and for further illustration and proof of some conclusions here stated with brevity, is referred to these books. In the present chapter I have tried to put together a summary statement of the outcome of extended inquiries.

yield for its labor and capital by turning, not to every industry in which it has some comparative advantage, but to those only in which it has the greater advantage,[1] And finally there are goods whose importation continues, even tho there is no obvious obstacle to their domestic production from soil or climate. These are things which *could* be produced to as good advantage at home as abroad; but they lack the comparative advantage, or lack a sufficient advantage. They do not measure up to the standard set by the dominant industries; the obstacle to their successful prosecution within the country is not physical, but economic. In this class belong also the industries which are protected and which would not hold their own without protection. They are in a position analogous to that of the strictly domestic industries in which labor is not effective, but which, being carried on of necessity within the country, have high prices made necessary by high money wages. The obvious difference between the two cases is that the circumstance which causes the strictly domestic industries to be carried on is an unalterable one, such as the difficulty or impossibility of transportation; while that which causes the protected industry to become domesticated, even tho it lacks a comparative advantage, is the artificial one of a legislative barrier.

What, now, are the causes of industrial effectiveness and comparative advantage? To put the question in other words, what are the industries in which a comparative advantage is likely to appear? and, more particularly, in what directions is the labor of the people of the United States likely to be applied with special effectiveness?

The answer to this question which is suggested or implied, even tho not explicitly stated, in most of the literature on the subject, is that differences in effectiveness and cost rest on physical causes. They are the consequences of climate, soil, the stores of mineral in different parts of the earth's crust. They are not the results of man's action; they merely respond to man's utilization. The most significant point of novel character which is brought out by American tariff experience is that side by side with the physical

[1] See what is said in Chapter 9.

causes of comparative advantage stand others which are often quite as effective. It would be going too far to say that the physical causes are shown to be of secondary importance. But human causes — man's ways of doing things — play so large a part and combine so constantly with the physical causes that it is often difficult to say which dominate.

Agricultural products have always constituted the largest part of American exports. They still remain so, even tho non-agricultural products contribute a greater share than they did thru the nineteenth century. A new country, with abundance of fertile land, finds its labor most effective in the extractive industries. Hence the United States long was, and still is, a steady exporter of wheat, meat products, cotton. In the same way Canada is now a heavy exporter of wheat. Wheat is specially adapted to extensive culture, and is easily transportable; it is the commodity for which nature gives a clear comparative advantage to a new country in the temperate zone. The international trade of the United States was long determined chiefly by the country's special advantages for the production of wheat and similar agricultural staples.

But it is not merely the natural resources which have told, but the manner in which they were used. From the first, inventiveness and ingenuity were shown. The United States early became the great country of agricultural machinery. Especially during the second half of the nineteenth century, the skill of the makers of agricultural implements and the intelligence of the farmers who used the implements were factors not less important than the great stretches of new land. Still another factor of importance was the cheapening of transportation. From the very beginning, the Americans have been energetic and successful in overcoming the vast distances of the country. Our railroads have cheapened long hauls as nowhere else. The most striking advances in this combination of machine-aided agriculture with cheap transportation were made in the last third of the nineteenth century. Then new lands were opened, and agricultural products exported, on a scale not before thought possible. It has already been pointed out that when the effectiveness of labor is spoken of, the

effectiveness of *all* the labor needed to bring an article to market is
meant; not merely that of the labor immediately and obviously
applied (like that of the farmer), but that of the inventor and
maker of threshing-machines and gangplows, and that of the
manager and worker on the railways and ships. In other industries, even more markedly than in agriculture, the labor of the
directing heads, of the planners and designers, tells in high degree
for the final effectiveness of the labor which is applied thru all
the successive stages. But in agriculture as practiced in the
United States the guiding and contriving mind tells more than
in the agriculture of any other country.

The heart of the country, the main source of its prosperity and
power, is in the great central plain, the valleys of the Mississippi
and Missouri. Here is the region of extensive cultivation, of
agricultural machinery, the one-family farm. True, during the
harvest season there is a heavy demand for agricultural laborers,
met in large part by transients. It is true, further, that the stage
of pioneer farming has been passed or is rapidly being passed,
that rotation is becoming more systematic and skilful, the land
more valuable, cultivation more intensive. Nevertheless this
remains the region of the one-family farm. The farmers "ride
on their stirring plows and cultivators" and in this way do most
of the work on their lands for themselves. No economic and
social situation of this kind has ever before appeared in the world's
history. Land in plenty, no density of population, the labor
power spread thin over the land, an agricultural output large per
unit of man-power but not large per unit of area; farms large in
acreage, and capitalistic production (in the sense that much
machinery is used); the labor of agriculture done mainly by the
owners of the soil; no sharp cleavage between land owners and
land workers; little inequality in economic and social status, a
high general level of prosperity; a landed class not rich and not
poor, not highly cultured but far from inert or dull. The phenomenon is unique in history.

What all this means with reference to the present inquiry is
brought out perhaps best of all by one striking episode: the

history and outcome of the endeavors to promote by protective duties the beet sugar industry.

The beet sugar industry of the United States, as it now (1925) stands, is in the main massed in the far west — California, Utah, Colorado, and the adjacent region. The agricultural belt of the central states has a very slender share. Only one state in this part of the country, Michigan, makes a considerable contribution to the supply. Barring Michigan, the production of beet sugar may be said to be confined to the Rocky Mountain and Pacific states.

The explanation of this geographical concentration does not lie in any obstacles from climate or soil in other parts of the country. The beet flourishes over a very wide area. An instructive pamphlet issued by the Department of Agriculture shows the zone in which the sugar-beet may be expected to "attain its highest perfection." This zone or belt, two hundred miles wide, starts at the Hudson, sweeps across the country, and includes a great part of the north central region. Yet in the last mentioned, the most important and productive agricultural region of the country, there is virtually no beet growing or sugar making, except, as just mentioned, in Michigan. And the fundamental reason for the absence of beet growing and hence of sugar-beet production in this region is to be found in the fact that agriculture is applied with *greater* effectiveness in other directions. It is not that the climate or soil or even the men make it more difficult to grow beets here than in Europe. It is simply that other ways of using the land are found more advantageous. The case is a representative one, and it will be worth while to consider it in some detail.

An excellent investigator on the agricultural aspects of the beet sugar industry has said : [1] "The growing of beets is not agriculture, but horticulture." All the manuals and pamphlets insist on the need of elaborate preparation, minute care, much labor directly in the fields. The planting of the seed does indeed take place by drills, the plants coming up in continuous rows. But after this

[1] Professor G. W. Shaw, of the University of California; see the pamphlet on Sugar Beets in the San Joaquin Valley. The passages quoted in the text are partly from Professor Shaw's pamphlet, partly from other sources.

first operation, painstaking manual labor is called for. When the young shoots come up, they need first to be blocked, then thinned. "Blocking" means that most of the beets in the rows are cut out by a hoe, small bunches only being left, about ten inches apart. These bunches are then "thinned"; every plant is pulled out by hand except one, the largest and healthiest. Essentially the same situation appears when harvesting is reached. The beets may be first loosened by a plow and by a lifter; but each individual beet must be pulled out by hand. Finally, they are "topped"; that is, the neck and leaves are cut off by hand with a large knife.

In sum, the growing of the sugar-beet calls for a large amount of monotonous unskilled labor. Not only does the typical American farm and farm community lack the numbers of laborers required; the labor itself is of a kind distasteful to the American farmers. The way in which this need of dull labor has been met is instructive not only as regards the beet sugar industry itself, but also as regards a general trend in the United States during the generation preceding the Great War. Almost everywhere in the beet sugar districts we find laborers who are employed or contracted for in gangs, an inferior class which is utilized, perhaps exploited, by a superior. In Colorado "immigrants from Old Mexico compete with New Mexicans (*i.e.* born in New Mexico), Russians, and Japanese." In Michigan, the main labor supply comes from the Polish and Bohemian population of Cleveland, Buffalo, and other large cities. As was said in a circular issued by the Department of Agriculture, "living in cities there is a class of foreigners — Germans, French, Russians, Hollanders, Austrians, Bohemians — who have had more or less experience in beet growing in their native countries . . . every spring sees large colonies of this class of workmen moving out from our cities into the beet fields."

In the general economic organization of the great central region, labor conditions of this sort play no appreciable part. Here the one-family farm dominates; there is nothing in the nature of an agricultural proletariat. And here there is no sugar-beet industry of any moment. It pays better to raise corn; there is a clear comparative advantage in corn growing. This grain is peculiarly adapted to extensive agriculture. It also lends itself readily to the use of machinery; corn can be "cultivated" between the rows by horse power. It is a substitute for root crops, and can be rotated steadily with small-grain crops. It is a direct competitor with the sugar-beet for cattle fattening. The advocates of beet raising always lay stress on the value of the beet pulp, the residue at the factory after the juice has been extracted, for cattle feeding. But corn is at least equally valuable for the purpose, and the typical American farmer raises it by agricultural methods which he finds both profitable and congenial. One man can grow forty acres of corn; he can plant only twenty acres of beets, and these he cannot possibly thin and top. In Iowa "the farmers are progressive, successful, and satisfied. In fact, this has been the main obstacle to installing the sugar industry there. The farming class of the state is accustomed to the use of labor-saving implements in the fields." This passage, taken from a publication of the Department of Agriculture, is one among many of similar tenor, all of which make propaganda for protection to beet sugar, and all are quite innocent of any understanding of the economic principles illustrated by their statement of the facts.

In the far West, where most of the beets are grown and most of the beet sugar is made, other factors enter. In two respects, the conditions are peculiarly favorable to beet growing: the climate, and the special advantages of irrigation. Physical causes are present which serve to give, in part at least, a comparative advantage.

The variety of the beet suitable for sugar making flourishes in a cool climate; but it needs plenty of sun. "Abundance of sunshine is essential to the highest development of sugar in the beet. Other things being equal, it may be said that the richness of the beet will be proportional to the amount — not intensity — of the sunshine." The cool region of cloudless sky in the arid west meets this condition perfectly. The irrigated regions of Colorado, Utah, Idaho, Montana supply just the right combination of climate and moisture: cool temperature, abundant sunshine, moisture exactly as needed, absence of moisture when harmful. California, where the industry first was undertaken on any considerable scale, and where it has grown steadily, has some special advantages on non-irrigated lands. Nature has given to a good part of its beet district the required combination of climate and precipitation.

These physical causes, serving as they do to give the beet sugar industry of the far West some degree of comparative advantage, have been reinforced by the fact that the competing product (cane sugar) encounters transportation obstacles in reaching the center of the country from the sea-board. Hence the beet sugar industry has here shown a great growth under the stimulus of protection. The growth is striking when compared with the absence of anything of the kind in the main agricultural region, which yet has climatic conditions similar to those of European countries where beet sugar production flourishes without any tariff support at all. It would carry us too far afield to inquire whether the net result is that the Western sugar producers are in a position to compete with other sources of sugar supply without protection. Apparently some part of the industry is independent of such support, but by no means all of it. These are questions of the balancing of forces, and concrete problems important for the legislator, which lie outside the field of the present investigation.[1] The case is significant for our purposes as an illustration of the way in which the interplay of physical and human factors combines to bring about or to take away a comparative advantage.

Essentially the same sort of situation, and the same explanation of what at first sight appear to be anomalies, are found in flax culture. Flax being an agricultural article, one might expect it to be produced with ease and with success in a country preëminent in agriculture. Yet in fact it never was produced in considerable quantities in the United States, and it quite dropped out of sight before the middle of the nineteenth century — that is, as soon as the country entered on its characteristic agricultural and industrial development. Attempts to stimulate its production by protective

[1] For an excellent account of various sugar producing regions, cane as well as beet, from which the United States is supplied, see P. G. Wright, Sugar in Relation to the Tariff (1924).

duties, tho repeated in tariff acts to our own days in a curiously perfunctory fashion, have been without effect. On the other hand, flax *seed* — as distinguished from the fibre to which the term flax is commonly applied — continued to be steadily produced. The explanation is identical with that which solves the beet sugar riddle. Flax fibre is a garden or handicraft product; flax seed is a grain crop. The first is a product of intensive agriculture, the second of extensive agriculture.

In the growing of flax for fibre we find the same characteristics as in beet culture, but even more marked. "Horticulture rather than agriculture — soil brought to the best garden tilth — seed sown preferably by hand — the field hand-raked — treading with boards attached to the feet and hand-spading — weeding by hand," — these are the terms used in describing the processes for growing the plant. Harvesting is done by hand; the plant is pulled up, not cut off. "Rippling" and "retting" follow; then comes "scutching" — a succession of laborious hand processes.

Quite different is the practice in growing flax for seed. Here the object is to get not long and fine fibre, but the maximum number of flowering heads that will bear seed. Virgin soil is best. All the modern farm apparatus is used in preparing the soil and planting the seed. In harvesting, machinery of the kind familiar in the United States, drawn by horses or tractors, quickly cuts the standing plants. Power machinery then threshes out the grain.

Flax seed is therefore, like wheat, suited to the frontier: easily produced by extensive culture, satisfactory in quality and homogeneous notwithstanding rough and ready processes, transported and marketed cheaply. Hence it has been a characteristic pioneer product in the United States, and its geographical center has shifted westward across the continent with the movement of the frontier. During the latter part of the nineteenth century and the early part of the twentieth it was grown in great quantities in various other virgin districts of the temperate zone — not only in the Northwest of the United States, but in Argentina and Canada also, the methods of production in the last two regions being copied from those which had developed in the United States.

One disturbing factor has done much to cause it to move quickly from one of these regions to another. A parasitic fungus readily attacks the plant. On fresh soils some years may pass before the wilt gets the upper hand; when it does, either there must be remedial measures or transfer to another region of virgin and uninfected soil. This peculiar difficulty explains the rapidity with which the crop flashes up in great quantities in one region, then disappears from this to appear in equal volume in another of the same type that is distant. As regards its general economic characteristics, flax seed belongs to those products of extensive agriculture in which the American farmer puts his energies to best advantage. And that advantage rests not merely on the physical basis of abundant good land and suitable climate; it rests also on the utilization of the natural resources thru agricultural machinery, cheap transportation, the minimum use of muscle and hand tools, the maximum use of intelligence and of elaborated machines.[1]

I turn now to another set of illustrations, derived from the tariff problems and tariff experiences of the United States with manufactured articles. The economic field is different, but the same principles hold.

The iron manufacture grew enormously during the period of high protection. How far the growth was caused by protection, how far was due to other causes, is a moot question, which I have considered in the volume already referred to.[2] What is significant for the present inquiry is that protection proved curiously uneven in its operations; in some branches of the industry was quite

[1] An admirable account of the contrast between the two phases of flax culture, and of the phases of economic history which it illustrates is given in an article by Mr. W. S. Barker, in the Quarterly Journal of Economics for May, 1917 (Vol. 31, p. 500).

Russia is (or was) a producer both of fibre and of seed, the fibre as a rule not of fine quality. I have been unable to secure information about the relations between this flax culture and the general agricultural conditions of Russia. Agriculture in Russia is extensive, and in some respects shows frontier conditions; but it is not machine-using agriculture. I suspect that the conjunction of flax fibre (not fine) with flax seed is connected with the co-existence of plentiful land and primitive agricultural methods.

[2] Some Aspects of the Tariff Question, Part III, especially Ch. 10.

without effect, in others was followed by great industrial development. The explanation of the differences is again to be found in the fact that the combination and interplay of human and physical causes, while serving to bring about in some directions a comparative advantage in the United States, yet proved by no means equally effective in each and every phase of the industry.

In two quite different parts of the iron and steel manufacture American producers have shown themselves able to produce cheaply, to command the home market, to export. These are on the one hand the heavy industry — crude iron and steel, beams, plates, rails, structural material; and, on the other hand, the making of tools and machines.

In the heavy industry, the richness of the natural resources explains much. The extraordinary coal deposits of the Pittsburgh region, and the no less extraordinary deposits of iron ore on Lake Superior, were the foundations for a burst of development unprecedented in history. But there was much more than this physical advantage. The coal and the ore were a thousand miles apart, and gave opportunity for long distance transportation — a species of industry in which, as I have already remarked, the Americans have achieved unique successes. It is not to be doubted that here, as in other achievements of transportation, a contributing factor has been the existence over the entire continent of absolute and permanent free trade. But still other human elements counted. Large-scale operations, mass production, elaborate plant, labor-saving devices thru standardization of products and of processes — these have been characteristic of American engineering and management. With these, partly as cause and partly as effect, have come the great industrial combinations, both vertical and horizontal, until the industrial unit in the iron trade has exceeded the wildest dreams of the preceding century. The familiar story need not be again rehearsed. Nothing brings into sharper relief the plain fact that here American industry has triumphed; and this not merely because of the bounty of nature, but in large part because of the peculiarly effective application of man's faculties.

As regards the more advanced manufactures of iron and steel, the emphasis shifts. Natural resources become a minor element in explaining the industrial achievements; human factors count most. The comparative advantage is found to rest chiefly on the national character and national aptitude, factors elusive of explanation yet persistent in effect.

A significant indication of the cleavage between industries that prove to have an advantage of this type and those that lack it is found in the export and import situation. Some of these finer manufactures of iron and steel have been steadily sent out of the country and sold in the open foreign market. Others, apparently of the same character, have been steadily imported, and this even in the face of high duties. How can both sorts of trade go on side by side?

Among the articles steadily exported are builders' hardware (such as hinges, locks, door knobs), saws and tools, machinery, cash registers, typewriters, sewing machines, electrical machinery and apparatus, locomotives. In the same class belong (tho not included among "iron manufactures" in the official statistics) agricultural implements and machinery. All have been sold to foreigners in large quantities, year in and year out thru several decades. For this trade there can be only one explanation. The things are made cheaper by Americans than by their foreign competitors, and therefore sold cheaper. In them we have a comparative advantage. Mechanical skill and ingenuity among the inventors and technical directors; organizing and managing capacity among the business leaders; steady and intelligent application by the rank and file in the workshops — all these count. Much also is due to the ability of the American business man in managing a well-devised plant and turning out a large quantity of uniform, standardized, perfected articles. It is significant that tools and implements of all kinds, made in turn with much use of other tools and implements, form the largest items in these exports. And it goes without saying that the domestic market for articles of this kind is supplied by the American manufacturers beyond peradventure.

And yet imports of articles of much the same kind — tools and machines — have continued; imports also of a variety of minor iron and steel products. These apparent exceptions, however, prove on closer examination not to run counter to the principle of comparative advantage; rather they serve to confirm it.

Thus, while the familiar sewing machine for domestic use is made in the United States more cheaply than in foreign countries, certain special machines — for embroideries and for factory work — continue to be imported. The explanation is that few of each special kind are wanted; the processes of manufacture cannot be standardized; the turning out of interchangeable parts by the thousand is not feasible. In making these handwork is called for in greater degree. Under such conditions the characteristic advantage of the American producer disappears. Where ingeniously perfected machinery can be applied in large-scale operations, the American is likely to hold his own, but not where a handicraft skill is needed for a special article.

Similarly, knitting machines have been both imported and exported. A circular automatic machine has been perfected in the United States, and is widely used for the commoner and cheaper grades of cotton knit goods; it is even exported. But a very elaborate German machine for knitting full-fashioned goods continued to be imported; because the fabrics for which it was used were more expensive, smaller quantities were marketable, and hence fewer of the knitting machines were used. Made as the machines were in comparatively small quantities, they were turned out more cheaply in Germany, and most of them were imported.[1]

Some kinds of cutlery, again, are steadily imported; others are not imported at all. Pocket knives have been regularly brought in from England and from Germany; and one of the extreme manifestations of protectionist spirit during the period 1890–1922 was in the high and elaborate duties on this article. Table cutlery, on the other hand, is supplied by the domestic manufacturer without

[1] I speak of the situation as it stood before 1914, and am not informed about the changes that may have taken place in later years.

competition from the foreigners; hence there has been no attempt
to levy particularly high duties. The explanation of the difference
between the two groups is not far to seek. Table cutlery, and more
especially table knives, are made in great quantities of a single
pattern. Automatic machinery, interchangeable parts, standard
patterns, mass production — here the Americans can outstrip
the foreigners. Pocket knives, on the other hand, are little
standardized. There is a bewildering variety of patterns; comparatively small numbers of any one can be put on the market. In
the same class belong carving knives. The Sheffield manufacturer
of these (a petty producer compared to the American table-knife
concern) can hold his own in the American market even in face
of high duties; so can the German "manufacturer," who is in the
main a middleman conducting an industry still in the stage of the
putting-out system. Hence it is that carving knives, like pocket
knives and unlike table knives, continue to be imported in face of
high duties.

The same trend runs thru the American textile industries. The
textile industries give scope for the special American aptitudes in
varying degree, the variations depending mainly on the nature of
the raw materials used. Where the material is homogeneous and
is adapted to treatment by machinery, the Americans can manufacture to advantage. Where it is uneven and does not lend itself
readily to rapid and continuous machine operations, they manufacture to less advantage; and then they clamor most loudly for
protection. Cotton and the cotton industry belong in the former
class; wool and silk, with their respective manufactures, belong
in the second.

I will not detain the reader with any prolonged account of the
development of the textile industries or with any consideration
of the special problems which they present — problems less easy
of solution on any one line of explanation than is the case with
agricultural products or iron and steel manufactures. It is well
known that the cotton manufacture is the oldest and strongest of
the textiles, and that its main body stands independent of pro-

tection. The woolen industry, on the other hand, nearly as old, has continued to need the prop of tariff support; and this to an extent not easy to explain satisfactorily. The manufacture of silks, the youngest of all, has grown with extraordinary speed to great dimensions, and has progressed toward independence in the degree to which its raw material has been made homogeneous and its products amenable to the machine. However different their degree of dependence on protection, each of the textile industries presents within its own limits differences and apparent anomalies analogous to those noted in agriculture and the iron trade. Most of the standard cottons, for example, are made to advantage within the country; but some finer goods and specialties continue to be imported. While most woolen goods need protection, some need protection more than others. Large groups of silk fabrics seem to be independent of protection; but other large groups have by no means reached that stage, and still others are imported in face of high duties. Everywhere we find within the same industry some branches that possess greater advantages than others, or less disadvantages.

The line of cleavage between those textiles that are made to advantage in the United States or with no great disadvantage, and those that labor under so great a disadvantage that they continue to be imported notwithstanding high duties, is most often that between cheaper and medium goods on the one hand, finer and more expensive articles on the other. When it is asked *why* this pervading difference, the answer commonly given is that the finer goods must be more carefully finished and call for more labor; therefore high wages are a peculiarly strong obstacle to their production in the United States. Where machinery can be much used, as with the cheaper goods (such as are made and sold in great quantities), the American producers can more easily hold their own without protection; the explanation, it is said, being that less of the expensive labor is involved and more use is made of machinery. But it requires no great economic insight to see that this only pushes the question back a step. Why is not the machinery itself more expensive? The machinery was made by labor. It is a commonplace in our general economic analysis that a commodity made with much use of machinery is the combined product of two sets of laborers — those who make the instruments and those who operate them. If *all* those whose labor is combined for producing the final result are paid higher wages than in foreign countries, why cannot the foreigners undersell where much machinery is used as well as where little is used?

The real reason why Americans are more likely to hold their own where machinery is much used, and where hand labor plays a comparatively small part in the expenses of production, is that Americans make and use machinery *better*. They turn to labor-saving devices more quickly, and they use devices that save more labor. Sometimes the machinery is lower in price than the same machinery when made abroad, because made with labor more effective. Sometimes it is the same in price, but is utilized better and made to turn out more product per unit of operating force. Sometimes, tho dearer in absolute price, it still is cheaper for use — cheaper relatively to its effectiveness. The result is the same, whatever the details of the differences. The same product costs less money in the United States than in countries not so adept with the machine process, and the same labor turns out more of the product. The question remains one of comparative effectiveness.

I would not be supposed to lay down the final word on this matter — least of all on the *causes* that lead to differences in effectiveness. The Americans, we say, have a greater aptitude in applying machinery. But why this national characteristic? To use a phrase of Professor Veblen's, something more than a taxonomic analysis is called for; we need a genetic explanation. How came it about that Americans developed their special traits? The same question arises with regard to other peoples, their industrial characteristics and their special advantages. The English have long been superior to the French in making the cheaper grades of woolens; the French have been their equals in some among the finer grades, their superiors in others. The French have long had an advantage in certain goods of luxurious or artistic character, such as handsome silks and chinaware; and again in certain sorts of minute and delicate mechanical devices.[1] The Swiss have shown an aptitude for labor-saving appliances and machinery greater than that of most of their neighbors. Germany, where handicraft methods of production seemed deeper rooted than in any other of the modern nations, shifted to the machine process in the latter part of the nineteenth century with surprising rapidity and success. Great Britain had the start in the machine methods and long maintained a preëminent position. While she cannot be said to have lost headway, still less to have moved backward, her position relatively to other countries ceased by the close of the nineteenth century to be that of unquestioned leadership. These differences and shifts have been the occasion for vaunting and vainglory, for national jealousy and recrimination. To the objective mind of science, they present questions of the greatest interest and of the greatest complexity. How are they to be explained? Are they based on the inheritance of racial traits, of which the explanation is to be found in biology? Or are they historical phenomena, quite unrelated to any physical or biological laws, originating perhaps thru the impetus of powerful personalities, persisting chiefly by imitation and habit? Political factors certainly have their influence. The free breath of democracy, the open road to every talent, unquestionably have been factors in the economic development of the United States, and of Switzerland also. Many and various questions arise.

It is beyond the scope of the present volume to consider these additional complexities. Like others on which our inquiry touches, they offer a fruitful field for further investigation. I know no more inviting set of topics for the right kind of economic history —

[1] Lord Lauderdale in a note to his Inquiry into the Nature of Public Wealth (2nd ed. 1818), p. 335, pointed out that even in the eighteenth century there was a well-developed difference in the character of French and English manufactures. The French excelled in fine cloths, rich silks, cambrics and fine linens, looking-glass, china, jewelry, and silversmith work. The English excelled in lower-priced cloths, silk ribbons and mixed goods, linens less fine, common glass, pottery and earthenware, hardware. Lauderdale ascribes the difference to the different distribution of wealth in the two countries. The greater massing of large fortunes and excessive luxury in France caused a demand for luxuries and so a perfecting of their manufacture; the more even distribution of wealth in England caused common articles to be in demand.

not the mere chronicle of what has taken place, but a search for the underlying forces and for the meaning of it all. The problems bear on important matters of economic policy, and indeed focus on the fundamental question of the weight and influence of the various political and legislative steps by which a people's economic development can be promoted. The familiar doctrine of protection to young industries is but one among the obvious aspects of this large group of problems. They are by no means to be neglected in any applications of the reasoning set forth in these pages. But for the present purpose — that of the verification of certain theoretical doctrines — we may accept the dictum of Adam Smith, who, with one of those flashes of insight so often found in the great Scotchman, remarked : "Whether the advantages which one country has over another be natural or acquired, is in this respect of no consequence. As long as the one country has those advantages, and the other wants them, it will always be more advantageous for the latter, rather to buy of the former than to make. It is an acquired advantage only, which one artificer has over his neighbor, who exercises another trade ; and yet they both find it more advantageous to buy of one another, than to make what does not belong to their particular trades." [1]

[1] Wealth of Nations, Bk. 4, Ch. 2 (Vol. 1, p. 423, Cannan edition).

CHAPTER 17

INTERNATIONAL PAYMENTS IN RELATION TO MONETARY SYSTEMS

WE proceed now to a different aspect of the problem of verification. The preceding chapters have dealt with the direction into which a country's labor and capital are turned, with the character of the national industries, with the accord of industrial development, with the theoretical forecast. These are matters of substantive outcome. What we have now to consider is not so much the substantive result as the mechanism by which the result is brought about.[1]

The mechanism is that of international payments. International payments, obviously a part of the general subject of international trade, have had much more attention in the literature of the subject, and especially in its recent literature, than comparative costs and international values. But they have rarely been treated in their relations to these underlying problems. I propose in the following chapters to examine them from just this point of view: to consider how the actual payments made by one country to another are related to the remoter and more fundamental problems of international trade. The inquiry will involve of necessity some consideration of still another field in economics, namely, the theory of money and prices. The present chapter, which is introductory in character, will be given chiefly to those aspects of monetary theory which are closest to the theory of international trade.

To begin, let it be emphasized once more that all the trade — virtually all — is carried on thru transactions between individuals

[1] The reader will bear in mind that this Part thruout is concerned with those countries only and those times in which the monetary systems are on a gold basis. The mechanism of international trade under inconvertible paper is reserved for treatment in Part III. It is the gold standard which has the wider and more enduring range, and is of the greater theoretical and practical importance.

in terms of money. In the ordinary course of affairs there is no conscious exchange of goods for goods. There are sales of goods, or payments for services which are liquidated in terms of money. Money, current funds, what the business man regards as cash, must be remitted from country to country. The illustrative figures presented in the first Part of this volume were worked out in terms of prices, and then in terms of money incomes, with the express object of directing attention to the details of the process by which eventual results were brought about. It is obvious that everything in the calculations rests on the assumption that the flow of specie affects the prices and money incomes of the trading countries. An inflow of specie causes prices and money wages to rise; an outflow causes them to fall. The whole train of reasoning rests, in this way, on the assumption of the quantity theory of money.

I say "in this way," because the quantity theory, when formulated in strict consistency with the premises from which it starts, involves something more than the mere proposition that an increase of the money supply raises prices, a decrease lowers them. Stated with logical accuracy, it involves the further proposition that the changes in prices are precisely in accord with the changes in the quantity of money: that prices double (the quantity of goods remaining the same) if money is doubled in quantity, are halved if the money is halved. As regards the mechanism of international trade, however, it makes no difference whether this precise formulation of the doctrine be accepted. It suffices if the course of prices and incomes be influenced merely in the stated direction. If an inflow of specie into a country causes prices and wages to rise, the consequences envisaged by the theory of international trade take place irrespective of the exact degree of correspondence between the two movements. It is not of importance for our inquiry whether there be adherence to the semi-mathematical and rigorously consistent formulation of the quantity doctrine.

In another regard, however, it is of great importance for the theory of international trade whether the relation between money movements and the level of prices be stated in a guarded or a loose way. Stated guardedly, the quantity doctrine examines the relation between *all* forms of the circulating medium on the one hand and the volume of goods (or "transactions") on the other. When set forth in this way, and with attentive consideration of the many and complex factors which enter into the determination of the total volume of effective money, the doctrine cannot, in my judgment, be controverted.[1] But the thing important for the mechanism of international payments, in relation to the theory of international trade, is not the validity of the complex and guarded doctrine. What signifies is a more special and limited proposition, namely, that the specie constituent has a peculiar and determinative effect on the range of prices. The specie which thus is of dominant consequence is such as moves freely from country to country in settlement of international balances; in our modern world, primarily gold. Yet gold is but a minor item in the heterogeneous list of things which make up the circulating medium of modern countries — bank notes and government notes, subsidiary coin, above all the great structure of bank credits and bank deposits. (I speak here, needless to say, of countries in which the whole mass rests on a specie basis, still leaving for later consideration the case of inconvertible paper.) This minor constituent, none the less, as it moves from country to country, is supposed to affect prices and wages, to cause changes in the quantities of goods exported and imported, to bring about notable readjustments in the terms of international exchange and in the prosperity of the trading countries.

The questions of the mechanism of international trade, then, become related not so much to the general reasoning of monetary theory as to the reality of the connection of prices with specie movements. They become questions on the one hand of the *sensitiveness* of prices to specie inflow and outflow, on the other hand of the ultimate *domination* of prices by these movements. No one can now reason, as Ricardo and Mill did, on the supposition that the circulating medium of a modern country consists exclusively of gold, or that an increase or decrease in the gold supply

---

[1] I would refer the reader to what I have said on this large subject in my Principles of Economics, 3d edition, Chapter 30.

brings a corresponding change in its total monetary supply or an immediate effect on its level of prices. But it is entirely possible that the total of the medium of exchange may be sensitive to gold movements — may shrink in some degree when gold flows out, expand in some degree when gold flows in. And it is also entirely possible that the gold movements may have a dominating influence on the monetary total; that this total is not only sensitive to them, but remains sensitive to continued movements of gold in the same direction, and that the direction is ultimately determined by them. To put it in another way, it is entirely possible that the course of prices in a country is sensitive to the international movement of specie, and also that in the long run the course of its prices is determined by that movement.

These two questions — of sensitiveness and of domination — are not unrelated. There could not be domination without sensitiveness; and continuing sensitiveness leads to domination. Nevertheless it will be convenient to consider them independently. We may turn first to the question of sensitiveness.

The forms of the medium of exchange (other than gold itself) which bulk largest in modern times are, on the one hand, paper money payable to bearer in the form of bank notes or government notes, and, on the other hand, bank deposits. Among these, government notes are obviously of the non-sensitive kind. Such, for example, are our own United States notes (greenbacks) and the Dominion notes of the government of Canada. Such were Reichskassenscheine of the pre-war German system. Bank of England notes are in the same class; they too are fixed in amount and indeed are in effect government notes. Most issues of bank notes, however, are in some degree flexible, and thus at least potentially sensitive. The deposits which constitute the other form of bank money, and which are by far the largest item in English-speaking countries, are least of all fixed in amount either by law or by custom, and are most of all — at least potentially — sensitive. Hence it is the connection between bank operations on the one hand and changes in prices on the other which must chiefly engage our attention.

The link of connection, it is hardly necessary to say, is in the bank rate of discount. The rate of discount tends to rise as bank reserves become less, to fall as they become greater. It is specie which is the variable and shifting constituent in the money available for bank reserves — the money that can always be used for payments *by* the bank. The other forms of money which may be permissible for such payments, such as government notes, are usually fixed in volume once for all. Hence it is the inflow or outflow of specie which primarily affects the discount policy of the banks. Their discount policy in turn affects the volume of accommodation which they offer to the borrowing public, and this in turn affects the volume of notes and deposits outstanding. In such fashion the international movement of specie may impinge promptly and effectively on the actual circulating medium of a country, on the general spirit and trend of its mercantile and trading operations, on the ups and downs of its price level.

Next, as regards domination — the ultimate consequences, not the immediate. Notes and deposits, so the usual reasoning goes, are in the last resort dependent for their volume on the specie into which they are convertible and on which they rest as on a foundation. The relation between foundation and superstructure may not be precise; a given basis of specie will not always support the same volume of bank money; but in the end an increase in the specie basis will lead to a roughly corresponding addition to the amount of active notes and deposits. As regards notes, the details of the legislation of the several countries necessarily affect the degree of correspondence. As regards deposits, legislation played its part, and still plays it, in the case of the United States, the one country where the law has specifically regulated the amount of the reserves which banks must hold against deposits. Elsewhere, in the absence of legislation, it is custom and the very necessities of the case which compel the banks to hold in their vault some legal-tender money and to keep their volume of deposit obligations in some relation to these holdings. In all the deposit-using countries the general tendency among competing banks is for each one to swell its business (*i.e.* its loans and deposits) to the maximum permitted by law or by custom or by the necessities of the banking and currency situation. With an increase in reserves, say thru an inflow of specie from abroad, deposits will increase too; with a decrease, deposits too will fall.

Further: the closeness of the connection between reserves and deposits may be stated in rigid terms or in flexible terms. In the days when the older legislation regulated the reserves of the national banks of the United States, it was not uncommon to speak of 25 per cent (*mutatis mutandis*, as the per cent required by law was different) as the fixed and unvarying reserve of American banks. Deposits, it was assumed, amounted to four times the reserve, and in that ratio regularly moved up and down with the reserve. More in accord with the actual course of events was the postulate that the relation is flexible. Even under these earlier legislative requirements and under the traditions built up on them, banks did not always and necessarily expand their operations when in possession of larger reserves than the law prescribed. Banks might wish to expand in this way; but the extent to which they could go depended on the temper of the business community. And so it is at all times and under all legislative conditions. The upbuilding of deposits on the basis of a given reserve does not proceed automatically. If the period be one of buoyancy, optimism, disposition to expand, banks will easily and quickly increase their loans and deposits. If it be one of caution and uneasiness, they will not be able to expand, even tho desirous of doing so and equipped to do so. During the upward phase of the business cycle, and especially in its later stages, when trade is active and the future looks bright, deposits will swell to the very utmost which reserves can support. Subsequently, in the trough of the downward movement, reserves become larger than the banks need or wish; nevertheless, they find themselves unable to extend loans and deposits and use their resources to the full. If, indeed, a smoothed curve be constructed, extending over a considerable period and including more than one business cycle, a close relation will appear; deposits will be found to move in a fairly constant proportion to reserves.

The relation is not unfailing; an element of the unpredictable remains. But, given a bank or a set of banks for which the ruling motive is the aim to secure the maximum profit, deposits will increase in the long run as reserves increase, and will decrease as reserves decrease.

Let us now take up once again the matter of sensitiveness. It is connected, obviously, with that of domination; yet it raises some problems of its own. They can best be considered by classifying countries according to the degree in which their monetary systems are sensitive. In some countries the conditions are (or have been) such that an inflow or outflow of specie might be expected to bring quick response in the banking and currency situation. In others the response is slow and uncertain.

The classic instance of marked and continuing sensitiveness is that of Great Britain, as her monetary system stood in pre-war days, and again stood after the resumption of specie payments in 1925. With a great utilization of deposit banking and a towering mass of demand obligations in the form of deposits, the banks habitually carried in reserves, as the basis of it all, the bare minimum necessary for the recurrent daily demands for cash over the counter. For the banking system as a whole no increase of money available for reserve could take place except thru the importation of specie. The Bank of England was the one source to which a joint-stock bank (the ordinary bank) could turn for cash. Bank of England notes were virtually gold certificates, varying in amount with the amount of gold held by the Bank. The Bank's holdings of gold in turn fluctuated chiefly with the conditions of international payments — the foreign inflow or the foreign drain. The Bank then, according to the extent of its gold reserve, made it easy or hard for the ordinary banks to maintain or replenish their cash, using its rate of discount to them as the means of regulating loans, thereby deposits, thereby command of cash. Being chiefly a bankers' bank, its discount rate to banks served to regulate the general discount market. The links of connection were close: gold inflow and outflow, bank discount rates, the loosening or restriction of loans and deposits, the temper and spirit of the business community, the trend toward rising or falling prices.

The influence thus exercised by gold holdings and by gold inflow or outflow was strengthened by still another circumstance; namely, that gold was the only kind of money available for ordinary cash transactions. Not quite the only kind, since subsidiary coin also played its part. But subsidiary coin is only the small change of the circulating medium, a minor element, whose amount is essentially the result, not a cause, of fluctuations in the volume of transactions and in prices. Gold, on the other hand, may be called the large change. Yet gold also, in such a monetary system as Great Britain had before the war, becomes of far less direct importance in effecting payments than the deposits. It is a minor element so far as used merely for hand-to-hand payments. As with small change, the amount in circulation is a result rather than a cause. When more goods are bought and sold, or the same goods at higher prices — when there are more people employed, or the same people employed at higher wages — banks find that more large change (gold coin) is called for over the counter. At all times that which recurrently comes back to them in the ordinary course of circulation tends steadily to flow out again. In times of rising activity, not merely as much tends to flow out as comes in, but more.

In this way a new sort of influence sets in. Since the gold which constitutes the large change is the only money available for bank reserves, the reserves themselves become subject to an internal drain. More active business and higher prices mean, for a system like that of Great Britain, that more cash is asked for over the counter; more gold or more Bank of England notes, or (since 1914) more government notes. While the volume of gold which circulates in ordinary transactions is proximately a result of higher prices, that same domestic stock of gold — the one and only item that has flexibility — becomes ultimately, and indeed by no long-sustained process, a force which presses on trade and prices.

Conversely, a decline in trade activity means that less gold is called for over the counter. Banks' holdings of gold tend to become larger than needed for the every-day calls. The reserves both of the ordinary banks and of the Bank of England itself become comparatively abundant; conditions which do not indeed lead automatically to larger bank loans and larger deposits, but which make expansion easy at a subsequent stage, when general trade conditions and the temper of the business community rise to the possibilities, as sooner or later they will hardly fail to do.

A somewhat different case, yet one in which the degree of sensitiveness is at least equally great, appears in Canada. It deserves attention because the experiences of Canada will be found in the sequel to be peculiarly instructive as regards some problems of verification.

The essentials of the banking system of Canada can be stated in a few words.[1] A small number of banks, most of them having individually large capital, large business, and many branches; a wide use of deposit banking; and, most significant for the present purpose, legal tender money partly gold, but mainly government paper issued on a plan virtually like that of Bank of England notes, and therefore dependent for its flexibility on an increase or decrease of the gold held against it by the government. The physical gold money is almost all in government vaults, the banks themselves using the government notes both as reserve and in counter payments. So far the system is very like the British.

The Canadian system differs from the British, however, in one important respect. The banks can issue notes, not indeed quite without limit (no bank may have notes in excess of capital), but with sufficient freedom to enable them to meet the daily demands for large change at their counters. Hence the particular kind of limitation on bank expansion which has just been described for Great Britain does not exist in Canada. Banking reserves and banking operations are not affected (virtually not) by any internal drain of gold. It is only an international movement which brings pressure on them. The situation as a whole presents the

[1] I refer to the Canadian system as it stood before the Great War, and as it stood again when the effects of the war had cleared away; neglecting, that is, the intervening period when there was not convertibility into gold.

simplest case — at least for recent times — of a banking system in which bank notes as well as bank deposits are allowed to grow or shrink freely, in which specie plays a very slight part in the circulating medium, in which the entire structure, while it rests on specie, yet rests on a slender basis of specie. In sum, it is one in which we may expect a high degree both of sensitiveness to the international flow of specie and of domination by that flow.

Somewhat different, again, and yet in many ways similar to Great Britain and Canada was the United States during the period from 1879 to 1914 — from the resumption of specie payments to the establishment of the Federal Reserve System. Deposits, functioning in the concrete form of checks, formed the largest constituent in the circulating medium. The eager competition of a multitude of banks, and the general atmosphere of enterprise and money-making, led each and every bank to expand to the maximum. That maximum was in part limited by law, in part was made somewhat elastic because of the difference in policy between the more conservative and the more venturesome institutions and directorates. It was affected, too, in no small degree by the factor of demand for counter cash and large change. Bank notes, while more elastic, more available for counter purposes, than in Great Britain, were much less so than in Canada. Issued as they were under the restrictions of the National Bank legislation, they responded very uncertainly to the varying calls for large change. During the period when the silver issues competed with them — a period, moreover, when the legislative restrictions fettered them most — they showed virtually no response to such calls. In the later period, after 1893, the fetters were less severely felt. Yet even then bank notes were issued only in very uncertain accord with fluctuations in the demands for large change; and, as regards an individual bank, hardly a trace of connection could be found between the circulation of that bank's notes and the calls on that bank for counter cash. The other items of hand-to-hand money — United States notes, silver dollars and certificates — were fixed in amount; tho the volume in actual circulation was affected somewhat by the operations of the Government Treasury (the "Independent Treasury"), whose policy it was to hold more of cash in its vaults at some times, at other times to push cash into circulation.

The gold was held by banks as reserves. A considerable part, nevertheless, was in everyday circulation, chiefly in the form of gold certificates. The total available was steadily swelled by the output of the domestic mines, which found its way regularly to the mints and to the channels of circulation or reserve. As regards quick drain or quick replenishment the supply was subject to the international movement only. Here was the one really flexible item. It was mainly from this source that a demand for larger bank reserves could be met; and it was thru this that a drain on bank reserves made itself felt most effectively. The dominating effect which the international movement might be expected to show was merely mitigated and concealed by the considerable supplies of gold from the domestic mines and by the heterogeneous character of the rest of the circulating cash. The case thus resembles in some essential features the British and Canadian: deposits swelled as a rule to the maximum; reserves not far from the minimum; bank discounts and loans, the money market and the tone of trade, easily and quickly affected by the cash holdings of the banks; those cash holdings having as their variable or flexible constituents the monetary supply of gold; this supply of gold swelled with increments from the domestic mines at a fairly steady rate, but subject to variation mainly from the international movement.[1]

In all countries using deposits and checks freely, the looseness of the connection between bank reserves and bank deposits leads not infrequently to a chronological order different from that assumed in the Ricardian reasoning. An inflow of specie may

---

[1] I say "mainly" from the international movement. It is true that the United States Treasury was at times a factor, endeavoring as it did to influence the banking and business situation by letting cash out from its holdings or impounding it. This endeavor to exercise a stabilizing influence, however, was not steadily maintained; it proved of varying and often of negligible effect. It was no more than a tentative and wavering precursor of the deliberate and well-equipped procedure for the same purpose which was subsequently incorporated in the Federal Reserve System.

follow, not precede, an enlargement of the circulating medium
and a rise in prices. So it may be, at least, for a short time,
even for a period of many months. Indeed, if there be further
forces at work than those merely monetary, it may remain so for
years.

This apparently anomalous sequence of events results from the
looseness of the connection between deposits and reserves; a circumstance which leads in so many directions to caution in making
hard and fast statements. Deposits, to repeat once again, are not
dependent on reserves in any automatic or mechanical way. In
times of buoyancy, loans and deposits expand, and prices tend to
rise. Unless the margin of cash happens to be at the very minimum, there will always be some play for an upward movement
without immediate pressure on the cash in hand. And if at the
moment the banks happen to have reserves not merely adequate
but abundant, the upward movement can go on for a considerable
time without strain of any kind. But as bank operations reach
the full amount which the cash reserves can easily support, the
rate of discount rises and money becomes tight. The expansion
of loans and deposits is not thereby necessarily checked at once,
still less does it cease entirely. The banks sail closer to the wind
and keep a sharp look-out, but they still find business good, and
do not cut their customers down. Thereupon specie begins to
flow in from abroad, tempted by the higher rates of interest on
current funds. The inflow thus follows the general expansion,
does not precede it. True, this is not the invariable order. The
flow of specie is dependent on conditions in other financial centers, and it will take place most easily and abundantly if there
is quiescence elsewhere, or less activity. But often enough its
inflow of specie will be proximately the result rather than the
cause of expansion.

This, however, is but a first stage, and by no means definitive.
Just as the tight money market attracts specie imports, the rising
prices attract commodity imports. Rising commodity imports
bring increasing obligations to make payments to foreign countries; and they tend to a reverse movement — a drain of specie.

The import of goods may readily come at a somewhat later stage than that of specie; since the movement of goods is more sluggish than that of gold. But come it will, and then the inward flow of specie will be followed by a current the other way. Prices cannot continue to advance indefinitely as they may during the first stage. On the contrary, they will tend to be brought back to a level that is in accord with the normal long-run relation between cash basis and credit superstructure. Just as a sustained inflow of specie will in the end push prices upward, so an upward movement of prices, even tho initiated merely thru deposit expansion, cannot persist unless supported by this same force — a sustained inflow of specie.

A sustained inflow of specie may of course be induced by other forces. There may be some cause of an extraneous character, acting of itself to make the balance of payments continuously favorable to the country in which expansion has begun. If, for example, the country is in the early stage of large borrowings — if a succession of loans from abroad is in course of being contracted — the proceeds of the loans will provide the means for paying for added imports. While advancing prices will tempt imports, the loans, so long as they continue, enable them to be paid for from year to year. They may even enable still more specie to flow in, and so give support to a still further advance in prices and still further imports. The process may go on *crescendo*, until at last there is a halt in the lending operations, not unlikely to be sudden, and marked by a financial and industrial crash. During the years of the upswing period, the import of specie into the borrowing country may seem to be due at each several date to the higher prices and the higher money rates to follow these, not precede them. But these higher prices could not be maintained, much less could move still higher, unless the flow of specie came to the rescue, so to speak. And it could not be a supporting factor for the persisting expansion unless there were some other force at work, such as an international loan. Of all this the experience of Canada, to be referred to presently, offers a striking illustration.

Differing widely from the monetary systems of the English-speaking countries are those of the Continent of Europe. In them also banking operations and currency supplies are intertwined, but in another way and with consequences not the same. The use of deposits and checks is small as compared with the English-speaking countries; a difference which alone entails fundamental differences in the working of the entire monetary mechanism.

A representative case for the Continent — representative, that is, for the purpose of the present inquiry — is, or rather was, that of France. With a specie standard and with specie convertibility (conditions happily so long maintained, and presumably to be restored in the future) the circulating medium consisted of gold, Bank of France notes, and silver in the form of the over-valued "limping" 5 franc pieces and of subsidiary coin. The silver is for our purposes negligible, being virtually fixed, moderate in amount, a passive element.[1] The gold and the Bank of France notes were the active elements, and they were also the flexible elements. The Bank's notes were not restricted in amount, or regulated as regards the conditions of issue. There was indeed a maximum, but it was never permitted to operate as a real restriction. A large amount of gold coin was in every-day circulation, and, what was more important, a great store was constantly held in the vaults of the Bank of France. A drain of gold for foreign remittance was easily met from the Bank's holdings; an inflow of gold from abroad was as easily absorbed in those holdings. The varying internal calls for cash, on the other hand, were usually met by notes paid out over the counter, mainly in the course of dealings with financial and commercial institutions. Internal movements of specie, out of the Bank and into it, tho subject to seasonal shifts and occasionally to commercial vicissitudes, showed no marked changes except over long periods of time. The Bank's great stores of gold served as a reservoir, mitigating and smoothing the effect of the one irregular factor, the international flow of gold. Its large

---

[1] I doubt whether the possibility of sending the 5 franc pieces to and fro between the countries of the Latin Union should lead to any significant qualification of this statement.

holdings of the metal, coupled with its power to issue more or less of notes as commercial transactions varied, enabled it to maintain its rate of discount at a singularly stable level. And that stability was a matter of deliberate policy. The dominant place of the Bank in the general credit and financial transactions of the country — its position as preëminently a bankers' bank, buttressed by its monopoly of note issue and its large "encaisse" — enabled it to impart stability not only to its banking policy but to the entire monetary and credit structure of the country.

As regards sensitiveness, it thus appears that France was in a situation by no means the same as that of Great Britain and the other deposit-using countries. What with the large circulation of actual gold, and the strong position and fixed policy of her great Bank, there was sluggishness in the response to an international movement of specie. True, that movement was watched with interest and even with concern by the French financial community. There was a steady disposition to influence it in the direction of promoting the inflow of gold. But it was not allowed to impinge quickly on discount rates, bank operations, bank credits. Nor could any foreign gold movement serve to increase or decrease effectively the total circulating medium, except over long periods of time. As compared with the total gold in France — that in circulation plus the Bank of France's holdings — the import or export of the metal in any one year, or over several years, was a small matter.

No doubt, gold was the dominant factor in the French monetary system. A steadily continuing increase or decrease of the country's gold could not fail to have its effect on prices. Domination thus there was, even tho not sensitiveness. But the situation serves to bring into sharp relief a factor which Ricardo and his followers habitually neglected — the element of time. Given time, a country whose circulating medium consists solely or mainly of gold must find its prices vary with changes in the gold supply. But the time required for any measurable effect on prices may be long; and while the long-drawn-out process is in course of operation, any number of other factors may also come into operation, strengthening or mitigating this one influence and always veiling it. Hence in such a country it is peculiarly difficult to trace the concrete working of the forces of international trade. There is nothing like the sensitiveness of the deposit-using countries, in which a great structure of credit money rests on a slender basis of reserves. There is the persistent steadiness of a circulating medium in which actual gold is used in a great mass of daily transactions.

It is not necessary to go further in the consideration of the monetary conditions of other countries of Continental Europe. Most of them, as they stood in the gold-standard days, presented features resembling the French. When the specie supply was less abundant, as for example in Italy and Austria, there was greater sensitiveness to gold movements. But it was then a sensitiveness rather of the standard of circulation than of the circulating medium itself, and raised questions more akin to those of trade under inconvertible paper than to those of trade with free gold movement. Where the gold supply was abundant and the metal was freely used in every-day payments, as in Germany and Belgium, there was resemblance to the French type, yet with variants. The German situation of pre-war days had some features of its own. Note issue was regulated and restricted; deposits and postal-checking accounts were coming into steadily greater use; the habits of the people in using money were changing almost as fast as population and industrial growth. The general result was that the monetary system, tho by no means so sensitive to specie flow as that of England — indeed, meant to be protected from disturbance by a deliberate bank policy — yet was less sluggish than that of France. But, to repeat, it is not necessary to go farther in this sort of description. What has been said suffices to show how great are the differences between countries, how complex and heterogeneous are the several monetary systems. Obviously it is needful to bear in mind the nature and the mechanism of these systems in any attempt to follow the working of the forces analyzed in the pure and simple theory — operating, as those forces must, thru specie movements and thru price changes.

We may turn for a moment to another and different case, that of the United States after the establishment of the Federal Reserve System.

The features in this system which are important for our purpose are the attenuation of reserves in the ordinary commercial banks; the accumulation of a great reserve of gold in the Federal Reserve Banks; and very flexible conditions for the issue of notes. The credit and money mechanism, one might imagine, thereby was made more sensitive, since the banks as a whole operated with less cash in hand. Yet in fact it was made less so because of the enormous store of gold concentrated in the Reserve Banks and the wide flexibility of note issue.

The law, as is well known (I assume the reader to be familiar with its main features), prescribes a minimum of 35 per cent against the deposits of the Reserve Banks, 40 per cent against the notes. But it was expected, when the system was established, that substantially more than the minimum would normally be kept — perhaps 50 per cent — at all events some very conservative and amply adequate proportion. While the proportion actually held during the war and for a short period after its close was not greatly above the required minimum, the unexampled post-war conditions soon brought into the United States such an influx of specie that the gold holdings of the Reserve System came to constitute a formidable problem, not because they were unduly small, but because they were quite needlessly large.

The point important for the present purpose is that the system was designed to regulate in some deliberate and systematic way the international gold flow and the effects of that flow on domestic trade and domestic prices. The system was expected to protect the country's financial and industrial structure against the impact of international gold movements, while yet it left the situation potentially sensitive, the degree of sensitiveness depending on the principles and policy of the governing official bodies. A great reserve in the Federal Banks obviously can serve as a buffer against external strain. Pressure from an inflowing gold supply may be easily absorbed by it; the Federal Banks can prevent the pressure from being transmitted to the ordinary banks and the general trade of the country. Conversely, an outflow may simply diminish the store held by them, again leaving the country at large undisturbed. And yet everything depends on the way in which the enormous store is handled. The system may be so administered as to render banking operations, credit adjustments, the trend of prices, closely dependent on the volume and the movement of the central reserve, and thereby on the imports and exports of specie; or it may make the dependence remote and uncertain.

At the time of the adoption of the system something like the European practice of pre-war days was probably contemplated: a normal reserve well above the minimum; not much attention to minor movements of the reserve, whether up or down, and these not allowed to impinge on the general credit structure; none the less, defense of the reserve, thru discount rates, whenever considerable and continuing drains set in; and, conversely, ready release from the reserve for seasonal or temporary remittances, indeed for very considerable outflow when the remittances swelled to dimensions much above the normal. But the establishment of any settled policy, the development of any traditions, was impossible either during the Great War or in the years immediately succeeding. I shall point out in a subsequent chapter[1] how anomalous was the character of the international trade of the United States during and after the war, and how different were the occurrences from anything contemplated in the theoretic analysis of the ordinary or "normal" conditions. It is enough here to note that the Federal Reserve System was designed to have a smoothed and moderated sensitiveness; one in which the movements of gold from country to country would be made smoother and less abrupt than in earlier days, and subject to some deliberate and methodical regulation; yet not in the end with effects different from those contemplated in pre-war theory and practice. It would seem probable that in time — when the far-ramifying disturbances of the war are at last effaced — some such situation will emerge. But it would now (1926) be quite rash to predict.

[1] Chapter 25, pp. 307–334.

CHAPTER 18

The Foreign Exchanges and the International Movement of Securities

Some further aspects of the movement of specie from country to country will be considered in the present chapter: the influence of dealings in foreign exchange, and the somewhat similar influence of the international movement of securities.

It is not within the scope of this book to follow the details of the mechanism of the foreign exchanges. The intricacies of the subject are adequately set forth in the books on this special subject, and need the less attention here because they are of little significance for the broader problems of international trade. There is occasion for no more than a summary statement of the way in which dealings and speculations in the foreign exchanges serve to postpone, to smooth, to reduce to a minimum, the actual transmission of gold.

If there were no such thing as speculative purchases and sales of foreign exchange, the rate (the price of bills on a foreign country) would always stand in one of three positions. It would be at the first position (par) when imports and exports exactly balanced; or rather, when the total of all payments, including non-merchandise items, exactly balanced. It would be at the second position (specie-export point), when the balance of payments was against the country; and at the third (specie-import point), when the balance of payments was toward the country.

In fact, the rate fluctuates all thru the range between the two extremes, and only by accident is it at any one time precisely at the parity point. This unstable and shifting situation is due to the calculations and trading of the bankers and brokers who buy and sell exchange. They sell forward, at less than the export point, when they believe the current of payments will turn the other way in due time; they buy exchange in advance, if they believe it can be done with profit in anticipation of a subsequent turn the other way. The rate of interest on short-time loans — the rate of discount — necessarily plays a large part in their operations. The transactions are often intricate, and are often on a great scale, involving millions in the aggregate, with an extremely small margin from which to eke out a profit. What is important for our purpose is that the general effect is to reduce the flow of gold to the minimum. The variations in the substantive transactions — in imports and exports — are thus made to offset each other. In the trade of the United States, for example, the autumnal excess of merchandise exports is made to provide means for paying for the usual spring excess of imports. And not only these fairly predictable oscillations are made to equalize each other, but irregular fluctuations also, in which the foreign exchange market has more of the gambling element. It would be pushing the point too far to say that gold flows with difficulty, or in the last resort only. It flows readily enough as soon as the necessary fractional profit can be figured out. But all the possibilities of securing the profit in other ways than thru the actual transport of gold are scanned with the same keen eye, and the other ways are utilized in the vast majority of the transactions.

The same smoothing of irregularities and discordances tends to be brought about by the virtual pooling of the foreign exchanges of the world as a whole. Not two countries alone are engaged in trade with each other, but many with many others. Commonly there will be discrepancies in the balance of payments between any two. The United States will sell more to Great Britain than Great Britain buys from the United States, but will buy more from Brazil than it sells to Brazil. Great Britain will buy more from the United States than she sells thither, but will sell more in Japan than she buys. In the talk of the street on international trade, and often also in the more pretentious talk of public men, much is made of the so-called "favorable" or "unfavorable" balances with individual countries. It is superfluous to remark that they signify nothing as regards the advantage secured by one country from its trade with that other country or with all countries. What they do mainly signify is that all those balances are handled by the exchange market as a series of connected items. The buying and selling of exchange by the dealers in the several countries bring it about that a payment due from the United States to Brazil for coffee is easily effected thru bills of exchange on London drawn against American exports of cotton to Great Britain. The dealers in exchange watch the whole financial world, and exert their ingenuity — spurred by remarkably keen competition — toward effecting remittances at the minimum expense. The actual transportation of gold is a comparatively dear way of settling the balances. Hence not only are present and future sales of commodities calculated or guessed at, present and future carrying charges in the way of interest worked out, but the existing and prospective supplies of bills on the several countries against each and every other country are followed with trained eyes. A present deficiency is met by a subsequent surplus; a debit balance payable to one country is met by a credit balance available against another country. Such is the net effect, in normal times, of the speculative operations of the professional dealers in the foreign exchange markets.

A similar smoothing and equalizing ensues from the holding by large banks, and especially by the great public banks, of bills of exchange on foreign countries and especially on gold standard countries. In pre-war days these were most commonly sterling bills; in post-war days they have often been dollar bills. Often they are treated as a "reserve," and in gold standard countries are often regarded as in effect the same as a gold stock. In whatever way law or custom treats them as reserve, they are in fact simply a means of enabling demands for remittances abroad to be met without trenching on actual gold. When deliberately held in considerable quantities, they serve, even more obviously than the speculative operations of the exchange dealers, to prevent the ups and downs of international payments from disturbing the monetary situation. They constitute a reservoir of foreign exchange from which an outflow can be easily met and into which an inflow can be readily absorbed. In connection with a discount policy aiming at the same result — the elimination or minimizing of a flow of gold — they have the appearance of dominating the situation. Sometimes, indeed, they are treated in the modern literature of our subject as if this were *the* factor that needed to be watched, wisely handled, adequately safeguarded; as if it were the core and substance of the problem of international payments. Altogether too much stress is thus put on the importance of a "defensive" bank policy, on the efficiency of this device toward maintaining stability of credit and prices. It operates essentially as the foreign exchange market does in the absence of any deliberate regulatory policy; and there is no clear evidence to show that under normal trade conditions it operates better. It is merely one of the several devices that enable international payments to offset one another with the minimum of friction.

Still another equalizing factor is the movement of securities that have an international market. They are sold between the great financial centers in a way that replaces or lessens the transmission of gold. Just as lending and borrowing have come to play a much larger part in international trade than was reckoned with in the earlier discussions, so have the sales and purchases of securities. This is true not only of those securities which had their origin in international loans, but of others also which at the outset had no international character but in the course of time have come to be quoted in the financial markets of different countries. They are bought and sold, sent this way and that, on a fractional difference in price. In the so-called arbitrage business — buying in one market with a view to reselling at once by cable in another — a great volume of transactions is carried on at an astonishingly small spread between buying and selling price, as is the case in the closely related purchases and sales of bills of exchange. In both sets of operations, the current rate on short-time loans is a commanding factor. In any given financial center, a tight-money market and a high discount rate tend to lower the prices of the "active" securities, and of the international securities among them; just as they tend, by increasing the carrying charges, to lower the price of exchange on foreign countries. An inflow of gold, which might be expected to take place toward the country of tight money, is replaced by an outward movement of securities. That movement of securities in itself tends to lessen the differences between the two money markets, both as regards security prices and interest rates, and so tends to lessen the immediate pressure toward a movement of gold.

These short-time transfers of securities from one market to another are not unrelated to the international investment operations, that is, the loans and interest payments whose more permanent effects have already been analyzed and will engage our attention further as we proceed. International loans take place thru the sale of securities which soon have an international market. Tho at the outset the effect of the loan is to cause a remittance in one direction only — from the lending country to the borrowing, from the country that has bought the bonds to the country which has sold them — the bonds or stocks at an early date come to be bought and sold in the financial market of both. They are likely to drift to and fro under the influence of the general conditions of trade and of the money market. Underneath this drift there remain the deeper currents. On the whole, securities are sold by the borrowing country during the earlier stage of its international investment operations, and move toward the lending country. And on the whole, when the borrowing country has grown to economic maturity, it tends to buy back its securities; a movement the other way sets in. The several flows intermingle, and at any given time it may not be easy to discern which is dominant — the more noticeable, which is impelled by the money markets of the moment, or the less conspicuous undercurrent which depends on the trend of investment.

The effects of the movement of securities are by no means always of the moderating and offsetting kind. A financial collapse, or a marked depression, in one financial market may cause securities to move thence to another, and so introduce a new substantive factor in foreign trade operations. It may lead to a shift in foreign exchange, a movement of specie, a disturbance of money markets, — all of which in turn have their effects on prices of commodities and on the sales of commodities between countries. Such, for example, was the effect of the agitation for the free coinage of silver in the United States in the first half of the decade 1890–1900. European holders lost confidence in American securities and sold large quantities of them in the New York market. After 1896, with the strong prospect of maintenance of the gold standard, renewed confidence in turn caused many of them to be bought back in the European markets. The international trade of Italy between 1880 and 1900 was similarly affected by fall and rise of confidence among foreign investors in Italian government securities. As will appear in the sequel, the entire effect of international lending operations is much less regular and predictable than the theoretic analysis would seem to indicate. The irregularity appears not only in the long-time swings of investment, in the changes of commodity imports and exports with swelling investments of capital and the subsequent swelling accumulations of interest payments; it appears also in those movements of securities, even less predictable, which are influenced by confidence, prestige, market availability. In ordinary times, when all goes smoothly, the existence of a large range of stocks and bonds which can easily move to and fro exercises a stabilizing influence on international trade. In times of disturbance, however, that same circumstance may become an independent cause of still further disturbance, and not least an independent cause of gold movements.

This sketch — so brief that it almost calls for an apology — of the various ways in which the international movement of gold may be staved off by various devices and reduced to a minimum, has been introduced in order to emphasize the complexity and the delicacy of the mechanism of international payments. This part of the economic world may be likened, indeed, not so much to a mechanism as to a sensitive organism that reacts to every quickening or slackening of its life-blood. There is sensitiveness, not impassive resistance. In the last resort, when all expedients for adjusting and equalizing the payments between nations have been utilized and exhausted, specie will flow in payment of balances. When trade is following its ordinary peaceful course, in a world not racked by political or economic cataclysms, it is likely to flow in small volume, even in driblets. Each driblet, slight tho it be, affects a susceptible spot, and tends to be minimized by reaction in some other part of the delicate adjustment. But if there be a succession of such influences — if there be a continued lack of equilibrium between a country's debits and credits — something more happens. There is then no way of resisting the inevitable readjustment. Sustained changes in the demand for goods, or continuing remittances on other than merchandise account, will show their consequences sooner or later in the international distribution of specie. *Then* the question becomes one of changes in prices and money incomes, and involves the somewhat different (tho not unrelated) problems of sensitiveness considered in the preceding chapter. And the question arises, too, whether in the slow process of adjustment toward the eventual outcome there may not emerge, when the final survey has been completed and the last consequences have been verified, a residuum of unexplained phenomena — puzzling occurrences that cannot be brought into accord with even the most guarded theoretical formulation.

All these considerations emphasize once more the importance of the element of time. Thruout the present economic system, with its intricate specialization of industry, its persistence in the grooves of custom, its repeated disturbance by an imperfect money system, there must be time for the fundamental forces to bring about their results. These forces are modified, counteracted, strengthened, by others of less strength but of more rapid operation; and they are themselves subject to change in the course of time. Hence the difficulty of tracing their operation in detail, and of seeing just how they work; indeed, of ascertaining whether they work at all in the way that general reasoning leads us to expect. It is only in outstanding and conspicuous cases that we can subject the general reasoning to specific verification. One such case will be considered in the next chapter.

CHAPTER 19

CANADA

As was remarked in a preceding chapter, Canada has a monetary system of the sensitive type, and may therefore be expected to show in its international trade a quick response to changing conditions. It happens that during the first decade of the present century the conditions affecting its trade did change greatly and conspicuously. The events of that decade have a quite unusual interest for the theory and practice of international trade.

The interest does not arise from the scale of the operations, or from anything unique in their general character. Canada was (and remains) a country of moderate size, with a population well under 10 millions during the period under consideration (7.2 millions in 1911). Her people then went thru a stage of rapid economic growth, due to the opening of the far Northwest and its unexpected and extraordinary development. There was a boom quite of the familiar type — rapid settlement of the new country, extravagant speculation in land and in securities, great extension of railways and allied enterprises. Feverish bursts of this kind are familiar in the history of new countries, and particularly familiar in the closely similar experiences of the United States. In its more overt aspects, the episode presents little that is new to the economist. But it has a special pertinence for the present inquiry because of one circumstance: a single influence — namely, borrowing on a great scale — was affecting the international trade of the country, and the modifications caused by this influence can be traced with quite unusual accuracy. I state the case somewhat too strongly in saying that the one influence alone was in operation; there were others, beside that of the great borrowings; but this last preponderated so enormously that the others could have but little effect in confusing the situation. In essentials the case is of a kind rare in economic experience, in that a single force was at work under conditions which enable us to trace its effects with certainty. The series of phenomena come as close to the conditions of an experiment — the deliberate isolation of a given force — as economic history can well supply. And there is the further favoring circumstance that the materials for tracing the outcome are ample, and have been analyzed with great labor and discrimination by a competent hand.[1]

During the last decade or two of the 19th century — in the period immediately preceding that which we are to consider — the international trade of Canada had the features to be expected in a country which has borrowed in the past. The stage had been reached where interest payable on the old loans over-balanced such new loans as continued to be contracted. Canada's commodity exports then exceeded her imports. With the 20th century, a new period set in, and all this was reversed. Heavy loans were contracted, virtually all being connected directly or indirectly with the settlement and exploitation of the West — Manitoba, Assiniboia, Saskatchewan, Alberta, and the rest. Beginning at a modest rate, the loans enlarged steadily, until in the later part of the period (1908–1913) they rose to two, three, and (at the very last) five hundred millions a year. The total sum borrowed by this country of moderate size amounted to billions of dollars in little more than a decade. The Great War, coming in 1914, suddenly stopped the movement. The experiment was then abruptly closed, so to speak, and could never again be renewed in quite the same simple and instructive fashion.

[1] Professor Jacob Viner's book on Canada's Balance of International Indebtedness, 1900–1913 (1924), of which this chapter is hardly more than an abstract, is a model monograph of its kind — exhaustive in the accumulation and analysis of the evidence, keen in the application of economic principles to the facts observed. I feel satisfaction in having taken the initiative in suggesting the subject to Professor Viner; the extraordinarily successful outcome of the research is due to his indefatigable industry and high intellectual ability.

Much is also due to Mr. R. H. Coats, Statistician of the Dominion of Canada. His report on Cost of Living (1915) supplied full and accurate material on price movements, arranged with unusual competence.

The total sums borrowed between 1900 and 1913 came to 2500 millions of dollars. By far the largest part came from Great Britain — not less than 1750 millions. The United States contributed 630 millions. An almost negligible remainder was lent by Continental Europe. So markedly preponderant was the share of the mother country that the case may be analyzed for most purposes as if this were the only source, tho the extent and the manner of American participation present some problems of their own, to be considered in due time.

It is in accord with the previsions of theory that these great borrowings led to complete reversal of the relation between commodity imports and exports. Instead of the previous excess of exports, Canada came to have a heavy excess of imports. The total excess of commodity imports during the 13 years was in round numbers 1.3 billions. The excess of imports, it will be seen, was less than the total of borrowings; a difference easily explained in view of the various other payments from Canada to Great Britain and other countries which were called for in the course of the operations — for accumulating interest on the successive loans, freight both on imports and on exports, and minor items such as tourist expenses and banking and insurance commissions. The details of the balance of payments we need not stop to analyze. It is enough to note the salient change brought about by the import of capital — a marked excess of commodity imports over exports. That this change should ensue is not only in accord with theory, but is confirmed, in the large, by the well-known experiences of all borrowing and lending countries. So far there is nothing noteworthy; it is familiar experience that loans and repayments of loans, interest remittances and the like, are in practise effected mainly thru the movement of commodity imports and exports. Much more instructive than this gross result are the various concomitants of the process and especially the working of the monetary mechanism.

The characteristics of the monetary system of Canada have already been described. It is one in which the superstructure is large in comparison with the gold basis, and in which therefore a

large expansion of the total circulating medium can result from a
relatively small inflow of gold. The inflow that took place was
not inconsiderable. Gold steadily dribbled into the country
the movement ceasing occasionally, in one or another year of
the period, but soon reviving again — with a total by 1913 of
$123,000,000. Almost all of the physical gold went into the
government vaults, Dominion notes being issued against the
accumulations. Whatever the process, so much of gold was added
to the basis on which the circulating medium rested. The effective
circulating medium, however, increased by a vastly greater
amount, the superstructure being enlarged approximately in the
same proportion as was the foundation of specie. The additional
Dominion notes (substantially the same thing as additional gold)
went chiefly into bank reserves. There they became the basis for
a great increase of bank deposits and bank notes. The total
demand liabilities of the Canadian banks of issue (deposits and
notes together) swelled from 350 millions in 1900 to over 1000
millions in the years 1911–1913. In round numbers, they tripled.
It may be noted that this increase, great tho it was, did not proceed quite in proportion to the enlargement of the base. The ratio
of cash reserves to demand liabilities became somewhat greater
in the last triennium; it reached 10 per cent, against about 7
per cent in the earlier years.[1]

Deserving of note is the circumstance that the expansion of
deposits and notes seems to have preceded rather than followed
the enlargement of reserve. The expansion often overstepped
the reserve increase. I have already pointed out [2] that such a
chronological sequence, while at first sight appearing to be inconsistent with the tenor of the Ricardian reasoning, represents
merely one of the modifications which must be attached to it in
view of the characteristics of deposit banking. In the case of
Canada this peculiarity of the situation was accentuated by the

[1] I have seen no explanation of this change. Possibly it was due to the fact
that the expansion took place mainly in a few of the very large banks; and there is
a general tendency for very large banks, having heavy demand obligations, to keep
a larger proportion of actual cash than do banks of moderate size.

[2] Chapter 17, p. 207.

relations between the Canadian banks on the one hand and those of New York and London on the other.

The nearest great financial center is New York, and the closest connections are with New York. As is always the case with outlying institutions, balances of the Canadian banks are kept in the metropolitan banks — in this case chiefly the banks of New York — and such balances constitute a "secondary reserve." The course of events in the mechanism of the lending operations would then be in general as follows. A loan would be negotiated in London, and funds there would be put at the disposal of Canadian borrowers. The Canadian banks would be informed of the successful London loan, and would be in turn ready to extend accommodation without delay to their clients at home. The funds available in London might be left there temporarily, to be remitted to Canada or New York, as might be desired; more commonly they would be transferred to New York, there remaining at call until transferred further to Canada. The Canadian banks could and would expand at once. Gradually, however, they would find their cash holdings not in accord with their swelling demand liabilities. They would draw on their New York correspondents for remittances; and thus finally the gold would flow into Canada which made possible the continuing expansion.

As is to be expected under conditions of this kind, the Canadian rate of exchange on New York — the price of New York funds in Montreal and Toronto — tended thruout the period to be favorable to the flow of specie into Canada. New York exchange was commonly at a discount in the Canadian cities, and Canadian exchange commonly at a premium in New York. Here, as in all the operations of the international exchange market, the transactions, tho in general associated with the remittances to Canada, sometimes turned the other way; exchange fluctuated and specie movements were irregular. But the same underlying trend persisted thruout our period. The steady continuation of this process — expansion in Canada, rising loans and deposits, reserves becoming again and again too scant, a rate of foreign exchange favorable to Canada, the replenishment of the reserves again and again thru the inflow of specie by way of New York — all this could persist only because of the continuing loans. Had it not been for the loans, the expansion of credit by the banks must have come to a halt. As it was, notwithstanding occasional interruptions, the round was repeated year after year. Specie did flow into Canada; the entire circulating medium did enlarge; in essentials, what happened did conform to the previsions of theory.

Next, and again quite in accord with theoretical expectation, prices in Canada rose sharply. Here, it is true, our experiment becomes somewhat impure. Another factor complicated the situation, namely the advance in prices which was taking place the world over. It will occur at once to the conversant reader that the level of prices in all western countries had begun slowly to rise in the years just before 1900, and that the rise became marked in the decade succeeding; a consequence, as is generally agreed, of the steadily increasing supply of new gold from the mines. What then is to be expected in Canada, on grounds of theory, is a rise *greater* than that appearing elsewhere. More particularly we should expect a greater rise than in Great Britain, the lending country. Precisely this is what happened. Whatever method of measuring the advance in prices be applied — weighted or "unweighted" mean, an index for all commodities or one for selected commodities — Canadian prices rose much more than British. Taking the year 1900 as the base (100), the weighted index for Canada was 136 in 1912, 132 in 1913. It was but 113 in Great Britain for both years. And as compared with the United States — a neutral country, so to speak — Canada again showed an exceptional advance. During the earlier years of the period, until about 1910, Canadian and American prices showed a roughly parallel upward movement; but in the later years, when borrowing was on the largest scale, the Canadian went distinctly higher.

For our purpose, however, this gross movement of prices is less significant than the price changes of the several separate classes of commodities — imported goods, exported goods, domestic goods. On grounds of theory we should expect not a uniform movement but a series of different movements. If the world level of prices had remained unchanged, we should have expected in Canada a fall in the prices of imported goods, and a rise in the prices of domestic goods. Exported goods in the long run would have shown a movement similar to that of the domestic, but with a lag which would for some time keep their prices either on the same low level as the imported, or in a position intermediate between that of the imported and the domestic articles. In the actual state of things, however — the world level of prices not stationary, but advancing — we should expect goods imported into Canada to show some advance in price, but a less advance than the domestic, and less advance than the exported also. With prices rising everywhere, we should expect domestic prices in Canada to rise more than the gross average in that country, and much more than the gross average elsewhere. This is precisely what happened. The prices of domestic goods in Canada rose from 100 in 1900 to a range as high as 161 in 1913. Imported goods showed an advance unmistakably less. During the earlier years of the period they remained on the whole unchanged, but began to advance after 1905, and reached their maximum, only 114, in 1913. Export goods moved in a range roughly half-way between these two, reaching 139 in 1912 and 134 in 1913.

The details of the price changes, still further followed, remain in accord with the previsions of theory. (Thruout, prices for 1900 are the base, 100.) A selected list of identical domestic commodities showed for Canada a rise to 162 by 1913; for the United States one only to 123 by the same year. Most significant was the change in wages and services. As has been said again and again, money rates of wages are the best single index of the movement of domestic prices. Canadian (weekly) wages rose to 145 in 1912, 149 in 1913. British money wages showed virtually no advance at all during the period; the United States showed an advance distinctly less than Canada — to 123 in 1911 and 127 in 1913. A novel and significant indication of the domestic price movements was the charge for hospital services (expense per patient per day), which rose to 145 by 1913. House rents rose to

162; business rents much more — the figure was 234 in 1913. An exceptional rise in business rents is a natural outcome of speculative furore and high business returns (high on the surface at least) such as characterize a boom period.

As has just been stated, the soaring course of domestic prices is in contrast with the lagging even tho upward movement of export prices. Most Canadian articles of export are of the kind which, when sent to foreign countries, constitute but a moderate fraction of the total supply there marketed. This is of course most clearly the case with wheat, the one outstanding crop of the new western region. Its sustained production and exportation was almost a matter of necessity. A cheap product of virgin soil, it would probably have continued to be placed on the market (tho in less amounts) even in face of falling prices. Moreover, something more than the mere cheapness of production affected the output and the exports. The pioneer farmers of the Canadian West had regard not merely to present costs. They were actuated not a little by the prospect of future accretion, the wish to secure the land and to build a property for the future. It is perhaps going too far to put this sort of case in the terms suggested by Professor Marshall in describing earlier phenomena of the same kind — that to the pioneer wheat is no more than a by-product in the process of acquiring the title-deeds.[1] But one need not be at all surprised that wheat grown under these conditions should be exported in great and increasing amounts, even tho it showed a rise in price not at all as marked as that of other Canadian goods. The same situation is seen in the case of flax-seed, also a characteristic product of pioneer agriculture.[2]

A more normal state of things — i.e. such as is to be expected on a priori grounds — appears in some other products which had previously figured largely in Canada's exports. They ceased so to figure, or at least tended toward disappearance. Articles like cattle, sheep, horses, bacon, butter, had been among the exports

---

[1] Principles of Economics, Book 5, Ch. 10, § 2 (6th edition).

[2] See the article, already referred to (pp. 187–188, above), by Mr. W. S. Barker, on Flax Fibre and Flax Seed, in The Quarterly Journal of Economics, May, 1917.

of the preceding period. These differ from wheat not only in that they are outside the class of pioneer products, but in that they had not been produced preponderantly for export. The domestic consumption had been large; they were nearer the verge of being once for all in the domestic class. Their exportation in some cases declined, in others ceased. The close commercial relations between the United States and Canada, and the particularly close relations of those Canadian districts which are nearest the border, caused some of them still to find their market in the neighboring country, yet with a clear tendency to diminution. But — to take one conspicuous example — cheese, which before had been made chiefly for export, now dropped out almost completely. It is not necessary to reproduce all the details of Professor Viner's investigation, or to note the exceptions to the general trend, sometimes easy of explanation, sometimes quite obscure. The reader is referred to his volume, in which the whole situation is unfolded. With hardly an exception, the phenomena of the export trade are as fully in accord with theoretical expectation as are the changes in prices and in money incomes.

Another aspect of the Canadian experience is in the trade between Canada and the United States. The contiguity of the borders of the two countries, and the consequent large trade between them, simplify a phase of the problem which as yet has hardly been touched — the relations between the borrowing country and third countries, i.e. countries other than the lender. In this case the United States was a third country; indeed, the only third country of any consequence.

In our theoretic discussion of the general effects of international lending and borrowing, it was pointed out [1] that under certain conditions the transactions may bring a movement of commodities into the borrowing country by a process that is simple and direct. That movement may take place without any flow of specie, without any disturbance of prices, without such intricate after-effects as have been described in the preceding paragraphs. This simpler course of events appears when the borrowers use the proceeds of

[1] See Chapter 12, pp. 124–127.

the loans once for all in buying additional goods in the lending country. The Canadians, for example, might have devoted the whole of the funds put at their disposal by the British lenders to the purchase *in England* of rails, locomotives, iron and steel, machinery. Did they do so?

Evidently not. An examination of the import statistics shows that the commodity imports and exports took no such simple course. They indicate a series of transactions more complicated, and more interesting to the student of international trade.

As between Great Britain and Canada, imports from the former did indeed increase, but not more than did the exports from Canada to Great Britain. And the *relation* between the imports and exports of these two countries remained virtually unchanged. Before the great borrowings began, Canada's exports, in the latter part of the 19th century, to Great Britain had exceeded her imports. They continued to do so between 1900 and 1913. The agricultural growth in the Canadian West led to an increase of grain exports to Great Britain so great that it quite equalled the increase of imports into Canada from that country. There was no net excess of commodity imports from Great Britain. But in Canada's trade as a whole an excess of imports did appear, and on a large scale; there was a great inflow of goods from other countries. And this inflow took place chiefly from the United States. During our period the total imports into Canada from the United States exceeded those from Canada into the United States by no less a sum than 1700 millions of dollars. Some excess of imports came into Canada from still other countries; but the amount from the other countries (300 millions in all) was small in comparison to that from the United States. In the main, it was from the United States that Canada got the goods which constituted the substance of what her loans yielded.

In part, it is true, the United States had a relation to Canada similar to that of Great Britain; she too was a lender. The Canadian loans in the United States during the period amounted to something over 600 millions. Probably the greater part of what was thus borrowed in the United States was spent there at once. But the excess of imports from the United States was much greater than the borrowings there. A round billion of dollars remains to be accounted for, not borrowed in the United States, yet leading to imports from the United States. Not only did Canada get from the United States the goods which the loans put in her hands; she got them mainly thru a process different from that of utilizing American loans directly for purchases in the United States.

The goods which Canada thus procured from the United States were of the most varied character. Some were capital goods, such as machinery, electric apparatus, railway equipment, coal, brick, cement, minerals. Some were consumers' goods, such as food and clothing. What was true in this regard of the United States was also true of the other countries from which came a substantial tho smaller flow of imports; with the minor difference that from these others the proportion of consumers' goods (such as sugar, tea, coffee) was larger.

Whether the articles that flowed into Canada were of the one class or the other — for producers' use or for consumers' — the chain of causation which brought them in was evidently an indirect one, not direct. And this is of no small importance for our problem of verification. In discussions of capital exports, it is often assumed that the adjustment of merchandise balances in such manner as to equalize the international payments is a simple matter. There is supposed to be really nothing here that calls for explanation; it is the most natural thing in the world that a country which lends capital should carry the transaction to its final stage by exporting merchandise in corresponding amounts. The same view is often held, perhaps by implication rather than explicitly, about the entire balance of international payments. The various items — import or export of capital, interest payments, freight charges — result in a balance of payments in favor of a country or against it; an excess of merchandise imports or exports then ensues by a quasi-automatic process, which calls for no special consideration. This simplification of the problem seems to me quite unwarranted. The experience of Canada shows how com-

plicated is the actual situation. It is complicated, to repeat, unless
the borrowing country uses the proceeds of the loans at once and
in full for purchases in the lending country; and this it will not
commonly do. Doubtless some part of the loans which Canada
placed in Great Britain were so used. But by far the larger part
of the loans made by the British were applied by the Canadians
to purchases quite outside of England. Not a little was used
in Canada itself, in payments for wages and materials in the construction work of railways and the like. A very large part was
used in the United States, but was "used" thru a process in which
the loans were quite in the background. The proximate forces
were simply that "money" was plentiful in Canada and prices
were high; in the United States there were goods of the kind that
Canadians wanted; individual promoters, builders, contractors,
traders in Canada found it profitable to buy goods from individual
concerns in the United States. The goods which it was thus
profitable to buy were partly consumers' goods, such as were in
demand by the Canadians — workmen and others — whose
services were wanted in the construction and agricultural operations, whose wages were high, who had plenty of money to spend.
Partly they were capital goods, also wanted in Canada in connection with these same operations. Money incomes and prices of
goods tended thruout to be higher in Canada; here was the proximate cause of the inflow of goods from abroad. Behind it all
was the actuating power of the loans, not operating directly, but
thru a mechanism far from simple.

All in all, this episode has unusual interest. So far as I know,
it serves to verify and confirm the essentials of the Ricardian
theory of international trade more completely and in greater detail
than any economic experience that has been subjected to scientific analysis. Not only this; it has a position similarly unusual
as regards the methodology of economics.

It is a commonplace that in economics, as in all the social
sciences, we are debarred almost completely from the method of
scientific experiment. We can never isolate a given force or set
of forces, never deliberately and rigidly arrange that one alone

shall be in operation, all others excluded. Therein our situation is unlike that of the chemists and physicists, or that which the biologists have succeeded in attaining within the last half-century. It is essentially like that of the geologists and geographers. These also are limited to the method of observation; they also cannot experiment. The reason for their limitations is indeed different from that which the economist must face. The geologists cannot experiment because the length of time over which their forces operate stretches far beyond the possibilities of man's operations; the same is true in the main of the geographers. The economist cannot experiment because he deals with human beings, and moreover with human beings in the mass — with large numbers and with mass phenomena. He cannot subject thousands of people to a given set of conditions, rigidly prevent the intervention of any other than the chosen factors, and unconcernedly let the consequences emerge. He can do no more than observe what takes place in the unregulated and changing world of affairs. He must watch with attention the confused march of events, discern the significant phenomena among the negligible, and patch together fragments of evidence which, tho they may tend to confirm a hypothesis, will but rarely constitute a continuous chain of evidence. The same is true of the geologist. He finds strata that appear and disappear, with gaps as they vanish across valleys or are buried beneath mountains and plateaus. It is thru long and patient observation, skilful hypothesis, visualizing of an imagined situation, excision of the accidental and the non-pertinent, that he establishes his generalizations or at least gives them plausibility. Such is the position of the economist, and such are his limitations. With all the refinements of observation which the development of statistical technique may bring, with all the accumulation of data thru economic history and description, the economist's generalizations can never have the exactness or the certainty which come from experimental confirmation.

Occasionally it happens, however, that there is a simple situation: a train of economic phenomena in which one cause alone is in operation. or is so predominantly in operation that others can be fairly set aside as negligible. The geologist sometimes has good fortune of the same kind ; an excavation lays bare a series of superimposed strata which tell their tale beyond misinterpretation. For the economist, the issue of inconvertible paper money has at times approached the same sort of simplicity ; yet even here the phenomena, tho they may be analyzed with ease as regards the outstanding train of causation, are often by no means easy of interpretation as regards important details. The Canadian episode described in the preceding pages unfolds itself as if planned for the economist's purposes. It comes as near to experiment as he can ever expect. A single cause came to operate on Canada's international trade — the import of capital. This is putting the case too strongly ; the isolation of the given cause was not perfect ; others also had some influence. But the import of capital was so great, overshadowed so completely all others, that there can be no error in attributing to this the main economic changes which appeared. We have a case in which on the one hand economic theory had been fully developed on deductive grounds — in which an analysis had been made of what might be expected to happen under given conditions. And on the other hand we have just those conditions actually present, and the ensuing series of phenomena passing before our eye with singular clearness. It is rare that the possibility of verifying the deductions of theory is found so successfully ; and it is of no little significance that for this particular sort of situation the conclusions of theory prove to be so completely verified.

CHAPTER 20

GREAT BRITAIN, I

THE international trade of Great Britain during the nineteenth century and the earlier years of the twentieth gives opportunity for illustrating and testing some conclusions of theory.

An inspection of the course of the imports and exports for the entire period, roughly a century, from 1830 to 1914, shows that a striking change in the relations between the two took place about the middle of the nineteenth century. During the first half of that century, until 1853, the recorded exports regularly exceeded the imports. After 1853, however, the contrary relation appears: the imports exceed the exports. The excess of imports is moderate at first, being from thirty to forty millions of pounds during the third quarter of the century. Beginning about 1873 it becomes more marked, increases irregularly but with hardly an interruption, often by leaps and bounds, and toward the end of the century rises to extraordinary dimensions.[1]

The turning point came in the middle of the nineteenth century; and on the face of the figures it came abruptly. In the year 1854, the recorded imports suddenly exceed the recorded exports. But this dramatic change — hardly to be expected on general principles, especially in view of the circumstance that the year was not one of crisis or other sharp overturn — proves on inquiry to be the evidence only of a change in statistical procedure. Until 1854 imports had been recorded on a basis of "official value" — arbitrary price figures for the goods. A change toward a more accurate reckoning, on the basis of the actual prices, was then made.[2] Thereupon the recorded import value shot up suddenly.

[1] Figures for the entire period are in the U. S. Statistical Abstract for Foreign Countries, of which the first number (and for a long while the only number) was issued in 1909. See pp. 40 *et seq.*

[2] See R. Giffen's Essays in Statistics, pp. 76–77. I know of no inquiries on the real relations between imports and exports during the earlier period.

236

The break in the figures at that date is thus explained, and is shorn of the striking significance which it might be supposed to have.

None the less the general trend of the figures for the middle years of the century indicates a change in the current of trade which in fact took place. Under the new and more accurate computation, imports not only exceeded exports at once, but continued to do so, and at an accelerating pace, as the years went on. It is probable that during the second quarter of the century the exports were greater than the actual imports; it is quite certain that thereafter the imports were greater than the exports.

The excess of imports which developed during the second half of the century is easily explained, or at least easily interpreted. It was the natural result of two circumstances. One was the stage which Great Britain had reached as an international lender, — the stage of maturity, so to speak. The process of making loans to foreigners had been going on for many years, and had been on a large scale from 1830 to 1850. Capital had been invested in the Continent of Europe, especially for railway construction, and it had been invested also over-seas, in North and South America. The American borrowings of all kinds were heavy after 1830; some of them with profitable result, others with disaster. Taking the operations as a whole, they had been remunerative, and a growing stream of payments of interest and income was setting in toward the lending country. As has already been remarked, capital export in its early stages, when the remittances from the lending country are not yet offset by payments due from the borrowing country, causes the lending country to have an excess of merchandise exports. As time goes on, the growing remittances — of interest and profits by the borrowing country or countries — come to exceed the fresh loans that are made to them, and the lending country begins to have an excess of imports in place of the previous excess of exports. This may be called the stage of maturity, a stage which comes more quickly if the annual accretion of new loans proceeds at a lessened rate, but is postponed if the process of lending, so far from slackening, goes on with increasing volume. In general the stage of maturity, the turning point, seems to have come in Great Britain shortly after the middle of the nineteenth century.

A second factor was the new position which Great Britain's shipping trade attained, or, to be more precise, the accentuation of its already dominant position. British ships had long done more than their share — their "fair" share of one-half — in carrying the imports and exports. With the advent of steam, and especially with the advent of iron steamships, an even greater part of the country's own carrying to and fro was done in British ships; and in the outside carrying trade — that between third countries — a similar extension took place. The result was a great increase in the earnings of shipping. This item also reflected itself in the excess of merchandise imports. The shipping earnings grew apace after the middle of the nineteenth century, and came to have a larger and larger importance for the international trade of the country, and for the balance of international payments.

The excess of imports, however, did not grow with steadiness. At times the upward movement relaxed, at other times speeded up. In a schematic analysis of the consequences of continuing loans, such as was made in the first part of this volume, it is convenient to assume that they are made at a steady rate — a given amount each year — under which conditions it is clear that in time the accruing interest on old loans will over-balance the new ones. In fact, however, they are made with great irregularity. The fluctuations are closely associated with the alternations and repression of industrial activity. During the recurrent upward stage of buoyancy and speculation, large loans are made; after each crisis there is a sharp reduction, perhaps complete cessation. Each of the successive cycles in British economic history during the last hundred years has been characterized by a great wave of foreign investment, followed by recession and quiescence. Meanwhile the item of income from the old and still outstanding investments has continued steadily to grow. The outgoing movement has been irregular; the incoming movement has been regular. The *net* outcome therefore has been, as regards these two forces, unsteady. While the tendency toward a growing excess of imports has been unmistakable, and has been beyond doubt a result of the uninterrupted growth of inflowing income, the irregularities of the outflow of capital have often caused a marked diminution of the net incoming balance. Even at a comparatively late stage, there were years when a net excess of exports still appeared, as in 1859 and 1872, and some when the balance was even, as in 1873 and 1886. The more common effect of bursts of capital export has been the diminution for the time being of the excess of imports — a phenomenon which, as will presently be pointed out, was noticeable during the first decade of the twentieth century.

These are familiar matters. The point that is less familiar, in connection with the theory of the subject, or at all events is not commonly considered, is the closeness and rapidity with which the varying balance of payments has found its expression in the varying balance of trade. The actual merchandise movements seem to have been adjusted to the shifting balance of payments with surprising exactness and speed. The process which our theory contemplates — the initial flow of specie when there is a burst of loans; the fall of prices in the lending country, rise in the borrowing country; the eventual increased movement of merchandise out of the one and into the other — all this can hardly be expected to take place smoothly and quickly. Yet no signs of disturbance are to be observed such as the theoretic analysis previses; and some recurring phenomena are of a kind not contemplated by theory at all. Most noticeable of all is the circumstance that periods of active lending have been characterized by rising prices rather than by falling prices, and that the export of goods apparently has taken place, not in connection with a cheapening of goods in the lending country, but in spite of the fact that its goods have seemed to be dearer at times of great capital export.

It must be confessed that here we have phenomena not fully understood. In part our information is insufficient; in part our understanding of other connected topics is inadequate. The

uneven stages by which the outgoing loans proceed are evidently
related to the stages of the business cycle. We know much more
of this matter than was known twenty years ago; yet it is only
about the recent cycles that we possess the more detailed knowledge
and the better understanding. The sequence and the interdependence of the several stages in the earlier days may have been
different. We know, too, more about the course of prices during
recent decades than we knew about prices in preceding times. It
is only of late that attention has been paid to the possibility, nay
the probability, of divergent movements in import prices, export
prices, domestic prices. Price indices usually are given for a
single lumped aggregate of all goods; whereas for the problem
of international trade series of separate indices are needed for the
different classes — domestic goods on the one hand, international
goods on the other. We do not know what degree of verification
of our theoretic reasoning would be found if the needed information were at hand — indeed, whether any verification at all would
appear, or only the uncovering of new perplexities.

The difficulties of verification become manifest when one com-
pares what we know about the movements of prices and incomes
with those that might be expected on theoretic grounds. What
we might expect *prima facie* is a general tendency to falling money
incomes and falling prices during the early stage, that of capital
export, running to the middle of the 19th century. Thereafter, a
reversed movement might be expected: rising money incomes
and rising domestic prices, with falling prices of imports. What
we find in fact is thus summarized by Professor Bowley,[1] an
observer whose competence is not to be questioned :

"From 1775 to 1815 prices rose, but incomes rose still more.
From 1820 to 1851 prices fell 35 per cent, while incomes remained nearly
steady.
From 1851 to 1873 prices rose 50 per cent, but incomes rose 60 per cent.
From 1873 to 1895 prices fell 45 per cent, while incomes fell, but rose
again to the 1873 level.
From 1895 to 1901 prices rose 12 per cent, but income rose 15 per cent."

[1] England's Foreign Trade in the 19th Century, 2nd edition, p. 106.

Here are phenomena which (so far as concerns the present inquiry) can be more easily explained away than they can be explained. The price changes up and down are the changes of all prices, as recorded by the usual index numbers; nothing appears as to any special changes in import prices or domestic prices. The movements of money incomes might be significant. They would be indicative of tendencies to gain or loss from the conditions of international trade, *if* they could be regarded as having been influenced solely by this factor. But they were of course influenced by sundry other factors as well — by the general downward trend of prices and incomes the world over between 1820 and 1850; by the sharp upward movement of similar wide sweep that followed the Australian and Californian gold discoveries; and so on thru the familiar fluctuations. And obviously there were other changes than those due to varying monetary conditions. Consider the commanding position which Great Britain held as a manufacturing country during the second and third quarters; the heavy and increasing demand for her products; the probability that the barter terms of trade thruout this half-century were favorable to her; and then the slow change during the last quarter of the century, the rise of rival manufacturing countries, the modified conditions of international trade and international competition. How disentangle the effect of any one among the many and various factors? How verify in the actual course of events the theoretic previsions?

A further circumstance calls for comment, one connected with the puzzling movement of prices and incomes, and connected, as these were, with the actual working of the machinery of international trade. It is the relation of the flow of specie to the changing phenomena and the changing relations.

The excess in money values of exports at one period and of imports at another appears to be in accord with the net balance of payments. This accordance is not peculiar to Great Britain. It is found in the international trade of all the countries of western civilization. So far we have a verification of theoretic analysis; the observed phenomena are such as general analysis leads us to expect. But just how is this result brought about? Is it in fact brought about in the way that theory lays down — by an initial flow of specie, subsequent movements of prices, and only in the end by the appropriate flow of merchandise? How far can we trace the sequence of events in detail, and so subject our deductive analysis to a rigorous test?

Here the phenomena again are baffling. The movement of specie is rarely considerable — considerable, that is, in comparison with the volume (in money terms) of the merchandise movements. When it does take place on a large scale, the explanation usually is to be found in other directions than are indicated by the general theory of international trade. Heavy and rapid transfers of specie from one country to another are, it is clear, usually the result of financial disturbances, of crop vicissitudes, of causes that exhaust their effects in a few months or at most in a year or two. And as regards the broad continuing movements of specie — those that are moderate in any one year, but are cumulative — the same sort of statement appears justified: they too seem explicable in the main on grounds other than are considered in our theorizing. The steady inflow of gold into Great Britain from 1850 to 1873, the equally steady inflow from 1896 to 1914 — these are obviously but one phase of the world's increased gold production. The growing supply was distributed among the different countries largely thru Great Britain, that country absorbing a share only. We may indeed reason on general principles that during such a period as that from 1850 to 1890, the general conditions of her international trade were such as would have tended in any event to turn the flow of specie her way. The actual inflow of specie, we may reason, simply was made greater by these general conditions than it would otherwise have been. Similarly we may argue that the occasional diminution of the inflow, its sporadic cessation or even reversal, are also explicable on general grounds ; they would have been more marked had not the world supply of gold been in process of enlargement. But all this clearly is to explain the facts in the light of a theory deemed sound, not to test the soundness of the theory by the facts. What we find is simply trickles of specie, small in comparison with the great streams of merchandise; a movement of the specie that on the whole is toward Great Britain, is fairly steady, tho sometimes faltering, occasionally reversed; with oscillations that can be plausibly explained, but can hardly be said to be observably and specifically in accord with the formulations of theory.

The best that we can do toward bringing this phase of theory into accord with the facts is to dwell again on the circumstance that the circulating medium of Great Britain thru the entire period was highly sensitive. Specie movements into the country or out of it, even tho small in comparison either with the country's total monetary stock or with the volume of merchandise imports and exports, none the less had a prompt effect on its credit and currency structure, and so on the movement of prices and money incomes. If they are steadily in the same direction, their effect is cumulative. Reasoning in this way, we can maintain that the observed movements, tho clearly the resultant of many and interacting factors, are yet not inconsistent with the general reasoning. This cannot serve as verification; but it is no ground for saying that there is failure of verification.

On the subject at large I venture to repeat what I have said elsewhere: [1]

"So insignificant are the ordinary movements of gold from one country to another, so likely to be disguised by eddies and cross currents due to the complexity of international dealings, that some writers have pooh-poohed the whole theory of the equalization of imports and exports thru changes in international prices. Yet without this theory it is impossible to explain the facts, and especially the equalization of the money value of exports and imports. The influence of the quantity of gold on prices, slow-moving as it is, and subject to all sorts of disturbing causes, is the underlying persistent force which determines not only the international distribution of specie, but also the variations in the purchasing power of gold in different countries and the greater or less extent to which those countries share the gains from international

[1] Principles of Economics, Ch. 33, Vol. 1, pp. 460–461 (3d ed.).

trade. . . . The comparative smallness of the ordinary flow is due mainly to the fact that international trade, long-maintained, has already brought about such a distribution of the precious metals, and such a range of prices in the several countries, that their exchanges balance very closely. It is only when great economic changes occur that a large movement of specie takes place; and even then it is commonly distributed over a period of several years."

CHAPTER 21

GREAT BRITAIN, II. THE TERMS OF TRADE, 1880–1914

I TURN now to a series of movements for which the data are more precise, and for which something in the nature of a specific test of theory is more nearly possible. The period covered is that from about 1880 to the outbreak of the Great War in 1914.

As already observed, the excess of imports over exports by this time was definitely established. Once established, we might have expected that it would grow; and grow, if not at a constant rate, at least with a continuing upward movement from year to year. But what we find in fact is a very irregular movement, by no means a steady maintenance of an upward trend. The payments from other countries to Great Britain on account of the "invisible items," as reflected in the excess of her imports over exports, showed for a number of years in the early part of the 20th century a decrease, not an increase. Between 1904 and 1914 the annual excess of imports declined heavily — from £177 million a year in the quinquennium 1900–1904, to £145 million in 1905–1909, and to £137 million in 1909–1914.

The explanation of this unexpected turn is to be found in a sudden burst of capital exports. This is the one item among the total of the invisible items that commonly shows, in a country that has reached the stage in which Great Britain found herself during the period in question, the greatest irregularity. It happened then to exhibit quite extraordinary changes. A great and sudden enlargement of loans to foreign countries marked the years of expansion that preceded the Great War. The accompanying chart indicates how extraordinary was the outflow.[1] On that chart are indicated, on the three lower curves, the main items which

[1] I have taken the figures on which the chart is based from Mr. C. K. Hobson's Export of Capital, pp. 197, 204; adding, however, those showing the excess of merchandise imports.

GREAT BRITAIN, 1880–1914.

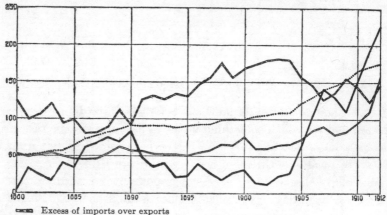

┉┉ Excess of imports over exports
┉┉ Income from abroad
══ Shipping earnings
── Export of capital

enter into the total of the "invisible" factors of Great Britain's trade: the inflowing income from investments, the shipping earnings, and the export of capital. It will be seen that the first of these, income from investments, shows a fairly steady growth from year to year, such as is to be expected. The second, shipping earnings, also shows a continuing growth, tho not one so steady. The two account for the balance of payments due *to* the country, and so account for the excess of imports (I disregard minor items). The new loans — the capital exports — vary to an extraordinary degree; and no variation is so striking as the upward burst in 1904–1914. The phenomenon, it may be noted, was not peculiar to Great Britain. A similar one appeared in Germany and France, indeed in all the capital-lending countries of Europe. With it went an equally striking expansion of the total volume of international trade, an accentuation of international competition, a yeasty and uneasy turmoil both in the lending and the borrowing countries — the various forms of trade rivalry, fomented by nationalistic sentiment and by economic jealousies and fallacies, which contributed so largely to the ensuing war. It was in Great Britain, then still by far the most important lending country, that the capital export reached undreamed-of dimensions.

The consequence was that for a decade or thereabouts the normal trend — so it may be called — of the country's international trade was interrupted. A glance at the uppermost line of the chart, which indicates from year to year the excess of imports over exports, shows that this excess grows until the close of the century. But with the year 1900 it ceases to grow; and after 1904 it declines sharply. Its movement shows an unmistakable inverse correlation with that of the capital exports. Thruout, as the capital exports rise, the excess of imports shrinks. Most significant for the present purpose is the fact that the marked expansion of foreign loans which began about 1904 is accompanied with an equally marked decline in the amount by which the imports exceeded the exports. It will be observed, further, that the correlation is direct and immediate. There is no indication of a lag; the change in the balance of payments and that in the balance of trade are synchronous. Of this exact concurrence, hardly to be expected on grounds of general reasoning, more will be said presently.[1]

Such a reversal of the normal movement — one so considerable, and persisting thru a decade — would presumably lead to noticeable consequences in the terms on which Great Britain got her goods from other countries. It would tend to make those terms less advantageous. Had the normal course of events continued — a growing increase in the excess of imports — they would presumably have become *more* advantageous from year to year. The reversal (or rather, marked slackening) of the current of payments might be expected to lessen progressively the gain of Great Britain from her exchange of goods with other countries.

On this precise topic, the greater or less gain secured by Great Britain from her international trade under these shifting conditions, we fortunately have significant evidence. The statistics inform us accurately about the imports and exports (in terms of money value); and it happens that the figures showing the amounts of the invisible items are almost equally accurate. Still more

[1] See pp. 259 *et seq.*

important for the purpose in hand is the circumstance that we have price figures of a kind not usually obtainable. The British Board of Trade publishes price figures separately for imported and exported articles, or rather, indices showing the movement of the prices of the two classes. The lack of separate price figures of this kind is one of the greatest obstacles to any procedure for testing the validity of the more complex parts of the theory of international trade. In the present case, as in that of Canada, just considered, we are fortunate in having the needed data.

Let the reader recall what has been said elsewhere [1] about the net barter terms of trade and the gross barter terms of trade. The net barter terms are those of the exchange of domestic goods for foreign goods in the very simplest manner, where nothing enters into the trade between countries except sales and purchases of merchandise. Then the net barter terms are the only terms that arise, and this is the only sense in which we can speak of the terms of trade. For the moment I ignore services; they will be considered presently. It is the goods transactions, thus considered as the sole items, which the Ricardian theory in its earlier formulation alone took into consideration. But as the non-merchandise transactions enter, there is occasion to distinguish. The actual international trade of any modern country may be separated into two parts: first, the exchange of exported goods for an equal money value of imported goods; second, an excess in money value of the imported goods over the exported goods, or vice versa (as the case may be), representing the balance of the non-merchandise transactions. The distinction, be it observed, is one of analysis only. What in fact takes place is that one unsegregated mass (or flow) of physical goods moves toward the country as imports, another mass moves out as exports. For a country having net payments due *to* it on the "invisible" account, the money value of the imports is greater than that of the exports; for a country in the reverse situation the money value of the exports is greater. The physical volume of the incoming goods (imports), as compared to the physical volume of the outgoing goods (exports),

[1] Chapter 11, pp. 113, 117.

will be larger for the country having an excess of imports in money value; that is, such a country will be getting a larger physical quantity of imports in exchange for a given physical quantity of exports than it would get if the money volume of the two were equal. This better relation (in physical terms) is of course quite different from the relations of the money value of the imports and exports; least of all can it be said that the latter (the difference in money quantities) serves as a measure or index of the rates of physical exchange. But those terms — the *whole* of a country's physical imports as compared with the whole of its exports — constitute the gross barter terms of trade.

We may proceed now to consider in what way we might measure changes in the way these transactions take place; how ascertain what modifications may arise in the terms on which a country barters its imports for its exports — both the gross and the net terms. The terms of course must always be advantageous to some extent, otherwise the exchange would not take place at all; but they may be more or less advantageous. There is a range of greater or less, a possibility of more favorable terms or less favorable terms. The device to which attention is now to be called enables us to measure the change, or the direction of change, toward a more or a less favorable situation. Let it be premised that they in no way indicate whether a country secures a large or a small share of the total gains which the international barter brings to all concerned — to other countries with which it trades as well as to itself — and which are divided between them. They only indicate in which direction the accretion of gain is changing; whether the gain, whatever it be in a given year, is less or greater in that year than in previous years or in subsequent years. It is *changes*, and changes only, both in the net barter terms of trade and in the gross barter terms, which we are able to follow.

The method by which changes in the net barter terms of trade are to be discerned was suggested by Professor Bowley as early as 1893.[1]

---

[1] England's Foreign Trade in the 19th Century, 1st edition (1893) p. 20. See also Changes of Prices of Imports and Exports since 1881, Journal of the Royal Statistical Society, 1897, Vol. LX, p. 437.

Suppose that the prices of both imported and exported goods are known, and that indices of these prices have been computed. We know then whether the prices of imports in any given year are higher or lower than in the year selected as base; and so as to the prices of exports. If now imports and exports in each single year are the same in money value, it follows that a change in prices registers accurately a change in physical quantity. If prices of exports have fallen, a given money value means a larger quantity; and conversely, if prices rise, a given money value means a smaller quantity. The mere movement of import and export prices thus registers changes in the physical quantities exchanged, *if* the total money value of imports in each year equals the money value of exports. The movement of prices shows the direction of the changes in physical quantities, and so of the changes in the net barter terms. The relation obviously is inverse. As export prices fall, more of exports are given; as import prices rise, less of imports are received. What is shown (to repeat) is merely whether more or less exports are bartered for a given quantity of imports than were bartered in a preceding year. We ascertain not whether the terms of trade in any year are in themselves advantageous or favorable, but only whether they have become more or less favorable than in the preceding year.

The method would be equally applicable if the imports and exports, tho not equal to each other in money value from year to year, maintained a constant proportion. If the imports were in money regularly 25 per cent greater than the exports, the reciprocals of the import and export prices would still show the relations of the changes in physical quantities. Their course would of itself suffice to show whether a more or less volume of exports was going out in exchange for a given volume of imports. In either case — equality or constant proportion — we can follow the direction of changes in the net barter terms of trade.

But, as need hardly be said, the suppositions underlying this method do not conform to fact. The imports and exports of no modern country are equal to each other in money value; nor do they bear a constant proportion to each other. In the case of

Great Britain we have seen how great the excess of imports has long been, and also how that excess has fluctuated from time to time. The net barter terms are a hypothetical matter. The phenomenon which we encounter in fact is that of the gross barter terms of trade — the relation between the unsegregated mass of goods coming in and the unsegregated mass going out.

None the less, it is possible to use substantially the same device for measuring changes in this relation also. We can construct indices of the trend of the gross terms. The following figures for Great Britain's trade in the years 1890, 1900, 1910, illustrate the procedure :

	Values of Imports and Exports (million pounds)				Derived Indices		
	Recorded Values		Values at Prices of 1900		Relative Physical Quantities (1900 = 100)		Relative Gross Barter Terms (6) ÷ (5)
	(1) Imports	(2) Exports	(3) Imports	(4) Exports	(5) Imports	(6) Exports	(7)
1890	356	263	333	278	72.4	98.6	136
1900	460	291	460	291	100	100	100
1910	575	430	525	438	114.1	150.3	132

Columns 1 and 2 give the actual money values of the total imports and of the total exports; that is, the values as recorded in official statistics. Columns 3 and 4 give these money values as they would have been at the prices of 1900. Possessing a separate index of import prices, as we fortunately do, we can readily compute what the money values of the imports would have been if the prices of the articles had remained unchanged — if prices had remained the same as they were in the year selected as base (1900). And so as to the exports. The prices being reduced to identical terms, a larger or smaller total money value necessarily indicates a larger or smaller physical volume. The adjusted figures of money values become measures of physical quantities. Columns 3 and 4, while they are money values (adjusted), thus show the increase or decrease of the physical quantities of the imports and exports. Columns 5 and 6 then show in what way the quantity *relations* of different years compare. The year 1900 is taken as the base for this purpose, just as it is for the price comparisons. The proportion of exports to imports — physical quantities — for that year 1900 is taken as 100. According as the proportion is found to be greater or less in another year, the figure is greater or less. The figures thus deduced for the several years give an index of changes in the gross barter terms of trade. Let it be borne in mind that here, as in the figures on net terms, we have nothing which indicates whether the terms are in themselves favorable for any given year. They indicate only the direction and extent of changes. There is nothing to show whether the barter terms of trade with foreign countries in 1900 gave Great Britain a large or a small share of the total divisible gain from foreign trade. But such as they were in 1900, favorable or not, it appears that in 1890 they were *less* favorable than in 1900; more of physical exports was given for each unit or given assortment of physical imports than in 1900. And it appears that in 1910 also the relation was *less* favorable than in 1900; then also more of exports was given in exchange for a given quantity of imports than in 1900.

We have then an index of the gross barter terms of trade. The chart on the opposite page shows at a glance the general trends from 1880 to 1913. First follow the dotted line, indicating the course of the gross barter terms of trade.[1] The terms of trade became markedly more favorable to Great Britain from 1880 until 1900. During these two decades less and less of exports went out in relation to the imports; a given physical quantity of imports was purchased for a steadily declining physical quantity of exports. After 1900 the tendency is the other way; more and more of exports are sent out, in comparison to the imports that come in.

The course of the net barter terms is indicated by the unbroken

---

[1] The figures on which the chart is based are given in detail in Appendix I, p. 411. Both for chart and figures, I make use of a paper printed in the Economic Journal, March, 1925.

line. The changes are in the same direction as those of the gross
barter terms, but less marked. From 1880 to 1900, a less and less
quantity of exports was sent out for a given quantity of imports;

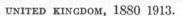

UNITED KINGDOM, 1880 1913.

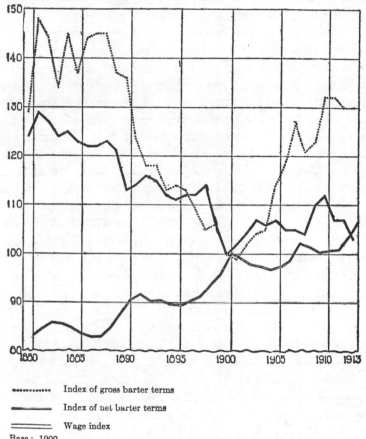

<dotted line> Index of gross barter terms
<solid line> Index of net barter terms
<line> Wage index

Base : 1900.

or rather, less and less of exports *would* have been necessary to
procure a given quantity of imports if the only elements in the
country's international trade had been the exchange of merchandise
imports for merchandise exports. After 1900 the trend is the
other way, becoming less favorable to Great Britain instead of

more favorable; the quantity of exports that would have served
to purchase a given quantity of imports shows a rise.

In the interpretation of the chart and of the figures on which it
is based a qualification needs to be borne in mind, tho one more
important as a matter of principle than as modifying the substantive results.   In the calculations on the net barter terms no
account has been taken of certain items which in strictness should
be recorded and weighed.   Chief among these are the earnings
from shipping services; others, less in amount but presenting the
same question of principle, are banking and insurance services and
the earnings therefrom.   Here we have items which are in the
nature of exports.   The British each year do work of freight and
passenger carriage for which they expect to be paid, and in fact
usually are paid, in that year.   The concrete way in which the
British community receives the payment is thru the inflow of
imported goods; it is the money yield of foreign goods sent to
Great Britain and sold there which pays for the shipping services.
If this were the only "invisible" item in Britain's foreign trade,
and if the recorded imports and exports, instead of being equal
in money value, showed an excess of imports precisely equal to
the money value of the shipping earnings, we could still treat the
situation as one in which imports and exports were equal.   Shipping services are exports, and are paid for by imports.   In such
case, in other words, we should have to consider solely the net
barter terms of trade; no other problem would be presented.

The significance of items of this kind, then, is different from
that of certain other invisible items, such as, on the one hand, new
loans made, and, on the other hand, income from loans made in
times past.   Income from past investments, for example, means
that Great Britain is now receiving payments (which take the
form of imported goods), while she is *now* giving nothing.   She
is sending out no goods or services in exchange.   The loans and
investments whose income flows in were made in the past, very
likely long ago.   The income accruing in the present is pure gain;
pure gain, that is, so far as concerns the present conditions of
international trade.   What Britain receives on this account affects

her gross barter terms of trade, but has nothing to do with the
net barter terms. The same is true, *mutatis mutandis*, of fresh
loans and investments. These also affect the gross barter terms,
but not the net barter terms. Of course they affect the gross
terms the other way. The export of capital means that goods are
sent out, but are not expected or stipulated to be paid for in the
current year. For the time being the goods go out from Great
Britain, but neither merchandise nor money comes in as payment.
Eventually, of course, income will be paid; and it will come in
the form of imported goods. Some annual payment may begin the
very next year, and presumably a return flow will set in (unless the
investment happens to be a complete failure) within a very few
years. In the end, even the principal may be repaid; and then the
payment made to Great Britain will be heavy and her merchandise
imports will be very greatly swelled. But all these transactions,
with their trend first one way and then the other, have a direct
effect, year by year, on the gross terms of trade only. They are
thus different from such transactions as are involved in shipping
services; these being part of the immediate volume of British
products which goes out from year to year and is paid each year
in the form of inflowing imports.

It follows further that in any strict calculations of the net
barter terms, and of changes in those terms, regard should be had
not only to the volume of shipping services, but also to their
prices — to the rates of freight. The index of export prices which
has been used in constructing the chart and the tables does not
include shipping, nor such minor items as banking and insurance
service. Therein it obviously fails to be inclusive. Doubtless the
materials exist from which shipping rates could be computed, and
the index of export prices thus made more accurate. I have not
endeavored to modify in this way the price indices, but have taken
them as they appear in the British sources — figures, that is,
derived from the prices of merchandise alone. It is possible that
corrected indices would show a different trend, but not probable.
I feel reasonably confident that no differences would appear such
as to invalidate the general conclusions here drawn. The point

is of importance not so much by way of indicating that the figures are to be suspected, as for the purpose of illustrating further the distinction between the gross and the net barter terms.

Turn now once more to the chart. The movements which it shows — the changes in the terms of trade — are in clear accord with what is to be expected on grounds of theory. That the gross barter terms should vary as they do, becoming more favorable until 1900, thereafter less favorable, is indeed easily in accord with theory. They will naturally fluctuate in the same direction as the balance of payments. When the balance of money payments due from other countries to Great Britain becomes larger, more goods move to Great Britain. As need hardly be said again, this increase in the physical quantity of the imports is not the same as the excess (or enlarged excess) of the money values of the imports, or in proportion to that excess. But it is in the same direction; it is but another phase of the same movement. We can easily understand, therefore, that the gross barter terms became more favorable during the period 1880 to 1900, when the excess of imports over exports was enlarging, and became less favorable after 1900, when the excess was declining.

More significant in its relation to theory, however, is the fact that the net barter terms move in the same direction. On grounds of deductive reasoning we have argued that when a country has payments to receive for other items than merchandise, the direct and simple exchange of goods for goods is also affected, and is affected to the country's greater advantage. Not only does it get a special and additional inflow of goods on the invisible account, but the main stream of goods, so to speak — that which comes in exchange for its own merchandise exports — reaches it on better terms. The course of prices for imports and for exports, and the physical volume of imports got for the exports, are such that it obtains a larger share of the total divisible gain from the international barter. And so it proves in this case. The net barter terms of trade are modified to the advantage of Great Britain during the period from 1880 to 1900, while the tendency to gains of this kind is checked from 1900. An elusive set of facts, of a kind not easy to put fingers on, is found within our grasp; a recondite theorem is confirmed.

I turn now to another aspect of the problem. The concrete way in which the inhabitants of a country get the benefit of more favorable terms of trade — gross or net — is that their money incomes rise, while the prices of imported commodities fall. With the same labor they can buy more of imported goods. More favorable terms of trade mean rising money incomes; less favorable terms, falling money incomes. We should expect in Great Britain a tendency toward rising money incomes from 1880 until 1900; thereafter either falling incomes, or a check in the upward movement.

Let the reader glance at the chart again. On it he will observe a lower line; it indicates the movement of money wages from 1880 to 1913. The slope is upward until 1900. Thereafter it shows no marked inclination either way, certainly not before 1913. The relation between money wages and the barter terms of trade is clear, certainly for the earlier period. As the terms become more favorable, money wages rise. After 1900, when the change in the barter terms is in the other direction, the rise in wages halts. Money wages remain nearly constant. The period after 1900 was one of rising prices and rising money incomes in the world at large; and the upward movement might be expected to show itself in Great Britain. Yet as regards money wages, there is no such tendency; a striking contrast to the conditions of the previous period, when they moved upward in the face of falling commodity prices. For the period as a whole there is unmistakably an inverse relation between the movement of wages and the changes in the barter terms of trade. It is precisely the sort of correlation we should expect on grounds of theory.

We may turn back now for a moment to the Canadian case, described in the last chapter. The international trade of Canada from 1900 to 1913 evidently followed a course quite the reverse of the British. Great Britain was not only a lending country, but was rapidly increasing her loans; Canada was borrowing heavily.

Canada had a great excess of imports; Great Britain had the equivalent of an excess of exports — a marked lessening of the usual excess of imports. These contrasts, as they appear in the present chapter and in that on Canada, are familiar to the reader. We have now to observe in what way they were reflected in the barter terms of trade. All the elements in the situation might be expected to bring it about that the terms became more advantageous to the borrowing country — to Canada.

The appended chart shows the direction and extent of the changes in the gross and in the net barter terms for Canada. It has been prepared in the same way as the chart for Great Britain on p. 253. The year 1900 is the base period, as it was for Great

CANADA, 1900–1913.

.... Index of gross barter terms
▬▬▬▬ Index of net barter terms
═══ Money wages

Britain. It will be seen that the trends of the two lower curves are markedly downward for the period as a whole. Whichever of the methods of measurement is applied — gross terms or net terms — it appears that Canada gave progressively less of physical exports in exchange for a given quantity of physical imports. As regards the gross barter terms, this progressive gain was the natural concomitant of the heavy borrowings. It was to be expected that Canada, getting a growing excess of imports over exports in terms of money, should also get more imported commodities in proportion to her commodities exported. But for the verification of theory it is particularly significant that the net barter terms also become more favorable. The Canadians not only got more of physical goods in proportion to the goods they sent out, but they got, on better terms, those imported goods which may be regarded as coming in payment for their own exported goods, and which had no relation to the borrowings. And these advantages are further reflected in the upper line of the chart, which shows the course of money wages in Canada. The movement of Canadian prices and wages has been fully described in the preceding chapters; the course of money wages is here charted merely in order to show the contrast, or rather the natural inverse correlation, between the course of money wages and that of the terms of trade. Just as the Canadian case is a simpler one than the British (being as it is an almost pure experiment in international borrowing), so the verification of general reasoning is more marked and more unequivocal.[1]

The question now suggests itself whether the monetary phenomena in Great Britain during this period show the same sort of accordance with theoretic reasoning as has been found for the terms of trade. Did gold imports and exports, bank loans and bank deposits, the total circulating medium and prices, move in the manner we should expect? To this question I am unable to give an answer. As regards Canada, Professor Viner's researches

[1] The figures on which the chart is based are given in full in Appendix II, p. 414, where due acknowledgment is also made to Mr. A. G. Silverman, by whom they were compiled.

may be fairly said to give one. There the verification of theory is almost conclusive. The British situation, however, was more complex than the Canadian. The specie movements, for one thing, had quite a different character. Gold was steadily flowing into Great Britain from the mines, and steadily flowing out to other countries. The South African gold — much the largest constituent in the rapidly accruing output — went first to London, and thence filtered out in irregular streams to other countries. Both imports and exports of gold were almost continuous, and represented in the last analysis nothing more than the process of distributing the new supplies over the world at large. None the less, each individual movement was determined proximately in the same way as if there had been no new gold at all — by the Bank of England's position, its reserve, its rate of discount, its relation to the British banks at large, the price of foreign exchange, the imports and exports of goods. To trace the connections between these monetary elements and the general problems considered in preceding chapters is a task which I have not found it practicable to carry out. It would be necessary to follow step by step the flow of gold into the country and out of it; the Bank's reserve holdings and discount policy; the reserves, the interest rates, the loan operations and the deposits of the commercial banks; the details of the price changes — in fact, the working of the entire banking and monetary mechanism. Not least, the flow of commodity imports and exports would have to be followed in detail. Such an inquiry might well yield results of significance not only for the problems of international trade, but for those of money and credit as well. In this matter, as in so many others, economic science needs much laborious and skilled statistical research for its enrichment and advancement.

One thing, however, stands out in the British phenomena. This is the unmistakably close connection between international payments and the movements of commodity imports and exports. And this closeness of connection, striking in the case of Great Britain, is found again and again in other countries also. International payments, tho they involve between the individuals directly concerned nothing more than remittances in terms of money, lead almost at once to transfers of goods. The movement of exports and imports — the substantive course of international trade — responds with surprising promptness to the balance of international payments as a whole. The promptness is surprising because each constituent transaction, to repeat, is purely in terms of money. When individuals in a country like Great Britain make loans to other individuals (or governments) abroad, they undertake to put at the disposal of the borrowers merely so much of purchasing power, so much "money." Yet the recorded transactions between countries show surprisingly little transfer of the only "money" that moves from one to the other — gold. It is the goods that move, and they seem to move at once; almost as if there were an automatic connection between these financial operations and the commodity exports or imports. That the flow of goods should ensue in time, perhaps even at an early date, is of course to be expected; it is a commonplace in the theoretical reasoning that this must be the ultimate outcome. What is puzzling is the rapidity, almost simultaneity, of the commodity movements. The presumable intermediate stage of gold flow and price changes is hard to discern, and certainly is extremely short.

I find it impossible to see how there can be a complete skipping of the intermediate stage — anything in the nature of an automatic connection. There is, of course, the case, discussed at length in the preceding pages, where no intermediate stage is to be expected at all; the case, namely, where those who make loans happen to stipulate also that the proceeds shall be used to buy specified goods of their own or of their associates. But in the "normal" case, which is exemplified in Britain's trade for the period just examined, purchases of goods are not thus tied to the loans; and it would then seem to be only some sort of roundabout process, some disturbance or readjustment of monetary and price conditions, that could lead to the movement of goods. Being roundabout, one would suppose that it would take time. And yet it appears to require practically none.

It is true that a searching examination of the presumable links of connection, such as was suggested a moment ago, might show that the process was not always so rapid as it seems to be on first inspection. The explanation of the speedy adjustment may be found in the sensitiveness of the British monetary system. It must be admitted, however, that a quick and close adjustment appears to exist in other countries whose systems are less sensitive. So far as I have been able to observe, it is found in the trade of Germany and France also during this very period, the decade or two preceding the Great War.   One might be tempted to say that the sensitive industrial organism always and everywhere shrinks from the loss of its lifeblood, the vital circulating medium; that it turns instinctively to some other way of meeting demands on the industrial structure.   But this is no more than a metaphor; it may suggest in what direction an answer should be sought, but gives no answer.

All in all, we have here a field quite insufficiently explored.   The plain outstanding fact is that the exports and imports of goods adjust themselves, if not at once, certainly with quickness and ordinarily with ease, to the sum total of a country's transactions with other countries.   The balance of payments is satisfied only to a slight extent by any shipment of specie, chiefly thru changes in the commodity sales and purchases.   And hence the corresponding changes in the barter terms of trade also appear with surprising promptness.

CHAPTER 22

The Franco-German Indemnity of 1871

The international trade of France during the period chiefly considered in the present series of chapters — the second half of the 19th century and the first decade of the 20th — had the features characteristic of a country which has long been exporting capital and is still doing so. . Her merchandise imports regularly exceeded her exports. As in Great Britain, loans had reached by the middle of the 19th century the stage where interest payments on what had previously been advanced to foreigners exceeded the annual outgo for new loans. Had it not been for the persistent new loans — the continuing export of capital — there would have been an even greater balance of payments in favor of France, and an even greater excess of merchandise imports. As it was, the "unfavorable" balance of trade was steady, and during the generation preceding the Great War tended to become greater.

There were other non-merchandise items in the international account. Such, for example, were the considerable payments on account of tourists visiting France and of foreigners domiciled there. The amounts were substantial and added to the excess of merchandise imports. These items, however, and other minor ones of similar tenor, and indeed the general course of the country's international payments, had not the somewhat spectacular character which we find in some of the non-merchandise transactions of Great Britain and the United States; such, for example, as the surprising remittances by American immigrants, or the British bursts in the export of capital. The international trade of France, like her internal commerce, moved on a comparatively even keel. A careful study of wages and prices in France, with attention to the

263

different movements of domestic and international prices over considerable periods, might yield instructive results. But no such study has been undertaken, and indeed the necessary statistical material is not readily available, perhaps not available at all. In general, the experience of France offers nothing of special note for the purposes of the present investigations.

To this general statement there is one outstanding exception. The Franco-German indemnity of 1871 does have a spectacular character, presents interesting questions, suggests something novel for the problems of verification and interpretation. The main features of the episode have been frequently and fully described; yet there are certain points, especially as regards the consequences of the indemnity for Germany, which remain obscure. The following pages give an outline of the essential features of the famous transaction, such as will enable the reader to follow the observations which I shall have occasion to make on the bearings of the case on some other and wider problems.[1]

The total sum which France was required to pay Germany under the Treaty of Frankfurt was 5.301 milliards of francs: 5 milliards indemnity, plus 301 millions interest on the postponed payments. Against the total was an allowance of 325 millions for the railroads of Alsace-Lorraine, which were taken over by the German Empire and whose owners were reimbursed by France. Thus there remained to be remitted to Germany the sum of 4,976 millions, almost exactly 5 milliards, the amount of the indemnity proper.

The indemnity was stated in the form of a lump sum, the 5 milliards. True, there was an arrangement for spreading the payment over time. But the time was so short that the obligation

---

[1] The literature on the indemnity is large. All accounts of it make free use of Léon Say's remarkable report, made as chairman of the Committee in charge, and printed in his collected works, Vol. I. Among accounts in English, the most complete is by A. E. Monroe in the Review of Economic Statistics, 1919; another, also complete, is in Moulton & Maguire's book on Germany's Capacity to Pay (1923). See also H. H. O'Farrell, The Franco-German War Indemnity and Its Results; N. Angell, The Great Illusion, Part 1, Ch. 6; Soetbeer, Die Fünf Milliarden, in Deutsche Zeit- und Streitfragen, 1874; papers by A. Soetbeer and E. Nasse in Annalen des Deutschen Reiches, 1875; Bamberger, Die Fünf Milliarden, Preussische Jahrbücher, 1875; Gutmann, Das Französische Geldwesen im Kriege. Most of these publications lay stress on other aspects of the case than are considered in the present chapter.

on France may be described as one for a lump sum to be turned over at once. In fact, this was what France accomplished, the payments being actually made in a less time than the treaty terms contemplated. The case therefore differs from other indemnities of modern times, since usually these have called for a series of payments spread over many years. Such was the case with the Chinese Boxer indemnities under the Treaty of 1901, and with the Turkish indemnity under the treaty of 1878; it is most noticeably the case with the reparations payments required of Germany after the Great War. The Franco-German indemnity was peculiar in calling for the remittance of a great sum in a very short period of time, a transaction unexampled in history.

Two tasks had to be performed by France in order to meet the obligation. One was to secure for the government treasury at home the funds which it must have in hand for the first move toward remittance. The other was to transfer these funds to Germany. The first task, a purely domestic one, was accomplished with an ease and success which astonished Europe and perhaps astonished Germany most of all. France floated two great loans, one of 1¼ milliards (round numbers) in 1871, another of 3 milliards in 1872. There was also a small surplus from the budgets of 1872 and 1873; the Bank of France made a small advance; in the main it was the two publicly floated loans that supplied the money. The credit of France, tho shattered for a time by the war and by the Commune, had been early strengthened by the Morgan loan of 1870, one of the most courageous and successful operations in the history of that famous house, and was completely restored by 1872. The great loan of that year (3 milliards) was enormously successful, being over-subscribed 10 fold and more. Before the subscription books closed, it had become clear that the offering would more than absorb the stated total, and fancy bids poured in from bankers and investors eager to secure shares in the final allotment.

The second task, that of transferring the funds to Germany, was met with no less success. Payments had to be made under the treaty mainly in German or French coin, or in bills of exchange;

to a small extent also in Bank of France notes. Bank notes were turned over to Germany to the limit permitted (125 millions). Coin was turned over to the amount of something over 600 millions. The remainder was handed to Germany in the form of bills of exchange — 4,248 millions in all, by far the largest part of the required total.

The operations by which France acquired the bills were of the most extraordinary character. Every banking house in Europe was induced to participate. The French Government opened offices of its own in London, Brussels, Amsterdam, Hamburg, Frankfurt, Berlin. Not less than 120,000 separate bills of exchange were bought, were marshalled so as to conform to the stipulated dates for instalment payments, and were finally handed over to Germany. The French genius for the orderly conduct of great transactions never shone more brilliantly.

Whence, now, came this great volume of bills of exchange? Not from a surplus of exports over imports — not as the result of the sale of French goods to Germany or other countries. True, the merchandise movements showed effects from the indemnity operations. For a year or two the usual current of France's trade was reversed. The excess of imports over exports which had characterized it for so many years was replaced for a short time by an excess of exports. During 1872 and 1873 French exports were greater than the imports by about 200 millions of francs for each year. But after 1873 the previous merchandise relation again appeared with hardly an exception; imports again exceeded exports. France paid the indemnity only to a small extent in goods; just as she paid it only to a small extent in coin or in Bank of France notes.

The one adequate resource was the great mass of accumulated French investments in foreign countries. These investments existed chiefly in the form of foreign securities held by Frenchmen. It was their sale that supplied most of the funds for the great loans and for the bills of exchange, the funds both for the domestic and the foreign tasks. This resource was not utilized deliberately, in the sense that the officials in charge consciously turned to it. It was thru an indirect process, and apparently one not expected, that the foreign securities of the French investors furnished the where-withal. Italian, Austrian, Spanish, Turkish, American (South and North) securities were sold by French holders; sold not only in Paris but in London, Brussels, Amsterdam, in Germany itself. The proceeds were used in buying their own country's rentes. The foreign holdings of the French were converted *pro tanto* into domestic holdings. The proceeds of the sales of rentes were in turn used by the French Government in buying bills such as Germany accepted under the treaty stipulations — bills on Paris, London, Brussels, Amsterdam, and in some part on Frankfurt, Hamburg, Berlin.

The French side of the story thus is clear and comparatively simple. It has been put on record in Say's Report with a lucidity and fulness unusual for operations of the kind. How much France paid and in what way she paid, is well known.

So far as concerns the theory of international trade and international payments, this (the French) side of the operation is in some ways instructive, in other ways little so. It is instructive in showing how important may be the part played by securities, especially when there is pressure for large remittances in a short space of time. When occasion arises for sending great sums from one country to another, it may be expected that specie (if available at all) will move first of all; securities next; goods last of all. A comparatively slight movement of specie may lead to a considerable movement of securities; whereas the next stage, that of the transfer of goods, may not set in on a large scale without a heavy preceding transmission of specie. Something of this sort might be foreseen in the case of ordinary commercial transactions. The French indemnity payment, however, was not at all an ordinary commercial transaction. It differed not so much because the remittance had to be made by the Government — for, after all, the French Treasury had to effect payments to Germany by the same mechanism which would have been used by private persons — but in the circumstance that France was able to take advantage of the exceptional position of her investors. The French Treasury needed great sums at once and was able to get them with surprising quickness by floating its loans.　French investors had salable foreign securities which they were tempted to sell in masses, putting the proceeds in the domestic rentes.　What happened under these circumstances (so fortunate for France) gives hardly any clue to what might happen under conditions such as would ordinarily have to be faced by a country required to pay a great lump-sum indemnity.

Nor does it indicate — I may remark in passing — what is likely to happen if a country has to make sudden heavy payments of a non-political character; as, for example, if there be great importations to meet a deficient harvest.　Floating securities (if available) are then likely to move quickly in payment of the imports.　But great quantities of securities held for permanent investment by thousands of scattered persons would not be easily dislodged.　The economist who is searching for illustration or substantiation of his theories is circumvented, so to speak, by the unusual conditions which existed in the French case.　He might expect to find the case a very pretty one for his purposes.　What would really happen if one country were called on to remit a huge sum to another within the short space of a year or two?　Unfortunately, any theoretical analysis he may make of the presumable outcome must remain theoretical.　The French experience helps hardly at all for the purposes of verification.　And if the case thus affords but slight instruction with regard to transactions of an extraordinary and even catastrophic character, it affords still less for the ordinary operations of international trade.

What of the other side of the case?　What did Germany get? What was done with the bills of exchange by which the bulk of the payments were made?　Here our information is very much less complete; at the same time, some light is thrown on certain more general problems of international payments.

As we have seen, the indemnity was received preponderantly in bills of exchange — on England, Belgium, Holland, and so on. What did the German Treasury do with those bills?　Did it call for the remittances of specie as they fell due?　or sell the bills in Germany, leaving it to the purchasers to collect in any way they pleased? And did specie flow into Germany; or securities; or goods? No certain analysis has been made, or indeed can be made (in view of the inadequate statistical data) of the concrete way in which the indemnity reached the German people, of the processes by which her economic status was affected. These fundamental aspects of the famous transactions have been singularly neglected in the literature of the subject; and it is possible only to piece together fragments of evidence and interpret them as best one can.

Tho we have no complete or summary statement from German official sources,[1] some specific applications of the indemnity funds are known. For two purposes the Government took actual specie — gold. A moderate amount of gold (120 million marks, or 150 million francs) was put in the war chest of the fortress of Spandau. There it was left intact for some forty years; in 1914, when the occasion finally arose to utilize it for military purposes, it proved a bagatelle, negligible for the exigencies of the Great War. It can hardly be said to have served a useful purpose at any time. Far more important, both as regards the amount of physical gold used and as regards the economic effects, was the establishment of the gold standard in Germany. The indemnity payments enabled Germany to get with ease an amount of gold ample for carrying out the transition from the silver standard to the gold. Ordinarily a country which thus remodels its monetary system has a serious financial problem on its hands. It must have in hand large funds, and must usually resort to taxation or loans in order to get them. Germany was spared this embarrassment and strain by the indemnity. She got the gold easily, and was able to take her time in disposing of the old silver currency which the gold displaced. Apparently something like 750 million francs were applied in this way. For these two accumulations of physical gold, war chest and gold currency, nearly a billion of francs was utilized.

The larger part of the indemnity funds still remains unaccounted for; nor is it important for our purpose to account for all, or to fol-

---

[1] No full statement — indeed no general statement of any kind — was ever publicly made by the German Government explaining what it did with the indemnity funds.

low the German Treasury operations in any detail. Considerable sums were used in clearing away left-over charges of the war, in building fortresses in Alsace-Lorraine, in "re-establishing" the navy, in providing pension funds for the disabled. More important were distributions to the old North German Confederation for paying off its debts — largely for loans and expenses of the war — and similar payments to the other States which were now united in the Empire. After these allotments for debt-payments had been made, still further distributions seem to have been made to the several States. Even so, the Imperial Treasury for years continued to have large funds in its hands, and invested them in various ways — in German securities, foreign securities, time bills of exchange on London, deposits in foreign banks. Concerning the significance of the last named types of investment something more will be said presently.

What now did the German people get — the German economic body, as distinguished from the Imperial Treasury?

To some moderate extent Germany got goods at once, an excess of imports. Just how much came to her in this way cannot be accurately ascertained. During the period after 1871 Germany showed an excess of imports over exports. The excess was no doubt greater than that which had probably appeared even before 1870; there was a net accretion in the merchandise account. But the statistics of foreign trade for the Zollverein, and even those of the first years of the Empire, are so untrustworthy that nothing exact can be made out. What alone appears clearly is that the excess of imports was moderate, and that, during the years in which France wound up her part in the operations, no large amounts reached Germany in this way. It was not in the concrete shape of goods, wares, and merchandise that the German people got the indemnity; certainly not so during the period when France was paying it.

A larger part was played by securities. If the German people had countered exactly on the French — if they had bought securities abroad precisely as the French sold securities abroad — the operations would have offset each other. The Germans would have got the indemnity in the form of foreign investments; not necessarily the identical ones with which the French parted, but the same in amount. They did buy foreign securities to some extent; but here again we have only hints and indications, no precise information. The debts of the former German States were paid off, and the former holders sought new investments. These were partly domestic; an extraordinary increase in new joint-stock companies took place.[1] In good part, the re-investment was in foreign securities and in foreign enterprises; and to this extent they represent something that the German economic body really got from the indemnity. Large investments were made in Austria, especially for Bohemian and Hungarian railway projects. They led in that country to a speculative boom the like of which had never before been experienced, and which culminated in the crash of 1873, the first stage in the world-wide crisis of that year. There is evidence also of the purchase in Germany of Italian, Russian, Turkish and American bonds. The Germans had begun the process of foreign investment before 1870; it was widely extended after that year under the stimulus of the indemnity operations. The attainment of the stage of settled and established foreign investments was quickened and facilitated. In sum, the Germans did get considerable credits and possessions abroad, and the subsequent movement toward expansion of this kind was fairly launched. But after all it was not in this way that the major part of the indemnity was used.

Obviously an important part of the entire problem is that of the commercial specie movement: how much specie went out of France thru the channels of trade, how much went into Germany? Here again our information is unsatisfactory. It is known how much specie was handed over directly by the French Government to the German Government, and how much the German Treasury took for the new gold currency. But how much went out of France thru commercial channels, and how much went into Germany in

---

[1] Soetbeer gives for example the following striking figures:
Total number of stock companies founded in Prussia:
During the 80 years 1790 to June, 1870 — 279 Companies
During the 30 months June, 1870, to the close of 1872 — 762 Companies

this way, is not to be ascertained. For the purposes of the present inquiry, fortunately, statistical precision or even approximation is unnecessary. It is clear that during the years 1872 and 1873 substantial amounts of gold left France. That country had had just the opposite experience in the previous decade; then there was an inflow of specie, not an outflow. After the exceptional years 1872 and 1873, the inflow again set in, being indeed the normal trend for France under her general economic conditions. Germany appears to have had an inflow of specie thruout the decade — and practically all of it was gold, tho in what amounts, over and above those which the Government Treasury received directly from France, cannot be stated with exactness.

What does appear clearly, however, and is the essential thing to be brought out for our purpose, is that the circulating medium in Germany was greatly swelled. Between 1871 and 1873 a large amount of the new gold coin was added, while practically nothing of the old silver was withdrawn. The fiduciary paper (government issues and uncovered bank-notes) was also substantially increased. The total money in circulation increased in the three years by fifty per cent; in round numbers from a trifle under 2000 to full 3000 million marks.[1] So sudden an increase, coming at a time when all the other conditions for expansion were present, naturally resulted in a sharp rise of prices and in a speculative orgy which culminated in the crisis of 1873. Then there was a check; yet soon a resumption of the upward movement. Thru the greater part of the decade gold continued to flow into Germany. Imports also continued to flow in, and there was a marked excess of imports over exports. Germany got both gold and goods; got something in a sudden burst during the immediate period of the indemnity payments, but much more in an almost continuous stream for many years thereafter.

It is this last-mentioned course of events — the continuous movement of goods and money toward Germany thru the decade following 1871 — that is of most interest as regards the general problems of international trade. What it indicates is that, whereas

[1] These are the figures of Soetbeer, Deutsche Zeit- und Streitfragen, p. 50.

France closed out her part of the transaction in short order, Germany spread hers over a considerable stretch of time. The German Treasury, as we have seen, received bills of exchange in amounts enormous for that age. The bills were by no means presented for payment as they matured. They seem to have been nursed; and the proceeds were utilized from time to time, in direct ways or indirect, as occasion arose. True, considerable quantities were turned into cash before 1873, especially for the purpose of securing gold for the new currency. But large amounts, apparently the major part, were fed on the market piece by piece, as financial needs appeared. Sometimes the proceeds of maturing bills were invested by the Imperial Treasury in foreign or domestic securities; sometimes they were left on deposit in London banks; sometimes they were re-invested in still other bills. As time went on, the foreign securities were gradually sold, the balances in London were drawn out; the bills in which the proceeds of the original bills had been re-invested were perhaps again replaced, but finally bills were presented for payment as they matured. Thus the operations of the German Government in the foreign exchange market were spread over a series of years. Correspondingly, the effect on the foreign trade of Germany — the movements of specie, of goods, of securities for private investment — were spread over the ensuing decade. And during that time, still other factors were modifying Germany's international trade. Her manufacturing expansion, so remarkable in later years, took its first great start. Her agricultural imports swelled in consequence of the rapidly increasing movement of grain overseas. As is almost always the case over considerable periods, no one factor was so dominant that its effects stood out conspicuously. The consequences of the indemnity operations, prolonged as they were into a period that seemed far removed from the initial stages, were intermingled with other phenomena, were disguised, concealed, buried in a confused general movement.

I suspect it is in some such way as this that we can explain other similar cases that have puzzled inquirers. What are the conse-

quences of a sudden remittance of very large sums? of a great
subsidy, for example, by one country to another? of a heavy
indemnity? How are payments of this kind effected, what are
their consequences?

There is a well known passage in the Wealth of Nations in which
Adam Smith refers to the subsidies which England made to Prussia
and her other allies during the Seven Years War (1756–63). The
remittances, he says, could not have been in specie, for the sums
exceeded the total specie circulating at home. They must have
been effected by sending out goods against which bills of exchange
were drawn by the exporters and then sold to the British Government. And according to Adam Smith the actuating force which
caused the resort not to money but to goods was simple enough.
The "merchant" who is engaged in foreign business makes a profit
on the exportation of goods, but makes none (or a very narrow one)
on the exportation of specie; he is naturally led to "exert his
ingenuity" toward selling goods abroad; and thus the transactions
are wound up thru an exportation of goods, not thru an outflow of
specie.

All this of course must cause the Ricardians to shake their heads.
In the language of the younger Mill they "applied to Smith's
more superficial view of political economy the superior lights of
Ricardo." [1] These superior lights would have led them to analyze
in quite a different way the successive stages in great payments for
subsidies or like operations. First there would be a sale of bills
on the foreign countries by the "merchants" (bankers) to the
Government; then a rise in foreign exchange to the specie exporting point. Specie flows out; prices fall in the remitting country,
and rise in those that receive its specie; *then* goods begin to be
exported; and so on, until equilibrium is again reached. It is not
necessary to follow the several steps into every detail, or to point
out the difference between a single great payment, like that of the
Franco-German indemnity, and a series of heavy payments spread
over many years. Essentially the same question arises in any case
where an extremely large remittance has to be made in short order:

[1] J. S. Mill's Autobiography, Ch. 1, p. 28.

how does the mechanism of international payments function under such an extraordinary strain? Adam Smith's explanation was hardly satisfactory in his own day; certainly it cannot be so in ours. True, it had a plausibility for the 18th century, because then the same individual was likely to be both an exporter, an importer, and a dealer in foreign exchange. Differentiation in the conduct of these several phases of foreign business had barely begun; the "merchant" was likely to carry on all of them. And hence Adam Smith, casting about for an explanation, might readily conceive that the merchant, engaged in varied and interlocking transactions, would turn to the alternative of sending goods abroad to meet his bills, even tho this obviously would be a troublesome and risky matter, above all in times of war. That he should find a greater profit in so doing — that is, in sending goods rather than specie — is obviously inconsistent with Adam Smith's own doctrine of the equality of profit in the employment of different capitals. But before quite ruling out Adam Smith's explanation, one would wish to know more of the way in which things actually went in those days. Bookman tho he was, he was hungry for facts, and his version of what was taking place in his time is not likely to be entirely without foundation. None the less, it hardly tells the whole story even for the 18th century; and it certainly can tell us very little of what happened under such exigencies in later days.

Ricardo and his contemporaries were confronted by the same problem.[1] During the Napoleonic wars great subsidies were made to the Continental allies of England, and then also it became a question just how the subsidies reached the beneficiaries and just how they influenced the movement of specie or that of goods. But the Ricardian explanation, as sketched a moment ago, also cannot tell the whole story. The process which the Ricardians pictured is one which takes time. Here, as in almost all their reasoning, they neglected the element of time, and assumed that the

---

[1] For an account of those discussions, see the valuable paper by Professor N. J. Silberling in the Quarterly Journal of Economics, May, 1924, especially pp. 416 *et seq.*

results which would presumably come in the long run do come at once and without a hitch. The mechanism of outflow of money, falling prices, increasing exports, declining imports — all this automatic readjustment — does not work out its results in one year, or two, or three. It has been abundantly set forth in the preceding pages how long a time must be allowed before the eventual consequences appear, before the final readjustment can be expected. It is not to be supposed that a sudden huge remittance can be really brought about in this way. If we picture to ourselves a situation such as Adam Smith tried to analyze — subsidies which exceeded in amount the whole circulating medium of the country — and imagine a sudden export of perhaps half of the specie, we must imagine further a collapse of prices, a complete disorganization of trade and industry, a chaos in which neither exports nor imports could move quickly or in large volume, from which recovery and readjustment would be long and disastrous. Clearly nothing of the kind happened in 1756–63. Nor can this sort of explanation fit the conditions of the Napoleonic period. The Ricardians imagined that changes in prices would follow quickly and smoothly from the inflow and outflow of specie; goods would also move in and out of the country with ease and promptness. The whole machinery would work without giving any trouble, without disconcerting either the business world or the public Treasury or the observing economist. This intellectually courageous simplification of the problem is quite out of accord with the experiences of their own times or of any later time when there was the sudden impact of a huge remittance.

What then has happened? What was the course of events in the Seven Years War? What in the Napoleonic period? What in the Great War of 1914–1918, when Great Britain advanced enormous sums to her allies?

I have no more than a provisional hypothesis to offer; no more than this, at all events, on the earlier cases. As will be seen when the extraordinary operations of the Great War come to be considered, they are susceptible, as regards the mechanism of international payments, of a comparatively simple explanation. The explanation certainly is easy as regards the heaviest and most conspicuous remittances of that time, those from the United States. The subsidies of the Seven Years' War and those of the Napoleonic period are by no means simple; nor is the Franco-German indemnity as regards the German side of that episode. My hypothesis is suggested chiefly by the Franco-German indemnity. The French side of this, as has been said, is easy to understand; it is the German experiences which suggest a clue.

That clue is in the *gradual* character of the process of liquidation. The absorption of the indemnity proceeds into the German economic body appears to have been spread over the greater part of the ensuing decade. If only time be given, great operations of this kind can be wound up without disastrous disturbance, nay, with hardly a consciousness of strain. In Professor Silberling's paper on the Napoleonic period there is an intimation of what may then have happened. The first of the English Rothschilds, we are told, was of inestimable service to the British Treasury in the business of sending funds abroad. While not a little, it seems, went in the form of specie, the greater part was remitted thru bills. The bills, one may guess, were drawn on Continental "merchants," who were indicated to the Treasury by Rothschild and were encouraged by him to meet the bills when presented. These obliging persons probably nursed them; were willing to hold or renew until settlement could finally be made, and enlisted others to aid them when their own means approached exhaustion. No doubt eventually they found the operations profitable, notwithstanding all the risks and delays entailed by the long years of warfare. And eventually the settlement from England was doubtless effected thru the export of goods. From time to time, as Continental bills came on the London market, based on the sale of goods, the Treasury bought them and used them for meeting their outstanding obligations to their drawees on the Continent. It is quite possible that the last settlements may have been postponed to the period of peace after 1815, when English goods flowed out in the great volume so often referred to in the literature of the time.

The same sort of thing may have happened in Adam Smith's day. The "merchant" could sell to the English Government bills on his friends and correspondents abroad, and those bills would be duly met; the Government's remittances would be effected. The foreign drawees would be willing to bide their time, hold the bills or extend them, enlist their own business associates in gradually carrying out a series of troublesome but eventually profitable operations. In this case, also, doubtless it was the exportation of goods that constituted the last stage in the transaction. But that process of exportation set in gradually, had the appearance of being sporadic and uncertain, stood in no direct and visible connection with the British Government's subsidies to the Continent. The economic historian may unearth one of these days evidence that will enable him to follow the course of these operations, both for Adam Smith's time and for the Napoleonic period. The evidence at best could be only fragmentary and symptomatic; as indeed we have seen it to be for the comparatively recent and conspicuous episode of the Franco-German indemnity.

A suggestion of wider scope emerges. It is that not only in such exceptional cases as the Franco-German indemnity, but in others of more common experience, the underlying forces bring about their effects thru a gradual process — a movement here and a movement there, with cumulative pressure in the same direction. Specie rarely flows from country to country in great volume over a short period of time. So it is with goods; they ordinarily are exported and imported with regularity, not with abrupt changes one way or the other. When a sudden large movement either of money or of goods does take place, it is likely to be due to a temporary cause, such as a deficient harvest, or a financial crisis in one country not shared at the moment in another; conditions quite different from those to which we give chief attention in the theory of international trade. The long-run forces which are the more common and are mainly considered in the theoretical analysis take time for their operation. Specie is moving from country to country in small or moderate amounts every year, every month, almost every day. But sometimes the movement is preponderantly one way, sometimes another; on occasions in a strong and steady current, but often with such irregularities and eddies as to make it difficult to discern its main course. So it is with goods. In these fluid and shifting currents the long-run forces exercise a constant tho unnoticed pressure.

CHAPTER 23

THE UNITED STATES, I. UNTIL 1900

THE international trade of the United States during the century preceding the Great War presents phenomena analogous to those of Great Britain. More especially the influence of loan operations is abundantly illustrated. The illustration runs, of course, the opposite way; the United States was a borrowing country, not a lending one. Statistical data on prices are unfortunately not available with as much detail as for Great Britain; and hence it is only in the more conspicuous aspects that the consequences of the capital movements can be traced or the conclusions of theory tested. It happens also that for the later years of the period, with which the present chapter deals (before the Great War), some complicating factors entered which probably would make any clear verification impracticable even with the most complete figures.

I do not propose to follow in detail the history of the movements in the country's trade. They have often been described, and the reader who is interested can readily turn to other sources of full information.[1] It will be enough for the present purpose to summarize the main happenings, and to note their significance.

The relation between exports and imports — that is, between their money values — is naturally the phase about which our information is most full and trustworthy. The accompanying chart shows how that relation stood from 1821 to 1914. For reasons which will appear in the next chapter, the chart is not carried beyond 1914.

As in Great Britain, so in the United States, there is a mid-way point between two main currents. The year 1873 marks a turn of the tide in the United States in essentially the same way as the year

[1] See especially the paper on the Balance of Trade of the United States, by C. J. Bullock, J. H. Williams, and R. S. Tucker, in the Review of Economic Statistics, July, 1919.

EXPORTS AND IMPORTS OF THE UNITED STATES, 1821–1914.[1]

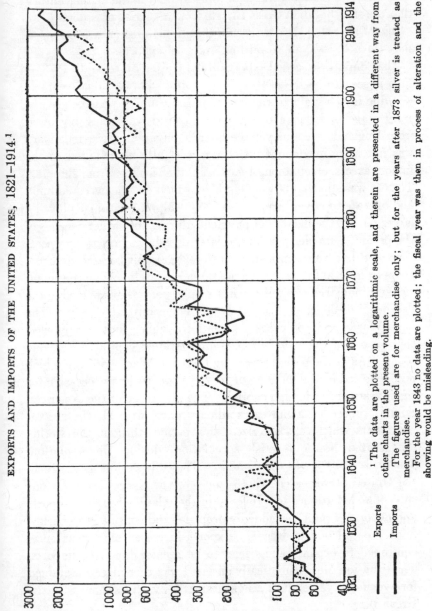

Exports ————

Imports ……………

[1] The data are plotted on a logarithmic scale, and therein are presented in a different way from other charts in the present volume.

The figures used are for merchandise only; but for the years after 1873 silver is treated as merchandise.

For the year 1843 no data are plotted; the fiscal year was then in process of alteration and the showing would be misleading.

1853 does for Great Britain. It was in the middle of the century that the shift began in Great Britain from an excess of exports to an excess of imports. It was in 1873 that the United States began to shift the other way — toward an excess of exports.

That imports exceeded exports in the United States until 1873 — such is seen to be the case, with exceptions in occasional years — was due in the main to the fact that the country was then in the early stage of its loan operations. Capital was being borrowed from England, while as yet the interest payable on previous loans was not large in amount. Other factors also contributed to the import excess, chief among them being the earnings from shipping. The era was still that of wooden ships, which Americans could build and operate to advantage. Relatively, shipping earnings played a larger part in the balance of payments during the earlier decades of the period, a smaller part in the later decades. Borrowing operations had not been considerable before 1830, but became so in the years from 1830 to 1837. Then, after a relapse following the financial and industrial crisis of the last-named year, they revived in the decade 1840–50, and attained large dimensions after 1850. The Civil War of 1861–65 checked them for a while ; but shortly after the war one of the great bursts of international capital movements set in. As in the period preceding the Civil War, so in that which now followed it, the building of railways was the main occasion for the investment of foreign capital. The expansion of the American railway proceeded at an extraordinary pace, with all the accompaniments which characterized this period thruout the world : exaggerated hopes, feverish speculation, devious manipulation. The crisis of 1873 was the nemesis. The collapse was as severe in the United States as elsewhere, and — what is significant for our subject — led at once to a reversal in the relation between imports and exports. Imports suddenly dropped, and continued to be low until the end of the decade. Exports increased almost at once, continued to expand, and began to be greater than the imports. The situation thus dramatically initiated was thereafter maintained for over forty years, until a new dramatic overturn came with the Great War.

There were interruptions, however; occasional stages when the change that set in with the crisis of 1873 was halted, even was temporarily reversed. For two decades, from 1873 to 1893, the situation hung in the balance; the excess of merchandise exports was not continuously and unfailingly maintained. British trade was then in a stage of similar wavering. The course of events on the one side of the Atlantic was in almost every respect the obverse of that on the other; the international trade of the two countries represented two aspects of one and the same series of operations. More especially, the loans of the one and the borrowings of the other were closely connected with the recurring alternations of activity and depression. The export of capital from Great Britain increased rapidly during the upswing stages of the several cyclical periods, and her excess of merchandise imports then declined; relatively, her exports became greater. During those same stages, the import of capital into the United States (chiefly from Great Britain) increased, and the imports of merchandise became greater. In some years of the period after 1873 the movement of capital into the United States was in such volume that the imports actually exceeded the exports, the capital borrowings being so great as to exceed all the other non-merchandise payments which the United States had to meet. This was the case in 1888 and 1889, and again in 1893.[1] The last-named year marks the end of this period of indecision. A sudden decline of imports followed the crisis of 1893, and the excess of exports over imports became not only marked but persistent. It was maintained steadily thruout the twenty years following, and became astonishingly great — a phenomenon to be considered presently in some detail.

In general all this is in accord with expectation. It is as much so as in the case of Great Britain, perhaps more completely so. The correspondence, or rather inverse relation, between the experiences of the two countries extends not only to the borrowing operations, but also to another item in the international account, namely, shipping earnings. While these became steadily greater for Great

---

[1] These are fiscal years, from June 30 to July 1, ending on July 1 of the year indicated.

Britain after the middle of the century, and contributed more and more to her excess of imports, they grew smaller for the United States during the decade from 1850 to 1860; and they came to a sudden end with the Civil War. The fear of capture by Confederate men-of-war caused the sailing vessels of the North to register under other flags or lie at anchor. By the time the war ceased, the day of sailing vessels had passed. Iron steamers took their place; and in building and operating these the British had a clear advantage. Ocean transportation to and from the United States was carried on in foreign vessels, and the charge for this service became a debit item for the country; it was met in the form of merchandise exports, and contributed to the recorded excess of exports over imports. In its main outlines this series of changes is again such as general reasoning would lead us to expect.

When it comes to details, the case is not so clear. The events are complex; the statistical material for test and verification is inadequate; and there are other difficulties, raising troublesome questions of principle.

The events are complex. They are so not least as regards the monetary conditions. During the larger part of the period before the Civil War, the United States was on a specie basis; after 1834 on a gold basis. The specie was held chiefly by banks, and was but a slender foundation for a large volume of notes and deposits. But the banking situation, as is well known to all students of the subject, was highly confused. Some approach to system and order was achieved during the decade immediately preceding the war (1850–60), especially in the seaboard region. But banking legislation and practise still varied greatly from one part of the country to another. The course of domestic and foreign trade, the extension of bank credit, and the changes in prices, were subject to a variety of forces, among which — especially in view of the fragmentary nature of the available information — it would be almost hopeless to discern any specific effects resulting from the course of international trade or from the international movement of specie.

True, for the period just before the Civil War (1850–60), the situation is not quite so beclouded. After the Californian gold discoveries, that metal was produced in abundance from the domestic mines. Most of it flowed abroad. It was an article of export, and had to be paid for in some way or other; it contributed its share to the then persisting excess of merchandise imports. Yet the gold was virtually an article of export, and the immediate cause of its movement from time to time was in the balance of international payments; and this balance on occasions was such as to bring about an actual inflow, and at other occasions caused the outflow to be less than usual. Monetary and banking conditions were then less chaotic than in preceding years; and the whole interlacing system of money, credit, prices, was clearly of the sensitive type. An attempt to trace the influence of the international movement of gold, or more accurately of the greater or less outflow of gold, might therefore seem not entirely hopeless. But these years of comparative clarity were few; and they were dominated by the great expansion which preceded the crisis of 1857, and by the depression following it. It is possible that an elaborate study of this one decade would yield results of significance toward testing the Ricardian theory of the relation between gold movements and prices. But the information on the pertinent matters is fragmentary, and at best the period is short. Even after painstaking sifting of the evidence, the direct effects of gold movements on credit and prices would probably remain obscure, and the long-run trends in the relations between domestic and foreign prices still more so.

After the Civil War, the national banking system brought about greater uniformity in the banking and credit situation. True, great banks were active outside the system, were unaffected by the federal legislation, and went their own way. As regards those within the system as well as those without, the structure of credit and money remained a sensitive one, as it had been before. But during the period from the close of the war to the resumption of specie payments — that is, from 1865 to 1879 — it was sensitive in other ways, and under the influence of other forces than is contemplated in the familiar theories of gold movements. The ordinary circulating medium consisted of inconvertible paper, and the entire structure of credit and money rested on inconvertible paper. The gold produced at the domestic mines continued to be exported, as it had been in 1850–60. And it was now solely and simply an article of export — a commodity exported precisely as any other metal would be. When it left the country, it did not deplete the monetary supply; it was not in circulation, and could not be. The movement of prices was necessarily controlled by quite other forces than the greater or less abundance of specie, the inflow or outflow of metallic money.

A conclusion of importance follows: namely, that one striking phenomenon of this period (1865–79) which we have found to be in accord with theoretical analysis, is — in a way at least — not at all in accord with it. This is the change in the relation between imports and exports which set in after 1873. True, a reversal of the kind — an excess of exports replacing an excess of imports — is what we should look for. But obviously it could not come about thru the mechanism contemplated in the Ricardian theory. Our expectation might be to find steps of some such sort as this: first, an abrupt stoppage (after the crisis of 1873) of loans made to the American borrowers; then a flow of specie out of the United States, to fill the gaps made in the balance of payments as the loans ceased; a fall in American prices because of the outflow of gold; and thereupon, at last, an increase in merchandise exports. But no such chain of events could possibly have appeared in the United States after 1873. The country's currency was not on a gold basis. No gold could flow out of its circulating medium because none (virtually none) was in it. The changes in imports and exports which we should expect did indeed take place. Prices did fall abruptly after 1873 — prices in terms of paper money. Exports rose, imports declined. But the immediate and direct links of connection in all these changes were with the phenomena of the business cycle, perhaps also with those of paper money; not with those of the international movement of specie. The general outcome was such as the ruling theory of international trade would predict; but the machinery by which it was brought about must have been quite different from that assumed in that theory.[1]

We have here, in fact, one phase of a set of problems quite different from those of specie prices and trade under specie ; the problems, namely, of paper money and of international trade between countries not having the same monetary standards. On these other problems something will be said in the concluding chapters of this volume.[2] Here I would point out that the episode of 1873 must lead us to pause and reflect. We find that the important substantive results ensue, even tho there be not that succession of events, that course of causation, that working machinery, which are integral parts of the general reasoning.

With the resumption of specie payments in 1879 there was a restoration of the monetary relations which the Ricardian theory of gold movements contemplates. The currency rested on a gold basis once more. Not only this : the system was again a sensitive one. The deposits, whose dominance in the circulating medium became more and more complete, constituted a structure which was easily swayed as alterations took place in the comparatively slender foundation of specie.

None the less, conflicting and unusual factors entered, and the difficulties of tracing the specific influence of gold movements remain almost insuperable. A supply of gold was indeed accumulated ; one which, tho not large in relation to the mass of credit which it supported, was in itself substantial. In the first years after the resumption of specie payments, there was a heavy influx of specie from abroad, caused by a combination of circumstances such as has frequently exercised a marked effect on the country's economic fortunes. Large crops at home, with deficient crops in Europe, led to heavy exports and to an inpour of gold, the immediate result being that the resumption of specie payments

[1] It is curious that Cairnes, who pointed out (Leading Principles, Part 3, Ch. 3, Section 7) the effects which the great borrowings had on the excess of imports over exports in 1867–73, and predicted the crisis and the overturn, never referred to the existence of the paper money régime, and apparently never perceived that the problem arose under conditions quite different from those considered in the rest of his discussion of international trade.

[2] See Part III, and especially Chapter 30.

was accomplished with unexpected success and finality. Thereafter, however, the movement of specie became indecisive. Some years showed a flow toward the United States, some years a flow the other way; nor do the alternations stand in any clear relation to the movements of prices or of merchandise imports and exports. The gold supply of the country did indeed steadily gain. But it grew by the simple process of the retention within the country of the product of the domestic mines. This indeed, thru the entire period from 1879 to the World War, was the process by which the United States procured the great stock of the metal on which its currency system rested.

It may be maintained, of course, that in this indirect fashion — the retention of its own product of gold — the country simply got its distributive share of the world's existing and accruing stock of gold, and that the entire process can be analyzed in ready consonance with the traditional theory. So it may be; there is not necessarily a conflict between the theory when applied with discrimination, and the facts when carefully examined. It does appear, for example, that immediately after the first two or three years (1879–81) the inflow of gold ceased; that there was then for a few years an even balance between imports and exports of the metal; and that during the subsequent stage of heavy borrowing (1885–89) there was again a substantial inflow. On the whole, the decade showed a large net gain of gold thru imports, over and above what was got from the domestic mines. It is to be noted, too, that during the second half of this decade — at the time when borrowing again was large, 1885–89 — the merchandise imports rose, while the excess of merchandise exports grew less, and in one year (1888) even ceased. All this is in accord with the presumable effects of borrowing. But the supposed *succession* of events is not to be clearly made out. It does not appear that the large increase in the country's gold holdings *preceded* the increase of imports or *preceded* the rise in domestic prices. A detailed examination of all the several phases might yield results confirmatory of the familiar reasoning, or might suggest considerable modification or correction. I suspect the latter is quite as probable as the former; but suspect also that the available statistical material would not suffice for establishing conclusive results.   Here, as in the larger sweep of the trade of the United States, the consonance of the general course of events with the received doctrine is undeniable, while yet it remains uncertain whether the several steps took place in the precise manner presumed.

In other respects also the situation in these years was perplexing. Monetary and credit conditions were affected by disturbing factors of quite an unusual kind.   The silver coinage, begun in 1878, injected into the currency system a new constituent, which grew by steady accretions side by side with the irregular movements of gold.   For a while the new silver money served in the main merely to displace national bank notes, but as time went on its influence was no longer neutralized in this way.   How much of the silver currency (used chiefly as pocket money) was simply in proportion to the general increase of population and production; how much of it was an injection into the circulating medium greater than sufficed to maintain the needed increment of money of this type and efficacy; how far it should be regarded as equivalent to gold that would otherwise have come in — here are problems that not only call for painstaking inquiry into the details of financial history, but involve conjectures and estimates which it seems impracticable to test with the available statistical material.

And in the end this very element, the silver issues, had still a further effect and introduced still a further complication.   The next decade (1890–1900) was marked by the climax of the silver controversy, the abrupt stoppage of the silver issues in 1893, the defeat of the silver advocates in the presidential election of 1896, the currency act of 1900 and therewith the definitive acceptance of the gold standard.   How disturbed were the events of the period, how extraordinary the swings from activity to depression, and then again from depression to activity, is familiar.[1]   The crisis of 1893 and the ensuing period of depression marked the middle of the decade.   Before it, and again after it, there happened to come on

[1] Dewey, Financial History of the United States, Chs. XIX, XX; Noyes, Forty Years of American Finance, Chs. VI–XII.

two occasions the same combination of crop accidents as in 1879–80. In 1890, and in 1896 once more, crops were abundant in the United States and deficient elsewhere. Exports of agricultural produce swelled. In the first episode (1890–91) the outflow of gold was checked; in the second (1895–97) a positive inflow took place. Between these fortunate years came the bitter period of depression, the desperate and finally successful endeavors by the United States Treasury to maintain gold payments, the deliberate importation of gold to that end. And when this struggle was over, came again a spectacular overturn — not only rapid revival in 1896–97, but a sudden great increase of exports during the last years of the decade, and with it a great inflow of gold.

Thruout this decade, still another element affected the international transactions — that of the flow of securities between the United States and Europe. During the first half, securities moved into the United States as European holders became fearful of the collapse of the gold standard. During the second half, confidence was re-established and heavy payments became due to the United States because of the spectacular increase of exports; and then securities were again sent to the country.[1] During the earlier stage, the sales of securities in the United States promoted the large outflow of gold which marked the years 1891 and 1893; during the later, they prevented the inflow from being as large (large it remained) as would otherwise have been the case.

These transactions in securities were as exceptional in character as were the other striking events of the decade. Under ordinary conditions some sort of regularity and predictability appears in this phase of international dealings. It is true that, commonly enough, securities move to and fro as a sort of balance-wheel, serving for the time being (like the dealings in foreign exchange and the international short-time loans) to smooth seasonal payments and unexpected remittances. They also show a long-time trend, according to the stage which has been reached in the position of a country as a borrower or lender. But of all these sorts of normality

[1] On the movement of American securities back to the United States in those years see S. v. Waltershausen, Die Handelsbilanz der ver. St. Amerika, p. 51.

there is little to be discerned in the period here under review. The fluctuations and abrupt reversals in political and economic influences led to currents in the security movements which could conform to no general analysis. They were part of a confused series of events, in which it would seem impossible to disentangle the effects of any one of the forces which "normally" act on international trade.

CHAPTER 24

THE UNITED STATES, II. 1900–1914

IN the period from 1900 to the Great War, the foreign trade not only of the United States but of all countries showed a comparatively even growth. The advance, tho halted somewhat by the crisis of 1907, and not proceeding at the same pace or in parallel lines in all countries, was world-wide; and it was extraordinary in extent. Allowance must be made, when scanning the figures, for the rise in, prices; the physical quantities did not increase as much as did the recorded money values. But with all needed qualification on this score, the advance appears still extraordinary. Something of the same sort had happened a half-century earlier, in the period from 1850 to 1860. Then too the volume of international trade increased by leaps and bounds. Then too, after all allowance for higher prices, the increase in physical terms remained astonishing. In both periods there was the phenomenon of greatly increased gold supply: from the Californian and Australian mines in the first, from the South African in the second. The added gold supply, it is pretty generally agreed, was the cause, or a dominant cause, of the general trend toward rising prices. This same cause is also often referred to as explaining the growth in international trade and indeed in world-wide production. It is not obvious why substantive consequences of such magnitude should ensue from the mere enlargement of the circulating medium, or rather of the basis on which the circulating medium rested. More probably, it would seem that the main explanation is to be found in the accumulated effects of improvements in transportation by land and by ocean, such as were made on so great a scale in the second quarter of the 19th century, and were again made in its last quarter, combined with the opening of new sources of supply for those raw material and food-stuffs for which cheapened transportation signifies most. Yet it remains striking that the physical movement of goods should enlarge so enormously at the very time when the gold supply also was in the stages of most rapid advance. There are questions here which have not been satisfactorily answered. As regards the present inquiry, however, they need not detain us, since we are concerned not so much with the total volume of international trade or with the causes which make it grow more or less rapidly, as with the relations between imports and exports and the causes of changes in these relations.

In the United States, the period from 1900 to 1914 presents some special problems in this regard. It has already been pointed out that by 1890 the stage had been reached where there was definitively an excess of merchandise exports over imports. The periods of wavering (1885–1890) and of confusion (1890–1900) were over by 1900. The United States had then become unmistakably a country in the later phase of borrowing operations. The interest payable on previous loans had risen to great amounts; the inflowing remittances from new borrowings were not great. The balance of the loan transactions led to net payments out of the country and so tended to bring an excess of merchandise exports.

But that was not all. Still other items entered, and made the international account as a whole far from simple, and the application or verification of general principles by no means easy.

First of all, it is to be noted that the excess of merchandise exports was very large indeed. The chart on the following page shows how extraordinary it came to be. When it rose in 1898 and 1899 to figures of 640 and 550 millions of dollars (respectively), the conditions were regarded as exceptional; and for myself, I recall that at the time it seemed impossible that an excess of this extent should persist. Yet something like it was maintained thruout the period to 1914. With but two exceptions (1909 and 1910) each single year showed an excess over 400 millions; and for the period 1900–1914 there was on the average an excess of over 500 millions per year. The aggregate money values of both exports and imports

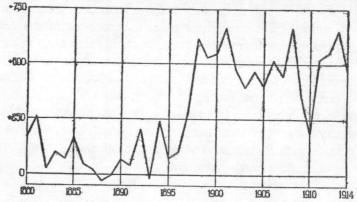

doubled; but the relation between the two showed on the whole little change. The excess of exports was fairly regular and always great.

The main explanation of this accentuated excess of exports is to be found in the appearance of a new item in the international account — new at least in its magnitude. This was the remittance of large sums by immigrants who had established themselves within the country to relatives and friends in their native countries.

These transactions were connected both as cause and as effect with that steady movement of hundreds of thousands of persons annually into the United States which is so conspicuous a feature of the economic and social history of the country during the period. That phenomenon was itself quite extraordinary; and it led to extraordinary international payments. The remittances, as was just intimated, were not merely the consequences of the immigration; they served also in good part to cause it. They were consequences in so far as the newcomers — often men in their prime, coming without families — were able to save a large part of their comparatively liberal earnings, and sent large sums home partly to support relatives, partly for investment there, in the purchase of land. But they operated also as a cause of immigration in that the funds were in good part sent for the purpose of enabling relatives at home to pay their passage money and join the first comers in the land of plenty and freedom. All in all, the total of the remittances made in these two ways rose to surprising sums. Their quantitative importance was hardly suspected until a careful investigation was made in 1907, when it appeared that the annual outgoings of this sort were not less than $200,000,000, and had been for several years at some such figure.[1] They became still greater in the years immediately following. Thruout the opening years of the century they constituted a very large item in the international balance of payments, and virtually a new one.

There were other changes also in the international balance sheet; changes, however, which were more in the nature of modifications of familiar items. Their character and extent is best shown by a comparison of accounts as we find them from time to time. It is not possible to follow the items year by year, or indeed to have much confidence in the precise accuracy of many of the figures. For the entire period preceding the Great War, the statistical material is less abundant and less trustworthy for the United States than it is for Great Britain. None the less the drift of the main changes, and the general consequences for the balance of payments, can be made out with sufficient clearness. I give statements which have come to my attention for certain years.[2]

(1) *1868–69*

Cr.			Dr.		
Net Exports	286.5		Net Imports	402.7
Gold Exports	37.5		Interest	80.0
New Loans	200.0		Freights	24.0
			Tourists	25.0
	524.0			531.7

[1] The matter was brought to the attention of economists and the financial public by a remarkable article contributed by Mr. C. F. Speare to the North American Review for January, 1908. A graphic account of the remittances by Italians to their home country, and of the social and economic consequences, is in R. F. Foerster's Italian Emigration of our Times (1919) Chs. 20, 22.

[2] No. 1 is from the Report of D. A. Wells as Special Commissioner of the Revenue for 1868–69. No. 2 is from a memorandum prepared by Sir George Paish for the United States Monetary Commission of 1909. No. 3 was laid before the Senate Committee on Currency and Banking in 1913 by a New York banker, Mr. J. F. Kent (see the published Hearings before that Committee, p. 2979). All the figures represent more or less of guesswork; they are serviceable chiefly as indicating the general drift during the period. This drift is brought about also in the second set of figures at the bottom of p. 296.

(2) *1908–09*

Cr.			*Dr.*		
	Net Exports	1675		Net Imports	1312
	Gold Exports	48		Interest	250
	New Loans and			Freight	25
	other items	184		Tourists	170
				Immigrants' re-	
				mittances	150
		1907			1907

(3) *1911–12*

Cr.			*Dr.*		
	Net Exports	2188		Net Imports	1618
	Gold Exports	8		Interest	200
	Interest to			Freight	50
	United States	50		Tourists	250
	New Loans and			Immigrants' re-	
	other items	100 @ 150		mittances	250 @ 300
		2346 @ 2396			2368 @ 2418

Some of the main debit items are separately stated in the following table. In it I not only repeat the figures for those items which appear in the preceding tables, but add further figures for the same items. These additional figures have been given at one time or another in somewhat fragmentary fashion, without any attempt to incorporate them in systematized balance sheets. They serve in some sort as checks or corroborations of the more systematic statements.[1]

		WELLS 1869	1894	WALTERS-HAUSEN 1901	PAISH 1909	KENT 1912
Credit Items:	Fresh Loans to United States	200			184	100 @ 150
Debit Items:	Securities Sold in United States		60			
	Interest and Dividends	80	95	114	250	200
	Freight Payments	24	23	53	25	50
	Tourist Expenses	25	47	84	170	250
	Immigrants' Remittances		40		150	250 @ 300

[1] The figures in the second column (1894) have been furnished by my colleague, Professor J. H. Williams, who discovered them in the New York Journal of Commerce, July 8, 1895, and the Commercial Chronicle, Vol. 60, p. 2, p. 632. Those in the third column (1901) are from S. v. Waltershausen's paper on Die Handelsbilanz der Vereinigten Staaten (1901).

In view of the scattered sources from which the figures are derived, it is surprising that they agree so well as regards the trend of the several items. The only striking case of irregularity is Paish's estimate for freight charges in 1909, which is undoubtedly too low.

The series shows in general such trends as might be expected. The item of fresh loans made to the United States — capital borrowings — is large (200 millions) in 1869, and sinks to somewhere between 100 and 150 at the end. There is a curious lack of quantitative data concerning it. Beyond question it fluctuated widely from year to year, just as did the capital exports from Great Britain, rising to great amounts in the years of expansion, sinking to little or nothing in those of depression. In the ominous year 1894, when there was fear that the United States would go to a silver basis, it came to less than nothing. Securities were then sent back to the country from abroad (as has already been mentioned) and the capital movement served to create a debit instead of a credit item — it was as if the United States had paid back money to foreign countries, not borrowed from them. The other side of the loan account, interest and dividends payable by the United States, remains a constant debit item, and, as may be expected in a country which borrows steadily even tho irregularly, a growing one. In the earliest year here noted (1869) the inflowing capital sums still exceeded the interest payable on the preceding loans. As time went on, interest payments rose, while new borrowings became smaller; considering the loan account as a whole, the debit item came to exceed that to the country's credit.

The other items — freight payments, tourist expenses, immigrants' remittances — all indicate growing payments due from the United States to other countries. Tourist expenses show a remarkable increase; estimated at 25 millions in 1869, they are put at ten times that sum in 1912. Freight payments double, from 24 to 50 millions. Immigrants' remittances, which appear suddenly in 1909 as if then a fresh item, had undoubtedly played a large part in previous years, being simply discovered after having grown rapidly since the beginning of the century.

Compare now the course of the balance of payments, as just analyzed, with that of the balance of trade, as described in earlier paragraphs. We find nothing which is out of accord with theoretical presumptions. The heavy payments called for by the various invisible items were met by an excess of commodity exports. That excess, which on first examination seems surprisingly great and continuous, appears, on consideration of the entire range of foreign transactions, quite such as is to be expected. So far theoretical reasoning appears to be verified.

When we proceed to probe the matter further, however, we are confronted by troublesome questions. They relate partly to the machinery by which this nicely adjusted balance of payments was brought about, and partly to the consequences for the barter terms of trade.

First as regards the machinery, and especially the distribution of gold between the United States and other countries. During the fifteen years 1900–1914 the same absorption of the domestic production went on as in the two decades immediately following the resumption of specie payments in 1879. In the later period (after 1900) the net result of the oscillating international movement — an inflow in some years, an outflow in others — was that the country neither got gold from foreign countries nor received it. The total imports of gold for the fifteen years exceeded the exports by 50 millions; a sum negligible for so considerable a period and for a country so rich and populous. During the same time, however, the United States was accumulating the gold yielded by her own mines. The domestic output of gold was (in dollars) from 80 to 95 millions a year. While a substantial part was used in the arts, the increase of monetary stock was still (in round numbers) 800 millions. Tho hardly any gold flowed in from foreign sources, an enormous amount was added to the circulating medium from domestic production.

The United States thus happened to receive, as the country's distributive share of the world's monetary stock of gold, the total of her own contribution to that stock. One might reason about the case thus. *If* the United States had produced no gold; *if* the country had not been growing in population and wealth more rapidly than other countries; *if* then the problem had been simply that of distributing the world's stock of gold (either constant, or growing very slowly from other sources) — the metal would have flown out of the United States in consequence of the country's heavy remittances on invisible accounts. Prices would have fallen there as compared with prices elsewhere, exports would have been stimulated and imports checked, and the balance of payments finally settled thru an excess of exports. This is the "orthodox" process by which the United States would have met the heavy payments for interest, tourist expenses, immigrants' remittances, and the like; this is the mechanism which would have brought about the definitive excess of merchandise exports.

The actual conditions were very different, and were very complex. While the United States was producing and also impounding very large amounts of gold, very large amounts were also being produced in other countries, notably in South Africa. The enormous addition which was being made to the entire world's monetary stock of gold was distributed among the several gold-standard countries by an irregular and devious process, with ebbs and flows for each and every country. The process of distribution was affected by the circumstance that the United States was itself a producing country. Moreover, it was a country growing rapidly in population and wealth, such as might be expected under any circumstances to absorb an increasing proportion of the world's gold. If there had been no gold mines at all within her own borders, some share of the newly accruing output in other regions would have gone this way. The extent of the share so coming in would have depended on her general position in international trade. It would have been larger if the barter terms had tended to become more favorable, smaller if they had tended to become less favorable. It is a curious result, but doubtless an accidental one, that the net outcome for the whole period should be the retention by the United States of precisely that amount which her mines produced.

I turn now to the barter terms — the substantive outcome. On this aspect of the situation, the data have been carefully sifted. We are able to state what was the course of prices for imported and exported goods, what the net barter terms of trade, what the gross barter terms. The charts on pp. 300, 301, show the main movements.[1] The period covered in them is that from the resumption of specie payments in 1879 to the outbreak of the Great War.

Chart I shows the course of the prices of imported goods and of exported goods. The general movements are such as might be expected. Allowing for cyclical variations, the trends for both are

CHART I.

IMPORT AND EXPORT PRICES, UNITED STATES, 1880–1914.

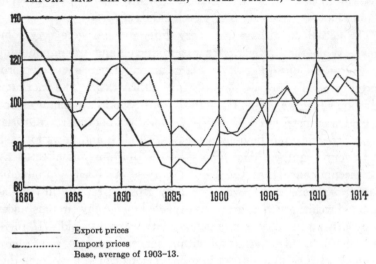

——————— Export prices

····················· Import prices

Base, average of 1903–13.

downward from 1879 to the close of the century; then, after 1898, upward until 1914. This was the general course of prices the world over during the thirty-five years. In the United States import prices fell somewhat faster than export prices during the earlier stage, more especially in the very first years (until 1885). During the later stage there is no significant divergence between the two; the trend is the same.

[1] See the paper by Mr. T. J. Kreps in The Quarterly Journal of Economics for August, 1926 (Vol. 40, p. 708), where the figures are given in detail and the mode in which they were calculated is explained. The figures most important for the present purpose are reproduced in Appendix III, p. 416.

The inquiry on this subject, suggested to Mr. Kreps by myself, proved to be much more laborious and difficult than anticipated; and the perplexing statistical problems were handled by him with high ability. The results, I may add, are significant not only for the problems of international trade, but also for statistical technique and monetary theory.

Chart II shows the movement of the barter terms of trade, both net and gross. The reader will bear in mind that in both a higher index number (rise of the curve) signifies that more of exports are being sent out for a given volume of imports; in other words, that the barter terms became less favorable to the United

CHART II.

GROSS AND NET TERMS OF TRADE, UNITED STATES, 1880-1914.

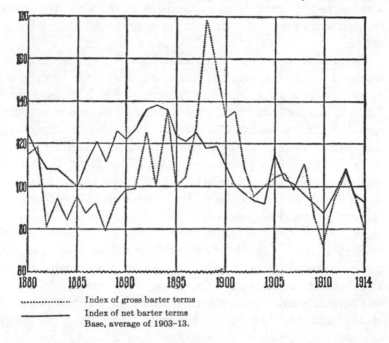

```
          Index of gross barter terms
          Index of net barter terms
          Base, average of 1903-13.
```

States. Conversely a lower index number (decline of the curve) signifies that less of exports are sent out for a given volume of imports and that the barter terms become more favorable.[1]

As already stated, thruout the period (except for sporadic years, 1888, 1889, and 1893) the exports exceeded the imports; the amount of the excess is shown on the chart at p. 294.

[1] The figures on which the curves are based were calculated on the principles already explained. See Chapter 11, pp. 113-122, and Chapter 21, pp. 248-252.

The course of the net barter terms has no very marked trend. Such trend as there is would indicate that the net barter terms were less favorable during the earlier stage (before 1900) than in the later. For about a decade — 1886 to 1896 — there is a discernible upward movement, *i.e.* less favorable terms. After 1900 there is no clear tendency to change. Certainly the net barter terms are quite as favorable after 1900 as before; if anything, more so during the later stage rather than less so. Tested in this way — as regards the net barter terms — the United States was exchanging its goods with foreign countries on no worse terms after 1900 than before.

The gross barter terms show great irregularity of movement, yet a general trend not dissimilar. The irregularity is to be expected, in view of the abrupt changes which repeatedly take place in the international trade of the United States. Agricultural commodities dominate in the exports, even tho less overwhelmingly so in the later years than in the earlier. The variations of the crops (notably cotton) from year to year, and of their prices, bring about sudden changes in the recorded exports. The disturbed conditions of the decade 1890–1900 also go far to account for irregular movements; especially a great burst, during the second half, in the exports of all kinds of commodities. The chart shows that in 1898–1900 the excess of exports took a sudden leap, and that the gross barter terms of trade became correspondingly unfavorable — the curve mounts. The physical volume of the exports was becoming much greater as compared with the physical volume of the imports. After 1900, however, this relation no longer appears. The gross barter terms of trade, like the net barter terms, indicate nothing that is noticeably unfavorable to the United States. It is true that the money value of the exports continued to exceed by very large amounts the money value of the imports — almost as much so as during the unusual years 1898–1900. Yet when correction is made for the prices of imports and exports, and a calculation is made of movements in the physical quantities of the two (as is done in this procedure) it appears that the United States was getting her total imports in exchange for her total exports on terms as advantageous as before, certainly no more disadvantageous. The curve of gross barter terms, like that of net barter terms, does not mount.

This is an unexpected result. It is unexpected for both accounts — the net account and the gross. On general principles we should look for terms of trade more unfavorable in the second stage. The excess in the money volume of the exports meant, to repeat, that the United States, in meeting the divers additional charges for immigrants' remittances, tourist expenditures, interest, and the like, sent out goods having a greater money value than the goods she bought. The process would presumably mean that the United States was pushing the sale of her goods in foreign countries, was offering them at lower prices, would send out relatively greater physical quantities — would have barter terms less favorable. It does not appear to have been so. The heavy debit items were met without this disadvantageous consequence. The case shows an outcome different from that in Great Britain and Canada during the same period. For these countries, the actual course of events proves to be in accord with theoretical prevision. For the United States it does not.

I am not sure that this anomaly can be satisfactorily explained. But there are at least possibilities of explanation. The two sets of cases — Great Britain and Canada on the one hand, the United States on the other — while alike in one respect, are unlike in others. Both in Great Britain and Canada one single factor was dominating the changing course of international trade. In Great Britain it was the great lendings, the capital exports; in Canada it was the great borrowings, the capital imports. But in the United States the situation was not so simple. We have grounds for believing that there was not merely the one new factor of heavy debit charges and heavy remittances. Other factors also changed, or at least were greatly modified or accentuated.

First to be mentioned is the accumulated effect of the protective tariff policy so long maintained by the country. Here there may be — we must speak in guarded terms — an illustration of the working of duties on imports, as set forth in Chapter 13. The consequences of such duties are the same as those of a decrease in the country's demand for imported goods. Indeed, a protective system may be said to amount in substance to a conscious and deliberate determination to buy less of imports; and the less of imports a country demands, the more favorable are the barter terms for the imports which it continues to take.

Signs of such tendencies are to be discerned in the international trade of the United States after 1900. The imports from European countries tended to slacken or remain unchanged, in face of a rapid growth in population and wealth. Those from tropical and oriental regions showed steady and rapid increase. The imports of textiles into the United States, for example, remained virtually stationary (in money value) for several decades preceding 1914, and showed a distinctly declining course during the particular period here under consideration. Meanwhile population was growing fast, and the domestic production of textiles was growing even faster than population. And a similar tendency is to be observed in the imports and the domestic production of other goods which European countries supply to the United States.

The growth of manufacturing industries in the United States during the half-century following the Civil War of 1861–65 is familiar. Beyond question it was promoted by the protective system. For the present purpose it does not matter whether the growth is regarded as healthy or unhealthy — such on the whole as conduced or did not conduce to the country's material prosperity. It may have led to the development of industries which remained dependent on tariff support and were in effect a burden on the country; or it may have led, thru the processes which are assumed in the argument for protection to young industries, to an eventually beneficial nurture of manufactures in which the country proved in the end to have a substantial and sufficient comparative advantage. Results of both kinds seem to have accrued.[1] The question pertinent for the present inquiry is merely whether a decline in imports,

---

[1] As I have tried to point out in my book on Some Aspects of the Tariff Question, to which the reader is referred for a detailed examination of the points here indicated.

ascribable to causes of this kind, did appear in special degree during the years (after 1900) when remittances to foreign countries
increased in special degree.   One may fairly contend that it did.
True, the protective system was little more stringent then than it
had been before; the changes in the tariff acts of 1897 and 1909
made no great general advances in the rates.   But the system had
had more time in which to work out its effects.   And the element
of time is quite as important here as in other parts of the field of
international trade, or in the economic field at large.   The tariff
system led to the growth of the protected American industries by
gradual stages, and was cumulative in its effects.   It was in the
later stages that the full effects appeared, both as regards the
industries that still remained dependent on protection and those
that no longer needed it.   And these full effects, as they were felt
after 1900, were to lessen the imports of large classes of goods.   It
was as if a decline in demand for European goods had set in.

There are still other possibilities.   Is it to be assumed without
further ado that the conditions of demand for the exports remained
unchanged thru the period, that the foreign demand schedules for
American products continued to be the same?   The increase of
exports from the United States which we have noted was accompanied by a change in their character.   Not only did they increase
in money value; their make-up changed.   The proportion of food
products, while varying greatly from year to year according to crop
conditions, on the whole became less.   Cotton retained a dominating position; copper and oil became more important.   Most
noticeable of all was the larger part played by manufactured
goods of various kinds.   Thus in the character of the demand
by other countries for the exports, as well as in that of American
demand for the imports, the conditions may be regarded as having
tended to make the terms of trade more favorable to the United
States, or rather to have prevented them from becoming less
favorable.

A change in demand is the most elusive among the factors which
act on the terms of trade.   Other factors, such as tourist expenditures, or capital import and export, can be specifically traced.

Even tho it be not easy to ascertain just how large are the sums involved, it can at least be known whether they exist and whether they are becoming larger or smaller.   But it is almost impossible to put one's finger on a specific increase of demand; verification is almost hopeless.   In the present puzzling case I see no way of testing whether the swelling exports from the United States were to any noticeable extent the results of an increase of demand.   It may be that a change of this kind set in, by the merest chance, at the very time when the heavier remittances had to be made.   The two forces would then tend to neutralize each other, that of increasing demand being reinforced by the working of the protective duties. The growing exports from the United States, and especially those of manufactured goods, may signify that there was an increase of demand from foreign countries; and they may thus constitute a factor which, if standing by itself, would have tended to bring gold into the country and to make the barter terms of trade more advantageous.   Or they may signify merely that the barter terms, under the pressure for growing remittances to foreign countries, were becoming less advantageous and that this pressure caused commodities of any and every sort to be exported in greater quantities.   There is no way of testing what was cause and what effect.

The topic is speculative.   We have a characteristic case of confused outcome.   Different forces have worked in different directions, and it is impossible to discern what is the quantitative effect of any one.   What has been said in the preceding paragraphs can serve in no way as verification of theory.   It is merely a resort to general reasoning, deduction, theory, as a means of interpreting a complicated and perplexing course of events.   The theory may help in explaining the facts; but the facts are not such as to substantiate any theory.

CHAPTER 25

The United States, III. After 1914

The present chapter deals with the international trade of the United States during the years of the Great War and of the period immediately after it. In carrying the narrative and analysis into this extraordinary and abnormal period, I depart from the plan of the previous chapters, which made no attempt to consider the war and post-war phenomena of European countries. The grounds for including the American experiences of this date are two. In the first place, the United States remained on a gold basis, and might be expected to illustrate the mechanism of international trade under specie conditions. Second, the events of the time led to unusual and striking operations bearing on our general problems.

On the outbreak of the war, in July, 1914, the immediate effects were almost as disastrous in the United States as in the warring countries. A severe financial crisis was precipitated, so severe that the New York Stock Exchange, for the first time since 1873, was closed, and remained closed for a longer period than ever before in its history. There was a heavy drain of gold out of the country; gold payments were virtually suspended; foreign exchange soared; extraordinary measures were taken by the banks to meet extraordinary emergencies.[1] But this stage of semi-collapse proved brief — so brief that it has almost faded out of memory. By the end of the year calm had been restored, and the export of gold ceased. The Stock Exchange opened in the early days of 1915. There was a slow revival of industry and trade during the first half of that year, a more rapid revival in the second half. By 1916 the war boom set in. It lasted thru 1917 and well into 1918. While a boom thruout, its economic characteristics were

[1] For an excellent account of this first stage see an article by Professor O. M. W. Sprague in the American Economic Review, Sept. 1915.

somewhat different in its earlier stage — that preceding the entrance of the United States in the war in March, 1917 — from what they were in the later stage, after that epoch-making date. We may begin by considering the way in which international trade was affected during the earlier stage, from about the middle of 1915 until the spring of 1917.

By 1915 a great demand for American products set in, almost entirely from the countries at war. Largely it was for commodities to be used directly in the war; but foodstuffs for civilians as well as for soldiers were also called for. Of the former sort were explosives; iron and steel; copper, brass, and zinc; automobiles, horses, leather. Breadstuffs, meat products, sugar, were of the latter.[1] The total of the exports suddenly increased, and continued to increase year by year, reaching sums never before dreamed of. The imports also rose, but by no means at the same rate; and an amazing excess of exports over imports developed. If that excess had already been unexampled for the fifteen years preceding the war, it was not only beyond example during the war, but almost beyond imagination. The exports were greater than the imports by two, three, four billions of dollars a year. These are of course money values only. In terms of physical quantity neither exports nor imports increased at the rate shown by the price figures. But as regards the problems of international payments — the mechanism of international trade — it is the money values that signify.

[1] For the calendar years 1914 and 1915 (I do not take fiscal years for this purpose) the exports of significant classes of articles show the following figures, in millions of dollars:

	1914	1915
Explosives	10.0	181.8
Chemicals, drugs, dyes, etc.	28.4	80.4
Brass and manufactures	6.8	54.8
Copper and manufactures	117.2	125.1
Zinc, except ore and dross	8.8	33.5
Iron and steel and mfs.	199.9	388.7
Automobiles and parts	34.2	111.2
Horses	17.5	94.8
Other animals	3.0	26.8
Leather and tanned skins and mfs.	67.9	156.1
Wheat and wheat flour	249.6	378.7
Other breadstuffs	60.7	149.2
Meat products	137.7	259.0
Dairy products	3.7	20.6
Sugar, refined	18.2	42.7

If ever a country could be made rich by a " favorable " balance of trade, the United States had its golden opportunity during these five years.[1]

And gold the United States did get. Altho during the brief period of acute depression — the last six months of 1914 — much gold had gone out, the return movement during the second half of the fiscal year (January 1 to June 30, 1915) was so great that there still remained a net excess of imports for that fiscal year as a whole. In the year 1916 the net imports exceeded 400 millions, and in 1917 rose to nearly 700 millions. Thru causes which will presently be noted, the inflow then was stopped, and in the years immediately following was even replaced by a moderate outflow. For two years, however, cash flowed into the United States in extraordinary volume.

Great as was this inflow, obviously it was not large enough to pay for the much greater exports of merchandise. The absolute amount of gold that came in was enormous; yet it was still small, when compared with the payments due for goods exported. Only in part was the excess of exports paid for by the transmission of hard cash. Other means of payment had to be provided, and

[1] I give the figures (in millions of dollars) of merchandise (including silver) imports and exports for the *fiscal* years (ending June 30) 1915–19.

Fiscal Year	Exports	Imports	Excess of Exports
1915	2820	1703	1116
1916	4393	2232	2161
1917	6368	2694	3674
1918	6059	3016	3043
1919	7534	3174	4359
Total for period	27,174	12,819	14,353

The net gold movements (excess of imports or exports of gold) during the same five years were:

Fiscal Year			
1915	25.3	excess imports	
1916	403.8	"	imports
1917	685.3	"	imports
1918	66.4	"	exports
1919	54.2	"	exports
Total for the period	993.8	"	imports

were found in the time-honored and inevitable resort of the hard-pressed — borrowing.

The first great loan operation came in September, 1915, when the Anglo-French loan of $500,000,000 was placed on the American market. Like other subsequent borrowings of the two governments, it was managed by the firm of J. P. Morgan & Co. Thruout the war, and indeed for the period after the war, that firm acted as financial agents not only for them, but for their European allies also. Its first operation, the "Africs" [1] loan of 1915, was simple enough. Government bonds, the joint and several obligations of Great Britain and France, having five years to run, were sold to Americans; being taken by banks and investment concerns, not without some pressure from the great house itself, and in course of time distributed among investors. The proceeds were used by the Morgans in order to pay for the American goods which had been or were to be bought by the two governments. The foreign purchasers, be it noted, were in the main not private persons, but the warring powers themselves. They bought not only war supplies of all kinds, but food and other necessaries for their civilians. Characteristic of purchases of the latter kind were those of wheat and flour, bought by the governments and then sold to their own population at a lower price than had been paid, lest a stir of unrest be aroused by the high price of bread. Not all the exports from the United States were accounted for by the various kinds of government buying; but it was these which played by far the largest part.

Other loans followed, and, as the war went on and spread over all the world, in such volume that the credit of the borrowers was strained to the utmost. Soon it became necessary to resort to less simple methods, and to attach to the loans which were placed in the American market something more than the bare obligations of the several governments. Secured loans were offered. Stocks and bonds of American railways and other enterprises, held in Europe in consequence of the long series of loans made in previous years by foreign investors to Americans, were now sent back to the

---

[1] "A. Fr." was the stock market abbreviation, commonly pronounced "Afric."

United States and put in the Morgan vaults as collateral to ensure the solidity and the ultimate payment of the bonds offered by them to the American public, now no longer borrower, but turned lender. These securities came chiefly from London. The British Government at first endeavored to bring about their transfer into its hands (by loan or purchase) thru friendly negotiation. But the urgent necessities led before long to stern measures. A full and detailed list of wanted bonds and stocks was prepared and published, and the holders were required to put them at the disposal of the British Treasury on pain of paying, as regards the income from them, an extra income tax of ten per cent (2 shillings in the pound). A committee was organized to manage the procedure, and it handled something like two billion dollars' worth of securities.[1] After the sober British fashion, the pressure on the owners was made as little irksome as possible; they could sell or could loan; and if they loaned, they were to receive, so long as actual sale was not found necessary, not only the interest or dividends accruing from their properties, but ½ per cent on the nominal value in addition. The French Republic took similar steps toward getting into its hands American securities owned by its citizens; but its more solicitous policy toward property holders led it to resort to bonus rather than compulsion. With the details of these operations we need not concern ourselves. They are part of the whole series of fiscal and economic measures, quite unusual in character, to which the governments were led by the stern exigencies of the war.

We may now consider in what way these two great movements, the flow of gold to the United States and that of securities, fit into the received version of the theory of international trade.

That gold should pour into the United States is quite in accord with the usual analysis. The huge exports had to be paid for, and a great movement of gold to the United States was to be

---

[1] The Report of the American Dollar Securities Committee, dated July, 1919, gives summary figures concerning these operations. The amount stated in the text (2 billions of dollars) includes the value of securities which the Bank of England gathered before the Committee got to work.

expected. It was to be expected, too, that the increase of the gold supply in the United States should bring about a rise in American prices, or at least should give the basis and the impetus for a rise; a consequence which did ensue. Of this aspect of the case (comparatively simple) more will be said presently. In other respects, however, things did not happen at all in the way which unvarnished theory would suggest. Indeed, they could not happen so. Prices abroad were not affected by the specie movement. The gold came chiefly from countries no longer on a gold basis — from the dead holdings or reserves of the central banks of England, France, and apparently Russia also. Each of these countries was on a paper basis, was hoarding its gold so far as it could, and was using it reluctantly and under pressure simply as an adjunct to military policy. Prices were determined by the conditions which obtain under inconvertible currency. Nothing like the Ricardian reasoning could be applicable as regards international trade : no assumption that there ensued a fall in prices in the European countries whence the gold came, thereby a stimulus to their exportation of goods to the United States, and so on. So far as concerns the inflow of gold the other way, into the United States, the Ricardian consequences might perhaps be perceived; not so as regards the flow out of the European countries.

When it comes to the borrowing operations, we are confronted still more patently by phenomena quite outside the range of the usual explanations. In relation to the substantive course of international trade — the movement of physical goods — the characteristic feature of the case was that the borrowings were caused by the exports, not the exports by the borrowing. Cause and effect ran in quite a different sequence from that which has been assumed in our general reasoning, and has been verified in our analysis of the earlier loan transactions of various countries. In all that has been said in preceding chapters, an export of merchandise has been treated as the *consequence* of an export of capital; either an indirect consequence, coming about thru price changes, or a direct consequence, following the immediate use of the funds in the purchase of the lending country's goods. But in this case it was the purchase of the goods for export which came first; thereafter came the efforts — efforts that grew desperate as time went on — to borrow in the exporting country itself the money means wherewith to make payment for these precise goods. It was not the loans from the United States that brought about the export of merchandise; it was the previous purchase of merchandise that led to the loans, the export of capital. The chain of causation is the reverse of what is ordinarily to be expected in the international borrowing operations and is ordinarily found in them.

I speak of an export of capital from the United States. In good part the outcome of the operations was not so much an export of capital as a repayment or redemption of past loans — a reimport of capital, if that phrase be permissible. To a considerable extent American securities were definitively returned by European investors, and were purchased by American investors. Dividends and interest that had been previously payable to European holders now became payable to American holders. In the readjusted balance of international payments the item of income from these securities, which so far had figured as a debit item for the United States, ceased to figure on either side. For the time being, the income item was insignificant; it was the enormous transactions on capital account that signified. As regards these transactions, it was immaterial whether the Europeans found the means of paying for their purchases of goods by selling obligations of their own in the United States or selling their holdings of American securities. In both cases it was the exports of goods that caused them to turn to the sales, and it was the unusual connection between the two sets of operations that gave the whole situation its peculiar character.

Proceeding now to the second great stage of the war operations, that which followed the entrance of our United States into the conflict, we find again phenomena of quite an unusual kind; in part similar to those of the first stage, in part different.

As regards the continued exports and the use of loans in paying for them, the situation remained in the last analysis unchanged.

But there was this important modification : the American Government now undertook to do the borrowing and to secure the funds
from American investors.   The Allies of the United States (as
they had now become) had strained their credit almost to the
breaking point.   With all the resort to collateral security, they
could float no more loans.   At the critical moment the United
States stepped in, issued to the American public its own securities,
and then put the proceeds at the disposal of its Allies by way of
loan.   It cannot be doubted that for the first year of the American
participation in the war this was the one substantial contribution,
over and above that of moral support and psychological effect,
which the United States made to the Allied cause.

The procedure was simple.   The Treasury issued the successive
series of Liberty bonds and was able to dispose of them to the
public; of this more presently.   The Allied governments continued their purchases of goods in the United States and the goods
were exported as before.   When payments for goods became due,
this or that government would notify our Treasury of the sums
for which it had need.   Thereupon the Treasury would instruct
the Federal Reserve Bank of New York to hold to the credit of
the government a stated sum; and the sum would be withdrawn
by the borrower, deposited with its bank or banker, and used for
payment of the American sellers of the goods.   All that the
Treasury had to show for its vast disbursements was a certificate
of indebtedness of a quite informal sort.   Extraordinary amounts,
hundreds of millions in a single transaction, were handled in this
way.   In minor cases involving much smaller sums, the procedure
was somewhat different.   For certain governments, sums specified in advance were put at their disposal in the Treasury, and
against these they drew as they saw fit.   And to some extent
also the advances were not used for the purchase of American
goods, but for remittance abroad to be used in any kind of
expenditure which the borrower desired.   But the characteristic
operations, and those which involved incomparably the largest
sums, were of the first kind.   The advances were still made from
time to time *after* purchases of American goods had been

settled; and the proceeds were used at once in payment for the goods.[1]

The real meaning of all this was little understood by the general public; nor for that matter by the banking fraternity, the government officials, financial writers. The huge exports were thought of as sales for cash by Americans to foreigners. There was much gloating over the vast " favorable " balance of trade that was being built up; what could do more to enrich the country? As for the loans to the Allies and the payments to them, here was no offset to the fructifying process, because " the money stayed in the country." It is obvious that in reality, thru it all, both in the first stage (when the loans were still handled by bankers) and in the second, of advances by the Treasury, the thing that happened was that Americans bought from Americans. One group of Americans produced goods which were exported; another group supplied funds for paying them. During the first stage the funds were supplied by the investors who bought the Africs and the subsequent issues floated by Morgan's. During the second stage they were provided by those who took the several issues of Liberty bonds. At a still later stage, and indeed during the later phases of the second stage itself, something came from income taxes and excess profits taxes. Thruout, however, it was

---

[1] An excellent detailed account of the Treasury operations is given in Foreign Affairs for April, 1925, by Mr. Albert Rathbone, who was Assistant Secretary of the Treasury at the time and was in charge of this phase of the Treasury's business.

The following figures from Mr. Rathbone's paper (p. 396) show what were the amounts of the advances to the several countries both for the period of hostilities, up to November, 1918, and for the subsequent period of winding-up. The figures are in millions of dollars.

PERIOD	GREAT BRITAIN	FRANCE	ITALY	ALL OTHERS	TOTAL
Apr. 24, 1917, to Nov. 15, 1918	3696	1970	1051	381	7098
Nov. 15, 1918, to Nov. 1, 1920	501	996	580	291	2368
Total	4197	2966	1631	672	9466

The form of certificate of indebtedness which the United States took from the borrowing foreign governments is given on p. 56 of the Report of the Secretary of the Treasury for the fiscal year 1919–20.

one set of Americans who furnished the funds for paying still another set of Americans. The actual merchandise — the iron and steel, copper, railway material, motor cars, cotton, leather, breadstuffs and meat products — went to foreigners. What came *from* foreigners was merely some scraps of paper, their governments' promises to pay; nay, in sundry cases nothing more than an entry on the books of the Treasury. Never was the nature of capital export exhibited more clearly. Goods go out, and for the time being nothing enters in return. And never before was the nature of capital export more completely misunderstood. The country was supposed to receive much and to relinquish nothing; whereas in fact it parted with much and received nothing.

The curious self-deception of the American public was largely due to the continued upward movement of prices, the continued war boom, the specious appearance of wonderful prosperity. And in this regard there is a sharp difference between the first stage and the second. The upward movement of prices which had begun in the latter part of 1915 and had become marked in 1916 went on with swifter pace thru 1917 and 1918. The reader may be assumed to be familiar with its character and its momentous consequences. What is pertinent to the problems of international trade is that during this second stage — 1917 and after — the price movement was the result of domestic causes only. During the first stage it had been otherwise. Then the great imports of gold (during the fiscal years 1916 and 1917) filled the reservoirs of the banks. The Federal Reserve System, established in 1913, was just getting on its feet. The inflowing gold supply made its way into the coffers of the Reserve Banks, and supplied the basis for a quick and sharp expansion of credit, deposits, and circulating notes. But when the country entered the war the inflow of gold ceased. It was no longer necessary for the Allies to muster every resource — gold, as well as loans and sales of securities — in order to pay for their purchases. The United States Treasury stepped in for them.

The operations of the Treasury, however, served to expand the circulating medium even more effectively than the gold imports had done. The disposal of the successive Liberty loans was accomplished by utilizing to the utmost the credit machinery of the banks of the Reserve System. Purchases of the bonds were fostered, indeed were fairly pumped up, by great subscriptions for which the banks supplied the funds. Billions on billions were disposed of by this forcing process. The banks made loans to the subscribers, creating deposits to their credit; checks against these deposits served to pay for the bonds; the Treasury again deposited the checks to its credit, and in due time drew its own checks in payment for the war expenditures (including the loans to the Allies). The large stock of gold held by the Reserve Banks enabled the expansion to take place without the traditional earmarks of an undue or dangerous procedure. Indeed, the one really important sign of excess and the one effective check of excess — the outflow of gold — could not have taken place anyhow. No one of the traditional links of connection between price changes and international trade was present: neither an inflow of gold as a cause of rising prices, nor an outflow as a check. The Treasury and the banks were able to go their way in raising the war billions by creating deposits *ad libitum*. And these deposits remained a permanent addition to the effective circulating medium — permanent, that is, in the sense of remaining in effect so long as the debts incurred by subscribers to the bonds continued to be carried by the banks. The deposits kept going round and round. First they were used by the Treasury in its various payments; and then used and spread broadcast by the contractors, merchants, manufacturers, farmers, soldiers, into whose hands the "money" flowed. As with the export of capital, so with these financial operations, the process was one of self-deception. The real efforts and sacrifices of the war were concealed. And in both cases, the really significant operations were purely domestic, quite divorced for the time being from international trade.

All this could not go on indefinitely. The phenomenal excess of exports could not possibly persist. The upward movement of prices must come to an end when the Treasury's war operations would cease. A process of readjustment was inevitable. With the end of the war the gap between imports and exports could not remain so vast. The prices of the commodities on which the war demand had impinged most directly — explosives, metals, foodstuffs — could not but plunge downwards. The general price level must cease to rise; presumably it would fall.

It is quite in accord with previous experience under analogous conditions that the revulsion did not take place immediately. For a few months immediately succeeding the armistice there was a halt, a taking of breath as it were. Then the business world made an endeavor to resume and maintain the mad pace of the war. So it was at least in the victorious and the neutral countries; and even the defeated made some such start. The full history of the speculative period which began early in 1919 and ended with the crisis of the autumn of 1920 is still to be written.[1] Much affected by the anomalous monetary conditions of the post-war period, it had all the characteristics of an inflationist craze. But both gold-standard countries and paper-standard countries; both those with wide use of deposit and check systems, and those making but slender use of that powerful mechanism; countries almost exhausted by the war and countries to which it had brought affluence — all alike went thru the same excitement and the same revulsion. Perhaps something of the kind was inevitable: a stage of release and buoyance, and then at last the slow and bitter process of recovery from the lasting effects of the desperate struggle.

The course of the international trade of the United States under these conditions was in accord with the general movement. Here too there was a false start, followed by a painful readjustment. For a considerable period the situation was one to which the ordinary formulae could not apply.

The figures of the imports and exports of goods, and those of the flow of specie, are curious. Consider first the calendar years from

[1] Not only its history, but its lessons with regard to monetary problems remain to be clarified. The causes by which the decline of prices was finally precipitated; the links of connection between that decline and the volume of credit and of currency; the part played by public finance and government deficits; the interaction of domestic trade and foreign trade — here are matters which give the economists much to reflect on.

1919 to 1921.[1]   The excess of merchandise exports remained extraordinary.   In round numbers it was four billions in 1919, three
billions in 1920, two billions in 1921.   Then it declined rapidly;
by 1922 it fell to amounts comparable to those of the pre-war
period (on this later stage more will be said presently).   The flow
of gold showed a movement of quite different character.   In
1919 there was a large net export (292 millions) ; [2] then a moderate
import in 1920; finally enormous imports in 1921.   The relation
between the two movements is quite the reverse of what one would
expect.   For the two years 1919 and 1920 (taking them together)
the excess of merchandise exports was still extraordinary; and
there was no net inflow of gold at all — on the contrary, a net
export.   In 1921, on the other hand, when the merchandise excess

[1] For convenience of reference, I give the figures (in millions of dollars) for exports and imports both of merchandise and of gold, for the entire series of calendar
years from 1919 to 1925.

Calendar Year	Merchandise (including silver)			Gold	
	Exports	Imports	Excess of Exports	Net Imports	Net Exports
1919	8159	3994	4166		292
1920	8342	5367	2975	95	
1921	4537	2572	1964	667	
1922	3895	3184	711	238	
1923	4240	3867	373	294	
1924	4701	3684	1017	258	
1925	5008	4293	716		134

[2] The export of gold during the calendar year 1919 was ascribed, at the time
and just after, to causes supposed to be of exceptional character.   The merchandise
imports into the United States were mainly from the Orient and South America,
while the exports were mainly to Europe (a contrast, it may be remarked, which
was of long standing in the foreign trade of the United States).   Ordinarily the
exports to Europe provide the bills of exchange which serve to pay for the imports
from the East.   But at this time, so it was said, the usual foreign exchange
operations could not take place.   Europe was on a paper basis, and could furnish
no exchange available for remittances to the Orient, where specie alone was accepted
in payments ; hence gold (and silver also) had to be sent thither from the United
States.   I am not convinced that this explanation of the export of gold is satisfactory.   The shuffling of the exchanges is not necessarily or usually prevented
by paper currency or dislocated rates of exchange.   The probabilities would seem
to be that the United States had actually more of money payments to make (in
gold terms) than she had to receive.   The point, however, is of little importance
for the general problems here under consideration.

of exports had fallen markedly, the imports of gold reached dimensions comparable to the most extraordinary year of the war period. In the fiscal year 1916–17, the gold imports had been 685 millions. In the calendar year 1921 they were not less than 667 millions. While the "favorable" merchandise balance declined, the imports of gold rose — just the contrary of what would be expected under a naïve conception of the theory of the case.

These phenomena, like the equally striking ones of the war proper, were due to causes clearly of a transient character. In 1919 heavy government payments on loan account were still made by the United States Treasury to foreign countries, the winding up of war transactions for which the government had made pledges.[1] There were also heavy government expenses abroad for the support of the American military forces and their return homeward. In 1920, again, there was a transient cause of a different kind. In the United States one of the outstanding phases of the speculative expansion of 1919–20 was a veritable craze for exports. It is most astonishing that the business world failed to realize that sales to foreigners of the character and volume which the war loans had made possible could not continue when the war conditions had ceased. Even in the face of the new and altered conditions, goods were sold on credit to foreign buyers, or were fairly shovelled out to foreign countries in expectation of ready sale there. The real situation was not grasped until collapse came in the second half of 1920. Then it appeared that many foreign buyers could not pay their debts, and that many goods sent in expectation of profitable sale had to be disposed of at sacrifice prices. Great sums were lost; a large part of the "credit balance" which had been gloated over during 1919–20 simply disappeared.

In the years succeeding there was a gradual return to conditions less abnormal. In 1921 there were still left-overs from the period of craze; but by 1922 something like order emerged, and was maintained for some years thereafter. Even so, it must remain

---

[1] See the figures on the Treasury advances after the armistice (Nov. 1918), given on p. 315 above.

doubtful at the date of writing (1926) whether the country's trade had settled to really permanent conditions. I hesitate to comment on the rapidly shifting situation; whatever is written on the subject now (1926) will be behind the times from the moment of publication, and will need to be supplemented and revised in view of what develops during the years following. The analysis which follows is designed mainly to show how long the post-war conditions in the United States retained an unusual character and how little they lent themselves to explanation on the lines of the general theory of international trade. I will begin by considering in turn the several items in the international account. While there were still temporary and erratic movements, others of permanent significance can be traced.

The temporary movements were mainly caused by the still disturbed conditions of European countries. Uneasiness about the monetary and political prospects led to anomalous transactions of considerable volume. Characteristic among these was the outflow from the United States of its *paper* money, much of it in small denominations. Being a thing stable and reckonable, this was used or hoarded in Germany, Austria, and other countries with disorganized currency. For the time being its outflow was equivalent to an export from the United States. Before long — by 1923 and 1924 — the paper straggled back; and its back flow became in turn equivalent to an import item. Similarly, uneasiness concerning the future caused foreign investors and property owners to transfer funds to the United States. Sometimes they bought American securities outright; sometimes they left "money" to their credit on the books of banking houses. These operations (most marked in 1923) were equivalent in their effects to the making of loans by Europeans to Americans. They brought an offset for the time being to the loans which were made at the same time by Americans to Europeans. This flurry became less marked after 1923. On the other hand, the European borrowings which had begun during the war and had been maintained even thru the period of greatest uneasiness, were resumed on a larger scale by 1924, and quite offset the effects of this flight of capital.

Partly permanent, partly of a temporary character, were the heavy remittances made from the United States to Europe for charity. The steady immigrants' remittances of the pre-war type continued, apparently unabated in volume. Large sums were also sent out to Central and Eastern Europe for momentary relief. The amounts of these payments were quite as difficult to ascertain with accuracy as they had been for the year before the war. They served, like the shipments of currency and the panic transfers of capital, to becloud the situation and make it more difficult to perceive the more permanent and more important developments.

The changes of a more enduring sort, which particularly deserve attention as regards general problems of interpretation and verification, were of three kinds: first, some approach to equality between merchandise imports and exports; next, a new situation in the international loan account; and finally, a new situation as regards the movement of gold in and out of the country. For the purpose of considering these, it will be convenient to consider in some detail the international balance sheet of the United States for the years 1922, 1923, 1924, 1925. I give the figures as they have been compiled by the Department of Commerce.[1]

It appears at once that exports and imports no longer showed such extraordinary discrepancies as in 1916–21. While exports continued to be the greater, the excess was not such as to rouse astonishment. In 1922 the "favorable" balance of trade was

[1] The figures of exports and imports in this table are not the same as those given for the corresponding items in the table on p. 319. The present figures are derived from the special compilation made by the Department of Commerce relating to the entire international balance (Trade Information Bulletin No. 399, April, 1926); whereas the earlier are from the routine statistics of the Department on the Foreign Commerce of the United States. The discrepancies arise because of certain adjustments (for smuggled goods, illicit liquor, and the like) designed to make the international balance sheet accurate. The amounts by which the two sets of figures differ are small, and quite negligible as regards the comments which follow in the text.

On all phases of this subject we are immensely better informed for the post-war than for the pre-war period. Inquiry concerning the amount of the invisible items was begun by Professor J. H. Williams almost immediately after the war, the results being published in the Review of Economic Statistics. The importance and interest of his pioneer work caused the task to be taken over by the Department of Commerce. Beginning with 1922 the Department has presented, and presumably will continue to present, annual systematic statements on the balance of international payments which are as accurate as the nature of the case permits and quite accurate enough for the main purposes of economic analysis.

THE INTERNATIONAL BALANCE OF PAYMENTS OF THE UNITED STATES, FOR THE CALENDAR YEARS 1922, 1923, 1924, 1925

Cr.	Years 1922	1923	1924	1925
Total exports of merchandise and silver	3930	4280	4731	5033
Tourists	60	100	100	100
Freight	71	65	76	75
Interest receivable	476	567	614	680
Securities sold, bonds redeemed, etc.	294	435	364	551
U. S. Government receipts, principal Allied debts	31	91	23	27
U. S. currency sent out	50	50		
Motion-picture royalties	50	60	70	75
	4912	5648	5978	6541
Excess of exports of merchandise and silver	726	387	1006	700
Net exports of gold				134

Dr.	Years 1922	1923	1924	1925
Total imports of merchandise and silver	3204	3893	3725	4333
Tourists	360	500	600	660
Immigrant remittances and like payments	400	360	355	360
Freight	64	73	68	83
Interest payable	125	150	150	165
Securities bought	326	54	114	90
New loans	637	363	795	920
U. S. currency sent in			50	62
U. S. Government payments	16	19	5	5
	5132	5412	5862	6678
Net imports of gold	238	294	258	

726 millions; in 1923 it was 387 millions; in 1924 it was 1006 millions; in 1925 again 700 millions. The figures are comparable with those of pre-war times. The money sums, to be sure, are larger than they were in the pre-war period. But prices being 50 or 60 per cent higher, an export excess of 726 millions, such as appeared in 1922, meant no more than one of 500 millions in 1912. The figures might reasonably be interpreted as showing that, as something like the normal conditions of peaceful trade was restored, something like the normal relation between the money value of exports and imports also was re-established. International trade apparently was again in its former grooves, functioning in a normal way.

This approach to equalization was accompanied by a similar equalization between the several invisible items. Here we find some old items, but also some new; and there is occasion for comment.

Among the old and familiar items, that of longest standing and steadiest character was the tourist expenditure. Not only did it persist; it became larger year by year. The growth in numbers of the well-to-do pleasure seekers caused this debit charge to grow, and to grow with much steadiness. True, in these later days there was a countercharge, also growing, because of the increasing expenditures by European travellers in the United States. None the less, the net debit against the United States remained large and tended to become steadily larger. Its tendency to rise is to be contrasted with a different tendency as regards the other debit item just mentioned: immigrant and charity remittances. Here we might expect a declining tendency, somewhat abrupt for the charity donations of emergency character, more gradual for those made by the immigrants. Yet up to 1925 there appeared no marked change. Taking all these items together, their total remained large and tended to swell rather than shrink.

Earnings from shipping now presented features quite different from those of the pre-war period. Before the war this item also had been almost entirely on the debit side of the account; but now it stood on the credit side as well. Ocean transportation, formerly carried on chiefly by foreign vessels, was to a considerable extent in American hands. The United States Government had entered on a great shipping venture; and while the venture was far from profitable for its Treasury, and still less a source of economic gain to its people, the gross receipts figure in the balance of international payments on the credit side. As it happened, the amounts payable for freight carried in American vessels served to offset almost exactly the corresponding payments to foreign shipping, so that on this score no net charge arose against the United States.

We turn now to the items connected with international borrowings.

Interest payments from the United States on loans of the past were still large, even tho unmistakably less than they were before the war. Notwithstanding the return and repurchase of securities during and after the war, considerable capital holdings were still in the hands of European investors, and interest on these (or dividends or profits) had still to be remitted.

But interest, like the shipping earnings, now figured on both sides. While there was still interest payable *from* the United States — a diminished amount, but still substantial — interest was also payable *to* the country from foreign debtors. And the credit item on this score, new as it was, had become larger than the debit item. Before the war, some 250 millions had been payable annually from the United States for interest and profits; by 1923 the annual sum had shrunk to 150 millions or thereabouts. On the other hand, the amount receivable, a sum negligible before the war, was now nearly 500 millions a year and more.

Equally large in volume, nay larger, was the capital movement; but almost entirely the other way. The United States had become a lender — an exporter of capital. This movement did not fairly set in until 1922. It was different in character from the enormous loans of the war, and different also from the short-time extensions of credit that played so large a part in the speculative period of 1919–20. After the collapse of 1920, and as part of the gradual revival, foreign loans of the ordinary kind began to be placed in the United States; not distress borrowings, or short-time purchases on credit, but loans of the permanent sort, designed for long-time investment. They were first made in large amounts in 1922. A relaxation of the movement came in 1923, the year of the Ruhr occupation; thereafter it proceeded at accelerating pace. The figures for these four years were:

1922 $637,000,000
1923 $363,000,000
1924 $795,000,000
1925 $920,000,000

As with every export of capital, the immediate effect was a swelling of the debit side of the account. A considerable offset on the other side arose because some loans of earlier date, chiefly loans which had been contracted by foreigners during the war, were repaid. And as part of the capital movement there must be reckoned the purchases and sales of securities in the open market. Transactions of this kind, as it happened, were made in both directions during the years in question. As has already been noted, the unsettled conditions of European countries led to the so-called "flight of capital" from various parts of the Continent, taking the form (in good part) of the purchase of American securities by uneasy property owners. On the other hand, venturesome Americans bought European securities in the expectation of profit from a future rise in their prices, partly for speculative turns, partly with a view to long-continued holding with invigorated management. The balance of the entire capital movement thus fluctuated from year to year; in 1923 it was even against the United States.[1] Comparing this capital movement with the interest payments, it appears that while the country had become a receiver of interest on its loans of the war and post-war periods, the capital sums which it was sending out exceeded the net sums due for interest.

This new situation of the United States is a curious phenomenon, as surprising as any in this whole train of surprising events.

[1] See footnote at the bottom of next page.

The way in which it differs from the ordinary or expected course of events — from the "normal" — deserves attention.

The transition from a borrower's position in international trade to that of a creditor ordinarily has taken place by a gradual process, spread out over decades or even generations. Even the transition from the earlier stages of borrowing to its later stages is usually spread over many years. Let us recapitulate. First, there is the initial stage, with an excess of imports as its concomitant; then, as interest accumulates, a gradual lessening of that excess; then a hesitating period, with a roughly even balance of imports and exports; finally, an excess of exports which serves to meet the accumulated interest payments. A half-century may elapse between the first and the last stages. Of this general character, as we have seen, was the succession of events in the international trade of the United States during the pre-war period. If thereafter the borrowing country grows rapidly in wealth, and accumulates capital very fast — as the United States did — it is to be expected that, in the usual course of peaceful trade, still another series of stages will appear. The country may begin to pay off its foreign debts, buying back the securities held abroad by foreigners and the properties owned by them within its own borders.

The following figures show both sides of the capital movement during the four years in millions of dollars:

Year	Credit		Debit	Net Credit (+) Net Debit (−)
	Outstanding Securities Sold, Foreign Bonds Redeemed, Principal of Inter-Ally Debt Paid		New Securities Bought (Fresh Loans) and Outstanding Securities Bought	
1922	325		1063	− 738
1923	526		417	+ 109
1924	387		909	− 522
1925	578		1010	− 432

I take these figures from the consolidated statement, just referred to, published by the Department of Commerce in 1926; but do not follow the practice of regarding the inflow or outflow of U. S. paper money (a minor item) as part of the capital movement.

While doing so, it will tend to have an even greater excess of exports than before. When this process is completed and the foreign investments have been absorbed, a further turn will appear; the excess of exports will cease. And if thereafter the country, waxing richer and richer, begins itself to lend to others, it starts on the original round, but from the other end, the initial export of capital being marked by an excess of exports. The last series of changes and transitions, like those preceding, one would expect to find slow and gradual, drawn out over a generation or two.

The remarkable thing is that the later transitions, involving the shift from an established borrower's position to the position of an established lender, should be compressed within less than a single decade. No doubt, even without the forcing process of the war, some growth in this general direction would have set in. The borrowing days for the United States were nearing their end by 1914. By that time there were already substantial outgoing loans, mainly to Canada and to Central America. It is quite possible, too, that even without any war the reversal of the transactions on capital account would have proceeded more rapidly than previous experience could foreshadow. The pace of industrial change in the United States has repeatedly exceeded all expectations. But with every allowance for the possibility that the conditions were ripe for the beginning of the new cycle, it is extraordinary that the country's position in the international capital market should have been so abruptly and completely revolutionized.

The nature of the causes at work is not indeed difficult to discern. On the one hand, we have the vast destruction of capital in Europe, especially on the Continent; and not only this, but the ensuing sharp curtailment of the savable funds from which new capital could be derived. In the United States, on the other hand, the war had the effect of adding to its savable funds, and perhaps in even greater degree to its new savings. Great windfalls and great fortunes resulted from the war boom; while at the same time the habit of accumulation extended thru all classes of society as never before. The propaganda for the sale of Liberty bonds of small denominations proved to be the initial stage in a remarkable spread of the investment tradition.   The bourgeois attitude permeated the social body as never before in this country or in any other.

At the date of writing (1926) it still remains to be seen how great and permanent were the changes in the international loan account between the United States and other countries.   Quite possibly the eventual outcome will prove to be less revolutionary than these first experiences seem to indicate.   Time may bring relapses and reactions.   The domestic demand for investment funds will continue to compete with the foreign, and may easily be so strong as to put a damper on the export of capital.   In foreign countries the stage will be reached in due time when their most pressing needs for reconstruction are satisfied and their own savings begin to be more nearly adequate for their ordinary capital operations.   But the pre-war conditions are clearly gone.   Henceforth lending operations and the loan account must play a quite different part from what they did before 1914.   And when all is said, the rapidity of the changes which took place, no less than their extent, remains extraordinary.

On the third general problem of this latest period, the new situation as regards the international flow of gold, the essential facts have been indicated already.[1]   The great imports of the metal during the war itself were succeeded during the year after its close by others no less great, tho spread over a somewhat longer time.   A temporary reversal of the current, and a sharp one, appeared in 1919, when nearly 300 millions went out.   But soon the main flow was resumed, and during the entire period from 1919 to 1924 the net amount that poured into the United States was nearly 1300 millions.[2]   What signifies for the present inquiry is not so much the volume of this movement, extraordinary tho it was, as its relation to the general theory of trade balances, specie flow, international prices, and international trade.

[1] See pp. 309, 318 above.

[2] The imports for 1920–24 were 1552 millions; deducting the exports of 292 millions in 1919, we have a net import of 1260 millions.

Even the most guarded versions of monetary and banking theory contemplate that some influence will be exerted on credit and prices by the flow of specie from country to country, while very great movements of specie are expected to bring prompt and far-reaching effects. It is true that during this particular period most of the countries from which came the imposing mass of gold were not on a specie basis. In their case it was not the circulating currencies of paper money, but dead hoards of gold that were subjected to the drain — conditions under which it is necessary to apply quite a different theoretical analysis.[1] The United States, however, was completely and unequivocally on a gold basis. Here it would seem that the received doctrine should prove valid. Yet nothing points that way. The outflow of nearly 300 millions in the year 1919 had no visible effect in checking the rise of prices at that time of violent speculative activity. On the other hand, the phenomenal inflow in 1921-24 — about a billion and a half of gold imported in four years — was coincident not with rising prices, but with a marked fall during the first of these years and with a stable level during the remainder. It was not the expected that took place, but quite the unexpected.

The explanation of this "abnormal" turn of events is familiar enough, and in a way is easy enough. It is connected with the surprising course which the development of the banking system took, a development quite unforeseen by its founders, puzzling and even alarming to those who had to administer it. The Federal Reserve System had been established in 1913 with the express design, among others, of making the country's currency system less sensitive to gold imports and exports. Deliberately, it had been made insensitive rather than sensitive. During the war and the years following, legislation had been enacted for rendering it insensitive to an even greater degree than had been contemplated at the start. All the country's banking reserves of gold were shifted into the coffers of the Reserve Banks. Much more effective toward the end thus had in view — that of accumulating a great reserve which should serve as a buffer against the

[1] As is more fully set forth in Part III, below.

impact of gold movements into the country and out of it — were the unexampled trade conditions of the war and post-war periods. All previous rules and traditions concerning the amounts of reserve which central banks should acquire and might be expected to maintain were shattered. The Federal Reserve Banks, guided in their policy by the Reserve Board and by their own officers as well, could hardly do otherwise than let their vast gold holdings serve as a reservoir into which and out of which gold might move by the hundreds of millions without affecting credit conditions, the price level, the currents of international trade. Neither inflow nor outflow had the effects which the received doctrines contemplate; nor indeed, so far as one can guess, could they have had these effects, under the conditions then prevailing, whatever the guiding authorities might have tried to approve or to veto.

It would carry us beyond the scope of the present volume to enter on the questions of monetary theory which are raised by these experiences. Questions of the same sort, and no less perplexing as regards their bearing on the theory of money and prices, are raised by the monetary experiences of European countries during the same years. When more time has elapsed and a nearer approach to a normal economic situation has been reached, the enigmas may prove less baffling than they appeared at the time, the eventual outcome more in accord with familiar doctrines. But it is clear that we must be cautious in applying the familiar doctrines of international trade to the interpretation of this quite extraordinary situation.

Take what is perhaps the most significant aspect of all: that equalization (approach to equalization) between the money values of imports and exports which, as we have seen, was reached by 1923. Such an excess of exports as that of the war years was obviously abnormal and could not persist. But the return to something like normal conditions was not reached by the process which our general reasoning leads us to regard as normal. The inflow of specie which would presumably ensue with the continuing enormous excess of exports was belated. When it did set in, after 1919, it came with a rush. And when finally the gold poured in, no rise in prices ensued, and no increased importation of goods was induced by rising prices. One would argue that such an absorption of gold could not go on indefinitely without enlivening and enlarging the circulating medium as a whole. Eventually there must be rising prices, then increased importations, and thus in the end a readjustment of imports and exports. But it was not eventually, it was promptly, that the equalization of the imports and exports took place. The insensitive character of the monetary system kept the price level impassive and unchanged; yet the new and presumably normal relation between imports and exports none the less was reached with comparatively little delay.

To put it in the fewest words, things just *happened* so. As regards the merchandise movements, an inspection of the figures shows that it was a fall in exports rather than a rise in imports which caused the money value of the two to become approximately equal. The European demand for American goods declined markedly, especially for American agricultural products. The Americans did buy somewhat more of imports, especially from the Orient and other non-European regions. But these ups and downs cannot be related to any general price movements of the kind contemplated in the theoretical analysis. There were also, as we have seen, irregular changes of one sort and another in the invisible items. The final state of the international account was the combined result of all the items, visible and invisible. The erratic shifts in the whole series of transactions and the final net relation between the debits and credits led first to a prolonged inflow of specie, and then, by the close of 1924, to a cessation of the inflow. The gold which did come in during 1920–24 had no traceable effect on the merchandise imports and exports. Neither did it have an effect on the other item whose marked fluctuations were important in the final balance of payments — the export of capital. To repeat, it all just happened. One can make out nothing in the nature of an ordered sequence, of conformity to rule or to reasoning.

It will prove most interesting to watch the course of events during the next decade or so, say till 1935. A common opinion

in 1923–25 was that the United States had then definitely reached
the stage of being an exporter of capital; that the causes which in
pre-war days had brought about an excess of exports no longer
operated with such magnitude as to enable the former "favorable" balance to be maintained; that if this basic cause of prosperity was to endure, the one way to assure the propitious result
was an uninterrupted series of loans to foreigners. I speak of
favorable balance and propitious result, because most persons
who discoursed on the present and the future, whether government officials or representatives of the business and financial
world, took the good old mercantilist view which these phrases
imply. A great volume of exports, and especially a great excess
of exports over imports, was regarded as a vivifying tonic for
business, and especially as the means by which a burdensome
surplus product of manufactured and of agricultural products
could find the necessary foreign market. It is a familiar attitude:
exports, and still more exports, are the indispensable condition of
sustained industrial vigor and of ever growing prosperity. True,
the new position of the United States as a creditor country was
admitted to entail a tendency toward growing imports; foreigners,
it was agreed, must pay the interest on their debts in goods. But
this was merely a stronger reason for lending more and more to
them, and so enabling the mounting imports to be offset by exports
mounting still more.

The dispassionate student will shrug his shoulders at all this.
His interest will be in other directions — in the shifts of the various items of the complex situation and in the play of the underlying
forces. The export of capital may wax and may wane. It will
hardly cease; but it may prove of less commanding importance
than commonly expected. The great excess of merchandise
exports over imports may continue, or may be succeeded by
an even balance, or may be replaced by an opposite relation —
an excess of imports. The whole balance of international payments, with all its interwoven and conflicting elements, subject as
it is to the possible decline or growth of almost every item, may
take a shape quite beyond any foreshadowing. Most interesting

of all, and perhaps most unpredictable of all, is the way in which
the monetary mechanism will operate. Will the currency system
of the country remain as insensitive to gold movements as it
came to be during the war and post-war periods? Will the whole
enormous gold stock be retained within the country? And if not,
what will be the method and what the results of its re-distribution?
Will deliberate policy and plans for a managed currency determine
its movements, or will its international distribution proceed after
all in that undesigned fashion which has so long been regarded as
part of the normal economic order? And, to come to our immediate subject, by what processes will the currents of international
trade be influenced? It may be presumed with confidence that
the fundamental actuating forces in the movement of merchandise
will still be the prices of goods in the several countries, and the
relative levels of their domestic prices and their money incomes.
But just how the prices of American goods, and the country's
general level of domestic prices and money incomes, will shape
themselves or will be shaped under the newly developed banking
and currency situation — he would be a rash man who ventured
to predict. And hence he would also be rash who ventured on
a prediction as to the ultimate structure of the country's
international trade, of its merchandise exports and imports, of its
balance of payments with other countries, of the greater or less
extent of its real gain from the total of all the transactions
taken together.

PART III

INTERNATIONAL TRADE UNDER INCONVERTIBLE PAPER

CHAPTER 26

The Underlying Principles

The theoretical analysis given in Part I of this book and the discussion of the problems of verification in Part II have rested thruout on the assumption that one and the same metal — gold — is the basis of the circulating medium of the trading countries, and moves freely between them. It is obvious, however, that the machinery of the flow of specie, of prices, of money incomes rising or falling because of the specie movement, of readjustment thru a new level of prices and money incomes in each of the countries — all this cannot operate, or at least cannot operate in the same way, where the monetary systems rest on different bases. Where there is paper in one country and gold in another, or gold in one and silver in another, the entire mechanism is different. The compensating, correcting, stabilizing influence of gold movements ceases to be operative. It becomes a question whether in its absence the substantive outcome also is different. How, for example, do our conclusions on the barter terms of trade apply? It has been among the major objects of the present volume to ascertain in what way and to what extent the general reasoning on the barter terms of trade is found applicable in the concrete working of international trade. That same problem presents itself where there are different monetary systems and dislocated foreign exchanges. The presumption no doubt is that the ultimate phenomena of trade between nations will not be essentially different because of differences in their monetary systems. Just as trade between individuals will presumably be conducted on the same terms under a money régime as under barter, and on the same terms under one monetary system as under another, so also with regard to trade between nations. But

337

precisely in what way do these results, similar tho we expect them to be, come about where the machinery in operation is dissimilar? and may there not be important substantive differences because of the fact of altered machinery?

One or two matters of phraseology may first be disposed of. I shall use "exchange" and "foreign exchange" when referring to bills of exchange and the prices at which the bills sell. Unfortunately we have not in English any term which is always and solely used to designate these things, like the German *Devisen* or the French *change*. The term "foreign exchange," which might readily be supposed to refer to the exchanges of goods between countries, *i.e.* to the substance of international trade, must be used, somewhat clumsily, when we discuss bills of exchange and the prices at which they sell in terms of another country's money. On the other hand, following the usage already familiar to the reader, I shall speak of the "terms of trade" or the "barter terms of trade" when referring to the substance of the trade between countries — to the physical volume of goods that go from one to another.

Further, I shall speak of "paper exchange" and "specie exchange," of "paper conditions" and "specie conditions," indicating by these phrases whether the trade takes place under a monetary standard which is the same in the trading countries or under different standards. There may of course be specie conditions which are not the same in the two countries — gold in one, silver in another; then the case becomes analogous to that of paper conditions and paper exchange. A general term for describing the conditions dealt with in the present chapter is "dislocated exchanges." Where the same money is used in the several countries — gold, as in the cases considered in the first two Parts of this book — we have connected exchanges. What we are now to consider is international trade under dislocated exchanges.

The older writers assumed that the main currents of international trade were not affected by the substitution of paper money for metallic, or by the circumstance that the trading countries might not have the same metallic standard. Differences between the monetary systems of the trading countries simply caused the counters of exchange in each of them to be different, nothing more. The followers of Ricardo had occasion chiefly to consider trade between a specie-standard country like England and another country having depreciated paper. In such case, they argued, the country of paper money would have prices higher than it would have under specie, according to the extent by which the volume of the paper was greater than the specie which would have circulated in its absence. The normal or ordinary rate of foreign exchange on the paper country would be high in the same proportion. The mere fact of prices higher in paper, and the higher "nominal" quotations of foreign exchange, would have no effect on the substantive trade. Imports and exports between the countries would move in just the same way and in the same volume as if both countries were on one and the same specie basis.

It seems never to have occurred to these writers to inquire what would happen if, under paper conditions, a *status quo* were disturbed. Suppose a given situation to have been established as regards paper currency, prices, foreign exchange: paper doubled in quantity, prices twice as high as before, a corresponding rate of exchange (sterling exchange, say, twice as high as before in terms of the paper money). Suppose then that something happens to disturb this established situation: a tribute or indemnity becomes payable by one country to the other; or a loan transaction enters, tourist expenditures; or — what might most readily have occurred to the older writers — an increase of demand takes place in one of the countries for the products of the other. What then? Would the "nominal" rate of foreign exchange remain the same? Would prices in the several countries remain the same? Would the physical volume of imports and exports be changed, and, if so, by what process? So far as I know, these questions were neglected in the older literature of the subject and have been hardly less neglected in modern times. That the Ricardians should have ignored them is in keeping with their general treatment of monetary problems. They regarded monetary disturbances as of little substantive importance, whether for domestic or international trade; the only significant consequence of inflated prices was that a new set of counters came to be used. We have learned how unduly simplified is this version of what happens in domestic trade; much more takes place within a country when paper money is put forth. Something more may happen also in the trade between countries.

The logical corollary of the Ricardian simplification of the problem has appeared recently in the purchasing-parity doctrine. That doctrine, as set forth more particularly by Professor G. Cassel, maintains that the rates of foreign exchange — the prices at which bills of exchange on one such country will sell in the currency of the other — are in accord with the range of general prices in the two; or rather, to state the doctrine more carefully, are in accord with the relative price levels — with the changes in general prices that appear in the two. If paper currency in country A is put out to such an extent that prices are doubled in that country; and if, on the other hand, paper issues in country B result in a quadrupling of prices in B; then in B bills of exchange on A will sell at twice the rates which prevailed before the respective paper issues. The new rates of foreign exchange will be on a parity with the altered price levels. In more refined and careful expositions of the doctrine this bald and simple statement is somewhat qualified. Account is taken of disturbing influences, of irregularities that conceal the main trend. Payments on other than merchandise account — government remittances, and invisible items of all sorts — are admitted to exercise for considerable periods an influence of their own on the rates of exchange, not directly connected with the price levels. It is admitted also that the actual dealings in bills commonly have a speculative character, and are affected for weeks and months by expectations and rumors concerning the economic and political future. But thru all the transactions, it is maintained, the same general trend appears — accordance of the foreign exchanges with the respective price levels; and in the end the first approximation is found to fit the facts. When once all the remittances, on merchandise account and on account of other items as well, have been arranged for and allowed for;

when the currencies and the price levels have settled down to some stabilized level — then the rates of foreign exchange will be found to be stabilized on the same basis. Fluctuations in the rates may take place above or below that settled basis, but will not bring any permanent departure from it.

This doctrine seems to me in need of modification. It fails to meet a question of fundamental significance: how are *changes* in the conditions of international trade — changes in the terms of trade between countries — brought about when there are dislocated exchanges?

Let us assume two countries *each* of which has an inconvertible paper currency. No money of either can enter the circulating medium of the other. No change in the balance of payments can cause a flow of money; goods only can move. The case is the same in principle as that of two countries one of which has a gold standard, the other inconvertible paper. It is the same, that is, if the gold standard is steadily and unfailingly adhered to in the one country, the paper standard similarly adhered to in the other. As a matter of fact it happens often enough in a paper country that its paper is not the sole and universal medium of exchange, gold remaining in use for some payments. Gold then may pass into the country and out of it, not merely as a commodity like tin or copper, but to some extent as a monetary medium also. Where this is the case, the trade between gold standard and paper standard countries presents some special complications. The situation is reduced to its simplest elements if we suppose two paper standards, and no money in either country which can pass to the other.

Further, let it be assumed that the monetary situation in both countries is stable. Whatever inflation or deflation there may have been, is definitive; each has settled down to a fixed monetary supply. Prices may be higher than they would be under a specie régime, or the same, or lower. But they are no longer subject to change because of increase or decrease in the volume of money. It is not the consequences of changes in the volume of money and in prices that we are now to examine, but the characteristics of international trade between countries having different monetary standards, and between which no money can pass.

The two countries may be imagined to be Great Britain and the United States; a paper pound in the former, a paper dollar in the latter — Bradburys and greenbacks. The range of prices in each country will be determined by the several quantities of pounds or dollars. The volumes of the respective paper money being fixed, the level of prices will remain unchanged in each so long as the volume of commodities remains the same. This states the result in the barest form of the quantity theory, the most extreme and perhaps most offensive. I will leave it to the conversant reader to make all needed corrections and qualifications on the score of spending habits or rapidity of circulation, expansion and contraction of credit, changes in the volume of goods and in their marketing, and so on. Let these internal conditions be supposed to remain unchanged thruout.[1]

Assume now that the quantity of paper pounds in Great Britain has not materially changed from the quantity of gold pounds previously used, and that prices in Bradburys are not materially different from what they had been under gold. In the United States, on the other hand, assume that the quantity of paper dollars has greatly changed, has doubled; and that prices in greenbacks are twice as high as they had been under gold. Assume that the rate of foreign exchange has settled down to figures conforming to the altered price conditions. Suppose that sterling exchange is quoted in New York at the figure of ten dollars to the pound, which would be equivalent to quoting in London (if this way of figuring foreign exchange transactions happened to be adopted there) one dollar for two shillings, or approximately one penny for four cents. Such, on the reasoning of the Ricardians and also on that of the purchasing-parity school, would be the established or normal basis of foreign exchange rates; and this rate of

---

[1] The exactness of the accordance between prices and monetary quantity is unimportant, I think, for the argument of the present chapter. Compare what was said above, Ch. 17, p. 198.

exchange would persist so long as monetary conditions within the two countries remained the same.

Assume further, as a starting point, that goods alone are the occasion for remittances between the countries. Their transactions are solely on merchandise account. The sums due in London for American goods sold to British purchasers are exactly equal in money value, at ten dollars for the pound, to the sums due in New York for British goods sold in the United States.

Now, in a situation thus simplified, suppose a new factor to enter. Something happens that disturbs the situation. Suppose there is a sudden burst of loans by the British to the United States. No other change takes place; there is a net addition to the remittances made from Great Britain. I assume a sudden burst, because the point to which I would now direct attention is brought out most clearly by supposing a change which takes place rapidly and on a large scale. One might choose for illustration an indemnity or tribute, or new interest payments by the one government to the other on a large debt. In practice of course it is rare that changes of this kind appear suddenly. The case of an indemnity comes nearest to being cataclysmic, and even that would doubtless give opportunity for an adjustment in some degree gradual. The modifications and qualifications that must be observed in applying the reasoning to changes that come by gradual stages will be presently considered. For the moment, attend to the simple case of a sudden and great increase in the payments that must be made from London to New York. Suppose the increase to be 25 per cent. Suppose, too, that this goes on year after year — is not a sporadic episode, but a steadily continuing series of remittances. It begins abruptly; it goes on at the same rate for a long time.

The American borrowers have sterling exchange at their command; they can draw on the London bankers who finance the loans. The supply of sterling exchange offered in New York is greater than before. The amount of the loans is (say) one quarter of the amount which British importers had previously been paying to Americans (remitting to New York) for merchandise bought.

Or, what comes to the same thing, the demand in London for "dollars," by the bankers who have to meet drafts sent them by their New York correspondents, becomes greater than before. The price of dollar exchange rises in London; the price of sterling exchange falls in New York. It is not material whether the transactions are carried on in the one market or the other, or partly in one and partly in the other. We may follow the traditional way of quoting exchange, so many dollars to the pound. For convenience we may treat the problem also as if all the transactions were executed in one place; the two to which resort is made in practice being in effect one connected market. Let the place be New York. Then 25 per cent more of sterling exchange is offered in New York. There is no more demand for sterling exchange than before; no more purchases of British goods are made than before, and no larger remittances have to be made to London.

The situation is of a kind not unfamiliar in economic analysis, that in which two fixed quantities meet. Such a situation was assumed in the old reasoning about the wages-fund; such too was assumed, and I think may still be reasonably assumed, in the reasoning which underlies the quantity theory of money. In the present case, there is in the foreign exchange market a given supply of sterling exchange, a given quantity offered for sterling. The price in Bradburys of dollar exchange will rise exactly in proportion to the increased quantity of sterling exchange offered. Exchange will go to $8.00 tc the pound. The same number of pounds will buy less dollars than before; the same number of dollars will buy more pounds than before. If all the transactions took place in London, and if quotations were made the other way — in terms of the amount of British money which one dollar would buy — then exchange would shift from a previous rate of 2 shillings per dollar to a new rate of 2s. 6d. per dollar.

The essential point is that the price of foreign exchange, the purchasing power of one currency in terms of the other, depends at any given time on the respective volumes of remittances. It results from the *impact* of two forces that meet. The outcome is simply such as to equalize the remittances; such that the money value of the two, expressed in the currency of either country, is the same. The price of foreign exchange thus may change without any movement in the general range of prices in either country. And it may change very much indeed. Therein, of course, the situation differs radically from that under gold-standard conditions. When gold is the standard in both countries, foreign exchange fluctuations remain within narrow limits, whereas the level of prices in each country, tho it changes but slowly, is subject to no restrictions at all analogous. When, however, there are dislocated exchanges — the monetary conditions in each country remaining constant, as here assumed — the level of prices in each country remains the same (subject to a minor correction presently to be stated) even under the impact of great disturbances in international trade, whereas the foreign exchanges may show wide and rapid fluctuations.

It is in this, respect — the possibility of wide fluctuations in the rate of exchange — that the conditions differ most obviously from those of transactions under the gold standard. When gold can flow from country to country, such a change in the balance of payments as has just been supposed does indeed bring its first impact on the quotations for foreign exchange. But those quotations must remain within the narrow limits of the gold points. Soon specie begins to move, and then further movements begin, in prices and in the movement of goods. Under paper-standard conditions, however, exchange may fluctuate widely, may soar or decline with the changing volumes of remittances; but nothing therein disturbs the general monetary situation.

This then is our first proposition, and a fundamental one. In the absence of a common monetary standard, the rate of foreign exchange depends on the mere impact of the two quantities on hand at the moment.[1]

We may proceed now to the next stage: how the movement of

---

[1] This general line of reasoning on the equalization of payments thru alterations in the rates of foreign exchange is fully worked out in a notable paper by Professor J. W. Angell, International Trade Under Inconvertible Paper, Quarterly Journal of Economics, Vol. 36 (May, 1922). Essentially the same reasoning underlies Hawtrey's compact treatment in his Currency and Credit (p. 61, 2nd edition).

goods, the substantive course of international trade, the eventual
price situation in the trading countries, the barter terms of trade,
are affected.

An early and almost immediate effect clearly is to stimulate the
movement of goods from the remitting country (Great Britain)
to the receiving country (United States). The British traders
who sell goods in the United States receive more than before for
the dollar exchange which they can put on the market. There is
something like a bounty on British exports, felt first by the merchants and middlemen, soon by the producers. The extent and
the duration of that bounty depend on the conditions under which
the goods are produced in Great Britain. If they are produced
solely for export, the bounty will be large and will last for some
time. Altho goods in stock may be pushed for export more
rapidly when the movement begins, altho the first stage may be
merely that of taking up the slack, no really effective addition
to the quantity exported can take place until more of the goods are
produced; and that takes time, perhaps much time. Such would
be the case, for example, with coffee exported from Brazil; the
domestic consumption is negligible, the export sale dominant, the
output very constant. If, however, there is a substantial domestic
consumption — if the output had previously been marketed partly
at home and partly in the United States — there would be some
shift from the domestic market to the foreign, and so some additional export of goods, some additional supply of dollar exchange
in London. Exchange will not rise in London as high as would
have been the case without these further exports. The extent
of the addition to the supply of dollar exchange will depend on the
extent to which consumption and sales in the domestic market are
curtailed. At the other extreme would be the case where the
domestic consumption had previously absorbed the greater portion
of the output, and the export had been but a small portion. Here
there is more easily a shift from the domestic market to the foreign,
and a larger and quicker addition to the supply of dollar exchange.
The extent and speed of these adjustments will be affected
obviously by the elasticity of the domestic demand. If that be

inelastic, there will be a slower decline of the domestic consumption, and a slower transfer of the goods to the export trade. The conditions both of domestic supply and of domestic demand will affect the duration of the bounty.

For a time, then, and very possibly for a considerable time, there will be *some* bounty. Prices of exported goods will be high in Great Britain, and export trade will be prosperous. Dollar exchange will be high in London and will probably remain high for a considerable period, tho with a tendency to gradual decline as exports increase. The increase of exports will take time, as in all cases where labor and capital shift from one industry to another; and the time is likely to be longer than economists have been in the habit of expecting.

Converse effects will show themselves in the United States. In New York sterling exchange falls; and Americans who have sold goods to British customers and who have sterling exchange to sell, get less dollars than before. Side by side with the tendency toward greater exports from Great Britain into the United States there will be a tendency toward less exports from the United States into Great Britain. American exporting industries will be depressed, and depressed according to the extent to which they are dependent on the export market. There will be the reverse of a bounty on exports, a handicap, a penalty. If the exporting industries have been producing preponderantly for the foreign market, as was so long the case and on the whole still is the case with cotton-growing in the United States there may be in those industries a long period of declining prices, depression, complaint. While importing into the United States will be profitable (the dealers and middlemen taking their shares of the gains from the growing business), exporting will be less profitable, middlemen as well as producers finding trade dull and profits small.

In the end, it is to be expected, these things will be evened out. The same sort of readjustment of commodity movements takes place as under a specie régime. More goods move from Great Britain to the United States. Fewer goods move from the United

States to Great Britain. The Americans gain in having more of imported British goods at their disposal. The British lose in having less of American goods at their disposal. That which happens — so we reason — under identical monetary standards, happens also under differentiated standards and dislocated exchanges. And apparently it happens thru a process quite as quick and effective. Time is needed for a readjustment of production in either case, and there would seem to be no *a priori* ground for expecting more time in one case than in the other.

What now about prices and money incomes in the two countries? And what about the foreign exchanges? Will the eventual outcome here also be the same as that under specie? I think not. In some essential particulars, conditions will be quite reversed. Under specie the level of domestic prices in each country will be changed — lowered in Great Britain, raised in the United States. But with dislocated exchange, the level of domestic prices in each will remain as it was before. Under specie it is the foreign exchanges that never vary, barring the minor fluctuations within the gold points. Under paper, however, a new and different normal quotation for foreign exchange will be established. Indeed, it cannot be said that there had been, or will be, *any* "normal" foreign exchange rate under dislocation; and herein our conclusion is quite different from that of the older British economists and from that of their modern successors of the purchasing-parity school.

Let me now elaborate and substantiate the theoretic conclusions thus summarily laid down.

First, as regards prices in the trading countries. Observe that in the contrasts between the two sets of price conditions which were indicated in the preceding paragraphs it was stated that domestic prices remain unchanged in both countries under dislocated exchanges. It is otherwise as regards imported articles. These become permanently cheaper than before in the United States, dearer than before in Great Britain. It is otherwise also, for a period, as regards exported articles. True, the prices of these in the long run will follow the course of domestic articles; they *are*, of course, domestic articles as regards the conditions of supply and of long-period price. But during the stage of readjustment, during the lag, exported articles will be somewhat higher in price than before in Great Britain, somewhat lower than before in the United States. Eventually, it is to be expected that exported articles in both countries will return to their former level; the only persisting change in both will be in the prices of imported articles.[1]

Consider how these changes would affect an index number of the usual kind, made up from the prices of a miscellaneous assortment of goods — domestic, exported, imported. Such an index would show one sort of result during the period of readjustment, another when that period was past and things had settled down.

In the United States the index number will register during the period of readjustment a fall in prices. Imported goods will be cheaper as the immediate consequence of the new rate of foreign exchange. Exported goods also will be cheaper. Domestic goods will be unchanged. The general price level will thus be shown by the index to be lower. As time goes on, the exported goods will no longer show a fall in price, *i.e.* the initial fall will be succeeded by a rebound to the original figures. Their producers will be led to lessen supplies in such way that the returns to them will be as great as to other domestic producers. But imported goods will have fallen in price definitively. When all has settled down, the general price level in the United States will be lower than it was before the disturbing influence set in, domestic prices (including those of exported goods) being the same as before but the prices of imported goods lower.

In Great Britain the other way. During the period of readjustment exported goods will be higher in prices than before; imported goods will also be higher; domestic goods will show no change.

---

[1] Lest there be misunderstanding, I would remind the reader that, for simplicity, various assumptions are tacitly made, as they have been in previous chapters. For example, constant costs are assumed, no individual domestic commodity being affected in price by the circumstance that under altered conditions of demand more or less of it is produced; no commodity shifts from the export to the import list under altered barter terms; and so on. Such assumptions may be made without affecting the validity of the present conclusions.

The general index numbers will register a rise. As time goes on and readjustment is accomplished, the advance in prices of exported goods will cease; they will relapse to the same level as at the outset. The advance in import prices will continue and will be accentuated. The general price level will thus show a rise, tho not so marked a rise as during the period of lag.

All these propositions rest on the premise that nothing happens to change the quantity of money in either country, or to change the velocity of circulation, the use of credit substitutes, and so on; nothing happens, either, as regards the general effectiveness of labor and the output of goods. I would lay stress again on the assumption of stability in the quantity of the paper money. In most discussions of international trade under inconvertible currency attention has been given chiefly to the consequences of changes in the amount of the money; most of all, when these are connected with the fiscal needs of the issuing government. I am concerned here with the other question, comparatively neglected: how the matter lies in its essence, so to speak — how it lies apart from the fluctuations and perturbations which the history of paper money so frequently shows.

A word further now as regards the assumed stability of domestic prices. That they remain unchanged may seem to have been laid down in the preceding paragraphs without sufficient consideration, let alone proof. It results from the fixity of the *total money income* of the population, from the fact that total spending power remains the same thruout (and also, we assume, the way in which the spending power is exercised remains the same). The whole of the goods, be there more or less of them, must sell for the same money sum. If then the output of goods remains constant, the price level will be unchanged; and moreover, in the absence of any cause affecting one article peculiarly, each individual article will remain likewise the same in price.

If indeed something happens to increase the total output of the goods, or the total output of any individual good, prices will be affected, even tho total money income remains unchanged and the income of each several producer unchanged. If, for example, at the same time with the international disturbances, it happens that a change takes place in the effectiveness of labor in producing a given article, there will be a change in the price of that article. If, say, the same labor produces twice as much of woolen cloth, woolen cloth will be one-half the price it was before. The general index number of prices will show a fall in prices; but the money income of the woolen producers would be the same (disregarding transitional effects) and the total money income of the population would be the same. *Other* prices would not be altered.

I may digress for a moment to point out an analogy between the case just considered — increase in the effectiveness of American labor in producing some particular article — and the more general case considered in earlier chapters, that of an increase in the British demand for American goods.[1] Suppose such an increase in demand, bearing in mind what it is the American exporters really do : that it is they who really supply to the American public the British goods which are received in exchange for the exports. The consequence of an increase of the British demand is that more British goods are got in exchange for each unit of American exports; hence the greater is the contribution which the American exporters make to the national dividend of goods and services. These particular products of American labor — so we may describe the things imported from Great Britain — fall in price. But nothing else is affected. The general level of domestic prices remains the same, and each several domestic price remains the same.[2] Similarly in Great Britain. The goods which come in from America are the product of the British labor which is given to the goods exported *to* Americans. That British labor

---

[1] See Ch. 4, p. 30.

[2] It need hardly be remarked that temporary effects on other prices are possible. Only if the elasticity of demand for woolen cloth were exactly unity would there be complete absence of effect on other articles. If the elasticity of demand were more or less than unity, there would be some transfer of purchasing power from woolens or towards woolens (as the case might be) and therefore an influence for the time being on the prices of woolen goods, a corresponding shift of labor and capital, a readjustment in the output of the woolens and of the other goods, and finally the state of prices indicated in the text. These possibilities may be neglected in the present inquiry.

now yields less than before. Less American goods are got per unit of the labor given to the British products that go out. Those goods, the American goods, rise in price. But here too no other prices are affected; the British domestic price level remains the same, and the price of each several British article remains the same. These propositions, as I need hardly say again, refer to the permanent results, the definitive stage; the reader will supply for himself the qualifications as regards probable temporary changes in the prices of exported articles and the quite conceivable temporary changes (indicated in the footnote) of some domestic articles.

Looking now at the broad consequences under paper régime as regards prices and money incomes, we find, as already intimated, changes essentially different from those to be expected under a specie régime, and yet, as regards the welfare of the trading countries, an outcome not essentially different. The mechanism is altered, but the substantial results remain the same. Under the specie mechanism the total money income of the population of each country, so far from remaining constant, becomes greater or less with the movement of the specie. Domestic prices likewise have their ups and downs. In the case chosen for illustration, that of larger payments from Great Britain to the United States because of a steady succession of loans, money incomes are lower in Great Britain, domestic prices show a fall, the general index of prices presumably registers a fall. Imported goods are dearer, and the British consumers are worse off in that they buy dearer imported goods with lower money incomes. Under paper, however, money incomes are the same and domestic prices are the same; the only difference is that imported (American) goods are dearer. The general index number records a rise in prices. The British consumers in this case also are worse off; with the same money incomes, they pay more for American goods. Here is the substantial outcome, the same under paper as under specie.

Conversely, of course, in the United States. Under specie we expect as a result of the increased British remittance to the United States higher money incomes, higher domestic prices, lower prices

of imports. Under paper, we must expect the same money incomes, the same domestic prices, lower prices of imports. Again
the mechanism is different under paper, the effects on material
prosperity the same.

Observe further (still having regard to the ultimate outcome) that
the goods exported from the United States to Great Britain, tho
dearer in Great Britain, are unchanged in price *in the United States*.
Similarly the goods exported from Great Britain, tho cheaper
in the United States, are the same in price *in Great Britain*.
The altered prices — American imports dearer in Great Britain,
British imports cheaper in the United States — are altered solely
because of the new rates of foreign exchange. Pounds sell for a
lower rate as compared with dollars. The price of dollar exchange
has risen in London; the price of sterling exchange has fallen in
New York. Tho the American prices of American exported goods
are unchanged, yet these, when translated into British prices on
the basis of the new quotation of exchange, mean higher British
prices for the goods. And the other way as regards British exports:
tho their prices are unchanged in Great Britain in British money,
yet when sold in the United States on the basis of the new quotation of exchange, they are put on the American market at lower
prices. It is the rate of foreign exchange which has altered, and
has definitively altered. That alteration takes place regardless
of the fact that monetary conditions in the two countries are
constant. It has no connection with any purchasing parity.
The rate of foreign exchange shifts to a new figure, not because of
price changes, but because of changed conditions of international
trade; the new figure persists; and it is itself the continuing and
permanent cause of the changes that ensue in the prices of goods.

A word more concerning one corollary from the reasoning which
has already been mentioned but deserves further attention. The
general range of all prices — the change in the price level measured
by an index number which is based on all commodities, imported
as well as domestic — would show in each country a change, and a
definitive change. And this change would be the opposite of
that to be expected under specie conditions. The index number

for the United States would show a fall, whereas under specie conditions the same train of influences would cause the same sort of index number to show a rise. In Great Britain, on the other hand, a rise in prices would be shown, as against a fall under specie.

This apparently anomalous conclusion arises from the fact that in the United States the sum total of physical goods, and so the volume of trade in terms of units of transactions, becomes larger. There are more imported goods than before. More goods are retained for domestic consumption than before, since exports are less. On the other hand, the total money income is the same as before. There is a larger supply of imported goods; and there are more domestic goods (or services), too, since more of the country's labor is given to making them than before. Domestic goods (including those exported) will be unchanged in price, but imported goods will be cheaper. The price level for *all* goods shows a decline. The people of the United States have the same money incomes as before, but can buy more goods. In other words, they get the gain from the better terms of foreign trade in that concrete form in which alone any real gain at all can be got: by having more commodities for their labor. And conversely in Great Britain. There, while the total of money incomes is the same as it was before the change in the conditions of foreign trade set in, goods are less in quantity. There are less imported goods, less too of domestic goods. Prices of imported goods are higher. With the same money incomes, the people of Great Britain will be able to buy fewer goods.[1]

---

[1] The general train of reasoning followed in the text was developed in a paper which I published in the Quarterly Journal of Economics, May, 1917. In that paper, however, I said (pp. 397–398) that in the United States, in such a case as has been supposed, there would ultimately be a fall in the prices of domestic goods as well as of imported. This proposition appears to me on further reflection unsound. The accurate solution, *i.e.* that based on unrelenting theoretical reasoning, would seem to be that the fall in price is confined to imported goods only, and that it is the lower prices of these alone that lead to the decline in the general price level and to the greater purchasing power of the stable money incomes.

This solution seems to me to follow from the constancy of total money income, which points to constancy in money wages and in all the money expenses of production. Individual money prices of domestic goods will remain unchanged, as do the expenses of production. The *proportion* of the total money income which is spent on purely domestic goods may become greater or less than before, this depending on the elasticities of demand for these goods and for the imported goods.

Still another aspect of the problem remains for consideration; namely, how the barter terms of trade shape themselves under dislocated exchanges. It is to be expected, on grounds of general reasoning, that the principles valid for specie conditions will prove applicable under paper conditions also. Nay, since under paper conditions there is no flow of money at all, and nothing moves from country to country except merchandise — an even closer resemblance to barter than under specie — it is to be expected that the fundamental causes which settle the barter terms will operate at least as effectively and surely. They do; and the preceding exposition indicates in what way.

The situation which finally emerges in consequence of a remittance operation such as has been used for illustration is one in which more goods move from Great Britain to the United States than before, less goods move from the United States to Great Britain. In the United States, prices of British (imported) goods are lower; in Great Britain prices of American (imported) goods are higher. The British have a less quantity of American goods than before. The Americans have a greater quantity of British goods than before. In other words, the barter terms of trade have altered to the advantage of the United States. And, as we have seen, the extent to which this change takes place, the degree to which the barter terms become more favorable to the United States, depends on the conditions of demand in the trading countries. The concrete way in which the British experience the less favorable conditions is that with the same money incomes they buy less of imported goods at higher prices; the concrete way in which the Americans experience the more favorable conditions is that with the same money incomes they buy more of imported goods at lower prices. The outcome is essentially the same as under specie conditions; the difference is that money incomes are stationary in both countries under paper, and vary inversely to each other under specie.

As just remarked, international trade under paper approaches the conditions of pure barter. Under specie we may indeed lay it down that the trade is in essentials one of barter, since overwhelmingly the largest movement between countries is that of merchandise, while that of specie is small. But under paper, it is not merely a matter of preponderance in the merchandise movement. Nothing at all moves except merchandise. No money flows from country to country. And yet, tho what takes place is the mere exchange of commodities for commodities, tho this essential characteristic of all trade and all exchange seems to be conspicuously in evidence, each individual transaction remains a sale for money. No individual trader is aware that barter is taking place. As under specie conditions, so under dislocated exchanges, the entire series of transactions between the countries is wound up without any understanding of the situation on the part of the individuals who consummate them, unless it be in the excessively rare case of a merchant or banker who has a grasp of the intricacies of theory. All works itself out thru the buying and selling of foreign exchange, the exchange quotations, the slow and unperceived shifts in the flow of goods from country to country, the gradual alterations in prices, the painful readjustment of the productive forces. The whole process operates *thru* the foreign exchange rate. But that exchange rate itself depends on the same factors on which the barter terms of trade also depend : on the extent to which a country values foreign goods, and chooses to consume these rather than the things which it can directly produce within its own borders.

Some obvious qualifications on the scope and nature of these general conclusions should be borne in mind. There are of course limits and bounds within which both the barter terms of trade and the foreign exchange rate are confined. Those limits are reached when the barter terms become so unfavorable to one of the countries that it can produce at home as advantageously as it is able to import. The wider the disparity between productive forces — the greater the absolute or comparative advantage possessed by a country — the wider the range within which the barter terms and the foreign exchange can fluctuate. So it is under specie conditions. The wider the disparities of advantages in production, the greater the possible differences of money incomes from country to country; and thus the greater are the possibilities that one country will gain markedly thru a high range of money incomes and low prices of imported goods, while another, having high import prices and low money incomes, gains much less.

It is not to be gainsaid that there is, in the rough and as a first approximation, a general accordance between the quantity of paper money issued, the advance in prices, and the rates of paper exchange; and thus a rough sort of purchasing-power parity. A doubling or quadrupling of the volume of currency will lead to something like a doubling or quadrupling of prices, and to disturbance of exchange rates of similar quantitative character. What is to be questioned is the doctrine of an exact relation, and especially that of a tendency to a long-run exact correspondence. And the important comparison, it must be borne in mind, is between domestic prices and money incomes in the several countries, not between prices measured by an index number made up for all classes of goods, international as well as domestic. It is a mere truism that the prices of international goods tend to fluctuate in close accord with the exchange quotations. The real problem lies in the movements of domestic prices and money incomes. Between these and the exchange rates there are not only temporary discordances (concerning which something will be said in the following chapter) but permanent ones. Divergences may arise, and are likely to arise, between the exchange rates and the general domestic price levels, divergences that rest on deep-seated causes. They are such as to persist however long a time elapses and however completely competition irons out the short-time phenomena.

The conclusions that emerge from this prolonged analysis as regard the purchasing-parity doctrine can be summarized in a few words.

There is no normal or settled rate of exchange based on purchasing-power parity. To be sure, if there be not only the elements of constancy just mentioned, but also constant conditions of demand for the exports and imports, and, moreover, constancy in the invisible items, *then* the purchasing-parity doctrine will hold.

Then it can be laid down that, if the quantity of money be doubled in a given country, and if prices be doubled in consequence, the rate of foreign exchange will settle down in the long run to a figure in accord with the change in its prices relative to prices in other countries. But if something happens to disturb the conditions of demand for exports or imports; or if invisible items enter which disturb the barter terms of trade — then the purchasing-parity doctrine does not hold. And if both sets of forces vary together, if there be changing monetary conditions, and also changes in the conditions of demand, and (or) in the invisible items, the doctrine does not hold. The exchange rate then may vary within limits that are potentially wide.

APPENDIX

In the following pages I work out in detail, and illustrate by figures, the lines of analysis followed in the body of the chapter, the object being to show with the explicitness of figures how the rates of exchange shape themselves, how prices shift in the trading countries, how sales and purchases are carried out in the moneys of the countries, how the barter terms of trade work themselves out. The reader to whom this sort of treatment seems otiose can omit.

The figures have not always been carried out meticulously to the last fraction. Here, as in other numerical illustrations used in the present volume, results in round numbers have been thought to suffice.

Let us suppose, as before, a situation in which the United States and Great Britain each have inconvertible paper. The American paper is more abundant (relatively to the traditional gold currency of the two countries) than the British. The rate of exchange with which we begin is £1 = $10.00; or $1 = 2 shillings. Following the existing and long-established practice, we may still quote the rate in the way first stated, that is, so many dollars to the pound. And we may assume, as in previous illustrative figures, that all the exchange transactions are carried on in New York.

The successive stages in a series of representative situations may now be followed.

(1) Begin by assuming a stage of simple equilibrium, in which the only dealings between the two countries arise from merchandise transactions. Let cotton stand for the goods exported by the United States to Great Britain, and steel for the goods which Great Britain exports. Suppose that

U. S. sends to G. B. 50 million cotton @ 4.8d. = £1,000,000
G. B. sends to U. S. 50 million steel @ $0.20 = $10,000,000

With exchange at £1 = $10, the goods exactly pay for each other. Exchange remains at this rate so long as there are no other transactions. The barter terms of trade, be it observed, are 50 of American cotton for 50 British steel.

(2) Great Britain next is called on to remit to the United States for loans the sum of £250,000 a year. The American borrowers can draw on London bankers to that amount. The amount of sterling exchange on sale in New York, which before was £1,000,000, now is raised to £1,250,000. The only persons who buy that exchange are the representatives in New York of the British steel firms which have sold steel for $10,000,000. That sum, no more and no less, these representatives have to convert into British funds; they want sterling exchange for remittance to London. And no one else wants sterling exchange. The amount offered for the sterling exchange on sale is then the precise sum of $10,000,000; the amount of exchange on sale is £1,250,000. The price of sterling bills — the rate of exchange — falls to $8.00; £1 = $8.00. At that rate the transactions balance. If exchange happened to be quoted the other way — if in London, say, it were quoted in terms of so many shillings to the dollar — the figure would be 2s. 6d. to the dollar, as compared with a previous quotation (on the same basis) of 2s. to the dollar. The pound is worth less in dollars than before; the dollar is worth more than before in pounds and shillings.

The barter terms of trade remain unchanged. The same quantities of goods pass between the two countries. Great Britain sends no more goods to the United States than before, and the United States no less goods to Great Britain: and yet Britain's additional payments to the United States are met. By a stroke of the pen, so to speak, without any alteration in the substance of things, the loan remittances are provided for.

(3) Consider now the consequences on the prices of the two commodities, cotton and steel. And here again begin by simplifying the case as regards the two articles. Suppose both to be primarily articles of export from the two countries, and their prices determined, in the first instance at least, by the conditions of the export market. Cotton continues to sell at 4.8d. in London, and steel continues to sell at $0.20 in New York. But 4.8d. in London, translated into American currency at the new rate of exchange, means less American money than before. Before the disturbance of foreign exchange, 4.8d. in London meant $0.20 in New York. Now, however, at the new rate of £1 = $8.00, 4.8d. in London means only $0.16 in New York. The price of cotton, while unchanged in London, falls to $0.16 in New York. On the other hand, the price of steel, remaining as before at $0.20 in New York, now realizes to the British seller more than before in London. At the new rate of exchange, the British seller gets for $0.20 in New York, not 4.8d. in London, but 6d.

Observe that these precise changes in prices — the one advantageous to the British steel sellers, the other disadvantageous to the American cotton sellers —

will appear only under our supposition that both articles are produced and sold for export alone; that is, only if all the American cotton is marketed in Great Britain and all the British steel is marketed in the United States. If part of the American cotton is sold and used at home, there will be a change of price in the same direction, but not of the same extent. The fall in the price of cotton will attract domestic purchasers and increase domestic consumption; some cotton will be withdrawn from export. Similarly, in Great Britain, the full rise in the price of steel just figured out (from 4.8d. to 6d.) will appear only if the British production of steel has been for export only. If there has been a domestic market for part of it, the rise in price will check domestic purchases, and a larger proportion of the output will be exported. The way in which the first impact of the new conditions of foreign exchange will be transmitted to domestic prices will thus depend on two factors: the extent to which the commodities are directed to the export market, and the extent to which there is extensibility of the domestic market — the elasticity of the domestic demand.

It was remarked a moment ago that the barter terms of trade remained unaltered in this first stage. So far as concerns the substantive trade, neither country seems to lose or gain. But there are the changes in prices, and these involve substantive effects of no small consequence. They entail losses to American producers, gains to British producers. Perversely enough, some British — the sellers of steel — gain from the fact that payments have to be made to Americans; and their gain is secured at the expense of the unfortunate American producers of cotton.

Something analogous, it will be recalled, happens under specie conditions. There the British send specie to the United States; an apparent loss, not a real one. The Americans receive specie; an apparent gain but after all an illusory one. More or less specie is in circulation, prices are higher or lower — this in itself does not alter the wealth of nations. Whether under paper or specie, a remitting country seems to lose nothing in the first stages.

(4) Proceed now to follow the operations thru their subsequent course. For the purpose of concentrating attention on the particular matters here under consideration — the rates of foreign exchange, prices in the two countries, the barter terms of trade — we may continue to set aside for the moment the effect on domestic purchases and domestic consumption, and treat the case as if the two commodities were produced and sold for export only. The price of cotton then will fall from $0.20 to the bottom figure of $0.16 in New York; the price of steel rise from 4.8d. in London to the top figure of 6d.

Evidently under these conditions the price of cotton is unattractive to cotton producers in the United States, while that of steel is attractive to steel makers in England. The tendency will be for the production of cotton to diminish in the United States, and for that of steel to increase in England. Eventually the output of both articles will be such as to make the position of the American cotton producers no worse than that of other Americans, and that of the English steel producers no better than that of other Englishmen. The *extent* to which the decrease of the American output of cotton will go depends on the nature of the English demand for that article; the extent to which the increase of English output of steel will go depends on the nature of the American demand in turn for this. The *rapidity* of the changes will depend on the industrial conditions. If the commodity is one produced with much plant — steel, for example — no great expansion can take place except by the slow process of addition to plant. If it is an agricultural product like cotton, grown on land not readily turned to other crops, the process of diminution in the United States will also be slow. Even more slow will it be if the conditions of production are like those in the vineyards of France or the coffee plantations of Brazil. On the other hand, a manufactured commodity made with comparatively little plant and from raw material that is abundant — like German cutlery — will respond quickly to the new conditions of demand and price.

Under any conditions, whether of slow or rapid changes, an intervening period of partial and unstable adjustment is to be expected. The price of cotton, in our illustrative case, will rise somewhat from the bottom point; the price of steel will fall somewhat from the top point. And the quantities of the goods passing between the two countries will shift correspondingly, less cotton going out from the United States and more steel going out from Great Britain.

Let it be supposed, for example, that the following situation develops:[1]

$$\text{U. S. exports 48 million cotton @ } 5\tfrac{1}{2}d. = \text{£1,100,000}$$
$$\text{G. B. exports 60 million steel @ \$0.18} = \text{\$10,800,000}$$

Great Britain continues to remit £250,000 on loan account. The total of sterling exchange offered then becomes:

From cotton	£1,100,000	
From loans	250,000 . .	£1,350,000

Whereas the demand (on steel account) is . . . $10,800,000

The rate of exchange resulting from the two quantities is £1 = $8.00.

The gross barter terms of trade here are 60 steel for 48 cotton. The net barter terms we ascertain (as before)[2] by taking separate account of the steel sales which serve to meet the loan remittances. In round numbers, eleven million steel at $0.18 will supply, with exchange at $8.00, the £250,000 needed. Deducting these eleven million from the total British export of sixty million steel, we have as the net barter terms forty-nine million of steel for forty-eight

---

[1] These figures would indicate that the English demand for cotton is inelastic: the quantity of cotton bought in London decreases but little with a rise in price from 4.8d. to 5½d. They would indicate, on the other hand, that the American demand for steel is elastic; with a fall in price from $0.20 to $0.18 the quantity of steel bought in New York increases a great deal.

[2] Cf. 113.

million cotton. The barter terms with which we started (p. 358, bottom) were fifty steel for fifty cotton. As the situation now stands, tho the net terms have changed very little, the gross terms are much less advantageous to Great Britain.

(5) A definitive stage will be reached when cotton has reverted (risen) in the United States to the price which prevailed before the disturbing factor entered, and steel in turn has reverted (fallen) in Great Britain to its former prevailing price. Until such a stage is reached, cotton sells in the United States at a price less satisfactory to its producers than with other American products; while steel sells in Great Britain at a price more satisfactory. The tendency must be for the production and export of cotton to diminish in the United States, for the production and export of steel to rise in Great Britain. The following figures indicate the nature of the stage which will finally be reached, and will be stable. They are illustrative figures only; they indicate not what stage will necessarily be reached, but in what manner a definitive outcome will be brought about.

The price of cotton in New York reverts (rises) to the original figure of $0.20. The price of cotton in London rises to (say) . . . . 6d. The price of steel in London reverts (falls) to the original figure of . 4.8d. The price of steel in New York falls to (say) $0.16

At these prices, the merchandise transactions may be supposed to be:

> U. S. exports 45 million cotton @ 6d. = £1,125,000
> G. B. exports 70 million steel @ $0.16 = $11,200,000

Sterling bills on sale in New York are:

From cotton	£1,125,000	
From loans	250,000 . .	£1,375,000

Whereas the demand (on steel account) is   . . . $11,200,000 Sterling exchange is £1 = $8.15.

The gross barter terms of trade are 45 cotton for 70 steel; having regard to these, the United States evidently gains much more from the trade than she did at the outset. Making allowance, as before, for the steel that provides for the loan remittances of £250,000 (12½ million of steel at $0.16, with exchange at $8.15), we get as the net barter terms of trade 45 of cotton for 55½ of steel. The new terms have finally become distinctly more advantageous to the United States than they were before the remittances set in. The British demand being inelastic, and the American elastic, it is to be expected that in the final adjustment the net barter terms will thus become less favorable to Great Britain, more favorable to the United States.[1]

[1] I am indebted to Mr. Dennis Robertson for calling attention, in a review published in the *Economic Journal*, not only to some misprints in the first impression of this book, but to a slip which there appeared in the discussion of the changed terms of trade.

CHAPTER 27

DISLOCATED EXCHANGES FURTHER CONSIDERED

WE may proceed to other problems, somewhat different. The questions now to be considered arise not in connection with the invisible items (such as tourist expenditures) but from influences of another sort. Merchandise movements, instead of following variations in the foreign exchanges, may set in of their own accord; they may precede the exchange variations. Under conditions of the type analyzed in the preceding chapter the remittances first set in; then the exchanges are affected; then prices shift; at last the imports and exports of goods are modified. In the cases now to be considered, on the other hand, the sequence in time and the causal connections run the other way. Changes in merchandise movements, in imports and exports, are the initial modifying factors. Thereafter come the readjustments of the foreign exchange rates and of prices in the trading countries, and also some further and complementary changes in merchandise movements.

In considering cases of this kind I shall proceed, as in the last chapter, on the supposition that the volumes of currency in the several trading countries remain constant. It is not the effects of continuing issues of paper and continuing advances in prices that are here examined, but the characteristics of trade under dislocated exchanges pure and simple. Let the reader disregard for the moment the possibility or even probability that paper money issues may be enlarged, and that the enlargement will bring effects of its own. For the purpose of the analysis that follows, assume a fixed amount of currency in each country.

A clear example of changes of the kind now to be considered — that is, where merchandise movements themselves cause exchange fluctuations — is that of an altered state of demand. Suppose two

countries, the United States and Great Britain, to be in the initial
position described in the preceding chapter (prior to the remittance
there considered).   There is a given rate of exchange, and a stable
adjustment of prices and of the barter terms of trade; all are
mutually related to one another and in proper accord.   An increase
of demand then sets in for American commodities in Great Britain.
Let it be an increase of demand in the strict sense, in the "schedule sense," to use Professor Fisher's phrase.   The British buy
the same quantity of cotton, but pay a higher price.[1]   Great
Britain then has to make larger remittances to the United States
than before.   The sterling rate of exchange is affected precisely
in the same way as when the added remittances on loan account
had to be made by Great Britain.   Exchange in New York drops;
the pound sterling can buy less dollars, and the dollar can buy more
of sterling.   The American cotton sellers neither gain nor lose.
They realize more pounds sterling in Great Britain, but no more
American dollars when they sell their exchange in New York.
The situation is odd; the British buyers of cotton lose, but the
American sellers of cotton do not gain.   It is the new rate of foreign
exchange which conjures up this paradoxical outcome, acting as a
sort of *deus ex machina*.

There are other consequences, however.   The new rate of foreign exchange has an effect on British exporters of steel different
from that on American exporters of cotton.   The British exporters
gain.   They sell in the United States (in this initial stage) exactly
as much steel as before, and receive for this unchanged quantity
not indeed more dollars in the United States, but more pounds
in Great Britain.   Then sets in a sequence similar to that
traced in the preceding chapter.   Imports of steel into the United
States from Great Britain swell; and the rate of exchange moves
back toward its former position (but not back all the way to the

[1] In order to isolate the effects of the change in demand, let it be supposed further
that the shift is from a British domestic commodity (one not entering at all within
the range of international trade) toward a commodity imported from the United
States.   The price of the British domestic commodity thereupon will fall below the
normal figure.   It will remain below that figure until its supply is decreased by a
transfer of labor and capital to the making of goods for export, which will in the end
serve to pay for the added American goods.

point where it stood before). Steel tends to become cheaper in the United States, and the people of the United States get a larger physical quantity of steel than before. The barter terms of trade are modified in favor of the United States. The *deus ex machina* is able to maintain its wonder-working efficacy during the period of transition only.

Still another possibility, nay probability, has now to be considered. Cotton has been treated as the only article of export from the United States, or rather as the representative and type of all the exports. In fact, however, every country exports a number of different articles. Each article has its own demand schedule, at home and abroad; each is subject to changes in demand quite independent of changes in demand for other articles. It is highly improbable that at any one time an increase of demand will take place for *all* the articles of export from a given country. When such an increase takes place for any one of the exported goods, the others are also affected under dislocated exchanges, but in a way quite different. As regards the exported goods for which the conditions of demand are unchanged, the new rate of foreign exchange operates as a check or restriction. It does so, at all events, in the first stages. The sterling exchange which the sellers of such goods have for sale commands a lower price than before, and they do not have the compensating circumstance that their goods sell in Great Britain for a higher price than before. In other words, these exports feel a chill because of the decline in sterling exchange which follows from the offerings of other exporters whose sales to foreigners do show an increase. And the consequence must be a lessened volume of those other exports. That decline in volume, again, is presumably no more permanent than is the initial decline in sterling exchange. It is part of a general process of readjustment, resulting eventually in a modified and settled rate of exchange (one settled in the sense of remaining constant so long as conditions do not again change) and in modified barter terms of trade. It is hardly profitable to follow out the ultimate possibilities as regards the exports not affected by the increase of demand. Like many other theoretic possibilities they afford plenty of scope for elaborated analysis, but little opportunity for verification in the actual course of trade.

Returning now to the initial effects on the article for which there is the increased demand, and on the rates of foreign exchange, we have to confess that here also the deduced conclusions are rarely subject to verification or correction from actual experience. An increase of demand is an elusive thing. Changes in demand doubtless are taking place all the time, but it is rarely possible to put one's finger on a specific case and keep it under continuous observation. Commonly an increase of demand sets in not by a sudden sweep of the kind assumed in the preceding pages, but by slow and gradual steps. The further changes which ensue under conditions of dislocated exchanges — the altered supply of sterling exchange and the shifts in the rates of exchange — also appear gradually. During their slow course they are likely to be offset or reënforced, as the case may be, by other changes occurring in the same period. And the reverse effect on other articles of export, caused by the change in demand for a particular article or group, appears also by insensible gradations, and would be no less difficult of disentanglement. It is only in time of war that an abrupt and extensive change of demand for a given article is likely to occur; but in time of war still other factors will also undergo great and sudden changes; and the entire situation will be even more complex and confused than in time of peace. I doubt indeed whether there are any conditions at all — war or peace, dislocated exchanges or gold exchanges — under which it would be possible to verify or substantiate by actual observation the theoretic conclusions on the effects of changes in demand which play so considerable a part in the literature on international trade.

Another case, however, belonging in the same class, can be discerned in the actual course of trade and its sequence followed. It is that of a change in supply, not in demand. Suppose there is abrupt increase in the quantity of a given commodity offered for export. In a country whose industries are chiefly extractive, just this frequently happens. If its exports consist largely of agricultural products, its international trade is subject to spasmodic changes because of crop fluctuations. There are abundant examples where a country having an inconvertible currency, and therefore dislocated exchanges, finds its international trade perturbed in just this way : Argentina, for example, the United States, Russia.

When such a country has a bumper crop, its exports suddenly increase. The price at which the increased quantity of exported goods sells in foreign countries will depend on the conditions of demand there, and also on the conditions of supply in the importing region — on the state of the crops all around. Demand ordinarily does not change, or changes but little. It is an abrupt change in supply that has to be reckoned with. At the risk of some repetition I will dwell on several aspects of situations of this sort which deserve attention.

The first of our general propositions on the course of international trade under dislocated exchanges is here most conspicuously substantiated ; namely, that at any given time the rate of exchange is the result of the impact of the momentary supply on the momentary demand. The enlarged exports and the consequently enlarged offerings of foreign exchange meet an unchanged demand. The rate of exchange declines abruptly. The actual course of events supplies abundant illustrations of this first stage, and there is abundant discussion of it in the literature of the subject. Observers of all kinds, both those versed in economic theory, and the financial writers and the business men, are familiar with the effects of crop fluctuations under dislocated exchanges. The formulation of the rationale of the case has not often been precise, but its general character is known to all. The pressure from the added exports has for its first effect that exchange on gold countries falls.

It is clear — I would emphasize the point — that such a decline in foreign exchange is the *result* of merchandise movements. It is the increased exports, the larger crop movements, that bring about the new rates of exchange, and cause them to be more "favorable" to the country from which the exports come. The sequence is obviously the reverse of that which appears when non-merchandise items cause the foreign exchanges to shift, and thereafter lead to larger or smaller movements of physical goods.

Next, these very fluctuations in exchange, while caused by merchandise movements, become in their turn causes of *other* merchandise movements. The new rates of exchange which are brought about by heavy crop exports operate as a damper on other exports. While they serve to stimulate all imports, they serve also to check some exports, the exports, namely, of those commodities whose conditions of supply and demand are not affected by the crop changes. This again is a consequence more readily observable than is the analogous phenomenon in the case of change of demand. The same general reasoning is applicable to both cases. An altered demand, like an altered supply, modifies the movement of certain items of merchandise; this affects the rates of exchange; this again affects other merchandise movements. The characteristic phenomena — first, the direct impact on rates of foreign exchange, and next the rebound on the movements of other merchandise — simply come more frequently and more unmistakably under our eyes in cases of change in supply.

The eventual effects of course are not the same as the immediate. As in the case of increased demand, so in that of increased supply, there is prolonged readjustment. The rates of exchange, the course of prices in the trading countries, the barter terms of trade, are gradually modified. The nature of the ultimate outcome is different according as there is an increase of supply or an increase of demand. An increase of supply from a country — an increased offering of exports from it — tends in the end to make its barter terms of trade less favorable, whereas an increase of demand for its products tends to make them more favorable. As regards ultimate consequences, the difficulties in the way of observation and verification are equally great in the two cases. It is only the first stages in the series of effects which are readily discerned even in the case of increased supply. Crop changes, while they are conspicuous and their immediate effects also are conspicuous, show no regularity. Even tho the output of agricultural produce may tend on the whole to enlarge, it enlarges at no steady rate — is likely to advance in one year, to falter or sink in another. Unmistakable as are the immediate consequences of the fluctuations in supply on the exchanges and on prices, the ulterior effects are usually obscure. Almost invariably they are interwoven with the effects of other factors, most of all with those of changes in the monetary policy and the monetary conditions of the country having paper currency. Even tho the immediate effects of crop fluctuations on the foreign exchanges in such a country are plain enough, the ulterior consequences of sustained changes in supply are in this sort of case, as in so many that stir the curiosity of the speculative economist, concealed in the disordered and confusing march of events.

I turn now to another problem, that of silver exchange. If one country has a gold standard, another a silver standard, the situation obviously is also that of dislocated exchanges. Gold can not flow *as money* from the gold-standard country into the silver-standard country. It can flow only as bullion, like any other commodity; and its transfer cannot affect prices in the silver country. Conversely silver can flow only as bullion into the gold country. Such was the situation as regards international payments and the foreign exchanges in the trade of Great Britain and most of Western Europe with the Orient after the demonetization of silver in 1873. It remained so for the trade with British India until the cessation of the free coinage of rupees in 1893, and for the trade with Japan until Japan adopted the gold standard in 1897. It still persists (1925) for the trade of the gold standard countries with China.

In this case we must have regard to a factor different from those hitherto considered. The money of each of the trading countries, while not available in other countries as money, is yet available as bullion, *i.e.* as merchandise. Paper money cannot move at all from the country in which it circulates. Silver, however, is a commodity valuable in itself, and can move from the silver country into the gold country; and of course it can move from the gold country to the silver country. Gold likewise can move both ways. As regards a paper country, to sell goods in it and so to have at one's command bills of exchange on it, means only that purchasing power in the paper country becomes available; nothing more. One can either sell the exchange, or (ordinarily the less convenient alternative) use the purchasing power in buying any goods of the paper country which one happens to want. The paper itself is worth nothing in any other way.[1] But the sale of goods to a silver country and the consequent possession of silver exchange mean that one can get a specified quantity of silver, a commodity which is readily vendible in any country. And similarly the purchase of goods from a silver country does not necessarily involve the purchase of exchange on that country as a means of effecting payment for the goods. Silver bullion can be bought in the open market and the silver itself transmitted. The converse is the case where goods move from a silver country to a gold country. The vendor who sends the goods from this silver country has command not merely of purchasing power in the gold country, but of gold itself; and for this as bullion he can always find a ready market in his own country or anywhere else. An alternative exists which is not present in the transactions between paper countries and gold countries; and the conditions on which the rate of exchange depends are more complex.

We may take for illustration the trade between India and Great Britain — the Indian (rupee) exchange as it was between 1876 and 1893, that is, between the year in which the great fall in the price of silver began and that in which the Indian mints were closed to the coinage of rupees. The general trend of the trade with the Orient need not be rehearsed. It led to a flow of specie toward the Orient, both of gold and silver. The gold moved to the silver country (India) as a commodity. The silver moved more

---

[1] I bar from consideration the minor and negligible movement of paper to and fro in the pockets of travellers. I set aside also (as quite exceptional) substantial purchases of paper money by speculators in a foreign country. Such purchases played a large part in the extraordinary phenomena of the German currency debacle of 1921–23, and, like the other phenomena of that episode, stand outside the scope of the present analysis. Indeed the whole German episode stands outside the analysis of what may be regarded as the normal case of inconvertible paper issues — that in which they do not reach the stage of collapse.

largely as a money metal, for coinage into rupees. It was the movement of silver to India and its connection with rupee exchange that constituted the main phenomenon and the conspicuous phenomenon.

I do not propose to undertake any detailed examination of this much discussed episode. Its general character is well known. The balance of payments was such that both silver and gold moved to India. When they reached India, both were largely hoarded. So far as hoarded, they did not enter the circulating medium, did not affect prices, signified nothing further in regard to international trade. The silver, however, was chiefly coined into rupees; and tho even the rupees went freely into hoards, the volume of the active money did increase, and domestic prices did tend to rise. But the rise was slow, so slow as to be observable only over a series of years. The vast extent of the country, its enormous and immobile population, the sluggish character of its entire economic life, made it possible for marked changes to take place in international transactions with much retarded effects in domestic trade. Thru long periods foreign exchange, imports and exports, and the prices of imported and exported goods, could vary as if they were quite in a realm of their own, separated by a wide gulf from the prices of Indian domestic goods and from the money incomes of the great mass of people.

Within the sphere of international trade, however, there was close interdependence. Imported and exported goods were directly and immediately affected. The gold price of an Indian commodity in Great Britain, its silver price in India, the rate of rupee exchange, and the price of silver bullion — all were tied together. And so as regards the silver price of a British commodity in India. If rupee exchange and the price of silver bullion became low — if many rupees could be got for a pound sterling — the silver prices of exported goods would rise in India and exports would be stimulated. Thereafter, with the increase of Indian exports, the gold prices of those goods would begin to fall in Britain, and rupee exchange would begin to be readjusted. And it is clear that a chain of events similar in character might start the other way. An increased movement of goods from India to Great Britain might set in because of an increase of demand for them; and this would lead to a rise in rupee exchange.

We have here merely another case of the sort of distinction just made for the case of paper money and paper exchange. The rate of rupee exchange may be the cause of merchandise movements, or the merchandise movements may be the cause of the rate of exchange. Rupee exchange might go up or down from causes which have no immediate connection with the import and export goods — from loans, interest payments, government remittances. Thereupon merchandise movements would respond to the new condition of exchange. Or, the other way, crops might fluctuate from season to season, or trade disturbances might affect the volume of Indian exports (cotton, say, during the American Civil War). Then exchange would respond to the new conditions in the movements of the goods. And, at a subsequent stage, other goods, not the originators of the disturbance, would be affected precisely as if the rates of exchange had been shifted because of non-merchandise transactions.

To this analysis, however, there must obviously be added, in the case of silver exchange, the consideration of a factor different from any that enters in the case of paper money and paper exchange. It is the price of silver bullion in terms of gold. The gold price of silver may alter from causes that have nothing to do with rupee exchange and nothing to do with the trade between the gold and silver countries. The price of silver may fall in London because larger quantities come from the mines, or because the demand for use in the arts declines, or because governments buy less silver for subsidiary coin. The price of rupee exchange will follow that of silver. Merchandise movements will then be influenced exactly as if the rate of exchange had been disturbed by loans or other non-merchandise transactions. The converse chain of events may also take place. Merchandise movements may themselves be a cause influencing the gold price of silver bullion. An increase of exports from India, or a decline of imports into India, will cause rupee exchange to rise, and this will bring a rise in the price of silver bullion.

To sum up. In the case of trade between gold and silver countries, three sets of forces have to be reckoned with: first, the substantive course of trade, the export and import of goods between the trading countries; second, the non-merchandise transactions; and third, the price of silver bullion in terms of gold. Any one of the three may change independently, and thereupon changes will be entailed in the others. In the actual course of events, it will rarely happen that one of the three does vary quite alone, the others remaining the same. In almost every case where one has clearly been active, there will be ground for suspecting that the others have not remained entirely inert. Hence room will remain for differences of opinion how far the final outcome had been due to any one, how far to the combined and interdependent influence of all. There may be clear grounds for supposing that at a given time one of the three forces has been the dominant one or major one. But it will hardly ever happen that there is no ground at all for supposing that the others have not also exercised an influence of their own. Commonly they will have contributed to bring about the outcome, not merely succumbed to the impelling operation of the single one. One set of closely connected phenomena — a single tho many-sided result — will be found; the prices of international goods, the rates of exchange, the prices of bullion, will all move with a common accord.

CHAPTER 28

Speculation, Pegging, the Gold Exchange Standard

WHAT has been so far said needs to be qualified and amplified by a consideration of the short-period movements of dislocated exchanges. Something in this direction has already been done in the preceding chapters. Tho these were concerned mainly with long-period results, they dealt also with some transition phenomena of short or of moderate duration. Still other phenomena of similar character will now be examined. Partly they are inevitable incidents of a transition from one stage of equilibrium to another, and in that sense are normal; partly they are of irregular character, not evincing any underlying trend.

The reader should bear in mind that the discussion is still confined to conditions relatively stable; that is, it proceeds on the assumption that the currency amounts are fixed. The consequences which arise from an increase or decrease in the quantity of paper are still ruled out, it being important, I am convinced, to distinguish between the consequences of the mere fact of dislocated exchanges and those which result from increase or decrease of the currency.

First, speculative dealings. In the case of dislocated exchanges and especially paper exchange, these are of much greater importance than under gold exchanges, and have very different effects.

Between gold countries the fluctuations in the rates of exchange are restricted within the narrow limits of the gold points. The ups and downs cannot in any event be great. And this very circumstance brings it about that usually they are not rapid. The purchases and sales are made chiefly by a small knot of bankers and brokers, professional dealers who are conversant with the general course of the market, experienced in its movements, well-

374

informed and cool. Their operations, as has already been said, exercise a stabilizing and smoothing influence.

In the case of paper exchanges, the situation is very different. The fluctuations may be great, often are rapid, often are difficult to foresee. The very circumstance that they are great and unpredictable brings in an element by which these irregularities are accentuated: speculation by the "outside public." Even the best informed and most experienced of dealers often do not know what the rates of exchange are likely to be in the future, and find themselves buying and selling from day to day more or less blindly. Side by side with them come the non-professional buyers and sellers, the "speculators" in the narrower sense. Foreign exchange being a standardized article, like wheat or cotton or securities, it can be bought or sold on a large scale by any one. Given this possibility, and given also large and rapid changes in price, persons of all sorts and kinds make their way into the market-place. Whereas with gold exchanges the margin of profit on any one transaction is small, and a large total gain can be got only thru a great volume of business spread over a considerable time, under paper there is the chance of quick turns and big profits from a few transactions, even from a single one. Chances of this kind, leading as they do to speculation by all sorts and conditions of men, lead also to manipulation, pools, rumors and lies — the familiar phenomena of a gamblers' market.

Whether speculation under such conditions serves to lessen fluctuations is no more clear as regards paper exchange than it is in the analogous cases of cotton, wheat, stocks. As regards gold exchange, speculative purchases and sales doubtless operate to lessen the rapidity and the range of the fluctuations. But where "the public" takes part, as in these other cases, the rapidity of fluctuations is probably made greater by speculation; the ups and downs are more frequent, and they are more abrupt. It may be, however, that their range is made less rather than greater. So good observers have been led to believe, and have been led to conclude that in this regard the outcome of wide-spread speculative dealings is on the whole good. But one should not be unduly optimistic about any one of the highly-organized and highly-speculative markets. It is not clear that incessant and feverish buying and selling, whether by financial magnates or by the riff-raff of the business world, has a benign and smoothing influence.

As regards paper exchange, the question for the present inquiry is on the relation between the speculative fluctuations and the underlying forces which in the end determine the rates around which they move. Here some distinctions must be made. The underlying forces may operate in sudden and almost spectacular ways, or they may operate slowly and inconspicuously. Under conditions of the first kind, speculation will be rampant, and fluctuations will be large, irregular, and rapid. Under those of the second, the rates are more likely to shift gradually, the outside public is not likely to be attracted by spasmodic ups and downs, and the action of the professional dealers is more likely to have an evening and moderating effect such as it has under gold exchanges.

A moderated situation may be expected, for example, if there is merely a change in commodity demand. Such a change usually sets in, as has been noted above, by gradual and inconspicuous stages. Suppose that the British demand for American exports becomes greater. The first trace of the effects is that the brokers find exchange on London more plentiful than before in New York. Dollar exchange tends to stiffen. The brokers themselves, and the speculative fraternity generally, may think that this is but a flurry, and they will readily sell exchange short, at some advance over the previous price. The additional supply of exchange which must be in the end provided to meet the short sales will come without strain for a while, merely by taking up the slack which usually exists in the available supplies, or by arrangements with London correspondents for meeting the bills for the time being. Gradually it will appear that there is more than a flurry; more American goods are being steadily bought in Great Britain, and more sterling bills are being steadily offered on the market. The underlying situation emerges. The impact of the continuing new offerings makes itself felt on the market rate, and a new rate of exchange becomes established gradually and (perhaps) smoothly.

So it is when there are other changes that prove to affect the exchange rate permanently but operate by slow stages, such as tourist remittances, or a series of loans made from time to time by the people of one country to those of another. Just how much the needed remittances amount to, how rapidly they will follow one or the other, how soon cease, is usually a matter for guesswork. Spread over a season, a year, even a couple of years, they gradually bring their pressure to bear on the exchange market, with ups and downs but none the less with a movement which persists in the same direction. Underneath the fluctuations and speculations there is the inevitable: the balance of payments must be met, and the first step in the settlement, the only one that is effective, is the readjustment of the exchange rate.

Where, on the other hand, new factors enter suddenly and on a large scale, the exchange market feels a great wave of influence at once. The rates move suddenly, yet move irregularly. This sort of thing happens, for example — to refer again to a case already used for illustration — when crop fluctuations cause abrupt shifts in agricultural exports. It happens, too, when remittances of a political or military nature have to be made once for all at a stated date. A quasi-catastrophic effect ensues, and, as need hardly be said, is accentuated if additional paper money issues are made or are expected. In all such cases the altered relation of offerings and takings in the market reflects itself at once in the exchange rates. And when sharp fluctuations are repeated and seem to have become habitual, the outside public is drawn in more and more. Speculation becomes rampant; fluctuations are intensified; the market may be rigged; the day-to-day quotations become quite unpredictable. Commonly enough, when this stage is reached, the speculation which has resulted from the disturbances is regarded as their cause, and there ensue legislative inquiries and government interventions. But here too, underneath all the irregularities, there is a steady trend, induced by the altered relation of the supply of bills to the demand; a trend which may be misunderstood but cannot be reversed or long checked. Speculation is caused by the new situation, and in turn causes the situation

to have new aspects; but it does not make the final outcome
different.

"Pegging" of the dislocated exchanges by government action
or by the action of powerful private interests, is in one way the
opposite from speculation, in another way not unlike it. It is the
opposite in that its design is to stop fluctuations, and thus to
discourage speculation and what are supposed to be the effects of
speculation. It has a similarity to speculation in that it cannot
override for an indefinite time the main forces that determine the
rates of exchange.

For purposes of prestige, a government may wish to prevent the
quoted rate on its money unit from sagging or falling. A great
bank or group of bankers may wish to support the rate for purposes
of profit on loans or on remittance operations. The end can be
achieved by simply buying in the market at a given price all the
exchange offered. The effect of such purchases is essentially the
same as if a new demand arose in the ordinary course of trade.
The relation of offerings and takings is affected in the same way,
and the exchange rate modified or maintained in the same way.
The quoted figure is still the result of the impact of the two forces.
The peculiarity of the case is merely that one of the forces, that
of demand, is so adjusted as to equalize the impact of the supply
at a given point. Not a specific quantity is purchased, but such a
quantity as will keep the rate of exchange at a specific point.
Whatever supply of exchange is offered will be bought at the set
price.

The extent to which pegging will influence the exchange rate
depends, of course, on the extent to which it is carried, on the
amount of money which the pegger is prepared to spend in buying
bills at the set price, and on the length of time for which he is prepared to keep up the process. With plenty of funds in hand, and a
courageous willingness to use them to the full, he can go far in
affecting the rates of exchange, and can maintain his rate for a long
time. And the conditions may be more favorable to him or less
so; more if the ordinary conditions of trade are interrupted or set

aside, less if trade is in its usual grooves. During the Great War governments were lavish in their expenditure for pegging, as they were for others, and in this direction as in others their operations often were not only recklessly extravagant, but of negligible effect for the military objects which were supposed to be promoted. But they did serve to peg the rates for long periods. The success in attaining this immediate object was made comparatively easy because the ordinary course of international trade was itself profoundly disturbed, and the ordinary transactions greatly restricted. The reflex influence which pegging exercises on merchandise movements, and on all international transactions, was impeded or even completely obviated.

In time of peace, however, and under normal commercial conditions, that reflex influence becomes strong, and in the end may bring the pegger's efforts to naught, unless indeed he has succeeded in adjusting his set rate to the figure which would prevail on the whole without his interposition. Both the imports and exports of goods will necessarily be affected if he tries to keep the rate at a different figure. Exports will be stimulated if the rate is set high as compared with current prices of exportable goods; or (the more common case) imports will be stimulated if it is set low as compared with the current prices of imported goods. The greater the discrepancies, the more strain will be put on the resources of the pegger.

Similar is the situation with the invisible items. These two will respond to stimulus or discouragement, as the case may be. It is true that the invisible items, and especially the sales and purchases of securities, lending or borrowing operations of all kinds, are subject to influences of their own. For short periods, and indeed for periods of considerable length — not only for months, but for a year or two — they are themselves affected by the rate. Short-time loans by financial houses, loans by governments themselves, may be made more or less easy of negotiation by the state of the exchanges; and the very negotiation of loans then has its effect on the demand and supply of bills and so on the maintenance of the pegger's figure. In this way pegging may long be successful in attaining its object; and it may seem to be indefinitely successful. And yet here also the long-run consequences are not to be evaded. The flow of loans from country to country depends in the end on the relative conditions of capital supply, just as the flow of commodities depends on the relations between prices; and any rates of foreign exchange which do not accommodate themselves to these fundamental forces cannot be permanently maintained.

The gold exchange standard is virtually a case of pegging, and what has been said in the preceding paragraphs applies. It differs chiefly in that the process is expected to be carried on for a longer time. The term pegging is commonly applied to the support or regulation of the exchanges for a few months or at most years. The gold exchange standard contemplates the permanent maintenance of a fixed rate of exchange, and the conduct of international trade for an indefinite period without the actual use of gold as circulating medium, and with no flow of gold from country to country in the process of adjusting the international balance of payments.

Often the design is to keep the ruling rate of exchange at the same point at which it would be if there were the complete gold standard. While the currency of the country which adopts the exchange standard is not made convertible into gold, international trade is to be carried on as if it were. Even tho there be a stock of the metal in the hands of a central bank or government treasury from which in emergency gold may be sent to other countries, no flow of specie is expected to take place in the ordinary settlement of international payments. It is the rate of discount at banks which is expected to serve as the lever for influencing the offerings of bills of exchange, the course of business and prices, and finally, the commodity exports and imports. The rate of discount, however, is not dependent on a changing stock of gold held by the bank or banks. It is deliberately managed — manipulated, if that word may be used without implication of ill — in order to influence both the rate of exchange and the flow of remittances in such way as to enable the normal specie rate of exchange to be maintained.

Essentially the same situation exists if the established exchange rate be quite different from what it would be under specie — if it be one adjusted to a currency which had been overissued. The currency is to be stabilized in terms of gold, even tho there is no return to specie payments. The equivalent of the currency to the gold money of another country (the pound sterling or the dollar) is fixed at a rate corresponding to the existing depreciation. At the rate fixed on this basis, the rates of exchange are to be held. As in the case just considered, a central bank is put in charge, or a government department of analogous character. There a stock of bills on foreign countries and especially on gold-standard countries is to be kept on hand; there bills are bought and sold at the fixed rate, and more particularly are available for those who have payments to make abroad. Fluctuations in exchange may go on, but they are of a minor sort, kept within a narrow range. Such minor fluctuations, combined with changes in discount rates, are expected to suffice for bringing about a balance of the international debits or credits.

It is beyond the scope of this book to consider the difficult questions of monetary theory and experience which are raised by the gold exchange plan. I will confine my comments to a brief notation, in the nature of a recapitulation, on certain fundamental points.

Obviously, as in the case of temporary pegging, so in that of the permanent gold exchange standard, the maintenance of the fixed rate is made the more secure if the government has large resources and is determined to use them freely. Bills on foreign countries can be bought, impounded as a reserve, and sold when called for. Additional bills can be got in a pinch by borrowing abroad; arranging, for example, with foreign correspondents that bills shall be met whenever drawn. Seasonal variations in the exchanges can be readily smoothed over, much in the same way as they are smoothed, without deliberate intent, in the ordinary course of dealers' transactions under the plain and simple gold exchanges. Fluctuations and oscillations over longer periods, too, can be taken care of. The effects of crop changes, often momentous for the season, can spread over time; and in time, with careful nursing, can

be made innocuous.   If the rate is set in fairly accurate correspondence with the prices of goods in the trading countries — regard
being had also to non-merchandise operations — the system can be
made to work indefinitely.   Not only this; it will represent, for a
country which is in financial straits (such as a depreciated currency
usually entails), a comparatively cheap method of getting rid of the
main evils of depreciation.   Stabilization on a gold basis is achieved
without the expense of securing any considerable supply of the
metal for actual use in the currency system.

The difficulties arise when the correspondence with the fundamental factors — relative prices and incomes in the trading countries — ceases to be even roughly accurate.   Contingencies of this
kind must be faced.   It is true that they may not come for a long
time, and when they do come, may emerge slowly and almost
imperceptibly.   So slow and obscure are they that most writers on
the subject ignore them.   Yet, as is indicated by the discussion in
the preceding chapters, it is these which in the end determine the
rate of exchange.   It is here that the gold exchange standard, like
pegging, meets its eventual test.   Changes from any established
situation, any current rate of exchange, however firmly it seems to
be imbedded, do occur.   Demands will change, new articles of
export and import will appear, the balance of international payments will need to be readjusted; then what?

The consideration of the gold exchange standard brings out once
again the connection, both in theory and practice, between monetary problems and the problems of international trade.   What
determines the course of prices?   It is on prices and price changes
that the movement of goods from country to country depends.
Can prices and money incomes change, permanently and considerably, without a change in the quantity of money?   And can
bank policy, bank rate of discount, the stimulation or repression
of industrial operations by bank credit, exercise not merely a
temporary influence, but an enduring one, on the course of domestic
prices and so on the currents of international trade?   That they are
of influence for a time, no one can doubt.   But how about the long-
run effects?   The rate of discount, after all, is but one phase of

the rate of interest at large.   While it fluctuates much, in each
country it still oscillates above or below the general rate of interest
on long-time investments.   And this latter rate for a given country
is relatively stable.   It tends on the whole to be higher in some
countries than in others.   The discount rate also tends to be higher
in some than in others.   Being permanently higher in one country
than in another, can its mere height exercise a permanent depressing
influence on prices in the country of higher rate?   Changes in the
rate, to repeat, have a first effect on loans, on deposits, on available
funds; on the temper of the business public also, and thus on the
active or sluggish movement both of the purchasing medium and of
the goods purchased.   But it would seem that it is degrees of movement or relative movements which alone are thus affected.   The
extent to which people use loans and deposits at any given time
may indeed be influenced; things may be speeded up or slowed
down.   But does not the use of loans and deposits (or of bank
money other than deposits) depend in the end on the ways and
habits of the people in handling their money incomes or purchasing
power? and so on the extent to which a given volume of legal
tender cash (or cash otherwise made actually acceptable) bolsters
up the structure of credit payments?   Can these forces be permanently modified by mere changes in the charge which the business community has to pay for short-time loans?   On the other
hand, the quantity of goods put on sale, and the way in which
they are put on sale — the flow of goods into the markets — also
depend on forces which in the last resort are independent of the
discount rates: the volume of production, and the ways and
habits of the people in buying and selling goods.   No doubt bank
rates and credit extension have their effects, both mechanistic and
psychological, on the production and distribution of goods as well as
on the ways in which people use their purchasing power.   But are
bank operations the determinants of continuing changes in all this
interplay of factors, and so determinants of prices one way or other,
up or down?

I cannot but believe that those who propose gold exchange
standards, stabilized exchanges, currencies managed by discount

rates, often fail to face the long-run problems. For a time, for a considerable time, arrangements of this character will serve. They may be highly useful in putting an end to violently dislocated exchanges, to sharply fluctuating prices (especially of international goods), to demoralizing uncertainties all around. It is their validity as goals of definitive monetary settlement that seems to me open to question. The problems, as needs hardly be said, are much wider than those of international trade and of money. They reach far into the whole nature and justification of private property and capitalistic enterprise. So far as concerns the restricted range of the present book, they center on the old and much debated question of the relation between quantity of money and prices: whether the adjustment of international trade can be brought about *without* changes in prices; whether, therefore, stable equilibrium can be attained *unless* there be (1) either a flow of gold from country to country, or (2) an adjustment of the prices of imported and exported goods thru varying (not permanently stabilized) rates of foreign exchange.

CHAPTER 29

INFLUENCE OF CHANGES IN THE VOLUME OF PAPER MONEY

I PROCEED finally to a subject which so far has been advisedly put aside : the influence not of dislocated exchanges in themselves, but of the process of dislocation. To put it in another way, the problem now to be considered relates to the influence not of paper money in itself on foreign exchange and international trade, but of changes in the volume of paper money. As between increase or decrease in volume, it is the former, expanding currency and progressive depreciation, that bulks largest in the literature on the subject, and has chief attention.

A common opinion is that enlarging paper money issues, rising prices, and exchanges disturbed in correspondence, stimulate exports and check imports. There is supposed to be inevitably a bounty on exports. Most writers who analyze this sort of situation fail to distinguish between progressive depreciation and established depreciation, not considering any such reasoning as has led in the preceding pages to the conclusion that the mere fact of depreciation and of dislocation may lead either to a bounty on exports or, according to the circumstances, one on imports. What they attend to is the more conspicuous phenomena : the effect of rapid additions to the volume of paper money, the consequences of rapidly rising prices, and of exchange quotations also rising rapidly. Then there is supposed to emerge a sudden increase of exports, and a danger to industries in the countries to which the exports go. When Germany resorted in 1921–23 to its extraordinary and indeed fantastic currency issues, many countries thought it necessary to defend themselves against the "exchange dumping" of German goods. Great Britain, France, the United States, Australia, were for a time panic-struck.   Before long the panic proved to have been little less than foolish, and the episode was almost forgotten, tho the precipitate legislation to which it led was kept on the statute books for an indefinite period.

In support of the view that the process of depreciation brings about an export bounty it has been urged that there is one circumstance which in itself brings about that result: the failure of wages to rise as fast as prices.   No doubt it is true that often enough, tho not universally or inevitably, money wages do fail to rise as fast as the prices of goods.   So long as the discrepancy lasts, the business class gains thereby.   Profits rise and business booms. And this presumably extends to the exporting industries.   Foreign exchange rises with everything else; the producer of exported goods receives more money for the same quantity of goods; his expenses in the way of wages fail to rise as much; he gets an extra profit, or a "bounty."

I submit that all this, however, shows merely that the exporter gains as much as do others who are in business; not that he gets any profit different from that which accrues elsewhere.   There is nothing to give a special fillip to the export industries.   There may be a bounty for the business class at large, but there is no special bounty for the exporters.   And only such a special bounty would serve to increase the volume of exports.

The situation, I may remark, is different with the other type of dislocated exchanges — silver exchange.   Here a special gain for the exporters presumably appears.   If there occurs, in a country having a silver standard, a rise in exchange on gold countries — in India, say, a rise in sterling exchange — the bounty on exports will arise.   It will arise, that is, from the mere fact that in the world market the gold price of silver has fallen.   In the silver country the prices of goods in general will not be affected; there is nothing in the lower prices which silver fetches in gold countries that will in itself change the price level of the silver country.   But the prices of its exported goods will be affected at once.   They will advance in correspondence (more or less complete) with the advance in foreign exchange.   I will not add to what I have already said, summarily enough, on this topic. What is to be noted here is the peculiarity of the silver exchange case : that the mere rise in silver exchange, if caused by a drop in the gold price of silver, raises in itself export prices and the profits of exporters, while it does not in itself affect other prices. Exports thus are stimulated ; the exporters get the bounty.

The silver-exchange case, however, does point to the way in which, as it seems to me, depreciating paper money and rising paper exchange may act as a bounty on exports. If exchange rises *more* than prices do, the prices of exportable goods will be affected more than other prices, and the export bounty will set in.

Imagine the countries to be Germany and the United States. Paper money is issued in Germany ; prices rise, but dollar exchange rises more than prices. German goods in general can be bought at prices which, tho higher, are not advanced as much as is the exchange rate. As German goods are exported to the United States, and dollar exchange is drawn against the shipments, the dollar bills sell in Germany at a comparatively high rate in marks ; there is a special gain, a bounty. On the first emergence of such a situation the gain is probably shared between the producers and the various middlemen. The German exporting merchants who buy from the German producer will get some of it, and the American importers will get some. If competition is keen between the dealers, the German producer will get the lion's share. In any case he will find business good. And he will be led to enlarge his operations and offer more of goods for export, continuing to pocket an extra profit so long as the gap continues between German prices and dollar exchange.

But events may take precisely the reverse course. Exchange may rise *less* than prices. Then there will be a special profit on importing ; a bounty on imports ; a damper on exports. There is nothing in *a priori* reasoning, and nothing in the history of paper money, to lead to a presumption that exchange will rise faster or slower, more or less, than prices. In the long run, the two will show roughly parallel movements ; so much is in accord with general reasoning and general experience. For considerable periods there may be divergence, and thus an effect either way on imports and exports.

Which of the two possible results will be found when paper issues are first put out, or when paper is in the first stage of added issue, will depend on the way the purchasing power is used. When a government resorts to paper, it does not scatter the money broadcast, as might be inferred from the way in which we often speak of the "issue" of paper money. The money is spent; it is applied to the purchase of goods or services. The effect on prices is first felt on the things for which the government bids. These may happen to be services and domestic goods; and then there will be no proximate effect on other domestic goods and services than those bought by the government, and none on imported or exported goods; hence no immediate change in the currents of international trade. As time goes on, the tendency to rising prices spreads in all directions. Those who sold the goods or services to the government have larger money incomes; they spend more, and the prices of other goods go up. I see no ground for supposing that under conditions of this kind there will be any special advance in the prices of either imported or exported goods; there will be nothing in the nature of a bounty either way. So far as concerns international trade, the case will be neutral.

If, however, the government — or the other persons first getting command of the paper money — uses its additional purchasing power for buying imported goods, or for making remittances to foreigners on other than merchandise account, the bounty on exports will arise. These purchases enter the market for foreign exchange, and the exchange rate rises on countries to which remittances are to be made. It rises more than prices of goods made at home, if indeed these rise in the first instance at all. The exporter who has exchange on foreign countries to sell makes an extra profit. He can sell his exchange (in Germany, say) at a higher price, while his expenses for the moment are no greater. As has just been said, the added margin of profit will doubtless be shared between him and the various middlemen. If exchange rises fast and far, if the margin of profit is great, there will be a likelihood that the German exporter will gain, while yet his goods are sold at lowered prices in the countries to which they go.

Something of this sort happened when the German Government increased its currency issues during a year or thereabouts immediately after the Great War. It had heavy remittances to make on reparations account; and it was the purchaser, directly or indirectly, of needed food supplies and raw materials. Exchange went up, exports were stimulated, exported goods could be delivered abroad at lowered prices, and there came the fright about "exchange dumping."

The continuance of such a situation depends not only on the continuance of the government issues and their use in buying foreign exchange, but on the ease with which increasing supplies of goods for export will be forthcoming. The quicker there are additional exports, the sooner will exchange go down from the unusual height. As in the case of an unchanging paper currency (considered in Chapter 26) this characteristic of the price situation is temporary or transitional. The producers of exported goods do not remain indefinitely at an advantage compared to other domestic producers. Some of the latter will transfer to the export industries; and those already engaged in them will expand. The quicker there are additional supplies of goods for export, and so additional supplies of bills on foreign countries, the sooner will exchange go down from its abnormal height. The ultimate outcome, supposing no further disturbing factors to enter, can be worked out in the same way as for the case of paper which is stable in volume. In the end there will be no special influence on exports and no special effect on the prices of exported goods. The flurry will subside, and (always on the supposition that no further disturbing factors enter) international trade will return to a normal course, with those possibilities of shift and change which have been already considered as possible for a country having a settled volume of paper.

As it happened, in the much discussed German post-war situation, additional supplies of goods for export were not at all forthcoming in large amounts. Such as could be had, were indeed exported during that brief period at great profit; a profit so great that they could be sold abroad at low prices and yet leave a handsome margin to be shared between the German exporters and the various trade speculators. But the volume of this trade was small, because Germany was bare of physical goods. For that very reason, the bounty, so long as the peculiar situation endured, was high on the few goods that were available.

The much-discussed German episode was exceptional in another respect. The paper issues early assumed such extraordinary dimensions that those phenomena emerged which are characteristic of a currency much distrusted and no longer circulating freely. What has been said in the preceding paragraphs tacitly assumes that the output of paper money proceeds in a quasi-orderly fashion, in such way that the currency continues to circulate in normal ways. So long as this is the case, it affects prices in the same way as any increase of the circulating medium, be it specie, convertible notes, mere deposit currency. But very great issues of paper, succeeding each other very rapidly, work in a different way. As is familiar in monetary theory, their effect will be catastrophic; in a sense, quite abnormal. The usual ways of handling money and of handling goods become quite upset; everyone who has the money wishes to get rid of it, to spend it, as quickly as possible; everyone who has goods is chary of parting with them for money. Then ensue the familiar phenomena of complete monetary collapse and complete demoralization of trade and industry. All is chaos; perhaps not quite without rhyme or reason, but very much less reducible to rule than what happens in ordinary experience and is premised in ordinary reasoning. The conclusions just indicated concerning the effects on international trade of continuing issues which are fairly moderate, are little applicable to this extreme situation. Foreign exchange, like everything else, fluctuates in price spasmodically, with little discernible relation to other prices. I doubt whether any trend toward its being higher or lower than the prices of exported goods or of imported goods is likely to appear. What happens is mainly the complete dislocation of all trade, and the deadening of all industry, the decline of transactions with foreign countries as well as within the country, breakdown all around. This is what took place in Germany when the issues of paper money, at first comparatively moderate, reached the farcical dimensions of 1923. The export bounty and the exchange dumping came to a speedy end. Quite different conditions appeared when the paper rubbish was finally swept away, and the newly stabilized mark system was established. *Then* emerged the situation which has been considered elsewhere — that of a stable currency, which it was designed to keep on a par with specie, but which had the essential characteristics of a gold exchange system.

We return to the main proposition; namely, that depreciating paper does not in itself lead to rates of foreign exchange that will stimulate either exports or imports. As with almost every general proposition on these matters, there are cases which may be regarded as exceptions to the rule. One such played a large part in the paper exchanges of the post-war period. Depreciating paper may bring about the "flight of capital." Investors may become uneasy from continued depreciation, may fear complete collapse, and may wish to place their possessions in secure form. They will then buy gold exchange, sending the funds to foreign banks; or may buy foreign securities. Germans and Frenchmen during the ominous stages bought dollar exchange, Swiss exchange, sterling exchange, or else securities of these countries. The rates, in terms of francs or marks for dollars, Swiss francs, pounds sterling, not only rose, but rose more than domestic prices. And this disproportionate rise operated to stimulate exports. A bounty arose in just the same way as it does when governments use paper money at the outset for meeting their own foreign engagements. I suspect that it was operation of the latter, direct purchase of foreign exchange by government, which played the largest part in the bounty experienced (so long as conditions had any calculability) in Germany, in 1922–23, whereas it was the flight of capital that played the more important part during the depreciation of the French franc.

Such a flight of capital is a natural or at least presumable consequence of depreciating currency; and its further concomitant, the special rise in exchange and the bounty on exports, may thus be said to be in a sense a natural result of progressive depreciation. It is of course not an inevitable result. True, it may easily ensue in a country having large accumulations of capital, large holdings of securities, a highly developed mechanism of international banking and of international security movements. But even in such a country, it will not necessarily appear. All depends on the extent to which confidence is shaken and the property owners become uneasy; which in turn depends not merely on the progress of depreciation, but on the course of domestic and foreign affairs in general.

CHAPTER 30

SOME EXPERIENCES UNDER PAPER MONEY

I AM unable to attempt anything in the way of extended test or substantiation of the lines of reasoning followed in the preceding chapters. Voluminous as is the literature on paper money and on international trade under paper money, little investigation has been made that would bear directly on this sort of analysis. The absence of inductive studies that might serve to confirm it or refute it is due partly to the changing and unstable character of the events themselves — paper currency issues commonly are subject to arbitrary and irregular fluctuations — but also to the lack of adequate statistical data. In the main I must ask the reader to take the theorems here laid down as theorems only, as abstract doctrines or preliminary approximations, subject to correction, possibly rejection, as further and more searching inquiry is made on the actual course of events.

Two episodes, however, may be considered for the light which they throw on the validity of this theoretic procedure. Both are paper money episodes; one in the United States, the other in Argentina. Both are comparatively recent, having taken place in the latter part of the 19th century. Both have been the subject of painstaking inquiry.[1]

The experience of the United States from the close of the Civil War in 1865 to the resumption of specie payments in 1879 is instruc-

[1] The evidence set forth in the following pages is derived entirely from Professor F. D. Graham's paper on International Trade under Depreciated Paper; The United States 1862–1879, published in The Quarterly Journal of Economics, February, 1922; and from Professor J. H. Williams's book on Argentine International Trade under Inconvertible Paper Money 1880–1900, published in the Harvard Economic Studies, 1920. Everything that I am able to adduce on the two episodes is taken from these admirable studies. My own interpretation of the results is not always quite the same as that of the authors; but I am indebted to them for everything that may be of value, and am glad to acknowledge my obligation.

tive in several ways. The country's currency was paper, and the volume of the paper remained virtually unchanged. The case was one of a stable paper currency, not of increasing issues. At the same time there were two stages in the period, marked by different conditions of international trade. Until 1873 there were heavy borrowings from abroad; after the crisis of that year the borrowings abruptly ceased and large repayments were made. As has already been noted, imports swelled rapidly during the first stage, and far exceeded the exports; while during the second the situation was reversed, exports exceeding the imports. As has also been noted, this change toward a " favorable " balance was quite in accord with theoretical expectation. Yet evidently it did not take place thru that mechanism of shifting prices in the borrowing country which is assumed in the received theory. Since the United States was on a paper money basis, the mechanism must have been different.[1] The case is thus adapted for a test of the theoretical analysis of the mechanism of payments under paper conditions. It is promising in still another way. In a situation otherwise changed but little, a single factor — that of the import of capital — varies sharply, first in one direction, then in another; and its influence might be expected to be separately discernible. As in the Canadian case,[2] we have something analogous to an experiment; one factor changes, while other things remain almost the same.

We may begin with the year 1866. By that time the influence of the war disturbances was no longer dominant, and something like normal conditions had been restored. In 1866–68 there was already substantial borrowing from abroad, chiefly of course from Great Britain; and with it a large excess of imports over exports (in terms of gold values). In 1869 the great spurt set in. The annual import of capital, which had been about 75 millions of dollars, ran to much larger sums — an average of about 130 millions for the quinquennium 1869–73. The borrowings were mainly for railway building, which was carried on with feverish activity. The whole period, it need hardly be said, was one of

---

[1] See Chapter 26, p. 343.　　　　　　[2] See Chapter 19, p. 222.

speculative ventures the world over, interrupted for a short space by the Franco-German war and then stimulated by the very operations connected with the indemnity of 1871. It was the up-stage of a world-wide business cycle. When the crisis came in 1873, loans to American enterprises ceased almost at once, and only such contracts and commitments were maintained as could not be undone. In a year or two, by 1876, there was even an opposite movement; a considerable repayment of loans was called for and was effected. So things ran until in 1879 a new cycle started; then under different monetary conditions, and with results not significant for the purpose in hand. The episode with which we are here concerned ended with the year 1878.

I have spoken of the currency situation as stable. It would be more accurate to speak of it as stationary. The total volume of paper money remained virtually the same. But population and the volume of transactions continued to advance. Setting aside the fluctuations, by no means negligible, in credit conditions and in velocity of circulation, there was a steady undercurrent of pressure on the money supply and so a tendency toward a decline of prices. The process was that often described at the time as "growing up to the currency," a very irregular growth, but one that on the whole did take place, and that needs to be allowed for in interpreting the long-run trend of the price movements.

Observe now on the chart (page 396) [1] what took place in the rates of foreign exchange and in the prices of goods. First, as to foreign exchange. The rates of exchange (sterling), and the quoted price of gold in terms of paper, necessarily moved together, and the price of gold may be used to indicate the course of exchange. That price, the gold premium, had remained fairly stationary, tho with some declining tendency, from 1866 to 1869, ranging from 140 to 135. In 1870, however, it fell sharply, and in the remaining years of boom, from 1870 to 1873, remained at about the figure 110. After the crisis the price of gold remained for a while still stationary, and indeed showed an upward trend in 1875. In the course of 1877 and 1878, it fell steadily, until at last, with the resumption of

[1] Based on Professor Graham's figures, pp. 237, 253 of the article cited above.

PRICES AND THE GOLD PREMIUM, UNITED STATES, 1867–1879.

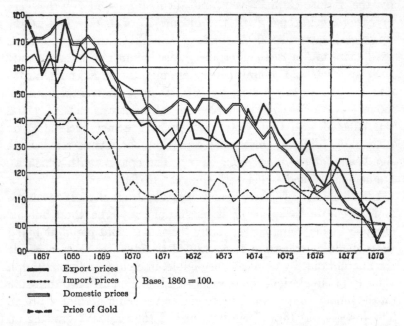

	Export prices	⎫
••••••	Import prices	⎬ Base, 1860 = 100.
	Domestic prices	⎭
▸◂◂	Price of Gold	

specie payments on January 1, 1879, the premium disappeared entirely and the new era of the gold standard set in.

Turn now to the prices of goods; and here, as the reader need hardly be reminded, it is not merely the general movement of prices that is to be considered, but even more the trend in the prices of the different classes of goods — exported, imported, domestic. As regards the general movements (indicated by an index number made up for goods of all three kinds), a relation to the specie premium is clear. Taking the entire period 1866–78, both prices and premium go downward; the country is growing up to the currency. But the rate of movement is significantly uneven. During the first stage, the price of gold in paper — that is, the gold premium — tends to be lower than the prices of goods; during the second, the price of gold is higher. After 1874, that is, almost immediately after the crash which took place in the autumn of 1873, there was a relative fall in the price of gold and of foreign exchange. A contrast of the same kind appears in the price movements, that is, the relative movements, of the domestic and the international commodities. The prices of export goods were low (setting aside irregularities caused by crop conditions) during the period of heavy borrowing and general expansion, from 1869 until 1873; while they were relatively high after 1873. The prices of import goods showed a similar drift, tho with a lag; they were low during the stage of expansion, especially during its later years, and they were high during the stage of depression, again most markedly so during the later years. Domestic prices showed movements inverse to those of the international goods. They were relatively high before 1873; after the overturn of that year they fell more sharply than did either import or export prices.

A tendency similar to that for domestic prices of goods appears with regard to money wages, the most important of all the domestic prices. In those industries which felt no influence of foreign markets or of foreign competition — those, namely, producing without foreign competition, and solely for the home market — wages showed a distinct upward movement from 1866 to 1873; and they showed a sharp decline after 1873. In export industries, on the other hand, and in industries subject to competition from imported goods, the movement of wages was virtually *nil* up to the time of the overturn; they showed no such advance as appeared in domestic industries. In the ensuing stage of depression, on the other hand, their movement, while downward, was much less so than in the domestic field. Relatively, they fell during the first stage, and rose during the second.

These phenomena, and more particularly the differences in the price movements of the several classes of commodities, are in accord with the theoretical analysis made in Chapter 26. The decline in the price of sterling exchange and of the gold premium during the years of expansion was the result to be expected from the heavy borrowings of that period. Abundant command of London funds was put at the disposal of American borrowers by British lenders. Under the impact of these offerings of sterling

exchange, its price tended to go down.   During these same years
the prices of domestic goods in the United States held their own
and money wages tended to advance.   After the crisis came the
contrary movements.   Foreign exchange and the gold premium
held their own, and in 1875 even showed a tendency to rise;
whereas domestic prices and money wages in the domestic industries sank at once and almost continuously.   In the very last stage,
in 1877 and 1878, just before the return to specie payments, the
gold premium gradually disappeared, and its movement was not
so noticeably at variance with the fall in domestic prices and wages.
At that closing stage all things were adjusting themselves to the
approaching gold basis; and the phenomena raise theoretical
questions of a different kind.

The substantive course of international trade — the actual flow
of goods and the recorded values of the goods — reflected the influence of these movements in foreign exchange and in the prices of
domestic and international goods.   During the first stage there was
a repression on exports; a burden, so to speak, or at all events the
reverse of a bounty.   The prices of exported goods were relatively
low, kept down as they were by the relatively low rates at which
foreign exchange could be sold.   After 1873, exported goods were
relatively high in price.   At a time when domestic prices in general
were falling fast, they were kept up by the sustained good rates
(until 1878) of foreign exchanges.   As regards import prices, what
is most significant is the lag in their movement as compared with
the export prices.   In the end they show, as is to be expected,
changes in correspondence with international prices in general.
But there is a preliminary period in each of the two stages in which
relatively a less movement appears in the import prices; and this
is the equivalent of a bounty during the initial years of the earlier
stage, of a burden or repression during the initial years of the
later stage.

We then have, as regards this bit of economic experience, an
explanation of the way in which, under paper exchanges, the excess
of imports was brought about in the first stage, that of exports in
the second.   The exchanges affected prices; and the price con-

ditions — always the proximate cause of movements in international trade — checked exports during the first stage, imports during the second. The mechanism was different from that of gold exchange prices based on the gold standard, but the substantive outcome was the same.

Not everything, however, is to be explained in this way. We must be on our guard here, as in all statistical and historical inquiry, against over-simplification in interpreting phenomena that are confused and complicated, often remaining obscure after the most painstaking examination. In the present case, for example, a further factor goes to explain the heavy imports into the United States during the years 1869–73. This was the direct purchase of British goods by the American borrowers. The way in which the balance of trade is affected by the direct linking of loans with expenditures in the lending country has been analyzed elsewhere.[1] These effects are the same under paper conditions as under gold conditions. So far as the proceeds of the loans were applied in part to the immediate purchase of goods in Great Britain, and so far as these purchases were additional to what would have been bought by Americans in any case, there was at once a movement of exports from Great Britain to the United States and an increase of imports into the United States. Operations of this kind could have no effect on the foreign exchange market or the gold premium in the United States, or the prices of goods in the United States. Such transactions call for no such recondite explanation as has been undertaken in the preceding paragraphs.

None the less, there remain transactions to which the simpler explanation cannot apply. By no means all the proceeds of British loans were used in direct purchases. A large part — the larger part, one would guess, for these particular operations — was cashed in by the borrowers, so to speak. Funds were wanted by them for use in the United States, and remittances to the United States were called for. And then we do need to resort to the more recondite explanation, and to search for evidence which will corroborate it.

[1] Chapter 12, p. 127

So far as concerns Great Britain, there is of course much less occasion to turn to an explanation based on the theory of dislocated exchanges. The gold standard having been maintained in Great Britain, and most of the country's trade conducted with other countries also having the gold standard, the mechanism of specie flow and specie prices was in operation for the larger part of her international trade. It is comparatively simple in theory, even tho, as we have seen, by no means without its complications in actual operation. At all events it is different from that of paper exchanges. Professor Graham has noted, to be sure, certain tendencies in the prices of British goods during the period in question which are quite in accord with the tendencies in the United States. They are in accord, that is, in that they show inverse movements of the kind to be expected under dislocated exchanges. The relations in Great Britain between her domestic prices and the foreign or international prices indicate a congruence (*mutatis mutandis*) with the analogous relations in the United States. But the evidence on this score is meager, and in interpreting it one can easily be led to discovering that which one has set out to find. It is the American phenomena which may be fairly said to verify the conclusion of theory.

Finally, it should be borne in mind that the episode covers a comparatively short period, and that only the earlier and transitional effects of changes in the balance of payments (in this case from the borrowing operations) are illustrated. There was no long-continued steady succession of loans; merely two marked stages of opposite character — unusually heavy borrowing during the first, abrupt cessation of the borrowing during the second. When loans set in afresh after 1879, the paper régime had come to an end. The features characteristic of dislocated exchanges are hence observable only for a scant decade. We are able to discern them for a period of transition only. Nothing can be made out as regards the eventual outcome. We do find that the transitional effects are such as the theoretical analysis has led us to expect; the price of foreign exchange is low, for example, during the stage of heavy borrowing, and the prices of export commodities are correspondingly low.   But there is nothing to show in what manner and to what extent the prices of exported goods and the rates of exchange would have eventually adjusted themselves if borrowing had gone on in the same way for many years.   The experiment did not last at all long enough to verify the conclusions concerning ultimate effects.   We are reduced, as so often, to fragmentary substantiation, to the necessity of piecing together scanty and scattered bits of evidence, to general presumption and inference.

Similar in some respects, different in others, was the experience of Argentina under a paper money régime.   It was similar in that there was international borrowing on a great scale, followed by sudden cessation of the borrowings.   It was different in that the Argentine paper money, far from being stable, fluctuated greatly in volume.

The period which is of interest for the present purpose runs from 1880 to 1900.   The Argentine borrowing took place during the first decade, and especially during the years just before 1890.   The abrupt cessation of borrowing came in 1890, and in the second decade there was no borrowing at all; on the contrary, nothing but payment of interest on old loans.   As in the case of the United States, the loans were made by British bankers and investors, chiefly for railway construction.   The Baring crisis of November, 1890 (the Barings had been the banking house mainly concerned), brought the operations to a sudden halt; that crisis has the same position in the Argentine episode as has the crisis of 1873 in that of the United States.   In both countries there was a culmination of speculation, with sharp revulsion to a period first of depression and standstill, then of gradual recovery.[1]

Further, the relation between the imports and exports of Argentina in 1880–1900 shows a close parallel to that which appeared in the United States in 1869–79.   Imports greatly exceeded exports until 1890; thereafter exports exceeded imports.   The overturn was as sudden and as complete in the one case as in the other.

---

[1] The suspension of the Barings came in November, 1890; in the Argentine the crisis was at its worst in the spring of 1891.

And the relation between imports and exports obviously was quite in accord with theoretical expectation, and with the experience of other countries under similar circumstances. The loans to Argentina were effected by an inflow of goods, not by an inflow of money; and similarly, when the reversal came in 1890 — when loans were no longer forthcoming and interest payments had to be made on the loans of the past — the payments thus due to other countries (Great Britain almost solely) were effected by enlarged exports of goods. The substantive course of trade, in Argentina no less than in the United States, was such as one must expect.

Argentina, to repeat, was on a paper basis, just as the United States had been. There were, it is true, differences between the paper régimes of the two countries; but none that were of consequence for the present purpose. Argentine money was issued by banks, under a system imitating the United States National Banking system of the same time. The Argentine law and its execution were so lax as to make convertibility into gold a mere pretense. Specie hence could not enter or leave Argentina in such way as to affect directly its monetary system or its monetary conditions. Gold, to be sure, was on hand in the country and did move in and out, sometimes in substantial quantities. But the movements did not impinge on the country's currency supply. It is not necessary to consider some aspects of the technique of foreign exchange dealings, which again present differences from those of the United States. Exchange was bought and sold in terms of gold pesos; hence the quoted rates of exchange showed stability. But the actual payments for exchange (sterling) were made in Argentine paper pesos. It was thus gold, not sterling exchange, which was directly the object of trading in terms of paper. The only thing that was quoted was a premium on gold in terms of paper. But the gold premium was in effect the rate of exchange; it was this to which an importer or exporter turned his attention when buying goods or arranging for remittances.

The important respect in which the Argentine case differs from the American is, as has already been said, that the Argentine paper currency was not stable in volume. The amount in circulation expanded greatly, especially during the closing years of the upswing stage. Between 1885 and 1891 the volume of paper outstanding more than tripled. The following figures summarize the story.

	PAPER IN CIRCULATION (MILLIONS OF PESOS)	PRICE OF GOLD IN PAPER PESOS (YEARLY AVERAGE)
1885	74.8	137
1886	89.2	139
1887	94.1	135
1888	129.5	148
1889	163.7	191
1890	245.1	251
1891	261.4	387
1892	281.6	332
1893	306.7	324
1894	298.7	357
1895	296.7	344
1896	295.1	296
1897	292.	291
1898	292.	258
1899	291.	225

The price of gold, it will be seen, rose in rough correspondence with the increase in the quantity of paper. The correspondence, however, is no more than rough. During the earlier years, from 1885 to 1889, the gold price rose less than did the volume of paper. In 1891, immediately after the crash, it showed a sharp advance; and it remained high until the middle of the decade, while the volume of paper remained nearly stationary. With the closing years of the century, a new era was ushered in. Proposals for return to a gold basis gradually crystallized, and in 1900 this salutary change was effected, the paper being stabilized on the basis of the market price of gold at the time — 227 of paper to 100 of gold. We have, then, a period of rapid inflation, a severe crisis, an ensuing stage of approximately stationary money and slowly declining gold premium, and finally of stabilization at the close.

The years which are of especial significance for the present purpose are those just before and just after the crisis. They show in what way the impact of demand and supply operated on the course of exchange and on the exports and imports of goods.

It will be convenient to turn first to the exports. Before 1890 there was a relatively low premium on gold, that is, a relatively low rate of sterling exchange. The low rate was the natural concomitant of the heavy loans then made to the Argentine. The borrowings in London being large, large sums of exchange on London were in the market, and the exchange rate and the gold premium tended to be low in Buenos Ayres. And this in turn tended to check exports. The Argentine exporter, selling for gold in London, got for his bills on London a price which was low in relation to the increasing volume of the paper, and low (presumably) in comparison with domestic prices. After the crisis the situation was reversed. Loans ceased, and the exchange market was no longer burdened by the sterling bills which Argentine borrowers had hitherto been offering. The effective rates of exchange, the gold premium, went up. The exporter now got in Argentine paper a much larger return for his goods; and exports advanced, both in quantity and in money value. In other words, the substantive course of trade — the deficiency of exports during the first stage, and the excess of exports during the second — was directly affected by the foreign exchange market. It was the varying price of exchange which brought about the relation between exports and imports. Our *deus ex machina* was in action.

Unfortunately the statistical evidence does not enable us to go much further than to reach this comparatively simple conclusion. To go beyond, one would need to know what was the course of domestic prices, and whether these advanced more than did export prices. In the last paragraph it was intimated parenthetically that one might presume they did. The gold premium failed to advance in proportion to the increasing volume of the paper, whereas prices in general, and domestic prices in particular, might be expected to do so. But this is no more than an expectation or presumption. The movement of prices under paper money inflation is always irregular, and its accordance with the rising quantity of paper is never exact or in form. There can be no certainty that full evidence, if attained, would substantiate the presumption that domestic prices rose more than did export prices. Here again we must supplement the fragmentary evidence by hypothesis and interpretation; we can do no more than resort to the very theories which we wish to test.

There is, indeed, one piece of evidence which may carry us a bit further. It appears that the prices of exported goods did not advance as fast or as much as the gold premium itself. On general principles, they might be expected to rise precisely in proportion to the premium, parallel to it. The fact that they rose less would accentuate the repression of exports resulting from the failure of both to rise in accord with domestic prices. But other causes than those connected with the loans might lead to the lag of export prices. The gold prices of the Argentine exports (among which wool, wheat, and maize were the most important) were determined by world conditions, and were subject to the crop fluctuations which obscure the general trend of agricultural prices. Their special conditions might easily be such as to depress the prices of the agricultural products having a world market, and to account for the exceptional movement of export prices in Argentina. Their failure to advance as much as did the gold premium is hardly to be related with any certainty to the Argentine borrowings and their influence on the course of sterling exchange.[1]

[1] In this regard, as in some others, I find myself unable to interpret all the phenomena of the Argentine episode in quite the same way as Professor Williams. He is inclined to the view that an issue of inconvertible paper operates in itself to stimulate exports and that therefore the failure of exports to swell during the years 1886–90 needs an explanation. As stated above (pp. 385–389) paper inflation does not in my judgment necessarily stimulate either exports or imports. The course of events in the Argentine before 1890 seems to illustrate the fact that there are some conditions under which the effect is to give a bounty on imports, not on exports, while after 1890 the illustration runs the other way — that there are other conditions under which a bounty on exports arises.

Something of the same sort is to be said of the relation between prices and money wages. Money wages in Argentina failed to advance in proportion to prices ; and business profits rose. They rose, it would seem, in all industries ; inflation served, as has been so commonly the case, to fatten profits all around, and to cut down commodity wages. This, however, was seemingly the outcome in industry at large, not in the export industries alone. While the lag in money wages appeared in the export industries, as it did elsewhere, the rise of profits, if I interpret the phenomena rightly, was here *less* than elsewhere. Unfortunately we lack the statistical evidence which would be conclusive on this point, as we do on the extent to which a rise in domestic prices took place.

It must be remembered, too, that the Argentine at this time was still in the early stages of pioneer development and that not only are the records inadequate, but the

The stage of reversal which followed the crisis of 1890–91 shows the operation of the same forces. The immediate consequences are easily seen. The price of exchange soared high in 1891, and remained high for several years thereafter. The large supply of bills on London which before had been available from the loans suddenly ceased. Those who needed to remit to London and were bidders for sterling bills had to pay a higher price in Argentine pesos. And this in turn made the prices of exported goods higher and stimulated exports; conversely, of course, checking imports. Such remained the situation for a year or two. Then ensued conditions more like those of paper not changing in quantity. The case becomes comparable to that in the United States during the years just preceding the resumption of specie payments. While the quantity of the Argentine paper remained stationary, the gold premium declined; Argentina, like the United States, had the fortunate experience of "growing up to the currency." There was financial and industrial recuperation, and finally the return to the gold basis. Those effects of paper money on international trade which are here under review were thus confined to a comparatively short span of time, the few years just before the crisis and just after it.

As regards imports, a qualification must be made similar to that just suggested in the case of the United States. The qualification is quantitatively even more important. The imports into Argentina (exports from Great Britain) were in greater part the direct result of the British loans. The funds borrowed were largely spent at once on British goods, especially on railway equipment; and these purchases would not have been made but for the loans, being specifically induced, or at least made possible, by them. The movement of exports under such circumstances takes place, as has already been abundantly explained, in quasi-automatic

very movements themselves were spasmodic and confused. Very possibly a more apt comparison with North American experiences could be made by citing an earlier episode in the history of the United States than that considered in the first part of this chapter; namely, that of the years from 1833 to 1837–39. Borrowings, inflation, marked changes in imports and exports, then took place in a manner and under conditions which have a curious similarity to those in Argentina a half-century later.

fashion and without perturbation of the foreign exchanges. Argentina procured from Great Britain in this period, and indeed in later periods also, a great part of her railway material by this simple process.

Not all, however, is accounted for in this way. Part of the proceeds of the loans were wanted by the Argentines for expenditures in their own country. In so far, there was remittance of funds from London to Buenos Aires, an effect on the foreign exchange market, a train of consequences analogous to that which appeared in the Argentine exports. Such goods as textiles, foods, drinks, tobacco, were more freely imported into the country because it was profitable to import them; because prices in the Argentine, translated into gold on the basis of the gold premium, made it profitable to bring them in. The fact that the gold premium was relatively low during the years 1886–89 made it easy to pay for such imports, and they streamed in. When the crash of 1890–91 came, and the gold premium soared, the converse effect was experienced. The gold premium remained high; domestic prices fell. Imports were harder to pay for, and the volume of imports declined.

It need not be said that the phenomena of these few years in Argentina are again only of the transitional kind. As in the United States during the corresponding period, conditions soon changed and trade was no longer carried on under inconvertible paper. This rapid change in the monetary situation makes it impossible to trace the long-run effects which one might expect under paper conditions. Among the long-run effects, the readjustment of the prices of export goods in such manner that they shall conform to the range of prices prevailing for the purely domestic goods is the most significant. It is also that which requires, as regards agricultural products, most time; and this not merely because of the obscuring influence of crop irregularities, but because the mobility of labor and capital is peculiarly uncertain in agriculture. In a country such as the Argentine then was, and indeed still largely remains — with great latifundia and great landed proprietors, the cultivators of the soil a submerged class, agricultural production mainly for export, cyclical disturbances extreme — there would be unusual difficulties in the verification of the broader theoretic deductions. We are unable to press the inductive inquiry beyond the first stage, that of phenomena essentially transitional. We must be content, as so commonly happens in such inquiries, with partial verification, with bits and scraps that seem to run true, but by no means tell the whole story.

APPENDIX

TABLES ON PRICES AND THE TERMS OF TRADE

GREAT BRITAIN
CANADA
UNITED STATES

I

GREAT BRITAIN'S TERMS OF TRADE, 1880–1913

The figures for Great Britain, as well as the chart in the text (Chapter 21, p. 246), are reproduced from the Economic Journal for March, 1925, where the reader will find also some further discussion of the results. For the table (pp. 412–13) and the notes explaining it, and for the chart, I am indebted to Mr. A. G. Silverman. The amount and quality of the work done by him, represented by these bare tabular results, can be appreciated only by persons who have themselves undertaken statistical research of the kind.

NOTES ON THE TABLE

Data in Roman are transcribed; data in Italics are computed.

Sources: for 1900 and subsequent years the data in Roman are published annually in British and Foreign Trade and Industry (e.g. Parliamentary Papers for 1912, Vol. 35, Cd. 6314, p. 9).

For the earlier years, 1880 to 1899, the data were obtained as follows:

Column A, British and Foreign Trade and Industry, 1854–1908, Cd. 4954, p. 19.

Column E, ibid., p. 19. Prior to 1899 the value of the exports of ships and boats (new) with their machinery was not recorded. The value of such exports is included in 1899 and subsequent years.

Column G, ibid., p. 53. These figures were computed by the Board of Trade from data published annually in the London Economist.

Column B, for the years 1880 to 1899 the figures were derived by dividing the declared value of total imports (not net imports) by the estimated value of these total imports at 1900 prices as computed from data published annually in the Economist (see British and Foreign Trade and Industry, 1854–1908, Cd. 4954, p. 53). Total imports were used because the estimated values of net imports at 1900 prices were not directly available. In applying the import price index thus obtained to the declared value of net imports (Column A) to obtain the estimated values of these net imports at 1900 prices (Column C), it is assumed that the import price index as calculated from data of total imports would not differ significantly from an import price index computed from net imports.

For 1900 and subsequent years,

Column B, figures are computed by formula $\dfrac{A}{C}$ or $\dfrac{\Sigma P_i Q_i}{\Sigma P_o Q_i}$ (Paasche's formula), which is the price index.

Column C, figures are derived by use of formula $\dfrac{A}{B}, \dfrac{\Sigma P_i Q_i}{\Sigma P_i Q_i} = \Sigma P_o Q_i$, which gives the estimated values at P_o prices.

Columns D and H are calculated as indicated. For the years 1880 to 1898, the figures in Column H, however, are computed with reference to the exports of 1900, without ships and boats (new) and their machinery. Since for 1900 the exports of ships, etc., were £9.2 millions, the exports excluding these items were for this year only £282 millions, not 291.

Column F, $\dfrac{E}{G}$ (1880–1913).

Column I gives the index of changes in the net barter terms of trade; Column J gives that of changes in the gross barter terms.

UNITED KINGDOM

VOLUME AND PRICES OF IMPORTS AND EXPORTS, GROSS AND NET BARTER TERMS OF TRADE

YEAR	Net Imports (Imports less Re-Exports)				Exports (Produce and Mfs. of United Kingdom)				$\frac{B}{F}$	$\frac{H}{D}$
	DECLARED VALUE (MILLION £)	IMPORT PRICE INDEX (1900 = 100)	Est. Values at 1900 Prices		DECLARED VALUE (MILLION £)	EXPORT PRICE INDEX (1900 = 100)	Est. Values at 1900 Prices		(1900 = 100)	(1900 = 100)
			ABS. VALUE (MILLION £)	RELATIVES (1900 = 100)			ABS. VALUE (MILLION £)	RELATIVES (1900 = 100)		
	A	B	C	D	E	F	G	H	I	J
1880	348	135	263	66.1	223	109	204	72.3	124	129
1881	334	134	249	64.1	234	104	225	79.8	129	148
1882	348	132	264	57.4	242	104	233	82.6	127	144
1883	362	124	292	63.5	240	100	239	84.8	124	134
1884	327	120	272	69.1	233	96	242	85.8	125	145
1885	313	113	277	60.2	213	92	232	82.3	123	137
1886	294	106	277	60.2	213	87	245	86.9	122	144
1887	303	105	289	62.8	222	86	257	91.1	122	145
1888	324	107	303	65.9	234	87	269	95.4	123	145
1889	360	108	333	72.4	249	89	279	98.9	121	137
1890	356	107	335	72.4	263	95	278	98.6	123	136
1891	373	107	349	75.9	247	94	263	93.3	114	123
1892	360	103	350	76.1	227	89	254	90.1	116	118
1893	346	101	343	74.6	218	88	248	87.9	115	118
1894	350	94	372	80.9	216	84	257	91.1	112	115

Year										
1895	357	*90*	*397*	86.3	226	*81*	278	98.6	*111*	*114*
1896	386	*92*	*420*	91.3	240	*82*	292	105.5	*112*	*115*
1897	391	*91*	*430*	93.5	234	*81*	288	102.1	*113*	*109*
1898	410	*92*	*446*	97.0	233	*81*	288	102.1	*114*	*105*
1899	420	*93*	*452*	98.3	264	*87*	302	103.8	*107*	*106*
1900	460	*100*	460	100.0	291	*100*	291	100.0	*100*	*100*
1901	454	*97*	470	102.1	280	*95*	294	101.0	*102*	*99*
1902	463	*96*	484	105.3	283	*91*	312	107.2	*105*	*102*
1903	473	*97*	488	106.2	291	*91*	321	110.1	*107*	*104*
1904	481	*97*	494	107.4	301	*92*	327	112.5	*105*	*105*
1905	487	*98*	498	108.4	330	*92*	360	123.6	*107*	*114*
1906	523	*102*	513	111.6	376	*97*	387	132.9	*105*	*119*
1907	554	*107*	520	113.1	426	*102*	418	143.6	*105*	*127*
1908	513	*102*	501	108.9	377	*98*	385	132.2	*104*	*121*
1909	533	*103*	515	111.9	378	*94*	401	137.8	*110*	*123*
1910	575	*110*	525	114.1	430	*98*	438	150.3	*112*	*132*
1911	577	*107*	541	117.6	454	*100*	454	155.7	*107*	*132*
1912	633	*109*	582	126.6	487	*102*	478	164.3	*107*	*130*
1913	659	*109*	604	131.2	525	*106*	497	170.8	*103*	*130*

II

CANADA'S TERMS OF TRADE, 1900–1913

The figures for Canada, (Chapter 21, p. 257 above), like those for Great Britain, have been compiled for me by Mr. A. G. Silverman. In this case, however, the task was comparatively easy, because the essential data are to be found, as is indicated below, in Professor Viner's book on Canada's Balance of International Indebtedness, and in Mr. R. H. Coats' invaluable report on Cost of Living.

It will be observed that this table (p. 416) is somewhat more full than that for Great Britain, in that it contains figures indicating the course of wages and of wholesale prices.

NOTES ON THE TABLE

[1] From a statement prepared for this book by W. A. Warne, Chief, External Trade Branch, Dominion Bureau of Statistics. Imports and Exports of Settlers' Effects, given in that statement, have been deducted from Net Imports and Net Exports, respectively.

[2] Constructed by Professor J. Viner from price quotations in Canadian Department of Labour, Reports on Wholesale Prices and in R. H. Coats' Cost of Living Report, Vol. II, pp. 250 *et seq*. See Viner, Canada's Balance of International Indebtedness, 1900–1913, Cambridge, 1924, p. 230.

[3] R. H. Coats, Cost of Living Report, Vol. II, pp. 427 and 431. These are indices not of actual earnings, but of weekly rates of wages.

[4] Export of Settlers' Effects were not available prior to July, 1900. Consequently only the exports of Settlers' Effects for the second half of the calendar year 1900 were deducted from the Exports of Canadian Produce for this year. This may introduce a very slight error in 1900 export figures.

CANADA

VOLUME AND PRICES OF IMPORTS AND EXPORTS, GROSS AND NET BARTER TERMS OF TRADE AND INDICES OF WAGE RATES AND DOMESTIC PRICES (1900 = 100)

	Net Imports (Total Imports — Exports of Produce)				Net Exports (Exports of Canadian Produce)				NET BARTER TERMS (B ÷ F)	GROSS BARTER TERMS (H ÷ D)	Indices of Weekly Wage Rates [3]		INDEX OF DOMESTIC WHOLE-SALE PRICES [3]
			Est. Values at 1900 Prices				Est. Values at 1900 Prices				UN-WEIGHTED	WEIGHTED	
	DE-CLARED VALUE [1]	IMPORT PRICE INDEX [2]	ABS. VALUE (A ÷ B)	RELA-TIVES (C ÷ 159.5)	DE-CLARED VALUE [1]	EXPORT PRICE INDEX [2]	ABS. VALUE (E ÷ F)	RELA-TIVES (G ÷ 167.1)					
	Million $	1900 = 100	Million $	1900 = 100	Million $	1900 = 100	Million $	1900 = 100	1900 = 100	1900 = 100	1900 = 100	1900 = 100	1900 = 100
	A	B	C	D	E	F	G	H	I	J	K	L	M
1900	159.5	100.0	159.5	100.0	167.1	100.0	167.1	100.0	100.0	100.0	100.0	100.0	100.0
1901	172.7	94.8	182.2	114.2	181.4	101.7	178.4	106.8	93.2	93.5	102.0	101.6	111.5
1902	197.2	92.5	213.2	133.7	206.4	102.8	200.8	120.2	90.0	89.9	104.3	103.8	118.5
1903	232.2	97.7	238.7	149.0	210.7	103.3	204.0	122.1	94.6	81.9	106.1	106.5	119.1
1904	232.3	94.0	247.1	154.9	187.4	104.0	180.2	107.8	90.4	69.6	108.8	109.3	119.1
1905	248.2	98.3	252.5	158.3	209.3	107.9	194.0	116.1	91.1	73.3	111.6	113.1	120.9
1906	291.5	107.3	271.7	170.3	237.0	115.3	205.6	123.0	93.1	72.2	114.5	116.5	122.8
1907	351.5	114.2	307.8	193.0	236.2	124.4	189.9	113.6	91.8	58.9	119.2	122.6	135.6
1908	269.7	99.5	271.1	170.0	245.9	119.9	205.1	122.7	83.0	72.2	121.1	124.8	133.6
1909	332.7	102.2	325.5	204.1	266.9	123.6	215.9	129.2	82.7	63.3	125.4	129.0	141.0
1910	414.9	105.0	395.1	247.7	277.9	125.7	221.1	132.3	83.5	53.4	129.7	134.0	145.7
1911	481.2	103.8	463.6	290.7	277.6	129.0	215.2	128.8	80.5	44.3	133.1	137.9	151.4
1912	615.3	113.1	544.0	341.1	339.8	138.8	244.8	146.5	81.5	42.9	139.3	145.0	161.8
1913	639.4	114.1	560.4	351.3	433.5	133.9	323.7	193.7	85.2	55.1	142.9	148.9	161.7

III

United States Terms of Trade, 1879–1913

The figures for the United States (see Chapter 24, p. 299) are derived from the paper published by Mr. T. J. Kreps in the Quarterly Journal of Economics for August, 1926 (Volume 40, p. 708). The inquiry in this case was more laborious than in the others whose results I have used, since it involved not merely the scrutiny and arrangement of statistical material already in existence, but the collection of the price figures themselves, and this from a variety of sources. For an account of the difficulties encountered in the apparently simple task, the devices that were used, the qualifications to be observed in interpreting the results, the reader is referred to Mr. Kreps's admirable paper.

The figures are here given not in the precise form of that in the original publication, but in an arrangement which permits of ready comparison with the figures for Great Britain and Canada. The rearrangement has been made for me by Mr. Kreps.

UNITED STATES

VOLUME AND PRICES OF IMPORTS AND EXPORTS, GROSS AND NET BARTER TERMS OF TRADE

YEAR (FISCAL)	Imports of Merchandise				Exports of Domestic Merchandise						
	DECLARED VALUE (MILLION $)	IMPORT PRICE INDEX (1903-13 = 100)	ESTIMATED VALUES AT 1903-13 PRICES		DECLARED VALUE (MILLION $)	EXPORT PRICE INDEX (1903-13 = 100)	ESTIMATED VALUES AT 1903-13 PRICES		B/F (1903-13 = 100)	H/D (1903-13 = 100)
			ABS. VALUE (MILLION $)	RELATIVES (1903-13 = 100)			ABS. VALUE (MILLION $)	RELATIVES (1903-13 = 100)		
	A	B	C	D	E	F	G	H	I	J
1879	445.8	124.5	374.0	27.7	698.3	96.5	719.6	40.2	129.0	145.1
1880	668.0	137.0	486.5	36.1	823.9	110.4	743.0	41.5	124.2	115.0
1881	642.7	126.7	507.5	37.6	883.9	110.5	795.0	44.4	114.7	118.3
1882	724.6	123.0	558.5	43.6	733.2	115.8	630.0	35.2	107.5	80.6
1883	723.2	116.1	621.5	46.1	804.2	102.8	779.0	43.5	107.9	94.4
1884	667.7	105.1	634.3	47.0	725.0	102.0	707.0	39.5	104.1	84.2
1885	577.5	95.4	604.5	44.8	726.7	95.3	759.0	42.4	100.1	94.6
1886	635.4	96.2	660.5	48.9	666.0	87.1	761.0	42.5	110.5	86.9
1887	692.3	109.5	632.0	46.8	703.0	90.7	771.0	43.1	120.9	92.0
1888	724.0	107.7	672.0	49.8	683.9	96.5	705.0	39.4	111.7	79.2
1889	745.1	116.0	642.5	47.6	730.3	92.4	787.0	43.9	125.7	92.4
1890	789.3	117.8	669.6	49.6	845.3	96.5	872.0	48.7	122.2	98.1
1891	844.9	113.4	745.0	55.2	872.3	80.9	979.0	54.7	127.3	99.2
1892	827.4	108.1	765.5	56.7	1015.3	79.7	1267.0	70.8	135.5	125.0
1893	866.4	113.2	764.0	56.6	831.0	81.9	1010.0	56.4	138.3	99.6
1894	655.0	97.0	675.0	50.0	869.2	71.2	1215.0	67.9	136.2	135.7

1895	732.0	84.9	861.0	63.8	793.4	68.9	1146.0	64.0	123.2	130.5
1896	779.7	88.6	857.0	63.5	863.2	73.1	1176.0	65.7	121.0	103.5
1897	764.7	84.1	875.5	65.6	1032.0	68.9	1489.0	83.2	125.0	126.8
1898	616.0	79.4	780.0	57.8	1210.3	68.1	1768.0	98.8	117.5	178.0
1899	697.1	86.6	804.5	59.6	1203.9	72.7	1647.0	92.0	119.1	154.4
1900	849.9	93.8	906.0	67.1	1370.8	86.2	1382.0	88.4	108.8	131.8
1901	823.2	85.5	962.5	71.3	1460.5	84.7	1715.0	95.9	101.0	134.6
1902	903.3	83.6	1078.0	79.9	1355.5	86.4	1561.0	87.2	96.8	109.1
1903	1025.7	88.2	1163.0	86.2	1392.2	94.8	1463.0	81.7	92.9	94.8
1904	991.1	92.6	1070.0	79.3	1435.2	100.9	1416.0	79.1	91.8	99.8
1905	1117.5	100.9	1108.0	82.1	1491.7	88.8	1672.0	93.4	113.5	103.9
1906	1226.6	102.0	1216.0	89.1	1718.0	99.3	1697.0	94.8	102.8	106.4
1907	1434.4	107.0	1340.0	99.3	1853.7	105.8	1760.0	98.3	101.1	99.0
1908	1194.3	94.8	1258.0	93.2	1834.8	99.3	1840.0	102.8	95.6	110.3
1909	1311.9	94.1	1395.0	103.3	1638.4	102.6	1590.0	88.8	91.7	86.0
1910	1556.9	103.3	1513.0	112.1	1710.1	118.3	1439.0	80.4	87.4	71.7
1911	1527.2	104.8	1458.0	108.0	2013.6	109.2	1817.0	101.5	96.0	94.0
1912	1653.3	112.7	1467.0	108.7	2170.3	103.6	2086.0	116.5	107.5	107.2
1913	1813.0	106.9	1696.0	125.7	2428.5	111.3	2170.0	121.1	96.0	96.4

INDEX

Absolute differences in costs, 3, 7, and Ch. 2, passim.
Advantage, superior, 23.
Angell, J. W., 345 n.
Angell, N., 264 n.
Anglo-French Treaty of 1860 (Cobden-Chevalier Treaty), 154.
Arbitrage, 218.
Argentina, international trade in, 401; foreign borrowings of, 401; and Ch. 30, passim.
Australia, how shipping charges enter into international trade statistics, 137.

Balance of payments, 99, 111; for Canada, Ch. 19, passim; for Great Britain, Chs. 20, 21, passim; for United States, 323, and Chs. 23, 24, 25, passim.
Balance of trade, 111.
Ballod, K., 164, 166, 168 n.
Bamberger, 264 n.
Banks of Canada, note-issues, 200, and Chs. 17 and 19, passim.
Bank of England, note-issues, 200, and Ch. 17, passim.
Bank deposits, ratio of specie to, 201; as related to business cycle, 202, 330.
Bank notes, flexibility of issues, 200.
Bank reserves. See Reserves.
Baring crisis, 401.
Barker, W. S., 188 n., 229 n.
Barter terms of trade, defined, 8; effect of changes in demand on, 101, 305; net terms and gross terms distinguished, 113; how affected by tributes and indemnities, 114; significance of phrase "less favorable," 117; by tourist expenditures, 119; by gifts or charitable contributions, 121; by loans, 254; by import duties, Ch. 13, passim; of Great Britain, Ch. 21; method of computing, 250; of Canada, 258; of United States, 299; under dislocated exchanges, 355.
Beet sugar industry, as illustration of principle of comparative advantage, 183.
Belgium, effectiveness of labor in, 171.
Böhm-Bawerk, 68.

Bounty on exports, under dislocated exchanges, 385; under silver exchange, 386; and Ch. 29, passim.
Bowley, A. L., 240, 249.
Brick, effectiveness of production in various countries, 164.
British India. See India.
Bullock, C. J., 280 n.
Business cycles, relation to credit expansion, 202.
Business profits, in relation to international trade, 81.
Butter, effectiveness of production in various countries, 171.

Cairnes, 44, 54, 67 n., 287 n.
Canada, sensitiveness of monetary system to gold flows, 205, 224; foreign borrowings of, 222; gold movements into, 224; effect of gold flow on prices in, 227, and Ch. 19, passim; price changes in, 228; trade of, with Great Britain and United States, 230; resemblance of Canadian experience to an experiment, 233; barter terms of trade, 258; money wages, 258.
Capital, represents application of labor, 68; how use of capital affects international trade, 71.
Capital and interest, 61, and Ch. 7, passim; note on Ricardo's and the author's method of analysing, 74.
Capital exports. See Loans.
Cassel, G., 340.
Charitable remittances, in relation to barter terms of trade, 121.
Coal, effectiveness of production in various countries, 163.
Coal-tar industry, in Germany and elsewhere, 57.
Coats, R. H., 223 n., 415.
Cobden-Chevalier Treaty, 154.
Comparative advantage, in relation to capital, 71; how influenced by use of machinery, 71; in agriculture and industry in United States, see Contents, Ch. 16; causes of, 180; as illustrated by the beet sugar industry, 183; by the flax industry, 186.

421

Comparative differences in costs, 3, 23, and Ch. 4, passim; relation to increasing returns, 83.

Cost, used in various senses, 3, 12, 161.

Cotton goods, effectiveness of production in United States and Japan, 174.

Credit, sensitiveness to gold flows, 200, 330.

Demand, elasticity of, 31; effect of changes in demand on barter terms of trade, 30, 101, 305; reciprocal international and reciprocal domestic demands, 54, 56, 92; significance of curve, 117; effect of changes in demand on barter terms of trade under inconvertible paper, 363.

Depreciation charge, in relation to interest charge, 69.

Dewey, 289 n.

Differences in labor costs, Ch. 15, passim.

Differences in wages, 44, Ch. 6, passim, 66.

Diminishing returns, 77, and Ch. 8, passim.

Disadvantage, inferior, 23.

Discount rates, relation to deposits, 201; relation to managed currency, 383.

Dislocated exchanges, defined, 338; barter terms of trade under, 355; international trade under, see Contents, Part III; fluctuations in foreign exchanges under, see Contents, Chs. 26 and 27; speculation in, Ch. 28; bounty on exports under, 385.

Domestic goods, 35, 40.

Domestic prices, 34, and Ch. 5, passim; relation to money wages, 40.

Domestic supply price, 12.

Duties on imports. See Import duties.

Effectiveness of labor. See Labor.

Elasticity of demand, 31.

England. See Great Britain.

Equal differences in costs, 3, 19, and Ch. 3, passim.

Exchange dumping, 385, 391.

Exchange rates. See Foreign exchanges.

Experiment, analogy of some economic experiences to, 233.

External economies, 84; in United States, 85.

"Favorable" balance of trade, 111; how affected by loans and interest payments, 127, 131; significance of, 112, 216; little understood by public, 315, 320. See also Balance of trade.

Favorable terms of trade, 30, 117. See also Barter terms of trade.

Federal Reserve System, relation of credit expansion to specie movements, 206, 213; operation of, during the war, 316; after 1913, 330.

Fisher, I., 364.

Flax industry, as illustration of principle of comparative advantage, 186.

Flight of capital, 321, 391.

Flour, effectiveness of production in Great Britain and United States, 170.

Flux, A. W., 167, 170.

Foerster, R. F., 295 n.

Foreign exchange rates. See Contents, Ch. 18; effect of speculation on, 215, and Ch. 18, passim; effect of pooling on, 216; between gold-standard countries, Ch. 18, passim; fluctuations under dislocated exchanges, see Contents, Chs. 26, and 27; impact theory of, 344; is there a "normal" under dislocated exchanges, 348; cause or effect of merchandise movements, 371.

Foreign investments, relation of, to international payments, 266.

France, effectiveness of labor in, see Contents, Ch. 15; monetary system of, 210; sensitiveness of monetary system to specie flow, 211; Franco-German indemnity, Ch. 22.

Franco-German indemnity, Ch. 22.

Free trade, does not lead to equalization of wages between countries, Preface, 38.

Freight charges. See Shipping charges and Transportation.

German chemical industry, in relation to non-competing groups, 57.

Germany, non-competing groups in, 57; effectiveness of labor in, see Contents, Ch. 15; Franco-German indemnity, Ch. 22; how affected by receipt of indemnity, 268; bounty on exports after the Great War, 388.

Gifts, in relation to barter terms of trade, 121.

Gold exchange standard, 380.

Gold movements. See Specie.

Graham, F. D., 393, 400.

Great Britain, comparison of British and Indian wages, 18; use of capital in 18th and 19th centuries, 71; increasing returns in 19th century, Ch. 8; how shipping charges enter into her international trade statistics, 136; British, Indian, and Continental wages

compared, 154; effectiveness of labor in, *see* Contents, Ch. 15; sensitiveness of monetary system to gold flows, 203; trade of, with Canada, 231; international trade of, *see* Contents, Chs. 20 and 21; capital exports of, 237, 246; earnings from shipping, 238; barter terms of trade, Ch. 21; movements of rupee exchange, 370; loans of, to Argentina, 401, Ch. 30, passim.
Gross barter terms of trade, 113, 248; method of computing, 250. *See also* Barter terms of trade.
Gutmann, 264 n.

Hobson, C. K., 245 n.

Ice, effectiveness of production in Great Britain and United States, 171.
Immigrant remittances, 294.
Immobility of labor, 17, 19.
"Impact" theory of rates of foreign exchange under paper currency, 344.
Import duties and barter terms of trade, 141, and Ch. 13, passim. *See also* Protective tariff.
Inconvertible paper, international trade under. *See* Contents, Ch. 26.
Increasing returns, 82; relation to comparative costs, 83; for England in the 19th century, 85.
India, British and Indian wages compared, 18, 154; effectiveness of labor in, 157, 163; demand for English goods, 157; flow of specie to, 157; effectiveness of labor in, *see* Contents, Ch. 15; movements of rupee exchange, 370.
Inferior disadvantage, 23.
Interest on capital, in relation to supply price, 62, and Ch. 7, passim; importance in international trade, 67.
Interest payments, on loans, 123, 128, and Ch. 12, passim.
Internal economies, 84.
International balance of payments, 99, 111; cyclical movements of, 128.
International goods, 35, 40.
International payments, in relation to monetary systems, *see* Contents, Ch. 17; mechanism of, 197, 273; relation to commodity movements, 260.
International prices, 34, and Ch. 5, passim.
International securities. *See* Securities.
"Invisible" items, 109.
Iron industry, how affected by non-competing groups in United States, 59; in England and United States compared, 168.

Japan, effectiveness of labor in, **174.**
Jevons, 158.

Kent, J. F., 295 n.
Kreps, T. J., 300 n., 417.

Labor, mobility in relation to international trade, 17, 19; effectiveness in various countries compared, *see* Contents, Ch. 15; causes of differences in effectiveness, 194.
Labor costs, differences in, *see* Contents, Ch. 15.
Lauderdale, 195 n.
Loans, 123, and Ch. 12, passim; effect on barter terms of trade, 254; foreign borrowings in United States after 1914, *see* Contents, Ch. 25; relation of United States Government loans to exports, 125, 314; to Argentina, 401, Ch. 30, passim.

Maguire, 264 n.
Marshall, 9, 53, 84, 88 n., 229.
Mercantilism, a popular point of view, 79.
Merchandise movements, relation of, to specie flows, 260; to export of capital, 312.
Mill, J. S., 4, 43, 54, 101, 136 n., 146, 199, 274.
Mining industries, 86.
Money costs, in relation to labor costs, 161.
Money wages, adjusted to effectiveness of labor, 21, 36; how far a sign of greater prosperity, 38; not necessarily equal between countries under complete free trade, 39; relation to domestic prices, 40; data on, 42; when high, not necessarily an obstacle to exportation, 79, 155; in relation to supply price, 115; in Europe and Orient, 154, and Ch. 14, passim; in Japan, 176; in Canada, 258. *See also* Wages.
Monroe, A. E., 264 n.
Moulton, 264 n.

Napoleonic period, mechanism of remittances during, 276.
Nasse, E., 264 n.
Net barter terms of trade, 113, 248; method of computing, 250. *See also* Barter terms of trade.
Non-competing groups, 44, and Ch. 6, passim; in relation to German chem-

ical industry, 57; in the United States in the textile industries, 59; in iron industry, 59, 66; as regards unskilled labor, 60.

Non-merchandise transactions, Ch. 11.

Noyes, 289 n.

O'Farrell, H. H., 264 n.

Ohlin, B., 171 n.

Orchard, J. E., 166 n.

Orient. *See* India.

Paish, G., 295 n.

Paper standard. *See* Inconvertible paper.

Passenger fares, 132.

Pegging, 378.

Prices, in different countries, 34, and Ch. 5, passim; relation to wages, 153.

Profits. *See* Business profits.

Protective tariff, not essential to the maintenance of high wages, 38; how related to superior business ability, 82; effect on barter terms of trade, 142, 145, 305; effect of, on the iron industry in U. S., 188; on textile industry in U. S., 192; on comparative advantages, *see* Contents, Ch. 16; in U. S., *see* Contents, Ch. 16.

Purchasing parity, doctrine of, 340, and Ch. 26, passim.

Quantity theory of money, 11; relation to theory of international trade, 198.

Rathbone, A., 315 n.

Reciprocal demand, international and domestic, 54.

Redfield, 165 n.

Rent, in relation to supply price, 62, 78; compared to business profits, 81.

Reserves, relation to deposits, 201, 207; in form of bills of exchange, 217; of Canadian banks, 225.

Revenue duties. *See* Import duties.

Ricardo, 4, 11, 43, 68; note on his method of handling capital and interest, 74; 86 n., 199, 211, 274, 275, 339.

Say, L., 264, 267.

Security movements, in relation to international balances, *see* Contents, Ch. 18; effect of, on exchange fluctuations, 218; a means of international payments, 266, and Ch. 22, passim; during the Great War, 310, 313.

Seven Years' War, mechanism of remittances during, 276.

Shaw, G. W., 183.

Shipping charges, 132, 134; statistical complications, 136; earnings from, by Great Britain, 238.

Silberling, N. J., 275, 277.

Silver exchange, international trade under, 369; bounty on exports under, 386. *See also* Dislocated exchanges.

Silverman, A. G., 259 n., 411, 414.

Smith, Adam, 196, 274, 275, 276, 278.

Social stratification, 53, 56.

Soetbeer, A., 264 n., 272 n.

Speare, C. F., 295 n.

Specie, flow of, from West to Orient, 157; production in Australia and California, 159; effect of flow on prices, 199, 208, 243, 260; relation to bank deposits, 201, 225; movements of, in settlement of international balances, *see* Contents, Ch. 18, 261; flow of, into Canada, 224; effect of flow of, on prices in Canada, 227; flow of, into United States after 1914, 309, 329; effect of flow of, on prices after 1914, 309, 329; distribution of world output of, after 1900, 298. *See also* Quantity theory of money.

Speculation, in foreign exchanges, 215, Ch. 4, passim, 375; in dislocated exchanges, Ch. 28.

Sprague, O. M. W., 307 n.

Sugar-beet industry, as illustration of principle of comparative advantage, 183.

Sugar refining, effectiveness of production in Great Britain and United States, 170.

Superior advantage, 23.

Supply price. *See* Domestic supply price.

Sweden, effectiveness of labor in glass industry, 171.

Tariff. *See* Protective tariff.

Terms of trade. *See* Barter terms of trade.

Textile industry, in United States, 59.

Tourist expenses, 119; in relation to terms of trade, 119; to distribution of wealth within a country, 120; of Americans, 324.

Transportation, effect of cost on terms of trade, 9; importance and influence of interest charge on railway transportation, 73, 181. *See also* Shipping, and Freight.

Tribute payments and the like, 109.

Tucker, R. S., 280 n.

"Unfavorable" balance of trade, 111; how affected by loans and interest payments, 127, 131; significance of term, 112, 216. *See also* Balance of trade.

United States, non-competing groups in, 56, 58; textile industry in, 59; use of capital, 71; special effectiveness of railway transportation, 73; great development of external economies, 87; how shipping charges enter into statistics of international trade, 136; effectiveness of labor in, *see* Contents, Ch. 15; protective tariffs in, *see* Contents, Ch. 16; comparative advantage in agriculture and in industry, *see* Contents, Ch. 16; protective tariff and textile industry, 192; aptitude in the use of machinery in, 193; ratio of reserves to deposits in national banks, 202; sensitiveness of monetary system to gold flows before 1913, 206; trade of, with Canada, 230; international trade of, before 1900, Ch. 23; from 1900–1914, Ch. 24; after 1914, Ch. 25; foreign borrowings of, Chs. 23, 24, 25, passim; gross and net barter terms of trade of, 299; relation of government loans to exports, 314; becomes net exporter of capital, 325, and Ch. 25, passim; international

trade under depreciated paper in 1866–79, 393.

Utilities, their bearing on the barter terms of trade, 30, 117.

Varying advantages, Ch. 9, passim.

Varying costs. *See* Contents, Ch. 8.

Veblen, 194.

Viner, J., 223 n., 230, 259, 415.

Wages, relation of low prices to high wages, 25, 48; differences of, within a country, 44, Ch. 6, passim, 66; differences between countries, 36, 39; relation to prices, 38, 153; comparison of English, British, and Continental wages, 154, and Ch. 14, passim. *See also* Money wages.

Wages and prices, in different countries, 34, and Ch. 5, passim. *See also* Money wages.

Waltershausen, S., 290 n.

Warne, 415 n.

Wells, D. A., 295 n.

Wieser, 156 n.

Williams, J. H., 280 n., 296 n., 322 n., 393 n., 405 n.

Window glass, effectiveness of production in various countries, 171.

"Yellow peril," 154.